Taking the High Road

JAMES A. JOHNSON METRO SERIES

**JAMES A. JOHNSON
METRO SERIES**

The Metropolitan Policy Program at the Brookings Institution is integrating research and practical experience into a policy agenda for cities and metropolitan areas. By bringing fresh analyses and policy ideas to the public debate, the program hopes to inform key decisionmakers and civic leaders in ways that will spur meaningful change in our nation's communities.

As part of this effort, the James A. Johnson Metro Series aims to introduce new perspectives and policy thinking on current issues and attempts to lay the foundation for longer-term policy reforms. The series examines traditional urban issues, such as neighborhood assets and central city competitiveness, as well as larger metropolitan concerns, such as regional growth, development, and employment patterns. The James A. Johnson Metro Series consists of concise studies and collections of essays designed to appeal to a broad audience. While these studies are formally reviewed, some will not be verified like other research publications. As with all publications, the judgments, conclusions, and recommendations presented in the studies are solely those of the authors and should not be attributed to the trustees, officers, or other staff members of the Institution.

Also available in this series:

On growth and development

*Edgeless Cities: Exploring the Elusive
Metropolis*
Robert E. Lang

*Growth and Convergence in Metropolitan
America*
Janet Rothenberg Pack

Growth Management and Affordable Housing
Anthony Downs, editor

*Laws of the Landscape: How Policies Shape
Cities in Europe and America*
Pietro S. Nivola

Reflections on Regionalism
Bruce J. Katz, editor

*Sunbelt/Frostbelt: Public Policies and Market
Forces in Metropolitan Development*
Janet Rothenberg Pack, editor

On transportation

*Still Stuck in Traffic: Coping with Peak-
House Traffic Congestion*
Anthony Downs

On trends

*Redefining Urban and Suburban America:
Evidence from Census 2000,* vol. 1
Bruce Katz and Robert E. Lang, editors

*Redefining Urban and Suburban America:
Evidence from Census 2000,* vol. 2
Alan Berube, Bruce Katz, and
Robert E. Lang, editors

On wealth creation

*Building Assets, Building Credit: Creating
Wealth in Low-Income Communities*
Nicolas P. Retsinas and Eric S. Belsky, editors

*The Geography of Opportunity: Race and
Housing Choice in Metropolitan America*
Xavier de Souza Briggs, editor

*Low-Income Homeownership: Examining the
Unexamined Goal*
Nicolas P. Retsinas and Eric S. Belsky, editors

*Savings for the Poor: The Hidden Benefits of
Electronic Banking*
Michael A. Stegman

On other metro issues

*Evaluating Gun Policy: Effects on Crime and
Violence*
Jens Ludwig and Philip J. Cook, editors

Taking the High Road
A Metropolitan Agenda for Transportation Reform

Bruce Katz and Robert Puentes, editors

BROOKINGS INSTITUTION PRESS
Washington, D.C.

Library of Congress Cataloging-in-Publication data
Taking the high road : a metropolitan agenda for transportation reform / Bruce Katz
and Robert Puentes, editors.
    p.   cm.   — (James A. Johnson metro series)
  Summary: "Examines the challenges facing U.S. cities, suburbs, and metropolitan
areas in light of the national debate on transportation policy—including finance,
decisionmaking, access for the elderly and working poor, and congestion—and provides
reform options that speak to leaders at the state, metropolitan, and local levels"
—Provided by publisher.
  Includes bibliographical references and index.
  ISBN-13: 978-0-8157-4827-4 (isbn-13, paper : alk. paper)
  ISBN-10: 0-8157-4827-2 (isbn-10, paper : alk. paper)
  1. Urban transportation policy—United States. I. Katz, Bruce. II. Puentes,
Robert. III. Title. IV. Series.
  HE308.T35 2005
  388.4'0973—dc22   2005012191

9 8 7 6 5 4 3 2 1

The paper used in this publication meets minimum requirements of the American
National Standard for Information Sciences—Permanence of Paper for
Printed Library Materials: ANSI Z39.48-1992.

Typeset in Minion and Univers Condensed

Composition by Circle Graphics
Columbia, Maryland

Printed by R. R. Donnelley
Harrisonburg, Virginia

CONTENTS

FOREWORD

Since the nation's founding, transportation has been vital to our prosperity, and it still is today. An active role in transportation policy and funding by our national government is vital. The last dozen years have seen strong leadership in this area, highlighted by approval of the landmark ISTEA bill in 1991 and its worthy successor TEA-21.

In my former role as chairman of the Rebuild America Coalition, an organization formed in 1987 to raise local and national infrastructure issues, I worked closely with congressional leaders on these bills. In this role, and as former mayor of Philadelphia and now as governor of Pennsylvania, I know firsthand the challenges and opportunities this national policy framework presents for our nation's cities and metropolitan areas.

Especially critical to the economic success of the nation is a bold and continued investment in transit. Throughout America, guaranteed federal funding has been of huge value because transit agencies have been able to plan and advance projects with a significant level of predictability. It is essential that such funding continue to enjoy budgetary protection just as highway funding is assured sustained support.

In December 2003 the Brookings Institution released a comprehensive report on economic and development trends in my state of Pennsylvania. Their good work received a lot of attention around the state and has helped me focus residents' attention on the need to reinvest in the economic vitality of the state's older cities, boroughs, and towns.

Taking the High Road is a collection of essays and policy briefs issued as part of the Brookings Metropolitan Policy Program's Transportation Reform Series. This volume offers provocative insights into the debate and discussion around the federal transportation law and offers a positive, progressive agenda for change. As this collection contends, unless transportation investments are considered in the context of other policies and priorities for economic growth, environmental stewardship, and reinvestment in existing places, a tremendous opportunity to strengthen this great nation will be lost.

EDWARD G. RENDELL
Governor of Pennsylvania

ACKNOWLEDGMENTS

The editors would like to thank Anthony Downs, Mark Muro, David Jackson, David Warren, and Amy Liu at the Brookings Institution's Metropolitan Policy Program for their wholly necessary guidance and assistance in the development of the policy briefs that constitute the chapters in this volume; Starr Belsky, who edited the volume for the Brookings Institution Press, as well as Inge Lockwood and Julia Petrakis, who provided proofreading and indexing services, respectively; and especially the myriad reviewers and commenters and those who provided input on the substance of the policy briefs. Their invaluable assistance and perspectives cannot be overemphasized.

The Brookings Institution extends appreciation to the many foundations that have made this volume possible: the John D. and Catherine T. MacArthur Foundation, the Ford Foundation, the Joyce Foundation, the Charles Stewart Mott Foundation, and the McKnight Foundation for their financial support of the Brookings Transportation Reform Series; the Johnson Foundation for hosting a major conference at the Wingspread Conference Center to launch this series; the George Gund Foundation, the Heinz Endowments, and the Rockefeller Foundation for their generous support of the institution's work around metropolitan growth, and the Fannie Mae Foundation for their inaugural support for the Metropolitan Policy Program.

PART ONE

A Metropolitan Agenda for Transportation

1

Transportation Reform for the Twenty-First Century: An Overview

Bruce Katz and Robert Puentes

In 1956 President Dwight Eisenhower signed the Federal-Aid Highway Act, creating the Interstate Highway Program, the largest public works program in our nation's history. But today, a decade after the completion of this vast network of highways, the country's transportation policy is languishing.

At its creation, the public agreed that this immense federal program was essential for the health, prosperity, and economic competitiveness of the nation. A sense of purpose and clear intent drove the program—to strengthen national defense, improve access to rural places and between cities, to create jobs and economic opportunity. The result has been the literal transformation of American life.

Congress wrestled with the program in the 1990s with passage of the Intermodal Surface Transportation Efficiency Act (ISTEA) in 1991 and the Transportation Equity Act for the Twenty-First Century (TEA-21) in 1998. These two key laws offered a new framework for thinking about transportation by assuring states and metropolitan areas of specific levels of funding and giving them the flexibility needed to design transportation mixes that met their needs. Spurred on by these reforms, a small but increasing number of states and localities began indeed to experiment with a more balanced mix including expanding and preserving highways, addressing the needs of older and newer communities, and deciding between building roads or enlarging public transit systems.

Transportation challenges remain, however, despite the revolutionary changes in policy adopted at the federal level. For that matter, many would contend that these challenges are worse than ever. Traffic congestion has increased. It has become a way of life in nearly every major metropolitan area and lasts well beyond the traditional rush hours. While congestion is increasing, air quality continues to worsen, raising serious health concerns. The transportation network is also aging. According to the U.S. Department of Transportation, about a quarter of the roads in urban and metropolitan areas are rated as poor or mediocre, and nearly a third of urban bridges are rated structurally deficient or functionally obsolete.

Transportation investments continue to have a profound impact on the pace and shape of metropolitan growth. Currently, the federal surface transportation law does as much as any cluster of programs to influence the spatial form and social fabric of our cities and suburbs. Most notably, a growing body of research based on actual investments clearly shows that major highway projects do not necessarily create new jobs or spur economic growth so much as shift economic activity around a metropolitan area.[1] The result is that cities and older suburbs frequently look on helplessly as commercial strips decline and infrastructure crumbles while growth follows new public investments in highways out to the suburban fringe. The extension and expansion of highways truly is what the late Daniel Patrick Moynihan called it: part of the federal government's hidden urban policy.[2]

Some urban thinkers and policymakers, like the late Senator Moynihan, have long recognized that so many of our country's challenges (transportation, environment, poverty, crime) cross the borders of political jurisdictions. As such, they can only be addressed meaningfully on a regional or metropolitan level; individual communities are generally too small and do not have the scope or scale to deal with these well-entrenched issues effectively. That message is starting to resonate as many metropolitan areas have begun the difficult process of reassessing transportation plans. Metropolitan devolution in the transportation arena has, in turn, sparked renewed interest throughout the country in broader metropolitan thinking and action.[3] But federal transportation laws are still deficient in many ways, and the implementation of the nascent reforms has not been uniformly positive. The nation continues to desperately need a frank and vigorous debate over the future of transportation policy.

To stimulate and inform such a discussion, the Brookings Institution Metropolitan Policy Program (then the Center on Urban and Metropolitan Policy) began in early 2003 to issue a series of papers designed to assess transportation reform. The series sought to frame the federal transportation policy debate around the most pressing challenges facing the nation's cities, suburbs, and metropolitan areas and to provide options for reform so policymakers could build on the progress and momentum of earlier transportation laws. But beyond the federal debate, the papers laid out an agenda that responds directly to those responsible for putting transportation policy into practice—especially leaders on the state, metropolitan, and local levels.

Those exploratory essays have been updated and incorporated into this volume and focus on issues most pertinent to strengthening America's metropolitan areas, raising as well some broader and longer-term policy implications, such as relieving traffic congestion and improving transportation access for the working poor and older Americans. Written in the context of the reauthorization of TEA-21, slated for 2005, they will continue to have relevance for years to come, even if Congress delays action. This volume provides a broad understanding of the challenges and informs this and future debates on transportation reform.

A Metropolitan Agenda for Transportation Reform

Bruce Katz, Robert Puentes, and Scott Bernstein lead off in chapter 2 by stressing that the nation's transportation policy is an agenda also to strengthen and support America's metropolitan areas. Outlining the broad reforms boldly initiated on the federal level, they note that these have not been uniformly implemented. For that reason, it is incumbent on Congress to cement and advance the gains achieved in the past decade and respond more forcefully to the pressing transportation needs of metropolitan America. To that end, they offer a comprehensive policy framework that calls for a two-step approach to thinking about further reforms.

First, Congress must strive to preserve the innovative framework of ISTEA and TEA-21 and ensure that states attend to the needs of their metropolitan areas. Federal reforms that place an emphasis on system rehabilitation and maintenance, improved operations, and alternative transportation development should be retained.

Congress, however, also should continue to go beyond earlier reforms. The authors show how implementation of the reforms appears to have fallen short of initial congressional intent in many states and metropolitan areas.

Therefore, Katz, Puentes, and Bernstein argue that to get transportation policy right in specific regions, Congress must also give metropolitan areas more powers and greater tools in exchange for enhanced accountability. This would help resolve three fundamental questions still outstanding as the federal law languishes:

First, who is in charge of transportation decisions? Current law puts state departments of transportation in the driver's seat on transportation decisions. Incredibly, metropolitan areas make decisions affecting only about 10 cents of every transportation dollar they generate, even though local governments within metropolitan areas own and maintain the vast majority of the transportation infrastructure.

Congress needs to overhaul the governance of transportation programs, recognize the primacy of metropolitan areas, and align the geography of transportation decisionmaking with the geography of regional economies, commuting patterns, and social reality. To this end, it should build on reforms of the 1990s and devolve greater responsibility and resources to metropolitan entities. These institutions are, after all, in the best position to use transportation funding in tandem with land use, housing, workforce, and economic development policies. Such a policy effort should require that state decisions be tied more closely to the demographic and market realities of metropolitan areas and the vision and priorities of metropolitan leaders.

Second, what solutions fit the transportation challenges of the modern metropolis? The current system's approach to transportation solutions is narrow and outmoded. Most state transportation departments, for example, still believe they can build their way out of congestion. Yet congestion is a product of many factors: low-density settlement patterns, employment decentralization, shifting consumption patterns, and market restructuring. That's why study after study shows that building more is not the best strategy for reducing congestion.

Congress, therefore, needs to eventually move beyond transportation-only solutions. ISTEA and TEA-21 made some efforts, mostly ignored, to integrate transportation decisions with local and regional decisions on land use, housing, and economic development. Those efforts should be expanded. At the same time, the new law should encourage the greater use of market mechanisms—such as tolls and congestion pricing—to ease congestion on major thoroughfares at peak traffic times. For example, the city of London is successfully experimenting with pricing schemes in the central business district.

Finally, how do we make transportation decisionmakers accountable? Federal transportation programs return more money to state and local governments than any other federal initiative involving physical infrastructure. Yet unlike other state and local bureaucracies that receive federal funding— state welfare departments, state education departments, local public housing authorities—state transportation departments are held to few performance standards.

Congress should, therefore, act to hold all recipients of federal funding to a high standard of managerial efficiency, programmatic effectiveness, and fiscal responsibility. To that end, a new framework for accountability should be developed that includes tighter disclosure requirements, improved performance measures, and rewards for exceptional performance. Congress also needs to create a transportation system that is more responsive to citizens and business. The more citizens and businesses inform transportation decisions, the better those decisions will be.

Financing the Transportation System

Perhaps no area of transportation policy generates as much contention, raises as many questions, or has been the subject of so many intense policy debates as the financing of the system. However, despite the attention, the debates and discussion around transportation finance are rather esoteric and often get caught up in larger conversations about taxes, economic growth, and equity.

Robert Puentes and Ryan Prince tackle this issue head-on in chapter 3 with a primer and policy discussion about the gas tax. Although the federal government, every state, and some localities levy this tax, it is still not widely understood, nor is it a popular focus of policy reforms. This is because there is much confusion around how the gas tax is imposed in each state, its rate, and the way it is collected and administered. It is also generally not clear how the state gas tax revenue is spent. Some states restrict the spending of this revenue for transportation generally; still others go further and restrict its use to highways only.

Through their research, Puentes and Prince found that the majority of highway funds are derived from federal and state gas taxes. State gas taxes alone made up 20 percent of all highway revenues in 2002 and are the largest single source of highway funding for the states. But after years of steady growth, federal and state gas tax receipts have begun to plateau and are actually declining, taking into account inflation. The authors point to the many reasons, including the states' reluctance to raise gas tax rates, and propose that this aspect of our nation's transportation finance structure is ripe for reform.

Martin Wachs builds on this analysis in chapter 4 by examining the broad trends in transportation finance. He shows that a complex partnership among many governmental bodies, continually influenced by numerous private, corporate, and civic interests, finances our nation's transportation system and that the nature of this partnership is changing. Originally offset by a variety of user fees, such as tolls and fuel taxes, the burden of financing transportation programs is gradually being shifted to local governments and voter-approved initiatives. This shift raises interesting issues for public policy. In the end, Wachs argues that expanded reliance on user fees remains the most promising way to promote equity and efficiency in transportation finance.

Several contributors go beyond the question of how transportation is paid for and examine what states are really doing with those gas tax revenues, including Puentes and Prince in chapter 3, where they note that thirty states restrict the use of their revenues to highway purposes only. Such restrictions, they argue, limit states' ability to finance mass transit, congestion and air quality improvement projects, and other options not related to highways.

In chapter 5, Edward Hill and his coauthors examine the thorny issue of how gas tax revenues are allocated spatially—across cities, metropolitan communities, and nonmetropolitan areas. Their analysis provides further evidence that the distribution of gas tax revenues within some states (in the form of transportation spending) appears to penalize cities and urban areas. Research in several states and metropolitan areas is starting to show that urban areas often act as "donor regions," contributing significantly more in tax receipts than they receive in allocations from their state's highway fund or through direct local transfers. Indeed, the geographic distribution of transportation spending has become an important and heated issue at both the national and state levels.

In the last reauthorization of the federal transportation bill, numerous states and constituencies called for a revised system of allocating states' shares of the Highway Trust Fund—more than 60 percent of which is generated by the federal gas tax. Some states argued that their shares of federal transportation dollars should be proportional to the amount of gas tax revenue they paid into the trust fund. Others wanted their shares determined by need. In the end, Congress addressed the problem of perceived funding inequities between donor and donee states by "guaranteeing" each state a return of at least 90.5 percent of the share of its contribution to the Highway Trust Fund.

Despite the embrace of this funding philosophy at the federal level, similar rules do not exist in most states. In Ohio the result is a spatially skewed pattern of state transportation spending that is essentially anticity and even antisuburb. In effect, funds are diverted away from the very places that struggle with the greatest transportation needs and pay the most in gas taxes.

Hill and his team examined the geographic pattern of state transportation spending in Ohio and found that between 1980 and 1998, Ohio's highway dollars were spent disproportionately in rural counties, which received more funding relative to their transportation needs than urban and suburban counties. One might assume that counties with high travel demands on its roads would receive more funds to deal with the resulting wear and tear, congestion, and other challenges to its road network. In Ohio, however, urban counties consistently took home a smaller share of state highway funds than suburban and rural counties relative to their amount of vehicle traffic (vehicle miles traveled), car ownership (vehicle registrations), and demand for driving (gasoline sales). On the flip side, rural counties received more dollars for each indicator of need than did urban or suburban counties.

At the same time, urban counties in Ohio contribute significantly more gas tax revenues to state transportation coffers than they get back in return, essentially acting as donors of transportation dollars to rural county donees. Gas and vehicle registration levies, in this regard, generate approximately 60 percent of Ohio state highway funds. Of these revenues, a significant portion is redistributed to localities for building, improving, and maintaining roads. But once again, urban counties fared worse than rural and suburban counties in comparison to what they paid into the system. Highway spending in urban and suburban counties matched neither the volume of gas tax funds generated in those counties nor their levels of transportation need.

Getting the Geography of Transportation Right

Two major tenets of ISTEA helped strengthen metropolitan areas by dramatically changing the manner in which transportation projects are selected: flexible funding and flexible programs, and the suballocation of funds directly to metropolitan and local government structures. These changes were significant. Flexible federal dollars made it possible for decisionmakers to consider a range of transportation projects that were previously ineligible for funding. Metropolitan suballocation changed the decisionmaking body for a portion of that funding and gave local officials the ability to spend federal transportation funds based on the unique needs of their region.

In chapter 6, Robert Puentes and Linda Bailey discuss the effect of the suballocation rule by analyzing spending patterns of state departments of transportation and metropolitan planning organizations (MPOs). Metropolitan areas, they contend, require greater control over the transportation spending so crucial to their dynamism. To support their case, the authors examine federal transportation policy since the end of the interstate highway era and find that only a few federal efforts explicitly serve to strengthen and support metropolitan decisionmaking.

They highlight four specific programmatic elements of the federal law that increased the ability of metropolitan areas to make transportation decisions: suballocated Surface Transportation Program dollars, the Congestion Mitigation and Air Quality program, the Transportation Enhancements program, and metropolitan planning funds. Although these are important efforts, they remain quite small, and the authors show how, taken together, federal law only gives metropolitan areas direct control over 7 percent of road and bridge funding under TEA-21.

This is disappointing, and Puentes and Bailey highlight important reasons why federal law should place more emphasis on metropolitan areas. First, local governments within metropolitan areas own the vast majority of the transportation network. Second, metropolitan transportation planning and programming is, by law, comprehensive and includes a wide range of stakeholders. Third, many states continue to penalize metropolitan areas in the distribution of transportation funds. Fourth, states are not fulfilling the promises of federal law. Last, there is a growing recognition that it takes more than transportation solutions to address transportation problems.

They then analyze spending patterns of MPOs and state departments of transportation and find that the former spend almost four times as much as the latter on transit investments—a basic local need. In the end, Puentes and Bailey argue that MPOs should be given direct control over more transportation money but not without first establishing a new framework for accountability and performance. Just increasing the amount of money these entities have to spend does not guarantee better decisions. Rather, tying these increased funds to performance goals such as enhancing accessibility, improving safety, or mitigating the increase in traffic congestion actually may do so.

In fact, MPOs are in a good position to deal with traffic congestion, which is essentially a regional phenomenon requiring regional approaches to lessen its negative impacts. Anthony Downs has literally written the book on metropolitan traffic congestion. Actually, he has done it twice with *Stuck in Traffic* (1992) and *Still Stuck in Traffic* (2004).[4] In these landmark publications, Downs examines the benefits and costs of various anticongestion strategies.

In chapter 7, Downs and Puentes examine the governance options needed for regional action and the conditions required to implement such policies. They make the case that traffic flows are regional in nature, not local or statewide. Only the coordination of transportation improvements with land use planning on the regional or metropolitan level could result in the most rational policies toward congestion. That is one of the reasons Congress established MPOs in the first place: to oversee surface transportation planning in major metropolitan areas.

But MPOs are not the only regional institutions that can carry out effective anticongestion policies. Downs and Puentes cite several examples throughout the country of other institutional arrangements, ranging from full metropolitan governments to single-purpose regional agencies and from voluntary governmental coalitions to public-private partnerships.

In the end, Downs and Puentes offer a sobering assessment of the potential for comprehensive, regionally based strategies for attacking traffic congestion as they conflict with deeply embedded attitudes favoring fragmented local governance over land uses. However, he seems convinced that the time has come to reexamine these obstacles and that ultimately broad regional solutions are inevitable.

Meeting Societal Needs in Transportation

Of course, transportation policy and spending is not just about building projects and moving vehicles. One of the most serious problems with the transportation debate so far has been the lack of focused and sustained attention to two of the nation's most pressing transportation challenges: transportation access for working families and mobility for the elderly.

To work, low-income adults need to *get* to work. However, traveling to jobs is frequently easier said than done, particularly for those without access to fast, reliable transportation. In almost every city, automobiles remain the fastest and most reliable way to get around. Moreover, the continuing decentralization of population and employment has exacerbated the isolation of many low-income families who lack reliable auto access.

In chapter 8, Evelyn Blumenberg and Margy Waller examine the serious transportation challenges facing low-income workers as they seek employment. Central to the argument is research evidence showing that the working poor require a range of transportation services to enhance their economic outcomes. Transportation is an essential link between low-income workers and jobs. They show how other strategies are important, too, such as urban reinvestment to bring jobs closer to low-income communities and housing strategies that help move low-income families closer to jobs. But, in the end, it is the transportation strategies that have the potential to immediately enhance geographic access to employment.

Blumenberg and Waller show how the transportation needs of the poor vary by metropolitan area and by neighborhood. Therefore, they provide a full menu of practical policy options, including automobile access programs, improved fixed-route transit services, and expanded paratransit and other door-to-door transit services. And although the authors' focus is on transportation, TEA-21 is not the only area of policy intervention they consider. Beyond TEA-21–related recommendations, such as augments to the Job Access and Reverse Commute program, they clearly explain how reforms incorporated into the Temporary Assistance for Needy Families program, the Workforce Investment Act, and other federal programs are also profoundly important.

Highlighting a different but potentially related issue, Sandra Rosenbloom points out in chapter 9 that the number of older Americans is expected to double over the next twenty-five years. All but the most fortunate seniors will confront an array of medical and other constraints on their mobility even as they continue to seek an active community life. Rosenbloom challenges the easy assumptions that underlie most policy debates on providing transportation to the elderly. She discusses how an aging society adds to a range of transportation problems and argues that as Congress debates reauthorization, it should consider special approaches to meet the mobility and access needs of the elderly.

To put the discussions about elderly mobility in context, Rosenbloom provides important demographic trends about elderly population growth, residential patterns, and transportation choices. Building on this, she debunks several myths about elderly travel needs and proposes a series of legislative and policy solutions that accommodate the preference of the elderly for a repertoire of travel options to give them freedom and flexibility in the face of declining skills.

Other Important Metropolitan Transportation Issues

In chapter 10, Edward Beimborn and Robert Puentes address the issue of metropolitan mobility from a different angle. They investigate the rules and regulations that govern the individual modes and find that federal transportation policy is essentially an unfair competition between highways and transit that can potentially distort local and metropolitan decisionmaking. Despite a number of reforms in the past decade, the authors show that federal rules remain stacked against transit, while planning, funding, and implementing highway projects is far easier. For example, under current law new transit programs only receive a maximum 60 percent federal share of total project funding, while the latest reauthorization language proposes a 50 percent or less match. Highway projects, on the other hand, continue to enjoy an 80 to 90 percent federal share. In addition, transit programs are subject to strict project criteria and justification, are required to address land use impacts, and are compared to and must compete with their peers before they can receive federal funding, whereas highway projects generally are not subject to such constraints.

The authors discuss these and other areas where new transit and highway programs are treated differently and how those differences lead to an unlevel playing field and inhibit comprehensive regional planning, management, and decisionmaking. A very telling example in Milwaukee demonstrates how these unbalanced rules may have skewed choices about what type of major investment project to pursue.

The last chapter makes the connection between mobility and security. Arnold Howitt and Jonathan Makler argue that although a number of positive steps have been taken in the years since the September 11 terrorist attacks, surface transportation has been effectively placed in a secondary tier of public services in terms of protective actions. Policymakers and senior public managers see highway and transit systems as genuinely vulnerable to terrorist attack; but among the many potentially exposed elements of American society, they have not been given the highest funding priority. In the end, the authors explore a number of ways in which surface transportation security needs to be enhanced to protect the mobility of the nation.

Conclusion

As the nation progresses into the twenty-first century, dramatic changes are increasingly evident. Market and demographic forces are fundamentally reshaping nearly every aspect of American life as the economy continues its shift away from manufacturing and toward the service sector. These economic forces, together with major demographic trends—population growth, immigration, aging, and internal migration—are radically changing the function of both metropolitan and nonmetropolitan areas and also thus altering the role and geographic scale of our national transportation policy.

The essays in this volume focus on realistic and pragmatic policies to address these changes. Given that they were originally conceived and written before TEA-21 expired, they also serve to illustrate how congressional inaction, mired by partisan bickering, interstate squabbles, and political rancor, has dampened the climate for meaningful reform.

Further reform will not come easily to the transportation sector. The deficiencies in transportation policies and practices are deeply rooted—in constituency and money politics, in state governance, and in the history of metropolitan development. Yet change must come if our nation is going to have livable communities, competitive economies, a healthy environment, and fiscal responsibility.

Yogi Berra is purported to have said, "You've got to be very careful if you don't know where you're going because you might not get there." The nation faces multiple transportation challenges that will not be resolved by pouring more and more money into a broken system. Systemic reform is needed and probably will only happen if transportation policy is vigorously debated in the public realm. Transportation is too important to get the silent treatment.

Notes

1. Marlon G. Boarnet and Andrew Haughwout, "Do Highways Matter? Evidence and Policy Implications of Highways' Influence on Metropolitan Development," discussion paper prepared for the Center on Urban and Metropolitan Policy (Brookings, August 2000).

2. Daniel P. Moynihan, "Toward a National Urban Policy," in *Toward a National Urban Policy*, edited by Daniel P. Moynihan (New York: Basic Books, 1970).

3. Devolution, as used here, refers to the delegation of certain authorities from a centralized level of government to a lower level. "Metropolitan devolution" in transportation refers to the provision of some planning and decisionmaking power to metropolitan or regional entities.

4. Anthony Downs, *Stuck in Traffic: Coping with Peak-Hour Traffic Congestion* (Brookings and Lincoln Institute of Land Policy, 1992); *Still Stuck in Traffic: Coping with Peak-Hour Traffic Congestion* (Brookings, 2004).

2

Getting Transportation Right for Metropolitan America

Bruce Katz, Robert Puentes, and Scott Bernstein

Since the debates and deliberations began in 2003 over reauthorization of the Transportation Equity Act for the Twenty-First Century (TEA-21), Congress has struggled with how to allocate about $300 billion dollars over six years to preserve, modernize, and expand the U.S. surface transportation system. The stakes could not be higher—for the country and particularly for its congested cities and suburbs.

Metropolitan areas are literally where America lives. Not only do eight out of ten people in the United States now reside in metropolitan areas, but these crucial places drive the economy. Together, these regions not only produce more than 85 percent of the nation's economic output but also generate 84 percent of America's jobs.[1] Increasingly, the metro areas are where the business of American life is carried on.

And yet, as Congress weighs reauthorization, most U.S. metropolitan areas—meaning most of America—face a series of enormous transportation challenges:

—Congestion is worsening in metropolitan areas of every size as regional economies continue to spread out in low-density ways.[2]

—Automobile dependency is on the rise as sprawl undercuts the viability of alternatives to driving alone, such as bus transit, heavy rail, light rail, biking, or carpooling.[3]

—The infrastructure network is aging, with about a quarter of the roads in urban and metropolitan areas rated in poor or mediocre condition, and nearly a third of urban bridges rated structurally deficient or functionally obsolete.[4] Yet, in many places, transportation decisionmaking still favors new construction, typically on the suburban and exurban fringe.

—There is also a growing spatial mismatch between jobs and workers as employment decentralizes and poverty remains concentrated in central cities.[5]

—Americans are now spending more on transportation than ever before, primarily because our sprawling metropolitan communities require families to drive longer and more often to satisfy their daily needs.[6] Since 1991 the nation's total transportation bill has grown faster than inflation.

—In addition, state governments—the major source of funding for local transportation needs—face unprecedented revenue shortfalls. At the same time, states and cities are being forced to spend millions to protect transportation hubs, such as ports and railways, from terrorism.[7]

In this context, the ongoing debate about the federal laws and programs governing highway, transit, air, and rail systems could not come at a more critical time for the nation's metropolitan areas. To put it bluntly, federal transportation programs return more money to state and local governments than any other federal initiative involving physical infrastructure, and they influence, as much as any cluster of programs, the spatial form and social fabric of our cities and suburbs.[8]

Furthermore, this is a time of substantial, though uneven, innovation in the transportation sector. Congressional reforms in the 1990s—the Intermodal Surface Transportation Efficiency Act (ISTEA) in 1991 and TEA-21 in 1998—gave states and metropolitan areas the certainty in funding and the flexibility in program design necessary to attempt new transportation solutions. Spurred by these reforms, a small but increasing number of states and metropolitan areas are experimenting with transportation policies that offer a more balanced mix between highway expansion and highway preservation, and between road building and transit expansion.

Thus the nation deserves more than a cursory debate and discussion about the federal transportation law. Therefore Washington should seize the opportunity to truly get transportation policy right for metropolitan America.

This chapter argues that Congress must strive to preserve the innovative framework of past reforms and go further to devolve power and decisionmaking on localities. In this respect, numerous encouraging examples of state, local, and metropolitan innovation provide a sound basis for retaining federal reforms that have worked. At the same time, the mixed record among states in implementing ISTEA and TEA-21 exposes the need for additional federal reform that gives metropolitan areas greater powers and more tools in exchange for enhanced accountability.

The State of Federal Transportation Law

Understanding where federal transportation policy should go to better serve the needs of localities requires first understanding where transportation policy has been. ISTEA and TEA-21, in this respect, took the first steps in revolutionizing federal transportation policy by recognizing and responding to the reality of metropolitan America. Overall, the laws enacted eight major changes.

Metropolitan Devolution

The reforms established a voice for metropolitan areas by devolving greater responsibility for planning and implementation upon metropolitan planning organizations (MPOs). These regional bodies were originally research organizations charged with advising state departments of transportation (DOTs). By enhancing the powers and responsibilities of MPOs, ISTEA and TEA-21 enabled metropolitan areas to tailor transportation plans to the realities of their distinct markets. MPOs are held accountable through a regular certification process intended to ensure adherence to statutory economic and environmental performance measures, to principles of effective citizen engagement, and to compliance with other applicable federal laws, including both the National Environmental Policy Act and Title 6 of the Civil Rights Act.

Reliable Funding

The reforms substantially increased federal funding across the board and guaranteed that federal gas tax revenues could not be diverted from surface transportation projects. The Minimum Guarantee Program ensures that a large portion of federal Highway Trust Fund dollars flows back to the states, based not on needs but rather on their share of contributions to the fund. The laws also required fiscal responsibility by confining metropolitan transportation plans to the actual availability of sufficient funds to complete, operate, and maintain projects.

System Preservation and Maintenance

ISTEA and TEA-21 recognized the importance of reinvesting in existing transportation systems and provided for their preservation. They stressed the use of advanced technologies for efficient data collection and the application of analytical tools to evaluate strategies for effective management and operations.

Funding Flexibility

The reforms afforded states and regions greater flexibility in spending federal highway and transit funds. Before ISTEA, highway program funds generally could not be used to finance projects of another transportation mode. Now, state DOTs and MPOs can employ a portion of highway funds for transit purposes. Such authority to flexibly allocate funds has provided states and MPOs, along with local political, corporate, civic, and constituency leaders, a greater opportunity to tailor transportation spending to regional needs and market realities.

Special Challenges

The new laws established a series of targeted programs to carry out important national objectives on the metropolitan level. Federal law now sets aside a portion of transportation funds for activities that mitigate metropolitan congestion and improve air quality. The Transportation and Community and System Preservation (TCSP) Pilot Program created incentives for linking transportation and land use planning. Another program, the Job Access and Reverse Commute (JARC) Program, helped provide more transportation alternatives for low-income workers in metropolitan markets.

Beyond Transportation

The reform statutes required transportation planning to move beyond simple mobility concerns and take into account social, economic, and environmental outcomes. The laws particularly tightened the linkages between transportation spending and metropolitan air quality. Enforcement of these linkages in Atlanta and other metropolitan areas confirms that they have toughened federal environmental supervision and provided another impetus for regional collaboration.

Citizen Participation

The laws greatly expanded the public's role in transportation decision-making. They required broad and inclusive public participation in the transportation planning process and mandated that this engagement be "early and continuing."

Open Government

The laws created, for the first time, a Bureau of Transportation Statistics (BTS) to enhance both planning and public access to information. BTS is working to improve the geographic analysis of transportation expenditures and their effect on metropolitan areas.

Taken together, all these reforms enacted over the past fifteen years represent a marked departure from past federal policies and practices, which had generally promoted a one-size-fits-all emphasis on road construction and new highway building. Each reform reflects a more sophisticated notion of the role transportation plays in building communities that are livable, competitive, and fiscally and environmentally sustainable. Several of them parallel recent reforms in federal housing and welfare policy by rejecting "made-in-Washington" solutions and devolving greater responsibility and discretion for program design and implementation upon officials closer to transportation problems. In sum, the reforms of the last decade represent a remarkable change of direction for the nation's beleaguered transportation policy.

Reform in Action: State and Metropolitan Responses to Federal Change

Have the reforms made a difference? Change, particularly in complex systems, does not happen overnight. In light of that, the impact of recent transportation reforms has so far been both profound and disappointing.

What has been profound has been the extent to which the two recent transportation bills attempted to respond to local regions' needs. This change in approach recast transportation governance, spending patterns, and behavior all at once.

Before ISTEA, regional transportation plans and programs were completely subordinated to federal-state highway planning. After ISTEA, metropolitan areas were not only permitted but required to establish transportation goals and objectives, so that transportation decisionmaking might respond more directly to the unfolding needs of particular regions.

At the same time, spending shifted with the new laws. During the 1990s, funding available for maintenance and repair of the nation's transportation system increased from $6 billion in 1991 to over $16 billion in 1999. By 2000 the overall share of highway capital funds spent on system preservation had risen to 52.0 percent—up from 44.7 percent in 1993.[9] Federal money spent on transit almost doubled, from just over $3 billion to close to $6 billion, and the amount of federal funds spent on bicycle and pedestrian projects grew from just over $7 million to more than $222 million over the same time period.[10] Many metropolitan areas also began the difficult yet important process of reassessing transportation plans and considering a broader range of transportation solutions.

Dramatic geographic reorientation also accompanied the changes. Public transit policies long associated with older, industrial metropolitan areas in the Northeast and Midwest have become conventional elements of transportation thinking in newer, growing areas in the Southeast and the Sunbelt. Metropolitan areas as diverse as Salt Lake City, Denver, Dallas, Charlotte, Las Vegas, San Jose, and San Diego have either built or are in the process of building light-rail systems. Significantly, these projects were undertaken because officials and civic leaders in these metropolitan areas believe their competitive future will be improved by transportation systems that promote greater efficiency and more compact development patterns, and provide workers with wider transportation choices.

Because of these shifts in federal policy and state and metropolitan spending, our nation now has hundreds more miles of rail service as well as millions more "route miles" of bus service. Planning and programming have generally improved with the enhanced involvement of local governments and the general public in transportation decisionmaking.

As a result, metropolitan travel habits are changing. Since 1995 the number of transit passenger trips has increased by 20 percent.[11] Transit ridership is now at its highest level since 1960. Even bicycle commuting grew by 5 percent during the 1990s according to the Census Bureau.[12] More recent indicators are beginning to show that automobile driving may be leveling off. For example, annual vehicle miles traveled increased by only 2.0 percent since 1999. Compare this to the 2.5 percent average yearly increase in the 1990s, 3.2 percent in the 1980s, and 4.3 percent in the 1970s.[13] While it is true that automobile travel still dominates in terms of absolute numbers, recent trends do indicate that the reforms on the federal level are having a substantial positive impact.

In sum, ISTEA and TEA-21 embedded in law, for the first time, the principle that America's metropolitan reality required an integrated, balanced, and regionally designed transportation system. As a framework, the laws are sound.

And yet the laws themselves are only part of the picture. Unfortunately, implementation of the new federal statutes has been seriously flawed—and in basic ways unresponsive to metropolitan needs. Most notably, many states have failed to utilize the tools and discretion afforded them by ISTEA and TEA-21 to meaningfully address the worsening transportation problems bogging down their metropolitan regions.

Insufficient Metropolitan Devolution

A major disappointment is the fact that, after ten years, most states have still not embraced the intent of federal law and devolved sufficient powers and responsibilities to their metropolitan areas. ISTEA and TEA-21 sought through devolution to better align the geography of transportation decisionmaking with the geography of regional economies, commuting patterns, and social reality. Thus the laws undertook to enlarge the responsibility of the regional MPOs in terms of transportation decisionmaking. However, that federal intent has largely been subverted. Although ISTEA and TEA-21 were designed to move transportation decisionmaking out of the back rooms and board rooms of the highway establishment, many state DOTs still wield considerable formal and informal power and retain authority over substantial state transportation funds. The governor and state DOT still have veto authority over MPO-selected projects. Although large MPOs (in areas with populations over 200,000) also have authority to veto projects, the reality is that the state receives and manages all the federal transportation money, as well as large amounts of state transportation money, and the state's political leverage is far greater than the MPO's.[14] In fact, a General Accounting Office report found that states often so dominate MPOs that in at least one case, the state DOT "was, in effect, the MPO."[15] The Illinois DOT, for example, is "heavily involved" in the metropolitan planning process in the Chicago region.[16] MPOs in other areas, such as Boston and New York, actually remain state agencies.[17] Such arrangements create an unfavorable climate for the flowering of federal policy reforms— and frequently cut against metropolitan interests.

Bias against Metropolitan Areas

Many states continue to penalize metropolitan areas in the allocation of transportation money. This penalty results from several biases. The first bias arises from the fact that federal law allocates the vast majority of federal money directly to state DOTs. Only about 6 percent of federal program funds are directly suballocated to MPOs and, even then, only to MPOs serving populations of over 200,000.[18] In fact, while federal transportation spending increased from ISTEA to TEA-21, the share of funds suballocated to MPOs actually *declined* as a share of total highway spending. All told, metropolitan areas make decisions on only about 10 cents of every dollar they generate even though local governments within metropolitan areas own and maintain the vast majority of the transportation infrastructure.[19]

A second bias follows from the way states distribute transportation revenues. Some states have developed distribution formulas based on transportation-related needs or on resident population, registered motor vehicles, and highway miles. However, others (such as Tennessee, Ohio, Arkansas, and Alabama) allocate a portion of funds evenly among their counties, regardless of their size, needs, and contribution to state funding pools. This holdover from the states' past years of active rural highway construction ensures that built-out urban counties fail to receive a sensible share of funding.

Another bias owes to the simple fact that the states own a substantial portion of the roads in rural areas; by contrast, local governments generally own many of the roads and the transit systems located in metropolitan areas.[20] This arrangement saddles local municipalities with responsibility for the roads in incorporated (more urban) places while states take care of roads in rural or otherwise unincorporated places on the suburban fringe.

Funding analyses in Ohio, Colorado, and Washington show how these biases affect metropolitan areas. In Ohio, rural counties receive much higher distributions of transportation revenues than do suburban and urban counties when allocations are compared to indicators of need such as population, vehicle registrations, vehicle miles traveled, and retail sales at gasoline stations.[21] In Colorado, the Denver Regional Council of Governments found that from 1998 to 2003, the share of transportation dollars allocated to the Denver metropolitan area had declined from 46 to 28 percent.[22] The decline in proportionate allocation destined for the metropolitan area occurred despite the fact that Denver boasted more job growth, people, and gasoline consumption than other jurisdictions in the state. The Denver metropolitan area receives only 69 cents in revenues for each $1 of tax revenue contributed.[23] Projections of transportation spending in Washington State found that from 1994 to 2013, the Seattle metropolitan area would raise 51 percent of the state's total revenues and receive 39 percent in return. In other words, Seattle serves as a net exporter of transportation (and gas tax) revenue, despite the critical role the metropolitan area plays in the state's economy.[24] An expanding set of emerging research and commentary is beginning to illustrate and explore these inequities in many other metropolitan areas, as well.[25]

Unlevel Playing Field between Highways and Transit

Another flaw in recent transportation reform that adversely affects metropolitan areas is that the rules governing transportation policy continue to favor roads over transit and other alternatives to traditional highway building. The federal government typically contributes 80 percent of the cost of road and new transit projects. However, Congress recently directed the Federal Transit Administration not to approve projects with more than a 60 percent federal share.[26] In addition, the Bush administration's fiscal year 2004 budget reaffirmed an earlier recommendation to reduce the federal match for transit projects to 50 percent beginning in 2004.[27] No such provisions burden roadway projects. This inequality between roads and transit is complicated by the fact that thirty states, unlike the federal government, prohibit the use of gas tax revenues for purposes other than road construction and maintenance.[28] Such rules make it inordinately difficult for transit projects to obtain additional funding, which they often must pursue through local ballot referenda or general revenue sources at the state and local level.

Other federal rules further tilt the playing field against transit. For example, strict project justification requirements and a demonstration of long-term financial commitment apply to new rail projects. Such oversight—while perhaps appropriate—far exceeds that applied to roadway projects. This, too, hampers development of the multidimensional transportation systems that businesses and workers require.[29]

As a result of these biases, states rarely utilize the funding flexibility allowed them by ISTEA and TEA-21. Data from the Federal Transit Administration illustrates that from fiscal years 1992 to 1997, only California, the District of Columbia, Massachusetts, New York, and Oregon transferred more than one-third of available funds from highways to transit—and six states transferred none.[30] Nationally, of the $50 billion available for innovation, only 6.6 percent ($3.3 billion) was spent on transit and other alternatives during the 1990s—and most of that shifting occurred in states with transit-intensive metropolitan areas, such as New York and California.[31]

Taken together, these biases ensure that state transportation policy pursued under federal law works against many metropolitan areas' efforts to maintain modern and integrated transportation networks.[32]

Inadequate Capacity

Another problem is that MPO as well as state capacity remains uneven. In a very real sense, the profession of transportation planning failed to keep up with statutory and on-the-ground changes in the 1990s. Even in recent years, state transportation planning has largely remained the province of transportation professionals versed in engineering and concrete pouring rather than urban planning, environmental management, housing, or economic development—and that has hampered state and local implementation of ISTEA and TEA-21's vision. Nor have circumstances been markedly better at the MPOs. In places as diverse as Albany, Dallas, Hartford, Minneapolis, San Francisco, and Seattle, MPOs are strong players in their regions and maximize their role in an effective way. These entities have built up the expertise of their staff to carry out the responsibilities of the new federal law. But other MPOs, particularly in smaller areas, struggle to fulfill their statutory responsibilities as well as implement local projects. Many lack adequate staff and financial resources. A recent analysis, for example, found that 58 percent of small MPOs (those representing populations of less than 200,000) cannot perform basic transportation modeling or forecasting. In addition, 16 percent of small MPOs do not even have a full-time transportation planner.[33] Exacerbating these problems are state lines. Thirty-eight of the nation's metropolitan areas encompass more than one state—including ten of the twenty-five largest—which significantly fragments local planning. The result is that for transportation very few effective metropolitan governance structures exist.[34]

Obstacles to Community Participation

Another disappointment is that many states and metropolitan areas alike undercut reform by flouting the spirit and intent of the new federal rules governing citizen participation. A number of states (such as Washington and Maryland) do include citizens on advisory committees that advise on selection of enhancement projects such as pedestrian and bicycle access or landscaping. In Denver and Albany, New York, MPOs have made public involvement central to their development of long-range "vision" plans. Yet, for the most part, states and metropolitan areas do not involve citizens in an "early and continuing" way in their transportation decisions, despite existing federal regulations requiring them to do so.[35] In addition, citizens rarely have ready access to transparent information on how and where their state and metropolitan bureaucracies spend federal transportation dollars. Incredibly, it is easier for citizens to discern where private banks and thrifts lend (thanks to the federal Home Mortgage Disclosure Act) than to determine where public transportation agencies spend. Ultimately this lack of transparency reduces the ability of employers, workers, and citizens in general to influence the regional transportation systems that so strongly shape economic competitiveness, development trends, environmental quality, and the nation's quality of life.

Inadequate Accountability and Performance Measures

Finally, TEA-21 failed to improve accountability and performance measures in a way congruent with its 40 percent spending increase over ISTEA. This laxity is astonishing, given the recent adoption by Congress and the White House of stringent performance standards for state grantees under welfare and education reforms, the annual performance requirements for all federal agencies under the Government Performance Results Act, and the sheer dollar size of transportation programs. To be sure, TEA-21 outlined seven criteria to be evaluated in planning highway projects: accessibility, economic development, efficiency, environment, mobility, safety, and system preservation.[36] These factors were to be "considered" in the metropolitan and statewide planning processes—and could, if adhered to, improve the quality of transportation planning and spending in metropolitan areas. However, TEA-21's additional funding did not hold states accountable for their performance regarding these factors. In fact, few performance standards were imposed. Furthermore, TEA-21 actually prohibits inadequate consideration of these factors from being contested in court.[37] This, too, has undercut reform.

Big-Ticket Challenges

Against this background, a number of critical transportation issues have emerged for debate. All of them involve fundamental aspects of American transportation policy, and all of them involve the nation's metropolitan areas.

Metropolitan Traffic Congestion

In the past two decades, traffic congestion has become a way of life in nearly every major metropolitan area. Between 1992 and 2000, the amount of time that travelers were delayed in metropolitan traffic increased by eighteen hours, or 41.2 percent.[38] No wonder drivers—stuck in traffic—increasingly demand relief. Even though neither ISTEA nor TEA-21 promised that, many naturally are looking to the federal government for help in addressing the mounting congestion problem. However, regardless of policy and market interventions, metropolitan congestion will continue to increase as the numbers of vehicles, drivers, miles traveled, and intercity trucks grow and as regional economies continue to decentralize along low-density settlement patterns. Fortunately, many are beginning to understand the fundamental connections between land use, housing, and transportation and to recognize that we cannot build our way out of congestion.[39]

Deteriorating Air Quality

As congestion increases, air quality continues to worsen in major metropolitan regions. Deteriorating air quality raises serious health concerns that are beginning to receive a great deal of attention. The Bush administration recently acted to modestly increase fuel economy standards for light-duty trucks and sport utility vehicles, and sent confusing signals about conformity with the Clean Air Act in cases scattered from California to Atlanta. At the same time, the Supreme Court, responding to scientific evidence, upheld new air quality standard measurements that better reflect the levels of air pollutants caused by car emissions. As a result, in April 2004, the Environmental Protection Agency designated 474 counties in 31 states out of compliance with the federal air quality standards of the 1990 Clean Air Act amendments for smog-causing ozone.[40] Some 150 million people live in these counties.

Crumbling Infrastructure and Functional Obsolescence

The transportation network is aging. Potholes, rough surfaces, rusting bridges: these are the realities of a deteriorating system. Recent analysis, moreover, estimates that the nation's aging infrastructure costs American drivers $5.8 billion in repairs each year.[41] Such costs subvert regional competitiveness and productivity by impeding the flow of people, goods, and services between America's cities and suburbs.[42] Furthermore, the very design of this aging infrastructure is becoming obsolete. Most cities and older communities now make do with a road and transit network that fits commuting patterns of the 1950s, when cities still functioned as regional hubs. Today, however, commute trips represent only 15 percent of all trips taken.[43] This fact—and the general obsolescence of much transportation infrastructure—undermines urban and metropolitan economies. In some cities, freeways block access to waterfronts and other assets and generally take up some of the most valuable real estate in the urban area (usually land either near or in the midst of the central business district).[44]

Growing Spatial Mismatch between Jobs and Workers

As economies and opportunity decentralize and working poverty concentrates, a "spatial mismatch" has arisen between jobs and people in the nation's urban regions.[45] In suburbs entry-level jobs abound in manufacturing, wholesale trade, and retailing—and hold out opportunities for people with basic education and skills. However, the absence of viable transportation options—combined with persistent residential racial segregation and a lack of affordable suburban housing—effectively cuts many inner-city workers off from regional labor markets. Quite literally, low rates of car ownership and inadequate public transit keep job seekers in the core from reaching many suburban jobs. Often, inner-city workers, hobbled by poor information networks, do not even know these jobs exist. This, too, undermines the competitiveness of metropolitan regions by reducing employers' ability to attract needed workers.[46]

Sticker Shock of Sprawl

Congestion and automobile dependence also affect the pocketbooks of citizens and commuters. The dominant pattern of suburban growth— low-density housing, a sprawling job base—has made residents and commuters completely dependent on the car for all travel needs. Partly as a result, household spending on transportation has risen across the country. Transportation is now the second largest expense for most American households, consuming on average 19 cents out of every dollar. Only housing-related costs eat up a larger chunk of expenditures (33 cents), with food a distant third (13 cents).[47] The transportation burden disproportionately affects the poor and working poor, moreover. For example, those in the lowest income brackets spent nearly 10 percent of their personal income on commuting in 1999—more than double the national average. The working poor who used their own vehicle to commute spent a larger share of their income (as do all workers) than those who are able to use transit.[48]

Inadequate State Funding

Despite these critical needs, states are not raising—or spending—enough revenue to meet the needs of metropolitan transportation networks. From the time the interstate highway system was originally authorized in 1956 to the present, increases in federal revenues have kept pace with inflation, but state revenues have not. Of the twenty-eight states that increased their gas tax since the passage of ISTEA, only one raised it as fast as or faster than inflation.[49] Since TEA-21 was authorized in 1998, two of the largest sources of new revenue for transportation projects are increases in federal revenues and increases in state debt. In fact, the percent increase in revenues from state borrowing in the form of bond proceeds outpaced the percent increase in revenues from new taxes and user fees by more than seven to one.[50] In 1999 the Governmental Accounting Standards Board approved Statement 34 on capital asset accounting, requiring consistent bookkeeping by state and local government for infrastructure investments.[51] This change requires state and local governments to account consistently for the depreciated value of their capital investments and to budget adequately to maintain their existing assets. The pressure to pay attention to these considerations has mounted in the wake of the recession and its effect on state finances. Forty states slashed their budgets by a combined total of nearly $12 billion in 2003—the largest amount since such records have been kept.[52]

A related problem involves state underspending on the Congestion Mitigation and Air Quality program, known as CMAQ. Under TEA-21, CMAQ allows states to disperse some $8.1 billion over the six-year life of the law to fund an array of activities, including transit projects and traffic flow improvements, to help metropolitan areas meet federal air quality standards. However, states have curbed that authority, according to Local Officials for Transportation, a coalition of elected officials that includes the U.S. Conference of Mayors, the National Association of Counties, the Association of Metropolitan Planning Organizations, and the National League of Cities. As a result, nearly $2.2 billion of CMAQ funds has remained unspent since ISTEA, depriving local governments of needed dollars for mitigating congestion problems and improving air quality.[53]

Each of these challenges shares a common origin. Despite the good intentions of ISTEA and TEA-21, a fundamentally antimetropolitan bias still pervades state and federal transportation policies and practices. Transportation reform matters because it offers our best opportunity to shape different growth patterns and manage these problems and so improve the next generation's metropolitan transportation network.

A Metropolitan Policy Agenda for Transportation Reform

So where do we go from here? One thing is clear: the debate around the nation's transportation laws should not revolve solely around money (see table 2-1).

Many of the urgings for additional federal spending are in response to the tremendous challenges outlined in this chapter. Coupled with that, states and localities are struggling under their own burdens of fiscal stress. Increased investments in transportation, the argument goes, illustrate the federal government's commitment to a range of issues, from safety and public health to jobs and economic growth to quality of life. The reauthorization debate around TEA-21 has made it clear that what matters more than the particular funding level of the reauthorization is how that money is spent and what impact it will have on most Americans.[54]

ISTEA and TEA-21 marked a sea change in federal transportation policy. In metropolitan area after metropolitan area, that change is apparent in many tangible ways. There is more funding for transportation alternatives, more focus on repairing and maintaining what is already built, and more integrated thinking about how transportation connects to other community priorities such as air quality, housing, and economic development. Furthermore, these changes reflect the shifting market and demographic realities of our country. In sum, they reflect what citizens say they want: more choices in transportation; metropolitan places that function efficiently for businesses, workers, and households; and more bang for the government buck (see table 2-1).

In keeping with that, the first order of business for Congress must be to retain the existing transportation reforms—specifically those initiated in ISTEA and TEA-21. The earlier reforms provide a solid foundation for a national transportation policy that is fiscally prudent, competitively wise, environmentally sound, and responsive to the changing demands of business and citizens. Congress, therefore, should continue to resist efforts to undermine the "flexible funding" provisions that allow decisionmakers at the state and local level to shift funds between highway and transit initiatives. It should reject bids to roll back environmental regulations in the name of project streamlining.[55] And it should maintain in federal law provisions that favor system rehabilitation and maintenance, improved operations, and alternative transportation development, rather than expansion of new highway capacity.

Yet Congress must also go beyond preserving past reforms. In many places, practice has not followed policy, so that implementation of the law

Table 2-1. Overview of Recent Federal Transportation Laws

Units as indicated

Law	Year	Total $ (billions)	Increase from previous		Demonstration or high-priority projects[a]	
			$ (billions)	Percent	Number	Total $ (billions)
Transportation Assistance Act	1982	72	...	...	10	0.3
Surface Transportation and Uniform Relocation Assistance Act (STURAA)	1987	88	16	21.3	152	1.4
Intermodal Surface Transportation Efficiency Act (ISTEA)	1991	155	67	76.9	538	6.2
Transportation Equity Act for the 21st Century (TEA-21)	1998	218	63	40.6	1,850	9.3
Transportation Equity Act: A Legacy for Users (TEA-LU; House proposal)	2005	284	66	30.3	4,128	12.4

Source: Federal Highway Administration, Office of Program Administration, *A Guide to Federal-Aid Programs and Projects*, FHWA-IF-99-006 (Department of Transportation, May 1999); Erich Zimmermann, *Bulldozed: How Taxpayers Get Leveled by Highway Pork* (Washington: Taxpayers for Common Sense, 2005).

a. Also referred to as congressional earmarks or "special projects in the home districts of individual members of Congress." Paul C. Light, *Government's Greatest Achievements: From Civil Rights to Homeland Security* (Brookings, 2002).

has fallen far short of congressional intent. The reasons for this are many: recalcitrant state bureaucracies that continued to operate "business as usual," insufficient tools and ill-designed programs, and a stunning lack of accountability and performance. The second challenge to Congress, therefore, is to build on the foundation of ISTEA and TEA-21 in a way that works to give metropolitan areas greater powers and more tools in exchange for enhanced accountability.

What follows is a set of general and specific recommendations for addressing the shortcomings elucidated here. It is the very minimum that Congress should do to ensure the effectiveness of the nation's transportation program.

Reform Governance

Metropolitan areas face a daunting set of transportation challenges—increasing congestion, deteriorating air quality, crumbling infrastructure, spatial mismatches in the labor market—that threaten to undermine their competitive edge in the global economy. The lessons of the past decade, however, show that existing governance arrangements and structures are not up to the task. MPOs and local officials have too little power; state transportation departments, too much. In many metropolitan areas, the proliferation of separate administrative bodies does not reflect the travel, environmental, and economic realities of twenty-first-century metropolitan America.

If local transportation challenges are to be met, metropolitan areas need a greater say in the design and implementation of transportation policy. This means the devolution promoted by ISTEA and TEA-21 must go further. Several steps are needed: The responsibility and capacity of metropolitan planning organizations needs to be expanded. State decisions must be tied more closely to the demographic and market realities of metropolitan areas and the vision and priorities of metropolitan leaders. Collaboration across administrative borders and modes (air, rail, highway, and transit) should be required. And, finally, a new cadre of broad-minded transportation professionals needs to be nurtured and sustained.

Expand the Responsibility and Capacity of MPOs. The roles and responsibilities of MPOs must be augmented. To that end, Congress should allocate substantial resources directly to MPOs (see discussion below). Congress should also preserve and strengthen the metropolitan role in transportation planning and spending; the existing TEA-21 set-aside for metropolitan transportation planning should be increased from 1 to 2 percent.[56] In addition, generous support should be provided to build the capacity of MPOs through technical assistance, professional training, and the sharing of best practices. To facilitate this, a special research program should be created at the national level to identify and evaluate innovative approaches to metropolitan transportation challenges. Finally, as described below, MPOs should be subject to heightened performance and accountability requirements.

Ensure State Decisions Reflect Metropolitan Realities. Even with further reform, state departments of transportation will continue to oversee the largest share of federal transportation resources. For that reason, it is critical that statewide transportation policies and practices strengthen metropolitan economies and respond adequately to metropolitan transportation challenges. Congress should therefore require that state transportation-governing bodies include political, business, and citizen representation from every metropolitan area in the state. Congress should also require state transportation departments to allocate federal resources in a manner that is consistent with objective needs and reflects the proportional contribution of gas tax revenues from different parts of the state. Finally, Congress should require that financially constrained state transportation plans incorporate locally defined metropolitan priorities.

Encourage State and Metropolitan Collaboration. In many regions of the United States, the geography of transportation decisionmaking—fractured by arbitrary political borders—fails to reflect the regional travel patterns of people or goods. Congress should therefore establish a pilot program (perhaps initially funded at $100 million a year) to support transportation planning for economic corridors and regions that cross state and MPO administrative borders. Planning in these corridors should involve all modes of transportation, including highway, transit, airport, rail, and port links.[57] In addition, Congress should require MPOs with contiguous borders to coordinate their plans. Where multiple MPOs within a single state serve a metropolitan area, the federal DOT should either mandate formal relationships between these MPOs or consider consolidating them.

Connect Rail, Air, and Surface Transportation. In 2003, for the first time in U.S. history, the statutes governing surface transportation policy (TEA-21), aviation (Aviation Investment and Reform Act for the Twenty-First Century), and passenger rail were slated to be considered during the same Congress. This offered a superb opportunity for policymakers to transcend the nation's past and current separation of those modes and end the separate treatment of inter- and intrametropolitan policies. However, although the aviation law was reauthorized in 2003, passenger rail and surface transportation action languished. Thus the United States is still the only industrialized country in the world that has not pursued an integrated approach to transportation policy. This ignores both travel and political reality. For example, the focus of the new Transportation Security Administration (TSA) has revolved almost exclusively around aviation-oriented passenger screening and technology for package and luggage screening—and yet some 91 percent of intercity travel occurs by car or bus.[58] That means the TSA's efforts do not address the largest share of intercity passenger travel. Likewise, the dislocations caused by the September 11 terrorist attacks underscore that the nation's economic well-being, as well as its strategic security, depends on metropolitan areas and the optimal functioning of our national travel system in an interconnected, redundant, and reliable fashion. Such links support our economy, preserve our basic freedom to travel, and provide for the strategic security of the nation. Our nation's transportation modes should be boldly connected, and Congress should consider them as they are: as connected entities of the transportation network.[59]

Build a Corps of Twenty-First-Century Transportation Professionals. A primary objective of transportation reform efforts must be to quickly build a core group of professionals capable of understanding and responding to the diverse and complex transportation challenges of our nation. To be successful, federal transportation reform requires a cadre of transportation practitioners familiar with metropolitan growth dynamics and expert in a broad range of disciplines, ranging from law, business, and finance to engineering, land use, and planning. Congress must, therefore, provide state DOTs and MPOs with the funds and guidance necessary to modernize their personnel and hiring practices. The DOT should augment the Metropolitan Capacity Building Program, for example, to identify gaps in the transportation profession and train and educate the next generation of transportation professionals. In particular, the DOT should work closely with the nation's universities to expose students in relevant disciplines to transportation issues and concerns. Such a "teach transportation" effort could ultimately attract a cadre of smart and able students to the profession. Congress should dedicate sufficient resources—say $50 million annually—to this critical area.

Provide Enhanced Tools and Policies

The challenges faced by metropolitan areas require more than governance reform, however. States and metropolitan areas also need access to broader, more flexible tools and policies. Thus the federal government needs to increase the resources that flow *directly* to MPOs. These institutions are, after all, in the best position to use transportation funding in tandem with land use, housing, workforce, and economic development policies. In addition, Congress needs to expand choices for metropolitan residents by providing a more balanced federal approach to highway and transit projects and by leveraging existing transit investments to promote more compact development. Finally, the new transportation bill should ensure that scarce federal dollars spur maximum use of the current road and transit network.

Increase the Funding that Flows Directly to MPOs. Congress should give MPOs greater resources and flexibility to tailor transportation solutions to the distinctive realities of individual metropolitan areas. Specifically, Congress should substantially increase the funding that is suballocated to MPOs, where the majority of the transportation challenges remain and the majority of funds are generated. Such funding should, at a minimum, include the portion of Minimum Guarantee funds that is "flexible" and not distributed by formula among the core programs ($2.8 billion in fiscal year 2002).[60]

In exchange for greater funding, MPOs would be subject to enhanced accountability measures (described below). For example, the DOT would be given the authority to withhold a portion of these additional funds to award exceptional performers. In addition, the planning and citizen participation requirements in existing law would be retained. The DOT would also be allowed to dedicate up to half a percent of the additional funds for annual capacity building and research efforts that further metropolitan governance in transportation.

Over time Congress should consider creating a broader transportation block grant to metropolitan areas, modeled after the successful Community Development Block Grant program. Such a block grant program could consolidate several categorical programs, including CMAQ, JARC, and the TCSP pilot program, as well as portions of major programs such as bridge repair. Such a block grant would provide metropolitan areas with the predictability of funding necessary to make long-term planning possible. Congress should then require the DOT to present a plan for a metropolitan transportation block grant in advance of the next reauthorization.

Level the Playing Field between Highways and Transit. Metropolitan areas fully understand the importance of transit to their competitive future. Yet, despite earlier reforms, federal policy and practice continue to place transit projects at a disadvantage. Therefore several reforms should be made. Congress should continue the funding guarantees for transit and ensure that the federal share for transit projects equals the federal share for highways. Thus the 80-20 split between federal and state-local funds for new fixed-rail transit projects should be reinstated, and Congress should allow community assets, such as parks and other infrastructure, to count as part of the state-local match. In addition, the new law should require equal treatment of proposed highway and transit projects. Roadway projects using federal funds should face the same level of scrutiny as new rail projects, for example. Similarly, long-range financial requirements for highway projects should be disclosed at program level, as they now are for transit projects. Finally, Congress should give incentives to states to remove legal barriers that currently prohibit the use of state gas tax revenues for transit purposes.

Facilitate Transit-Oriented Development. The federal government has a special chance to leverage the billions that have already been invested in rail and other fixed-route transit projects. Two key opportunities exist. First, metropolitan long-range planning requirements should contain a provision requiring the consideration of alternative regional land use scenarios incorporating policy goals or regional visions rather than simply extrapolating from past trends. Second, a key criterion for allocating transit funding should be the consistency of local land use plans and zoning codes with transit-supportive land uses. Beyond that, federal law should also require that federal funds for the provision of key infrastructure (such as transit facilities or bridges) be tied to requirements for transit-supportive design and should provide guidelines on the functional integration of transit and the surrounding uses.[61] Finally, Congress should direct the DOT to work with the Department of Housing and Urban Development on a special effort to realize the real estate potential of transit stations. This initiative could involve a range of activities (such as research, technical assistance, and joint agency planning) and could provide a helpful forum for local government officials, transit operators, private sector developers, financial institutions, and secondary mortgage market entities.

Use the Market to Mitigate Congestion. The mounting transportation pressures on metropolitan areas occur at a time of severe fiscal constraint, pervasive frustration with congestion, and increasing opposition to road expansion. As in Europe, this requires a firm national commitment to make maximum use of existing road capacity and expand transportation alternatives. The new transportation bill should, therefore, augment efforts to use state-of-the-art technology and communications to encourage market responses that would relieve congestion, including road pricing. Advances in pricing technology (including electronic toll collection systems) and pricing schemes (such as congestion pricing) should, in particular, be explored and applied. Congress should, to that end, triple funding for the Value Pricing Pilot Program to $25 million a year and provide the DOT with expanded resources for research and communication efforts in this area. These funds should be used for demonstration activities, and once this market-based approach takes hold, public funding incentives should no longer be needed.

Enforce and Augment Requirements for Accountability and Reward Performance

At a time of economic uncertainty and fiscal stress, the nation needs to get the most out of its transportation investment. Despite delivering large funding increases to states and metropolitan areas, ISTEA and TEA-21 held state and metropolitan transportation bureaucracies to few standards of performance. Future transportation spending should be linked to a higher standard of managerial efficiency, programmatic effectiveness, and fiscal responsibility. To that end, transportation reform efforts should establish a new framework for accountability that includes tighter disclosure requirements, improved performance measures, and rewards for exceptional performance. Congress also needs to create a transportation system that is more responsive to citizens and business. The more citizens and businesses inform transportation decisions, the better those decisions will be.

Establish a New Federal Framework for Accountability and Performance. As with other areas of domestic policy, a new framework for transportation accountability and performance should have several elements. First, Congress should require state DOTs and MPOs to disclose their program and spending decisions in a transparent, accessible, frequent, and continuous manner. State and metropolitan entities should, at a minimum, disclose their spending patterns by political jurisdiction and origins of the revenue used. To the greatest extent practicable, disclosures should take advantage of recent advances in geographic information systems and provide citizens with easy-to-read state and regional maps that chart and chronicle core highway and transit investments. In addition, given the recent increase in highway debt financing, state departments should routinely disclose bond requirements and obligations.

Second, the federal government should require state and local metropolitan transportation agencies to maintain information systems that annually measure progress on indicators of national significance. These indicators might include mitigating congestion, improving public health, improving air quality, lowering transportation costs, and expanding transportation options for target groups (such as the elderly or low-income workers). The law should also require transportation agencies to set annual performance objectives in each of these critical areas. As with disclosure of spending decisions, agency performance objectives (and progress toward meeting those goals) should be shared with the general public in an accessible manner.

Finally, federal law should establish consequences for both excellent and poor performance. Congress, in this regard, should allow the DOT to maintain a small incentive pool to reward states and metropolitan areas that consistently perform at an exceptional level. The department should also give high performers relief from regulatory and administrative requirements. By the same token, the federal DOT should consider possible intervention strategies for consistent low performers. (In designating high and low performers, DOT should take into account the difficult challenges facing state agencies and MPOs in large metropolitan areas.)

There is substantial federal precedent for such an accountability framework. Congress, for example, established a management assessment system for public housing agencies and created a performance measurement and reward system in the 1996 welfare reform law. The transportation system of governance and finance shares many similarities with these other areas of domestic policy—and should operate under similar accountability.

Increase Practical Opportunities for Citizen and Business Participation. Congress has already required that citizen participation in transportation planning be "early and continuing." Yet compliance with this requirement in an industry unaccustomed to public input has been sporadic at best. Congress needs to ensure, therefore, that transportation agencies have the resources and guidance necessary to carry out the law and that the DOT has the mandate to enforce it. It should be tasked, in this regard, to provide clear guidance on what constitutes performance regarding citizen participation and should establish mechanisms to evaluate agency adherence to these guidelines. Congress should also provide a new $100 million incentive fund to encourage state and metropolitan experimentation with state-of-the-art technologies for engaging citizens in public debates. The same fund could be used to expand the use of computer mapping tools to illustrate disparate spending patterns and to make such information widely available on the Internet.

Conclusion

Congress should make no mistake: great potential exists to build on the gains of previous reform efforts and help improve the economic vitality and environmental quality of metropolitan areas. Yet this potential will only be realized if congressional leaders confront the metropolitan realities of the twenty-first century and understand that yesterday's solutions cannot address tomorrow's challenges.

In that vein, Congress faces a two-step challenge. It should, first and foremost, do all it can to retain the slate of federal reforms that began in the early 1990s. These reforms have unleashed a wave of energy and innovation across the country that is beginning to fashion winning solutions to the pressing transportation challenges that face our metropolitan communities.

But Congress should go further. Metropolitan transportation challenges will only be fully addressed if metropolitan areas are given more powers, greater tools, and higher capacity to get transportation policy right for their places. Yet these reforms must come with a quid pro quo: the federal government must demand greater performance and accountability from its state and metropolitan partners. This federalist exchange—of greater flexibility in exchange for more responsibility—lies at the heart of other major federal reforms over the past decade, and it will be critical to the success of transportation policy over the coming decades.

The stage is set, therefore, to take federal transportation policy to a new level of effectiveness and impact. The stakes are very high: metropolitan (and national) competitiveness, environmental and community quality, and fiscal efficiency all depend on such progress.

Metropolitan political, business, and civic leaders are ready to go the next step. Is Congress up to the task?

Notes

1. DRI-WEFA, *The Role of Metro Areas in the U.S. Economy*, report prepared for the Seventieth Annual Meeting of the U.S. Conference of Mayors (Lexington, Mass., June 6, 2002) (www.usmayors.org/70thAnnualMeeting/metroecon2002/metroreport.pdf [January 2005]).

2. The twenty most congested metropolitan areas make up more than one-third of the nation's economy. See Senate Committee on Environment and Public Works, testimony of Ron Sims, 107 Cong., 2 sess. (March 19, 2002).

3. See Robert Burchell and others, *Costs of Sprawl—2000* (Washington: Transportation Research Board, National Research Council, 2002).

4. Department of Transportation (DOT), *Status of the Nation's Highways, Bridges, and Transit: 2002 Conditions and Performance Report to Congress* (2003), exhibits 3-6 and 3-28.

5. Keith R. Ihlanfeldt and David L. Sjoquist, "The Spatial Mismatch Hypothesis: A Review of Recent Studies and Their Implications for Welfare Reform," *Housing Policy Debate* 9, no. 4 (1998): 849–92.

6. Bureau of Labor Statistics, "Consumer Expenditure Survey" (www.bls.gov/cex/csxstnd.htm [April 2005]), Standard Tables 1984–2002.

7. Federal agencies have provided security-related technical assistance and training and sought to enhance networks of relationships between state and local transportation officials. They have not been able to provide much targeted financial support, however, to defray costs incurred in response to the terrorist attacks and the subsequent heightened security alerts—let alone to provide dedicated subsidies for the capital costs of improving highway and transit system security. See Howitt and Makler, chapter 11 in this volume.

8. See Office of Management and Budget, *Fiscal Year 2005, Analytical Perspectives: Budget of the United States Government* (2004).

9. DOT, *2002 Conditions and Performance Report*, exhibit 6-13.

10. Surface Transportation Policy Project, *Ten Years of Progress: Building Better Communities through Transportation* (Washington, 2002).

11. American Public Transportation Association, *Transit Ridership Report* (Washington, 1997 and 2005).

12. Bureau of the Census, *1990 Census of Population and Housing and Census 2000*.

13. See Puentes and Prince, chapter 3 in this volume.

14. Bruce McDowell, "Improving Regional Transportation Decisions: MPOs and Certification," discussion paper prepared for the Center on Urban and Metropolitan Policy (Brookings, 1999).

15. General Accounting Office, *Urban Transportation: Metropolitan Planning Organizations' Efforts to Meet Federal Planning Requirements*, RCED-96-200 (1996).

16. General Accounting Office, *Surface Transportation: Many Factors Affect Investment Decisions*, GAO-04-744 (2004).

17. McDowell, "Improving Regional Transportation."

18. States are required to spend funds in smaller urbanized areas but do not actually suballocate these funds to the areas. The suballocated funds, about $12.4 billion since 1992, come from small apportionments from the Surface Transportation Program. MPOs receive no direct funding from the major federal programs—interstate maintenance, bridge repair, and the national highway system. In fact, states are under no statutory obligation to suballocate funds from the Congestion Mitigation and Air Quality Program, even though that program's specific focus is metropolitan. See *Code of Federal Regulations* 23, sec. 133(d)(3) (1999). See also Senate Committee on Banking, Housing, and Urban Affairs, *Hearings on the Implementation and Reauthorization of the Public Transportation Provisions of the Transportation Equity Act for the 21st Century*, testimony of H. Brent Coles, 107 Cong., 2 sess. (June 13, 2002).

19. Ron Thaniel, "Barr Leads Mayors' Call for Dealing with National Crisis in Metropolitan Congestion," *U.S. Mayor Newspaper*, December 9, 2002 (www.usmayors.org/USCM/us_mayor_newspaper/documents/12_09_02/barr_leads.asp).

20. Nationally, local governments own more than three-quarters of the 4-million-mile roadway network and over half of all bridges. DOT, *2002 Conditions and Performance Report*, exhibits 2-3 and 2-4.

21. See Hill and others, chapter 5 in this volume.

22. Denver Regional Council of Governments, "Transportation Funding Equity?" (www.drcog.org/index.cfm?page=TransportationFundingEquity [February 2005]).

23. During the debate over reauthorization of ISTEA, the issue of donor versus donee states dominated the discussion. The resulting "minimum guarantee" provision ensures that each state receives at least 90.5 percent of its share of contributions to the Highway Account of the Highway Trust Fund.

24. Washington State recently recognized this disparity and created a statewide program designed to funnel 13 percent of gas tax revenues to urban areas. Washington Research Council, "Referendum 51 Gets Us Moving, Safely, Again," Policy Brief 02-13 (Seattle, October 2002).

25. For a national scan, see Environmental Working Group, *Metropolitan Areas Get Short End of Federal Gas Tax Funds* (Washington, 2004). For regional analyses, see the following—Atlanta: Duane D. Stanford, "Metro Roads Shortchanged: Funding Formula Steers Cash to Rural Highways at the Expense of Gridlocked Atlanta Motorists," *Atlanta Journal-Constitution*, September 28, 2004, p. A1; California: Adrian R. Fleissig and William F. Gayk, *Distribution of State Transportation Funding* (Sacramento: California State University Center for California Studies, 2003); Houston: Catherine Rentz Pernot, *Transportation Funding Equity: The Local Pie Is Strangely Sliced* (Houston: Gulf Coast Institute, 2003); Pennsylvania: Anne Canby and James Bickford, "Highway Investment Analysis," draft paper (Philadelphia: 10,000 Friends of Pennsylvania, 2003); San Antonio: Bill Barker, "Gasoline Tax Shortchanges Big-City Drivers," *San Antonio Express-News*, January 19, 2003; St. Louis: University of Missouri-St. Louis, *Analysis of Metropolitan St. Louis State Transportation Fiscal Flows* (St. Louis: Public Policy Research Center, 2001).

26. *Making Appropriations for the Department of Transportation and Related Agencies for the Fiscal Year Ending September 30, 2002, and for Other Purposes.* H. Rept. 107-308, 107 Cong. 1 sess. (Government Printing Office, 2001).

27. Office of Management and Budget, *Budget of the United States Government, Fiscal Year 2004—Appendix*, Title 3-General Provisions, sec. 321 (2003).

28. See chapter 3.

29. See Beimborn and Puentes, chapter 10 in this volume.

30. Robert Puentes, "Flexible Funding for Transit: Who Uses It?" report prepared for the Center on Urban and Metropolitan Policy (Brookings, May 2000).

31. Surface Transportation Policy Project, *Ten Years of Progress*.

32. For example, despite increasing ridership, since 1987 the total fleet of subway ("heavy rail") cars has actually been reduced, the percent that are over age has nearly tripled, and their average condition has deteriorated. DOT, *2002 Conditions and Performance Report*, exhibit 3-41.

33. Association of Metropolitan Planning Organizations, *The Case for Increased Metropolitan Planning Funds* (Washington, 2002)

34. Anthony Downs, "The Devolution Revolution: Why Congress is Shifting a Lot of Power to the Wrong Levels." Policy Brief 3 (Brookings, 1996).

35. *Code of Federal Regulations* 23, sec. 450.316 (2002). See Daniel A. Rodriguez, "Infrastructure and Social Equity: Lessons from Transportation," paper presented at the First Annual Conference on Infrastructure Priorities, Washington, October 24–26, 2001.

36. *Code of Federal Regulations* 23, sec. 134(f)(1)(A-G); 23, sec. 135(c)(1)(A-G); 49, sec. 5303(a)(1)(A-G) (2002).

37. *Code of Federal Regulations* 23, sec. 134(f)(2)(A-G); 23 sec. 135(c)(2) (2002).

38. Anthony Downs, *Still Stuck in Traffic: Coping with Peak Hour Traffic Congestion* (Brookings, 2004), p. 22.

39. See Transportation Research Board, *Strategic Highway Research: Saving Lives, Reducing Congestion, Improving Quality of Life—Special Report 260* (Washington: National Academies Press, 2001); Transportation Research Board, *Curbing Gridlock: Peak-Period Fees to Relieve Traffic Congestion—Special Report 242* (Washington: National Academies Press, 1994); General Accounting Office, *Surface Transportation: Moving into the 21st Century*, GAO/RCED-99-176 (1999).

40. Environmental Protection Agency, "Final Rule to Implement the 8-Hour Ozone National Ambient Air Quality Standard-Phase I," *Federal Register* 69, no. 84 (April 30, 2004): 23857-951.

41. American Society of Civil Engineers, *2001 Report Card for America's Infrastructure* (Reston, Va., 2001).

42. Other costs to be considered are the costs of crashes, disabilities, respiratory disease, air-pollution-induced building deterioration, and wasted time. Indirect costs could be as high as direct costs.

43. Bureau of Transportation Statistics, *Highlights of the 2001 National Personal Transportation Survey*, BTS-03-05 (DOT, 2003).

44. Milwaukee, San Francisco, and Portland, Oregon, have all successfully removed their waterfront-blocking freeways. See Charles Lockwood, "Destroy a Freeway, Save a City," *New York Times*, August 21, 2001, p. A19.

45. See, for example, Margaret Pugh, "Barriers to Work: The Spatial Divide between Jobs and Welfare Recipients in Metropolitan Areas," discussion paper prepared for the Center on Urban and Metropolitan Policy (Brookings, 1998); Bruce Katz and Kate Allen, "Help Wanted: Connecting Inner-City Job Seekers with Suburban Jobs," *Brookings Review* 17, no. 4 (1999): 31-35; General Accounting Office, *Welfare Reform: Implementing DOT's Access to Jobs Program in Its First Year*, GAO/RCED-00-14 (1999).

46. It is important to note that spatial mismatch is not just a "people to jobs" problem but also a "jobs to people" problem caused, in part, by massive metropolitan decentralization.

47. Bureau of Labor Statistics, *Consumer Expenditures in 2002*, Report 974 (Department of Labor, 2004).

48. See Bureau of Transportation Statistics, *Commuting Expenses: Disparity for the Working Poor* (DOT, March 2003); and Surface Transportation Policy Project and Center for Neighborhood Technology, *Driven to Spend: The Impact of Sprawl on Household Transportation Expenses* (Washington, 2000).

49. That state is Wyoming, which started out with the third lowest rate in 1992. See Puentes and Prince, chapter 3 in this volume.

50. Federal Highway Administration, *Highway Statistics 1999* (DOT, 1999), table SF-21; *Highway Statistics 2002* (DOT, 2002), table SF-21.

51. The Governmental Accounting Standards Board is an arm of the Financial Accounting Foundation. Similar to its sister organization, the Financial Accounting Standards Board (which sets accounting rules for corporations), the government board sets accounting rules for units of state and local government. Statement 34 governing these rules for capital asset accounting was adopted for the first time in 1999 and took effect for prospective requirements in 2003. See National Cooperative Highway Research Program, *A Review of DOT Compliance with GASB 34 Requirements*, Report 522 (Washington: Transportation Research Board, 2004).

52. National Association of State Budget Officers, *Budget Shortfalls: Strategies for Closing Spending and Revenue Gaps* (Washington, 2002).

53. Humberto Sanchez, "Local Officials Urge a Boost in Next Surface Funding Law," *Bond Buyer*, February 11, 2003, p. 5.

54. Federal programs actually represent only a very small percentage of the total dollars available—about 28 percent of the approximately $154.8 billion in total governmental expenditures for transportation in 1999. This is just a small slice of the overall $1.572 trillion national transportation tab. Almost all of the transportation expenditures are private expenditures. For data see Rosalyn A. Wilson, *Transportation in America 2001*, 19th ed. (Washington: Eno Transportation Foundation, 2002). Calculations are by the authors.

55. Despite contentions to the contrary, a recent report from the Federal Highway Administration concluded that most delays in transportation projects were due to short-funding on the state and local level and not to environmental regulations. Federal Highway Administration, *Reasons for EIS Project Delays* (DOT, 2000). Subsequently, a GAO report found the highest rated approach for reducing delays was to improve coordination among partners. General Accounting Office, *Highway Infrastructure: Perceptions of Stakeholders on Approaches to Reduce Highway Project Completion Time*, GAO-03-398 (2003).

56. For example, see *Metropolitan Congestion Relief Act of 2003*, H.R. 3611, 108 Cong. 1 sess. (GPO, 2003).

57. This program is intended to be less project specific than the existing National Corridor Planning and Development Program.

58. That is, trips of more than fifty miles one way. Bureau of Transportation Statistics, *National Transportation Statistics 2003* (DOT, 2004), table 1-39.

59. For example, the Reconnecting America project proposes a new approach to intercity travel by integrating aviation services (particularly the 58 percent of flights shorter than 500 miles) with rail and intercity bus service (www.reconnectingamerica.org [January 2005]). See also House Transportation and Infrastructure Committee, Subcommittees on Aviation and Railroads, *Joint Hearing on Planes, Trains, and Intermodalism: Improving the Link between Air and Rail*, testimony of Hank Dittmar, 108 Cong., 1 sess. (February 26, 2003).

60. Federal Highway Administration, *Computation of Apportionment of Minimum Guarantee Funds Authorized for Fiscal Year 2002* (DOT, 2003.)

61. See Dena Belzer and Gerald Autler, "Transit Oriented Development: Moving from Rhetoric to Reality," discussion paper prepared for the Brookings Center on Urban and Metropolitan Policy (Brookings and Great American Station Foundation, 2002).

PART TWO

Financing the Transportation System

3

Fueling Transportation Finance: A Primer on the Gas Tax

Robert Puentes and Ryan Prince

With debates about traffic and taxes urgent now, few issues have become as contentious as how to pay for roads and transit. Amid these disputes, few controversies remain as heated as those surrounding the motor fuel excise tax known as the "gas tax."

Initiated originally at the state level, the gas tax has been widely used in public finance since the 1930s, when states introduced the levies to pay for expanding the highway system. Today, revenue generated by the 18.4-cents-per-gallon federal excise tax makes up the bulk of federal highway funds. Similarly, revenue from the state gas tax constitutes the largest source of financing for spending at the state level, although funding tends to be spent on a greater variety of purposes.

The average state tax rate in 2004 is just over 20 cents. Although every state levies a gas tax and depends on it as an essential source of funds to pay for transportation projects and programs, many citizens and professionals still find the gas tax issue confusing and contentious. The confusion results in part from differences in the state rules governing the imposition, rate, and administration of the tax. Further complicating the debate is the fragmented nature of the tax, the unclear relationship between the state and federal gas taxes, and the arcane system of transportation finance overall.

The contention surrounding the gas tax stems from policymakers' resistance to taxes in general and the often inequitable distribution of its revenues within states. Equally controversial is most states' exclusive dedication of the gas tax to highway purposes. This forces transit and other projects to seek other sources of funding and places them on a less advantageous footing.

To help dispel this confusion and controversy, this chapter undertakes to describe the use of federal and state gas taxes and to assess their impacts on state and local transportation systems and funding. To that end, this chapter relates the history of the taxes, details the rules governing the use of associated revenues in every state, and assesses the flow and distribution of gas tax revenues at the federal, state, and local levels. At the end are various proposals to improve current use and distribution of gas tax revenues to support the development of more balanced, multimodal transportation networks.

What Is the Gas Tax?

At both the state and federal levels, the gas tax is a levy imposed on the sale of motor fuels on a cents-per-gallon basis.[1] Economists identify the gas tax as a user fee because it generally applies only to individuals purchasing gasoline for motor vehicle use on public highways.[2]

However, it is important to note that neither the federal nor state gas taxes are true user fees in the sense that the end user explicitly pays the specified tax at the point of purchase. Rather, both the state and federal gas tax are "manufacturer's excise taxes." The first entity in the state to refine, distribute, or wholesale gasoline (and other motor fuels) pays the stipulated tax rate. Often, the tax-paying entity is a distributor, importer, refiner, retail manufacturer, licensed dealer, supplier, or wholesale distributor.

The initial taxpayer incorporates the levy as an additional cost in its production process. To compensate for the added cost, producers incorporate the gas tax into their wholesale price and pass it through to the end user (the consumer), resulting in higher retail gasoline prices. Although the consumer is not directly taxed, that is ultimately how it functions. In fact, some states explicitly acknowledge this transfer.[3]

The Department of Energy has allocated an expense to each of the constituent parts in the gasoline supply chain and has derived percentages for each component's contribution to retail prices. This analysis reveals that from 2000 to 2005, federal and state taxes constituted the second highest proportion of the retail price of gas. Crude oil, the primary resource

Figure 3-1. Components of the Retail Price of One Gallon of Gasoline, Average, January 2000–February 2005

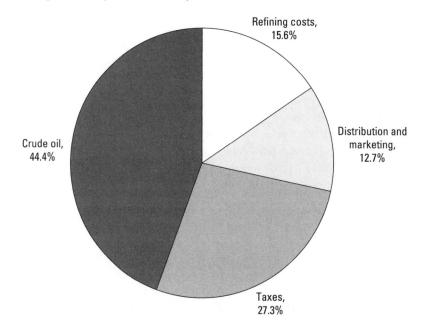

Source: Department of Energy, Energy Information Administration, "Gasoline Components History" (tonto.eia.doe.gov/oog/info/gdu/gaspump.html [2005]).

component of gasoline, has consistently contributed the highest proportion and majority of cost to the retail price (figure 3-1).

Since 1978 the federal government has exempted local units of government from paying the federal gas tax. In contrast, several states continue to impose the gas tax on local public entities. For example, in Wisconsin, the state levies a gas tax on local governments and school districts. In all, thirty-two states levy their gas tax on purchases made by local entities for highway purposes.

History and Current Role

In 1919 Oregon became the first state to enact a gas tax, and within ten years, every state had followed suit. Both Alaska and Hawaii instituted motor fuel taxes upon receiving statehood in 1959. The specific impetus behind the state gas tax was to finance the nation's growing roadway system and to alleviate the burden on other funding mechanisms, such as bond issuance and property taxation.[4]

Today, gas tax receipts are the most important source of revenue for aggregate state highway spending. However, the gas tax is collected, administered, and spent according to complicated and unique provisions that sometimes vary greatly from state to state.

In the majority of states, the tax is collected monthly from the manufacturer and administered by the state's department of revenue, tax commission, or similar agency. In some states, the tax is administered by the department of transportation. Each state distributes the funds based on an intricate and complex formula. A small portion of the receipts usually goes to the department of revenue or similar agency to cover the expenses of collecting the tax. Funds also occasionally flow to water transportation, such as harbor and watercraft programs, or are applied to nontransportation purposes, such as fish and wildlife programs.

The majority of the gas tax proceeds, however, flow to various repositories for spending on the transportation system—often a transportation trust fund, the state department of transportation, or the state's general fund. From these repositories, a portion of the revenue is typically distributed by formula to counties, cities, and other localities, but principally, the state departments of transportation retain the funds.

The federal gas tax was first levied in 1932 along with other excise taxes in an effort to mitigate a mounting fiscal crisis and to help balance the federal budget. Initially, Congress intended to use the gas tax to address immediate budgetary concerns, and the tax would lapse when the budget was balanced. Indeed, Senate Finance Committee testimony confirms that the federal gas tax was originally intended to be temporary. Furthermore, there was a clear sentiment that it should continue to serve principally as a fiscal tool for states to pay for highways.[5]

Contrary to original intent, the federal gas tax has remained and through periodic, incremental increases has produced a sustained cash flow to federal coffers. Its functional role, however, has changed dramatically. Initially, receipts from the federal tax accrued in the general fund, with congressional discretion for appropriation. That meant that revenues generated from the gas tax were not explicitly bound to highway or transportation infrastructure spending. Instead, highway funds were subject to the same allocation process applied to domestic discretionary spending. With the passage of the Highway Revenue Act of 1956, however, federal gas tax revenues were earmarked for roadway spending only. This law established the current Highway Trust Fund (HTF), which remains the principal repository for receipts from the federal gas tax.

Figure 3-2. Highway Trust Fund Receipts for Fiscal Year 2003[a]

Billions of dollars

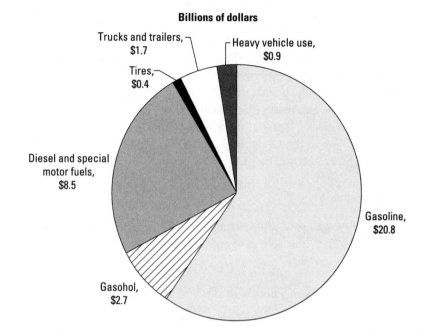

Source: Federal Highway Administration (FHWA), "Table FE-10: Status of the Federal Highway Trust Fund," in *Highway Statistics, 2003* (Department of Transportation, 2003).
a. Total = $35.1 billion.

Congress has periodically extended the gas tax beyond its initial expiration date in 1972. The most recent continuation accompanied the reauthorization of the Intermodal Surface Transportation Efficiency Act of 1991 (ISTEA) as the Transportation Equity Act for the Twenty-First Century (TEA-21) in 1998. Congress has also elected to periodically increase the federal gas tax to generate additional revenues and to realign trust fund receipts with inflationary pressures in the transportation and construction industries.[6]

The federal gas tax rose from 1 cent per gallon in 1932 to 4 cents in 1960. The tax remained unchanged until the early 1980s. At that time, the proceeds of the gas tax were still being deposited into the HTF for highway-only uses (the "Highway Account"). In 1982 Congress passed the Surface Transportation Act, which, for the first time, split gas tax receipts into two accounts. Beginning in 1984, 1 cent of a new 5 cent increase in the gas tax was placed in the Mass Transit Account for capital projects, with the remainder held in the Highway Account.

Today, the tax on gasoline is still the principal source of revenue for the HTF, and the HTF is the principal source of funding for federal-aid surface transportation programs (figure 3-2). In 2003 the gas tax accounted for 59.2 percent of all HTF receipts.

However, not all HTF revenues are spent on the highway system. The 18.4-cents-per-gallon federal gas tax is still deposited in the HTF but is now divided as follows: approximately 15.44 cents accumulates in the Highway Account, with the remainder distributed to the Mass Transit Account (2.86 cents) and the Leaking Underground Storage Tank trust fund (0.10 cents).[7] Nearly $18 billion of the $20.8 billion generated by the federal gas tax went into the Highway Account in 2003.[8]

Findings

This analysis shows several important findings regarding the federal and state gas taxes and their role in overall transportation spending. Here are several of the key results.

Majority of Highway Funds Are Derived from Gas Tax

The gas tax generates considerable revenues for transportation because of the sheer quantity of gasoline consumed in this country.[9] In fiscal year 2002, $135.9 billion was raised from federal, state, and local sources for highway programs. Receipts from federal, state, and local fuel taxes accounted for 39.9 percent of all revenues available for highway funding.[10] Combined with other taxes, fees, and user charges, these revenues exceeded $80 billion, or 59.4 percent of all highway expenditures (table 3-1).

More than half of the highway revenues are generated from state taxes, fees, tolls, and general revenue. Of the funds, state fuel taxes make up the largest revenue category, generating about $27.8 billion, or 20.4 percent of all highway revenues in 2002.

The largest percentage of federal and state transportation revenues is generated from taxes, fees, and user charges—such as tolls. At the federal level, nearly all (94.0 percent) of the revenue is generated from these sources. A large percentage of state funds (72.6 percent) is also derived from these sources, although the role of other sources, such as bond proceeds, is becoming more significant.[11] Proceeds from bonds have increased by nearly 60 percent since 1997. By contrast, only a small portion (8.2 percent) of the local revenues is generated by taxes, fees, and user charges. This is generally due to localities' inability to administer taxes as determined by the state.

Table 3-1. Revenue Sources for Highways, 2002

Thousands of dollars, except as indicated

Type of revenue	Federal	State	Local	Total	Percent
Fuel taxes	25,384,197	27,810,045	999,821	54,194,063	39.87
Vehicle taxes and fees	2,598,739	16,650,808	751,179	20,000,726	14.72
Tolls	0	5,214,951	1,355,000	6,569,951	4.83
Property taxes	0	0	6,488,000	6,488,000	4.77
General fund appropriations	1,484,000	4,738,952	14,111,000	20,333,952	14.96
Other taxes and imposts	235,000	5,977,175	9,370,000	15,582,175	11.46
Bond issue proceeds	0	8,014,466	4,733,000	12,747,466	9.38
Total revenues	29,701,936	68,406,397	37,808,000	135,916,333	99.99[a]

Source: Federal Highway Administration (FHWA), *Highway Statistics, 2002* (Department of Transportation, 2002).
a. Value less than 100 percent is artifact due to rounding.

The impact of the gas tax can also be seen in breakouts of individual states' revenue sources for highways. As table 3-2 illustrates, from 1995 to 2003, the state gas tax represented the primary source of highway funds for ten states. Federal payments (mostly from the federal gas tax) represented the largest share and are the primary source in thirty-four states. Kentucky is the only state in which vehicle taxes are the primary source. Five northeastern states—Connecticut, Delaware, Massachusetts, New Jersey, and New York—rely most heavily on bond proceeds.

Gas Tax Receipts Are Beginning to Plateau

Gas tax revenues at the federal level have risen from $125 million in 1933 to a high of $21.2 billion in 1999. Since then, total federal gas tax revenues have declined from $21.0 billion in 2000 to $20.6 billion in 2001 and have ticked back up to $20.9 billion in 2002 (figure 3-3).[12]

The inflation-adjusted data illustrate a much different picture of the historical growth of the federal gas tax and its corresponding receipts.[13] After controlling for inflation, revenues increased from $1.7 billion in 1933 to a high of $24.0 billion in 1994. The change in real revenues over time represents an increase of more than 1,000 percent. Figure 3-4 shows a prevailing upward trajectory for revenues, accompanied by frequent fluctuations in the effective tax rate. Periodic bouts of heightened inflation without commensurate tax rate adjustments are responsible for the majority of fluctuations. Thus, as the real value of the dollar declined, the effective tax rate also declined.

Until recently, receipts have trended upward despite variations in the overall trajectory of the real tax rate. Aside from a brief period in the 1970s

Table 3-2. Revenues, by Source, Used by States for State-Administered Highways, 1995–2003[a]

Percent

State	Motor fuel taxes	Vehicle taxes	Tolls	General funds	Other imposts and sources[b]	Bonds proceeds	Federal payments	Local payments
Nevada	42.8	16.3	0.0	0.9	3.2	6.5	29.6	0.6
North Carolina	38.7	12.7	0.1	3.2	15.3	1.2	28.5	0.3
Louisiana	38.3	10.2	2.7	16.6	1.9	4.3	26.0	0.0
South Carolina	37.4	7.9	0.1	3.9	2.5	9.9	37.7	0.6
Montana	37.0	8.1	0.0	0.0	1.0	0.0	53.4	0.4
Texas	36.9	17.7	1.8	0.2	3.1	3.0	33.6	3.5
Tennessee	36.5	15.5	0.0	5.0	4.9	0.0	36.6	1.5
Alabama	35.3	12.6	0.0	2.0	1.3	0.1	47.2	1.5
Pennsylvania	34.6	15.6	10.5	2.7	3.9	7.8	24.4	0.5
Ohio	34.1	5.2	7.0	1.1	4.0	12.9	34.1	1.6
Nebraska	33.2	7.8	0.0	4.6	16.1	0.0	30.8	7.5
Arkansas	32.9	11.1	0.0	3.3	3.0	8.8	40.1	0.8
Mississippi	32.9	10.7	0.0	2.1	9.0	8.6	36.0	0.7
Oregon	32.2	22.5	0.0	4.1	3.5	3.2	34.0	0.6
Idaho	30.7	17.8	0.0	0.0	0.0	0.0	50.4	1.1
Missouri	29.6	11.9	0.0	0.6	13.2	6.8	36.9	1.0
Minnesota	29.2	28.9	0.0	3.2	7.6	2.7	27.2	1.2
Wisconsin	28.8	13.4	0.0	0.0	2.5	13.9	37.2	4.1
South Dakota	28.4	2.7	0.0	0.0	16.7	0.0	50.3	1.9
Maine	28.0	10.7	10.7	12.7	1.3	7.4	29.2	0.0
West Virginia	27.7	20.5	4.7	3.9	1.8	7.2	34.1	0.0
Washington	27.2	21.9	6.6	1.2	3.0	13.3	25.4	1.3
Colorado	27.1	12.7	0.0	6.4	10.3	17.2	25.0	1.4
New Hampshire	25.4	15.4	15.5	0.6	4.2	6.6	31.1	1.3
Utah	25.3	7.1	0.0	17.5	3.7	20.2	25.9	0.4
Michigan	25.2	15.7	1.7	9.4	5.0	6.0	35.5	1.5
Florida	24.7	13.9	12.7	0.6	5.6	15.6	24.9	2.0
Indiana	24.6	7.9	5.3	2.9	2.5	19.3	36.3	1.3
Rhode Island	24.5	8.6	3.6	1.2	1.3	16.5	44.3	0.0
California	24.4	23.5	4.0	1.7	7.0	0.0	31.3	8.1
Connecticut	23.0	10.6	0.0	1.5	7.9	29.2	27.6	0.2
New Mexico	22.9	19.9	0.0	0.4	2.9	18.9	34.7	0.3
Virginia	22.8	18.6	3.3	2.8	17.4	12.9	20.8	1.4
Vermont	20.9	26.5	0.0	0.4	3.6	0.4	47.7	0.5
Georgia	20.4	9.5	1.2	5.9	14.1	8.0	40.5	0.4
Arizona	20.0	8.1	0.0	3.8	16.8	15.3	25.4	10.6
Oklahoma	19.5	12.2	13.6	2.0	4.1	18.1	29.4	1.1
Illinois	19.3	23.0	12.8	1.1	3.6	10.7	29.1	0.4
Iowa	19.0	15.9	0.0	4.8	26.2	0.0	34.0	0.0
New York	18.7	9.7	17.9	4.3	3.2	25.3	20.7	0.2
Kentucky	18.7	38.1	0.9	3.8	5.9	2.1	30.6	0.0
Maryland	17.9	21.6	10.9	0.9	8.5	7.4	32.4	0.4
Hawaii	17.2	15.8	0.0	1.3	5.3	19.9	40.5	0.0
Wyoming	16.2	11.4	0.0	0.3	4.8	0.0	66.8	0.4
North Dakota	14.8	9.9	0.0	7.3	2.2	0.0	62.9	2.9

(*continued*)

Table 3-2.   Revenues, by Source, Used by States for State-Administered Highways, 1995–2003[a] (*continued*)

Percent

State	Motor fuel taxes	Vehicle taxes	Tolls	General funds	Other imposts and sources[b]	Bonds proceeds	Federal payments	Local payments
Delaware	14.4	12.4	19.9	6.5	5.0	*24.8*	17.0	0.0
Kansas	14.3	8.2	5.7	1.7	19.8	23.3	*25.4*	1.8
Massachusetts	11.8	6.3	6.1	15.5	5.3	*34.4*	20.6	0.0
New Jersey	7.6	7.3	16.9	3.5	4.8	*45.2*	14.8	0.0
Alaska	4.5	5.0	3.4	23.6	4.8	2.6	*56.2*	0.0

Source: FHWA, *Highway Statistics, 1995 through 2003,* table SF-3.

a. States are ranked by gas tax share of revenue. Figures in *italic* represent the largest percent of revenues for each state.

b. Includes a wide variety of other taxes and fees such as rental car surcharges, severance taxes, casino revenue, cigarette taxes, general sales taxes, mineral lease and oil royalties, inspection fees on nonhighway fuels, lubricating oil taxes, and corporate income taxes.

Figure 3-3.   Federal Gas Tax Rate and Revenues, 1933–2002

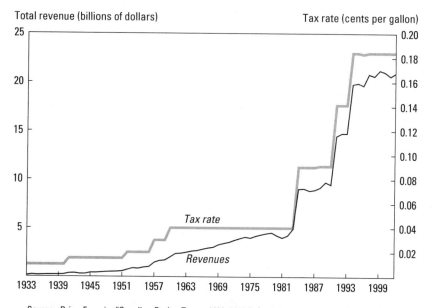

Source: Brian Francis, "Gasoline Excise Taxes, 1933–2000," *Statistics of Income Bulletin* (Winter 2000); Internal Revenue Service, "Historical Tables and Appendix," *Statistics of Income Bulletin* (Spring 2004), table 21, "Federal Excise Taxes Reported to or Collected by the Internal Revenue Service, Alcohol and Tobacco Tax and Trade Bureau, and Customs Service, by Type of Excise Tax, Fiscal Years 1996–2004"; FHWA, *Highway Statistics,* various years (Department of Transportation).

Figure 3-4. Inflation-Adjusted Federal Gas Tax Rate and Revenues, Current Dollars, 1933–2002

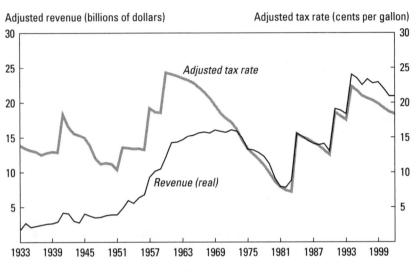

Adjusted revenue (billions of dollars)   Adjusted tax rate (cents per gallon)

with high inflation and volatility in world crude oil prices, inflation-adjusted revenues from the gas tax have consistently trended upward.

In inflation-adjusted dollars, the tax rate reached its highest level in the early 1960s, exceeding 24 cents per gallon. Beginning in the 1970s, the real tax rate descended into a trough and by the early 1980s had reached its lowest level, about 7 cents per gallon.

In 1984 Congress responded to the decline in the real gas tax rate with the first rate increase in twenty-three years. Thereafter, incremental increases have stabilized the real rate throughout the 1990s. The adjusted tax rate had, however, peaked by 1995. Accordingly, since then, adjusted revenues have declined by 13 percent.

Although inflationary pressures have affected the real tax rate, the sustained growth in population, per capita automobile ownership, automobile travel, and gasoline consumption have contributed immensely to the stability of the HTF over time (figure 3-5). Until recently, growth in both vehicular miles traveled (VMT) and fuel consumption has more than offset the inconsistent adjustments to the gas tax rate. VMT has risen both in aggregate and per capita terms with a commensurate, although not as extreme, increase

Figure 3-5. Conditions Underlying Growth in Fuel Consumption at the National Level, 1960–2002

Percent increase

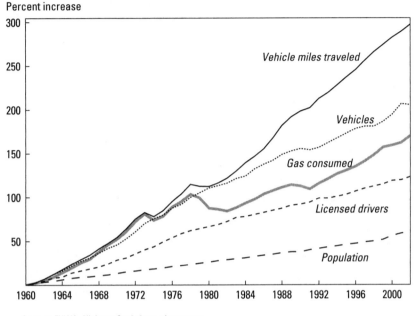

Source: FHWA, *Highway Statistics,* various years.

in fuel consumption. Of course, although increases in the indicators illustrated in figure 3-5 all contribute to additional gas tax revenues, they also add additional costs and place additional stress on the transportation network.

An analysis of the most recent data indicates that the rapid increases in these indicators may be leveling off. Perhaps most important is the leveling off of annual VMT. Recent data from the Federal Highway Administration (FHWA) show only a 2.0 percent average yearly increase in VMT since 1999. Compare this to the 2.5 average yearly increase in the 1990s, 3.2 percent in the 1980s, and 3.7 percent in the 1970s. Similarly, the growth in gasoline consumed also increased by an average of 1.7 percent since 1999, compared to 3.2 percent in the 1970s. Several factors explain this, including the increased fuel efficiency of some vehicles and slow, but steady, growth in the proliferation of alternative fuel vehicles.[14]

The leveling off of VMT is a generally positive trend for metropolitan areas in terms of the effects on externalities such as air quality and traffic

Figure 3-6. Aggregate State Revenues and Average (Weighted) Gas Tax Rate, 1933–2002

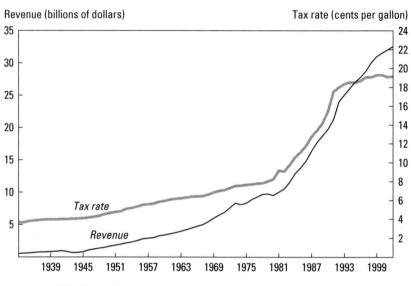

Source: FHWA, *Highway Statistics,* various years.

congestion. However, all these trends taken together ultimately jeopardize the overall stability of the HTF.[15]

In addition to the federal tax, all fifty states impose an excise tax on gasoline. Since 1933 revenues at the state level have risen from $518 million to approximately $32.6 billion in 2002 (figure 3-6).

Throughout its existence, the average tax rate at the state level has remained somewhat higher than the federal tax rate. This difference reflects the historical role of states as the principal financier of early highway construction. Despite the current federal role in highway funding, states retain responsibility for state and local roads outside the federal purview. In addition, federal policy requires that states provide a matching fund in proportion to federal expenditures for local projects. Given the funding requirements and roadway responsibilities, a powerful incentive exists for states to depend on and expand the state gas tax to finance highway projects. Accordingly, most states have continued to increase their gas tax rate, with the average rate consistently exceeding the federal rate. State tax receipts have in this fashion increased substantially

Figure 3-7.   Inflation-Adjusted Average (Weighted) State Tax Rate and Revenues, Current Dollars, 1933–2002

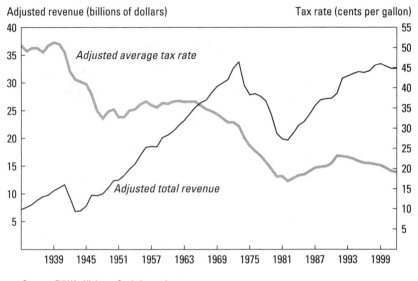

Source: FHWA, *Highway Statistics,* various years.

over time. Aggregate state tax receipts have benefited from the trends that have also until recently elevated federal receipts.

State revenues, however, were not unaffected by the excessive inflationary pressures that arose in the late 1970s and persisted through the early 1980s. Figure 3-7 shows that net receipts, adjusted for inflation, fell precipitously throughout that period. The decline in state revenues was even more severe than that experienced at the federal level. Total state gas tax receipts, adjusted for inflation, began to decline from a high in 1973 of $34 billion to a low in 1982 of less than $20 billion (in real terms). Federal receipts declined by $7.2 billion whereas net receipts, aggregated at the state level, declined by $14 billion.

Unlike federal revenues, state receipts from the gas tax have yet to eclipse the "real" revenue level of their 1973 peak, despite sustained increases in the effective tax rate commencing in the 1980s. As state gas tax revenues begin to level off, states will need to cap their transportation budgets or come up with additional revenue to finance the increasing needs of the transportation network. Throughout the nation, states are making arduous decisions about how to finance their transportation networks over the next several years.

Map 3-1. Gas Tax Rates per Gallon across the United States, 2004

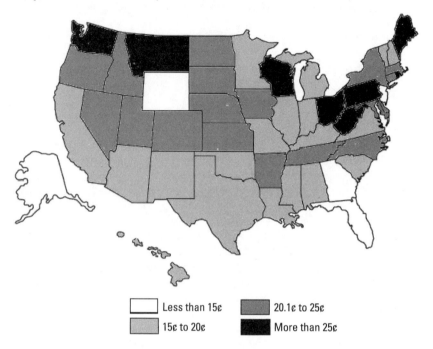

	Less than 15¢		20.1¢ to 25¢
	15¢ to 20¢		More than 25¢

Source: FHWA, *Highway Statistics, 2003* (Department of Transportation), authors' calculations, and a variety of state sources.

States Are Not Raising Their Gas Taxes

Each state imposes its own taxes on wholesale motor fuel, and the rates have changed over time. For example, the tax rate ranges from a low of 7.5 cents in Georgia to 30 cents in Rhode Island, the highest in the nation. The median and average rates are 20.5 cents and 20.7 cents, respectively. Appendix 3-B shows each state's current gas tax rate.[16]

Although wide variation exists among individual state gas tax rates, no regional or geographic trends correlate strongly with the tax rate variations across the United States (map 3-1). The average gas tax is only slightly higher in the Northeast (22.2 cents) than it is in the Midwest (21.7 cents), West (20.6 cents), or South (19.2 cents). States as diverse as Montana and Rhode Island have rates above 25 cents (among the highest), while Wyoming and New Jersey have tax rates below 15 cents, among the lowest in the nation.[17]

During the 1990s, the only states that drastically reduced their nominal tax rate were Connecticut, New Mexico, and New York. In 1996 Connecticut's tax rate exceeded that of all other states. Newspaper accounts suggest that excessive retail prices forced state officials to take action.[18] In response, Connecticut reduced its tax rate by 2 cents in 1997, 4 cents in 1998, and 7 cents in 2000. By 2004 nine states' tax rates were as high as or higher than Connecticut's. Nebraska's gas tax rate declined three times, from 25.9 cents in 1996 to 22.8 cents in 2000, but has since returned to 24.8 cents. Only Alaska and Georgia have maintained the same nominal tax rate since 1980.

Legislative discussions or public referenda to increase the state gas tax are often contentious, particularly in recent years. Indeed, as figure 3-6 illustrates, during the 1990s, the average tax rate leveled off considerably after the dramatic increases of the previous decade. This is not to say that states avoided raising their taxes during this period. Since 1992 thirty-two states have increased their gas tax. However, the amount of the average increase fell from 5.8 cents during the 1980s to 2.1 cents since 1992.

Some of this can be explained by the economic expansion that was taking place during the 1990s, the increase in revenues being generated from the gas tax, and the higher levels of overall federal funding that followed ISTEA and TEA-21. These laws not only infused the states with more federal transportation dollars than ever before, but they also gave states the flexibility to spend the funds as they saw fit.

Although most states raised their gas tax during this period, only one raised it enough to keep pace with inflation. Of the thirty-two states that have increased their gas tax since the passage of ISTEA, only Wyoming raised it as fast as or faster than inflation (and Wyoming started out with the third lowest rate in 1992). Although the nominal percentage change was 11.9 percent, in real terms, the average tax rate declined by 17.5 percent. In other words, many states do not have the same buying power, in terms of gas tax revenue, that they did in 1992 (table 3-3).

In several instances, state gas tax revenues have not kept pace with rising transportation budgets. This hinders states' abilities to raise matching contributions to meet requirements for federal funding. Thus borrowing has increased. In Rhode Island, for example, of the $133.9 million in state gas tax receipts spent on transportation in 2001, the state allocated $28.4 million for debt service. In this state, transportation expenditures, including debt retirement, have risen faster than gas tax receipts.[19] In Virginia debt service required 1 percent of the state's highway construction funds in 1989. That figure has risen to 13 percent by 2004 and will rise to 20 percent by 2009.[20]

But Rhode Island and Virginia are not alone in their escalating commitments of revenue to debt service and bond retirement. In 2002 eight states

Table 3-3. Nominal and Real State Gas Tax Rates, 1992 versus 2004[a]

Cents per gallon, except as indicated

State	1992 tax rate	1992 rate adjusted for inflation	2004 tax rate	Change in tax rate	Percent change in tax rate	Inflation-adjusted change in tax rate	Percent change in inflation-adjusted tax rate
Connecticut	26.00	35.10	25.00	−1.00	−3.85	−10.10	−28.77
New York	22.89	30.90	22.60	−0.29	−1.27	−8.30	−26.86
Alabama	18.00	24.30	18.00	0	0	−6.30	−25.93
Alaska	8.00	10.80	8.00	0	0	−2.80	−25.93
Arizona	18.00	24.30	18.00	0	0	−6.30	−25.93
Colorado	22.00	29.70	22.00	0	0	−7.70	−25.93
District of Columbia	20.00	27.00	20.00	0	0	−7.00	−25.93
Georgia	7.50	10.13	7.50	0	0	−2.63	−25.93
Hawaii	16.00	21.60	16.00	0	0	−5.60	−25.93
Illinois	19.00	25.65	19.00	0	0	−6.65	−25.93
Louisiana	20.00	27.00	20.00	0	0	−7.00	−25.93
Maryland	23.50	31.73	23.50	0	0	−8.23	−25.93
Massachusetts	21.00	28.35	21.00	0	0	−7.35	−25.93
Minnesota	20.00	27.00	20.00	0	0	−7.00	−25.93
Oklahoma	17.00	22.95	17.00	0	0	−5.95	−25.93
South Carolina	16.00	21.60	16.00	0	0	−5.60	−25.93
Texas	20.00	27.00	20.00	0	0	−7.00	−25.93
Virginia	17.50	23.63	17.50	0	0	−6.13	−25.93
New Jersey	10.50	14.18	10.50	0	0	−3.68	−25.93
Nebraska	24.60	33.21	24.80	0.20	0.81	−8.41	−25.32
Mississippi	18.20	24.57	18.40	0.20	1.10	−6.17	−25.11
Iowa	20.00	27.00	20.50	0.50	2.50	−6.50	−24.07
Nevada	24.00	32.40	24.75	0.75	3.13	−7.65	−23.61
New Hampshire	18.60	25.11	19.50	0.90	4.84	−5.61	−22.34
Tennessee	20.00	27.00	21.40	1.40	7.00	−5.60	−20.74
New Mexico	17.00	22.95	18.50	1.50	8.82	−4.45	−19.39
Oregon	22.00	29.70	24.00	2.00	9.09	−5.70	−19.19
North Carolina	21.90	29.57	24.60	2.70	12.33	−4.97	−16.79
California	16.00	21.60	18.00	2.00	12.50	−3.60	−16.67
Kentucky	15.40	20.79	17.40	2.00	12.99	−3.39	−16.31
Rhode Island	26.00	35.10	30.00	4.00	15.38	−5.10	−14.53
Arkansas	18.70	25.25	21.70	3.00	16.04	−3.55	−14.04
Pennsylvania	22.35	30.17	26.00	3.65	16.33	−4.17	−13.83
Idaho	21.00	28.35	25.00	4.00	19.05	−3.35	−11.82
Indiana	15.00	20.25	18.00	3.00	20.00	−2.25	−11.11
Delaware	19.00	25.65	23.00	4.00	21.05	−2.65	−10.33
Washington	23.00	31.05	28.00	5.00	21.74	−3.05	−9.82
South Dakota	18.00	24.30	22.00	4.00	22.22	−2.30	−9.47
Florida	11.60	15.66	14.30	2.70	23.28	−1.36	−8.68
North Dakota	17.00	22.95	21.00	4.00	23.53	−1.95	−8.50
Ohio	21.00	28.35	26.00	5.00	23.81	−2.35	−8.29
Vermont	16.00	21.60	20.00	4.00	25.00	−1.60	−7.41
West Virginia	20.35	27.47	25.65	5.30	26.04	−1.82	−6.63
Montana	21.40	28.89	27.00	5.60	26.17	−1.89	−6.54
Michigan	15.00	20.25	19.00	4.00	26.67	−1.25	−6.17

(*continued*)

Table 3-3. Nominal and Real State Gas Tax Rates, 1992 versus 2004[a] (*continued*)

Cents per gallon, except as indicated

State	1992 tax rate	1992 rate adjusted for inflation	2004 tax rate	Change in tax rate	Percent change in tax rate	Inflation-adjusted change in tax rate	Percent change in inflation-adjusted tax rate
Utah	19.00	25.65	24.50	5.50	28.95	−1.15	−4.48
Missouri	13.03	17.59	17.00	3.97	30.47	−0.59	−3.36
Wisconsin	22.20	29.97	29.10	6.90	31.08	−0.87	−2.90
Maine	19.00	25.65	25.20	6.20	32.63	−0.45	−1.75
Kansas	18.00	24.30	24.00	6.00	33.33	−0.30	−1.23
Wyoming	9.00	12.15	14.00	5.00	55.56	1.85	15.23
Average	18.55	25.05	20.66	2.11	11.93	−4.38	−17.50

Source: FHWA, *Highway Statistics, 1994* and *2004*, authors' calculations, and a variety of state sources.
a. States ranked by percent change in inflation-adjusted tax rate.

each allocated more than 50 percent of gas tax receipts spent on highways to service debt. Throughout the past decade, the amount of revenues in state transportation budgets allocated to debt service has increased substantially. Since 1990 aggregate outstanding bond obligations have increased by approximately 70 percent (in inflation-adjusted dollars). The use of gas tax receipts for debt service has remained relatively stable in proportion to disbursements, increasing from approximately 7.7 to 8.6 percent.

As state revenues plunged due to inflationary pressures in the late 1970s and early 1980s, many state legislatures aggressively raised their tax rates. In 1981 twenty-four states (an unprecedented number) increased their tax rates by an average of about 2.2 cents per gallon.[21]

While the majority of states legislated periodic increases in their gas tax, other states have indexed rate increases to fluctuations in some measure of inflation, such as the consumer price index, published by the Bureau of Labor Statistics. Other states index the tax to a baseline retail price of gasoline or to an inflation index gauging changes in the highway construction and maintenance industry or state revenue needs.[22] Also, New York and Connecticut impose a gross receipts tax on petroleum corporations operating in their states. The tax rate (translated into the conventional cent per gallon levy) increases commensurately with growth in revenues of petroleum firms operating in the state.[23]

These alternative tax structures, also known as a "variable rate tax," have emerged as an effective strategy to increase the tax rate and offset declines in revenue without the politically acrimonious task of tax increases by the legislature or through public referendums. Since 1980 twenty states have employed some variant of the variable rate tax. Although several states subsequently repealed the indexing mechanism (only eleven employ indexing today), inflation indexing remains an important option for augmenting revenues for transportation funding, regardless of inflationary pressures.

Many States Restrict Gas Tax Revenues for Highway Purposes

Beyond their tax structures, states also distinguish themselves on the basis of their regulations governing how gas tax receipts can be spent. Originally conceiving the gas tax as a user fee, many state legislatures continue to employ legal means to link gas tax receipts with highway expenditures. Thirty states earmark gas tax revenues for highway or roadway projects only. The remaining states allocate a portion of revenues to other expenditures.

Some states broaden the scope of receipt allocations to include all transportation expenditures, including mass transit. In a few instances, state provisions stipulate the decoupling of tax receipts from transportation expenses altogether and allocate a certain portion of receipts to the state general fund, or in the case of Texas, a special education fund.[24] Generally, the states' statutory and constitutional stipulations fall under one of three typical arrangements:

—The first and most exclusive categorical provision dedicates all gas tax receipts to public roadway development, administration, and maintenance. Frequently this regulation is embedded in state constitutions, and when it is, the wording is generally explicit.[25] Twenty-two states maintain constitutional restrictions.

—In eight other states, statutory restrictions enacted by the legislature dedicate revenues to highway uses. The statutory provisions are presumably more amenable to reform than constitutional mandates.

—The remaining twenty states and the District of Columbia have less stringent requirements and generally allow for a multimodal approach to the disbursement of gas tax receipts. The exact provisions and the amount of available flexible funding vary considerably among the states. Most often, the respective state codes have provisions that dedicate funds to general transportation purposes, with moderate allocations to other transportation programs, such as mass transit, congestion mitigation, and environmental impact mitigation.

Table 3-4 shows that from 1998 to 2002 three states (Alaska, Pennsylvania, and West Virginia) spent more than 90 percent of their gas tax receipts on state highways. By contrast, New York state statutory provisions allocate net gas tax receipts (less the costs of administration) to a variety of transportation modes. The state's provisions outline a complex formula for distributing the receipts to several alternative trust funds. Since the passage of TEA-21 in 1998, New York's state gas tax has generated approximately $7.3 billion in receipts. Following the statutory disbursement formula, the state spent $4.0 billion (55.8 percent) on "state-administered highways," transferred or directly spent $1.2 billion (16.5 percent) on local government–administered roads, and allocated $1.8 billion (25.7 percent) to fund mass transit. Maryland's spending was also balanced during this time: state highways, $1.2 billion (33.7 percent); local roads, $1.3 billion (36.4 percent); and transit $779 million (22.5 percent).

Notwithstanding several anomalies, the many states without exclusive provisions adhere to a disbursement formula somewhat analogous to that in New York. Aside from administrative costs and nominal allocations to general funds, most states apportion the substantial majority of gas tax receipts for highway expenditures and, to a lesser extent, general transportation expenses.

Few states spent a relevant portion of their gas tax receipts on transit between 1998 and 2002. Only eleven states spent more than 5 percent of their receipts on transit, and only five states—New York, Connecticut, Rhode Island, New Jersey, and Maryland—spent more than 15 percent. In each of these states, statutory provisions set aside substantial portions of net revenues for mass transit funding.

But these figures do not tally all transit funding from gas tax receipts. The District of Columbia and states such as Massachusetts, Pennsylvania, and New Jersey have made sizable investments in mass transit through flexible spending provisions by contributing a substantial portion of gas tax receipts and other revenues to their respective state transit authorities with appropriations from the general fund. Each fiscal year, the state legislatures of New Jersey and Massachusetts allocate funds for mass transit through the appropriations process. However, the accounting process used by the FHWA separates gas tax receipts and appropriations to fund mass transit agencies, thanks to the two-step process involving the general fund. In 2002 direct state mass transit revenues from the general fund were $498 million in Pennsylvania, $252 million in the District of Columbia, $125 million in Michigan, and $60 million in Massachusetts. (See appendix 3-A, "Methodology.")

Table 3-4.   Disposition of State Motor Fuel Tax Receipts, 1998–2002[a]

Percent

State	For state-administered highways[b]	For local roads and streets[c]	For mass transit purposes	For general fund and nonhighway uses[d]
New York	55.8	16.5	25.7	1.9
Connecticut	67.6	5.6	22.8	3.9
Maryland	33.7	36.4	22.5	7.3
Rhode Island	59.5	4.9	18.4	17.3
New Jersey	63.1	13.6	16.9	6.4
Massachusetts	56.1	32.4	11.5	0
Delaware	89.7	1.5	8.8	0
Wisconsin	44.9	43.9	8.3	2.8
California	52.6	40.2	6.6	0.6
Florida	67.4	18.2	6.2	8.2
Michigan	40.8	53.7	5.5	0
Virginia	79.4	14.7	5.0	0.8
Vermont	53.4	22.3	3.8	20.5
Washington	51.3	45.7	2.0	0.9
Missouri	64.3	31.5	1.8	2.3
Maine	85.2	13.2	1.5	0.1
Illinois	44.1	54.2	1.5	0.2
New Hampshire	69.2	19.0	1.3	10.5
Pennsylvania	90.2	8.3	1.2	0.2
Montana	88.6	10.4	1.0	0
Texas	67.3	0.3	1.0	31.4
Wyoming	67.6	28.2	1.0	3.2
Ohio	47.0	49.0	0.9	3.0
South Carolina	76.3	12.9	0.9	9.8
South Dakota	81.6	12.9	0.8	4.8
Oregon	61.3	35.8	0.7	2.2
North Carolina	88.3	9.4	0.7	1.6
Georgia	73.9	14.9	0.6	10.6
Minnesota	51.0	48.2	0.6	0.1
North Dakota	38.8	60.1	0.6	0.5
Tennessee	60.7	32.9	0.5	5.9
Colorado	62.7	36.8	0.5	0
Hawaii	81.5	0.8	0.5	17.2
Utah	67.3	31.6	0.5	0.7
Iowa	38.0	61.5	0.5	0
Nebraska	52.0	42.7	0.4	4.9
Arkansas	65.8	32.4	0.4	1.3
Mississippi	64.5	32.5	0.4	2.6
Kansas	46.3	52.5	0.4	0.9
New Mexico	71.2	19.8	0.4	8.6
Oklahoma	54.6	33.6	0.3	11.5
Idaho	46.0	47.6	0.2	6.2
Louisiana	89.2	10.6	0	0.1
Nevada	69.9	27.7	0	2.4
Alaska	93.0	3.0	0	3.9
Indiana	51.7	48.3	0	0
Alabama	60.9	35.5	0	3.6

(*continued*)

Table 3-4. Disposition of State Motor Fuel Tax Receipts, 1998–2002[a]
(*continued*)

Percent

State	For state-administered highways[b]	For local roads and streets[c]	For mass transit purposes	For general fund and nonhighway uses[d]
District of Columbia	1.2	98.8	0	0
Arizona	53.0	45.1	0	2.0
Kentucky	55.3	37.5	0	7.2
West Virginia	100	0	0	0
Average	62.6	29.2	3.6	4.5
Median	62.7	31.6	0.7	2.3

Source: FHWA, *Highway Statistics, 1998* through *2002*, table MF-3.

a. States in *italic* do not have a highways-only restriction.

b. Includes capital outlay, maintenance and administration, highway law enforcement and safety, and debt service.

c. Includes direct expenditures by state and transfers to local governments.

d. Includes local and state general nonhighway purposes.

Conversely, some states appear to allocate a percentage of gas tax revenues for mass transit despite explicit constitutional or statutory provisions that prescribe expenditures for highways only. The FHWA data suggest that appropriations have somehow circumvented constitutional or statutory provisions. This may indeed be the case for some small projects that are tangentially transit related, such as the construction of park-and-ride lots and high-occupancy vehicle lanes.

In Washington State, which maintains a constitutional restriction on the use of the gas tax, state law also allows gas tax revenues to finance the state's extensive ferry system, operated by the state department of transportation. Ohio, which also has a constitutional restriction, nevertheless permits its department of transportation to spend gas tax revenues on transit-related construction, such as railway bridges, but explicitly restricts their use for transit operating assistance or vehicle purchases. Nevertheless, as table 3-4 illustrates, the portion of gas tax funds spent on transit by most states remains comparatively minute.

Overall, exclusive dedication of gas tax revenues to highway purposes matters because it may prevent states from using federal funds—often difficult to raise locally or through other sources—for transit. In this connection, a 1993 General Accounting Office report pointed out that without access to state gas tax revenues, some transit systems often have to rely almost exclusively on funding derived from local sales taxes, which is often inadequate to meet their needs.[26]

Gas Tax Distribution Often Penalizes Cities and Urban Areas

Provisions regarding the distribution of gas tax receipts within states may, on their surface, seem geographically unbiased. However, in states with certain statutory provisions, the gas tax appears to penalize cities and urban areas in favor of rural areas or those on the suburban fringe.

In several states, urban areas act as "donor regions." These areas contribute significantly more in tax receipts than they receive in allocations from their state's highway fund or through direct local transfers. Research has demonstrated this fact explicitly in states as diverse as Colorado, Ohio, Missouri, and Washington.[27] This imbalance is likely also found in other states with comparable levels of urbanization and similar distribution formulas.

Two major factors affect the distribution of gas tax receipts within states. The first is the categorization of each state's roadways as either "state administered" or managed by local governments. The second factor is the formula used to distribute funds among local governments.

In most states, the maintenance of local streets and roads is considered a municipal responsibility. Each jurisdiction must determine its own spending priorities and revenue sources. By contrast, some unincorporated area roads are state maintained (simply because they are not located in a jurisdiction) and are not necessarily funded by local coffers. In such cases, these roads are often built, maintained, and rehabilitated from resources at the state and county levels. This provisional vagary directs a substantial portion of funds away from cities and older suburban areas that should be able to rely on the same pool of funds for their roads. Instead, they must rely on municipal income, property taxes, and other fees.

To ensure gas tax proceeds are spent equitably within the state, many states also have developed a distribution formula based on some combination of resident population, registered motor vehicles, and highway miles. However, several states (such as Tennessee, Arkansas, Ohio, and Alabama) distribute a portion of the funds evenly among all counties, regardless of size or need. The result is that built-out urban counties fail to receive their share of funding and lose out to less populated exurban counties, whose tax receipts remain tied to their "rural" categorization. This antiurban bias in Ohio is clearly illustrated in chapter 5 of this volume.

Historically, many states enacted distribution formulas while actively constructing the state highway network.[28] Often the investment needs for rural highway construction greatly exceeded the fiscal requirements in urban areas. Property taxes, general funds, and local bond issuance provided ample revenue during the initial era of urban highway building for rapidly growing cities and their surrounding suburbs. Now, with many older municipalities facing a stagnating local tax base, transportation investments increasingly compete with myriad other expenditures in a constrained budget environment.[29]

In Washington State, this distortion manifests itself in, by far, the state's most urbanized metropolitan area: Seattle. The Washington Research Council analyzed the distribution of transportation spending in the state from 1994 to 2013 and projected that the Seattle metropolitan area would raise 51 percent of the state's total revenues and receive 39 percent in return.[30] In other words, Seattle serves as a net exporter of transportation (and gas tax) revenue, despite the critical role the metropolitan area plays in the state's economy.

Washington State recently recognized this disparity and created a statewide Transportation Improvement Account, which is designed to funnel gas tax revenues to urban areas. Programs include an arterial improvement program designed to direct state funds for local government transportation projects to city and urban county arterial roads. The Transportation Improvement Account currently receives 13 percent of the gas tax revenues.

Colorado's gas tax redistribution formula also reflects this inequity. The state has experienced tremendous population and economic growth since 1960. The Denver metropolitan area has captured much of this and in 2000 accounted for more than 60 percent of the state population, 58 percent of registered motor vehicles, and 66 percent of statewide employment.[31] Projections suggest that metropolitan Denver will continue to absorb an increasing share of state population and job growth. Nevertheless, Colorado retains a rural bias within its formula used to distribute gas tax receipts. After administrative costs, the code allocates 65 percent of the first 7 cents to the state highway fund. The highway fund must distribute 25 percent to counties and 9 percent to incorporated municipalities, with the remainder earmarked for state-administered highways. The statute allocates revenues from other portions similarly.

The Denver Regional Council of Governments has addressed the outcome of Colorado's antiquated allocation formula.[32] Its research found that from fiscal year 1998 to fiscal year 2003, the share of transportation dollars allocated to the Denver metropolitan area had declined from 46 to 28 percent. The decline in proportionate allocation destined for the metropolitan region occurred despite the preeminent position held by Denver in both demographic and economic terms, as well as in gasoline consumption. The regional council's report indicated that the Colorado formula for distributing revenues results in gross inequities. Based on its calculation, the Denver metropolitan area receives only 69 cents for each $1 of tax revenue it contributes.[33]

On the other hand, California has enacted a model distribution formula that provides equity and flexibility. The state's formula for spatial distribution reflects the fundamental role its metropolitan areas play in enhancing the state's economic competitiveness. Indeed, the provisions require that allocations to both counties and cities reflect the proportionate contribution of each unit of government. In counties, the proportional distribution relies on each county's tax receipts, registered motor vehicles, and, for a smaller share, the percentage of county roads in relation to the total number in the state. For cities, each allocation relies on a city's population in proportion to the state population. Although population figures are not an exact proxy for tax receipt contributions, population correlates highly with automobile ownership.[34]

Conclusions and Policy Recommendations

Gas tax receipts have generally increased throughout the last several decades, despite volatility in the real rate of taxation and downturns in the business cycle. The resilience of gas tax receipts reflects the underlying spatial, demographic, and economic transitions under way in metropolitan America that have resulted in decentralized, automobile-dominated metropolitan areas. Commuting distances are increasing, as is the number of noncommuting trips for otherwise mundane activities.

Several trends, however, may begin to flatten the growth of gas tax revenues. Recent data suggest, for example, that the tremendous growth rate in vehicular miles traveled is slowly abating.[35] Moreover, efforts have been made to improve air quality by improving the fuel economy of the American vehicular fleet, and the consumption of alternative fuels appears poised for sustained growth. These phenomena may temper the growth in gasoline consumption in the future. In turn, these converging influences will affect anticipated gas tax revenues and, by extension, transportation expenditures, unless changes in tax policy and transportation spending occur at the federal and state levels. In view of that, states should consider the following policy recommendations to ensure appropriate levels of funding for future transportation needs and to meet the modern challenges facing metropolitan areas.

Allow Application of Gas Tax Revenues to Balanced Variety of Transportation Modes and Projects

Provisions in recent federal laws that allowed the "flexible" dedication of transportation funds to either roads or their alternatives revolutionized surface transportation policy. Unfortunately, many states have failed to complement these reforms and continue to limit how transportation funds can be spent. As a result, even though the federal government recognized the benefits of flexible spending and the devolution to local decisionmaking in transportation, states continue to follow a more centralized, detached process.

Although states must necessarily allocate a substantial portion of gas tax receipts to highway-related expenditures, roads-only policies should not encumber funding decisions. Metropolitan areas, the drivers of state economies, require balanced transportation networks to move people and goods. Restricting the available resources to roads only inhibits a balanced network by greatly limiting the ability of transit agencies and others to pursue sufficient funding.

Furthermore, states would undoubtedly make better use of federal funds by removing the roads-only exclusion. By committing a portion of revenues to transit, states would increase their ability to meet federal matching requirements. Currently, states are unable to take advantage of these federal initiatives because they are often unable to come up with their share of the match.

Reconfigure Formulas to Avoid Penalizing Urban and Metropolitan Areas

At the federal level, TEA-21 responded to the demands of donor states with the Minimum Guarantee Program, which mandated a 90.5 percent guaranteed rate of return based on each state's tax receipt contribution to the Highway Account of the HTF. (As of this writing, the Senate's reauthorization proposal increases the return to 95 percent). A similar policy at the state level would ensure an equitable redistribution of state tax receipts among each state's counties and municipalities. Furthermore, states should also require that counties allocate receipts to municipalities based on a rational measure of proportional contribution and need. The concentration of population and economic growth in metropolitan areas necessitates that states change their redistribution formulas to better support these places.

Expand State Gas Tax Exemptions to Local Public Agencies

Although the federal government exempts localities from the federal gas tax for their municipal vehicle fleets (including school buses), more than half of the states do not. State exemptions would provide considerable tax relief for local jurisdictions—particularly large urban places—at a time when officials are working to achieve a balance between easing the burden on revenue sources, such as property taxes, and providing public services. The Wisconsin Alliance of Cities recently found that Milwaukee would save about $700,000 a year with such an exemption.[36]

Of course, states are wrestling with tremendous budget issues of their own. Notwithstanding the curious practice of one government taxing another, exempting localities would be consistent with federal policies and would provide direct tax relief for urban residents.

Institute Reforms, then Consider Gas Tax Increases

Only after states have removed the restrictions on gas tax spending and taken steps to ensure urban areas receive an equitable distribution of gas tax and general transportation revenues should they consider increases in the gas tax. Reform *must* be coupled with any such increase.

In recent years, the growth in gas tax revenues, which states are accustomed to receiving, has leveled off. This comes at a time when nearly every state is facing budget deficits. As a result, states do not have the financial wherewithal to address a wide variety of transportation concerns.

To maintain funding levels and avoid leveraging alternative revenue sources, state legislatures should consider increasing their state gas tax and implementing appropriate indexing mechanisms. Indexing the state gas tax to a reasonable measure of inflation would rationalize the process of increasing the tax rate and allow revenues to keep pace with rising costs. Furthermore, it would reduce the need for state legislatures to use general fund appropriations to compensate for shortfalls in transportation spending. Indexing tax rates is an efficient means to ensure stable tax receipts and reliable transportation budgets. However, none of these steps should be taken until the aforementioned reforms are put in place.

Disclose More Information about Gas Tax Collection and Allocation

In response to the hot donor-versus-donee debate on Capitol Hill in 1998, the federal government provided a wealth of information about states' contributions to and disbursements from a wide variety of transportation funding sources, including the gas tax. States, however, do not release comparable data and information.

States should remedy this gap. They should take immediate steps to provide information on the geographic sources and redistribution of gas tax revenues within their states. The focus of such information should be to ensure that redistribution formulas properly reflect contributions and that urban and metropolitan areas receive allocations that fairly reflect both the transportation revenue they generate and their critical roles in the states.

Appendix 3A. Methodology

Many of the transportation figures regarding transportation finance are derived from the *Highway Statistics* series published by the Federal Highway Administration's Office of Highway Policy Information. This annual publication provides a wealth of information on vehicles and drivers, transportation finance, and the extent of the transportation system. Particular emphasis is placed, naturally, on the roadway network. The highway data in the summary are reported to the FHWA by the states.

The FHWA cautions users that although the data meet reporting requirements for highway program activities, they are derived from a very broad range of sources—other federal agencies, the states and their agencies, metropolitan planning organizations, and the local governments. As a result, the quality and consistency of the information is difficult to discern. For example, the data in table 3-4 may not necessarily reflect the exact amount of disbursements because of reporting discrepancies. The table reports revenues produced by the excise taxes on motor fuel, and, therefore, the revenues include tax receipts collected from the sale of all types of motor fuels. In certain instances, states reported receipts in lump sums, thereby requiring the FHWA to estimate disbursements.

Users are further cautioned that because of the many differences among states, comparisons between them are tenuous. Each state is, of course, different, with unique roadway characteristics and transportation policies. For the purposes of this report, we endeavored to account for these differences through notes in the narrative as well as judgment in presentation. In fact, to some extent, it is those laws and regulations that we chose to examine and identify. Our intent was not to scrutinize the precise percentage of transportation revenues or spending but rather to gain a general sense of how funds are collected and distributed within states and which rules and restrictions govern those funds.

Information about states' policies regarding individual gas taxes is derived from an extensive investigation into state constitutions and relevant statutes. The FHWA Office of Highway Policy Information also provides helpful information on the provisions governing each state's disposition of gas tax receipts.

Disaggregated data for local revenue shown in table 3-1 were not available for all categories. Percentage breakdowns from previous years were used to divide the figures. For the data in and discussion about figure 3-3, we relied on information collected and presented by the Internal Revenue Service, given that the Department of the Treasury collects most of these taxes.

Appendix 3B.   State Gas Tax Rates and Restrictions and Authorities

State	Gas tax rate, 2004 (cents per gallon)	Indexed tax rate	Exclusive highway provision	Type of exclusive provision	Constitution and statute section with stipulations
Alabama	18	No	Yes	Constitutional	Amendment 93
Alaska	8	No	Yes	Statutory	Sec. 42-40-10.G
Arizona	18	No	Yes	Constitutional	Art. 9, sec. 14
Arkansas	21.70	No	Yes	Statutory	Sec. 26-55-206
California	18	No	No	. . .	Part 2, chap.10, sec. 8503
Colorado	22	No	Yes[a]	Constitutional	Art. 10, sec. 18
Connecticut	25	Yes[b]	No	. . .	Sec. 13b-61a
District of Columbia	20	No	No	. . .	Div. 8, sec 47-2301
Delaware[c]	23	No	No	. . .	30 - IV - 5110
Florida[d]	14.30	Yes	No	. . .	Title 14, sec 206.46(3)
Georgia[e]	7.5	No	Yes	Constitutional	Art. 3, sec. 9, para. 6
Hawaii	16	No	No	. . .	Sec. 1-14-243-6(6)
Idaho	25	No	Yes	Constitutional	Art. 7, sec. 17
Illinois[f]	19	Yes	No	. . .	Sec. 35-505.8
Indiana	18	No	Yes	Statutory	Sec. 6-6-1.1-801.5
Iowa[g]	20.50	Yes	Yes	Constitutional	Art. 7, sec. 8
Kansas[h]	24	No	Yes	Constitutional	Art. 11, sec. 10
Kentucky[i]	17.40	Yes	Yes	Constitutional	Sec. 230
Louisiana	20	No	No	. . .	Art. 7, sec. 27
Maine[j]	25.20	Yes	Yes	Constitutional	Art. IX Section 18
Maryland	23.50	No	No	. . .	Title 2, sub. 11, sec. 2-110
Massachusetts[k]	21	No	No	. . .	Chap. 64A, sec. 13
Michigan	19	No	No	. . .	Chap. 205, 205.45, sec. 5
Minnesota	20	No	Yes	Constitutional	Art. 14, sec. 5
Mississippi	18.40	No	Yes	Statutory	Title 27, chap.055, sec. 11
Missouri	17	No	Yes	Constitutional	Art. 4, sec. 30B
Montana	27	No	Yes	Statutory	Title 15, chap. 70, sec. 101
Nebraska	24.80	Yes	Yes	Statutory	Chap. 39, sec. 2510
Nevada	24.75	No	Yes	Constitutional	Art. 11, sec. 5
New Hampshire	19.50	No	Yes	Constitutional	Part 2nd, art. 6A
New Jersey	14.50	No	No	. . .	Art. 7, sec. 2, para. 4
New Mexico	18.50	No	Yes	Statutory	Sec. 7-1-6.9

(*continued*)

Appendix 3B.   State Gas Tax Rates and Restrictions and Authorities
(*continued*)

State	Gas tax rate, 2004 (cents per gallon)	Indexed tax rate	Exclusive highway provision	Type of exclusive provision	Constitution and statute section with stipulations
New York	22.60	Yes[b]	No	. . .	FIN: Sec. 6-89(a-e)
North Carolina	24.60	Yes	No	. . .	Sec. 136-16.8
North Dakota	21	No	Yes	Constitutional	Art. 10, sec. 11
Ohio	26	No	Yes	Constitutional	Art. 12, sec. 5a
Oklahoma	17	No	No	. . .	Sec. 68-500.6(A)(3)
Oregon	24	No	Yes	Constitutional	Art. 9, sec. 3A
Pennsylvania	26	No	Yes	Constitutional	Art. 8, sec. 11
Rhode Island[l]	30	No	No	. . .	Sec. 31-36-20
South Carolina	16	No	No	. . .	Sec. 12-28-2725
South Dakota	22	No	Yes	Constitutional	Art. 11, sec. 8
Tennessee	21.40	No	Yes	Statutory	Sec. 67-3-2001
Texas[m]	20	No	No	. . .	Art. 8, sec. 7a
Utah	24.50	No	Yes	Constitutional	Art. 13, sec. 13
Vermont	20	No	No	. . .	Sec. 23-28-3106
Virginia	17.50	No	No	. . .	Sec. 58.1-22-89
Washington	28	No	Yes	Constitutional	Art. 2, sec. 40
West Virginia[n]	25.65	Yes	Yes	Constitutional	Art. 6, sec. 52
Wisconsin[o]	29.10	Yes	No	. . .	Sec. 78.015
Wyoming	14	No	Yes	Constitutional	Art. 15, sec. 16

Source: FHWA, *Highway Statistics, 2004*, and a variety of state sources.

a. There is some dispute in Colorado about this constitutional provision. Article 10, section 18 of the state's constitution declares that all "railroads shall be public highways." Thus the limitation that gas tax revenues be used "exclusively for the construction, maintenance, and supervision of the public highways" could include rail and guideways.

b. Gross receipts tax on petroleum producers. Tax rate increases with growth in revenues.

c. Delaware indexed its tax rate beginning in 1981 but has subsequently established 23 cents as a static rate.

d. The Florida constitution explicitly designates fuel tax receipts for highway purposes, but statutory provisions apportion a certain amount to mass transportation projects.

e. The Georgia code does not stipulate a highway trust fund per se but does earmark all proceeds from motor vehicle excise taxes for highway expenditures.

f. Illinois's variable rate applies only to gasoline purchased for consumption in a commercial vehicle.

g. In Iowa, gas tax is effective July 1, 2004.

h. Kansas's constitution authorizes taxation of motor fuels while statutory language mandates disposition to highway fund; 10 percent of appropriation to municipalities allowed for expenditure on bicycle and footpaths.

i. In Kentucky, new rate is effective third quarter 2004.

j. Maine, through a legislative determination, allocates a nominal portion of revenues, based on prorated share, to certain recreational uses. Also, Maine does index; see Glenn Adams, "Motorists to pay 0.6 cent more in state gas taxes on July 1" (http://news.mainetoday.com/apwire/D838TM3O2-169.shtml [June 18, 2004]).

k. Massachusetts abolished its variable rate tax at the end of state fiscal year 2001.

l. Rhode Island stopped indexing its gas tax in 1996.

m. Texas has provisions for allocation of one-fourth of its gas tax revenue to a fund for aid to public schools.

n. In West Virginia, the consumer sales and service tax is variable.

o. The tax rate in Wisconsin is effective April 1, 2004.

Notes

1. Certain states and local governments impose an additional tax on retail gasoline sales, but this chapter focuses specifically on the excise tax imposed on motor fuel as reported by the states to the Federal Highway Administration (FHWA).

2. The vast majority of states provide refunds or exemptions for gasoline purchases intended for nonhighway use.

3. See, for example, Indiana Code, sec. 6-1.1-20: "The distributor shall initially pay the tax on the billed gallonage of all gasoline the distributor receives in this state. . . . The distributor shall then add the per gallon amount of tax to the selling price of each gallon of gasoline sold in this state and collected from the purchaser so that the ultimate consumer bears the burden of the tax."

4. Jeffrey Brown, "Reconsider the Gas Tax: Paying for What You Get," *Access* 19 (Fall 2001): 10–15.

5. Brian Francis, "Gasoline Excise Taxes, 1933–2000," *Internal Revenue Service, Statistics of Income Bulletin* (Winter 2000–2001).

6. With the passage of the Revenue Reconciliation Act of 1990, Congress appropriated HTF revenues to mitigate an increasing budget deficit. After balancing the budget, Congress passed the Taxpayer Relief Act of 1997 and returned revenues from the 4.3 cent tax increase, instituted in 1993, to the HTF.

7. The Leaking Underground Storage Tank trust fund was created to help states clean up leaking fuel storage tanks that can pose an environmental and health hazard in terms of contaminated groundwater and soil.

8. The "Highway Account" has not actually been named as such. For the purposes of this chapter, it refers to those revenues in the Highway Trust Fund not designated for the Mass Transit Account or Leaking Underground Storage Tank fund. In fact, the Highway Trust Fund would be better named the "Surface Transportation Trust Fund" to reflect its broader perspective beyond roadways.

9. Over 172 billion gallons of motor fuel were consumed in the United States in 2002. FHWA, *Highway Statistics 2002* (Department of Transportation, 2002).

10. This figure includes gasohol and special fuels.

11. Although the federal highway data present it as such, it is questionable whether bond proceeds should be included here as "revenues." Bond proceeds must be repaid in the future, along with the interest payments, presumably by other sources of revenue, such as the state gas tax revenue, or from general funds.

12. Internal Revenue Service, "Historical Tables and Appendix," *Statistics of Income Bulletin* (Spring 2004), table 21, "Federal Excise Taxes Reported to or Collected by the Internal Revenue Service, Alcohol and Tobacco Tax and Trade Bureau, and Customs Service, by Type of Excise Tax, Fiscal Years 1996-2004"; Louis Alan Talley and Pamela Jackson, "Gasoline Excise Tax—Historical Revenues: Fact Sheet," Report RS21521 (Congressional Research Service, Library of Congress, March 3, 2004); and Louis Alan Talley and Pamela Jackson, "The Federal Excise Tax on Gasoline and the Highway Trust Fund: A Short History," Report RL30304 (Congressional Research Service, Library of Congress, 2000). Note that for the analysis in this section, we relied on revenue raised by the gas tax irrespective of where it was spent, as reflected in the preceding tables, which focused on highway spending only. See appendix A, "Methodology," for more details.

13. To account for inflation, we have used the Bureau of Labor Statistics, *Consumer Price Index—All Urban Consumers* (Department of Labor), table 1, 2002. Dollar amounts presented are in 2002 dollars.

14. The fuel efficiency of the American vehicle fleet is a confusing but important point in terms of the impact on gas tax revenues. The average fuel rate of all passenger cars was 22.1 miles per gallon (mpg) in 2001, the highest rate ever. However, since 1988 the overall fuel economy of "light vehicles" (cars plus light-duty trucks) has declined to 20.4 mpg, an approximate 8 percent decrease. According to the Environmental Protection Agency (EPA), this decline is attributable to the proliferation of sport utility vehicles. EPA, *Light Duty Automotive Technology and Fuel Economy Trends,* Report EPA420-S-01-001 (2001).

15. See Wachs, chapter 4 in this volume, for further discussion of this issue.

16. The "effective" tax rate is higher in certain states that impose a sales tax on the retail price of gasoline, in addition to the gas tax rate on wholesale prices. Arkansas, California, Connecticut, Georgia, Hawaii, Idaho, Illinois, Indiana, Kentucky, Louisiana, Michigan, Nebraska, New York, South Carolina, Tennessee, and Wyoming all impose a sales tax on the retail purchase of gasoline.

17. New Jersey is an interesting case. The reported tax rate in New Jersey does not include a gross receipts tax levied on petroleum companies operating within the state. That tax equates to approximately 4 cents per gallon. By contrast, the reported tax rate in New York and Connecticut includes those states' gross receipts tax. Also in New Jersey, the percent of highway revenues generated from tolls is the second highest in the country, trailing only Delaware. They are the only two states in which toll revenue exceeds gas tax revenue (see table 3-2).

18. Fran Silverman, "Gas Prices to Trickle Down at Pump: Many Stations to Drain Supply then Pass on Tax Cut," *Hartford Courant,* July 2, 1998, p. D1.

19. Bruce Landis, "Highways, Bridges, RIPTA Face Crisis," *Providence Journal-Bulletin,* August 11, 2002, p. A1.

20. Whittington Clement, "More Drivers, More Cars: New Demands Tax State's Road System" (www.transportation.virginia.gov/SecTran/ClementColumn-No1.cfm. [February 2005]).

21. Before 1980 there were no great differences between the states' gas tax rates. In 1976 all but three states had gas tax rates between 6 and 9 cents, with one below the range and two above. By 1983 the range was dramatically broader: 6.5 to 14 cents, with just one state below. See J. H. Bowman and John Mikesell, "Recent Changes in State Gasoline Taxation," *National Tax Journal* 36, no. 2 (1983): 163–82.

22. Ibid.

23. For the purposes of this analysis, we have included the gross receipts tax among the variable rate alternatives.

24. Because of this education fund, Texas does not earmark all its gas tax receipts for highways. However, all the remaining receipts are spent almost exclusively on highways.

25. The Arizona example is illustrative: "No moneys derived from fees, excises, or license taxes relating to . . . the use of vehicles on public [roadways] . . . shall be expended for other than highway and street purposes." See Arizona Constitution, art. 9, sec. 14.

26. General Accounting Office, *Better Tools Needed for Making Decisions on Using ISTEA Funds Flexibly,* GAI/RCED-94-25 (1993).

27. See Denver Regional Council of Governments, "Transportation Funding Equity?" (www.drcog.org/index.cfm?page=TransportationFundingEquity [February 2005]); University of Missouri–St. Louis, "Analysis of Metropolitan St. Louis State Transportation Fiscal Flows" (St. Louis: Public Policy Research Center, 2001); and Washington Research Council, "Referendum 51 Gets Us Moving, Safely, Again," Policy Brief 02-13 (Seattle, October 2002). For a discussion of the situation in Ohio, see Hill and others, chapter 5 in this volume.

28. Nevada has not changed its redistribution formula since the 1930s.

29. See Robert Puentes and Myron Orfield, "Valuing America's First Suburbs: A Policy Agenda for Older Suburbs in the Midwest," report prepared for the Center on Urban and Metropolitan Policy (Brookings, 2002).

30. Washington Research Council, "Referendum 51."

31. Bureau of the Census, "County Business Patterns" (www.census.gov/epcd/cbp/view/cbpview.html [2000]).

32. Denver Regional Council of Governments, *2003 Annual Report* (2003).

33. During the debate over reauthorization of ISTEA, the issue of donor versus donee states dominated the discussion. The resulting "minimum guarantee" provision ensures that each state receives at least 90.5 percent of its gas tax contribution to the HTF. See chapter 5 in this volume.

34. Texas recently developed a statewide Metropolitan Mobility Plan for addressing transportation needs in metropolitan areas. As part of this plan, funds from the Texas Department of Transportation are no longer allocated on a per project basis. Rather, allocations to metropolitan areas are now based on an assessment of need (for example, traffic population and other factors). Texas Department of Transportation, "Texas Metropolitan Mobility Plan: Breaking the Gridlock" (Austin, 2004).

35. See Don Pickrell and Paul Schimek, "Growth in Motor Vehicle Ownership and Use: Evidence from the Nationwide Personal Transportation Survey," *Journal of Transportation and Statistics* 2, no. 1 (1999): 1–18, and Surface Transportation Policy Project, "Transit Growing Faster than Driving: A Historic Shift in Travel Trends," Decoding Transportation Policy and Practice Brief 3 (Washington, May 29, 2002).

36. Wisconsin Alliance of Cities, "Position Paper on Local Government Gas Tax Exemption" (www.wiscities.org/gastaxposn.htm [2001]).

4

Improving Efficiency and Equity in Transportation Finance

Martin Wachs

Ever since the widespread adoption of automobiles, the American highway system has generally been financed with "user fees"—money collected from those who use the roads. Tolls and fuel taxes, which levy charges roughly proportionally to travelers' use of roads, have been the most common.

However, tolls have traditionally been costly and difficult to collect because of the need to construct toll plazas and staff them with salaried workers. In addition, revenues from fuel taxes have for three decades been rising more slowly than program costs as legislators have become ever more reluctant to raise them to match inflation. As a result, the burden of raising funds for transportation programs is gradually being shifted to local governments and voter-approved initiatives that are, in most instances, not based on user fees. These shifts have resulted in new sources of revenue, especially local sales taxes, that have increasingly come to pay for transportation infrastructure.

In fact, seemingly modest local tax increases enacted as short-term solutions to immediate problems are setting a major national trend. Without any deliberate or conscious change in policy, transportation finance is gradually devolving to local governments and lessening its reliance on user fees. User fees are, however, more efficient and more equitable than local sales taxes for transportation projects. In the short run, increases in fuel taxes are viable and practical. In the longer term, tolls collected electronically promise to be the most appropriate and flexible method of user fee financing.

This chapter outlines the relationships that define federal, state, and local roles in financing transportation systems. It summarizes some of the most pressing problems that regions and the nation face in paying for the growth, management, and maintenance of the American transportation system. And it argues that continued or expanded reliance on user fees remains the most promising way to promote efficiency and equity in transportation finance.

Roles and Responsibilities for America's Roads

Although some depict the different governments involved as a "layer cake," with local governments at the bottom and the federal government at the top, it is probably more realistic to view transportation governance as a "marble cake," with local, regional, state, and federal interests mixed together through multiple programs in which different governments cooperate, compete, regulate, and represent their unique concerns. Federal policy is often shaped by state and local interests, and state funding commitments are often made to maximize the receipt of federal funds.

When measured in terms of lane miles or surface area, local roads compose the vast majority of the nation's transportation system. Local roads are built, maintained, and operated mainly by counties, towns, and cities (see table 4-1). However, beyond busy activity centers, local roads are often characterized by low traffic volumes and, as such, account for a minority of all travel. In 2003 urban and rural local roads together carried only 13.2 percent of all vehicle miles traveled (see table 4-2).

These roads are critical because they provide the most direct access to homes, businesses, and institutions. Local roads and streets enable travelers to make the first and last part of every trip; they also support postal and parcel deliveries, emergency services by police, fire and ambulance services, trash collection, and a wide range of similar services. Local streets also are the rights-of-way for telephone and electric power lines and pipes that provide gas, water, and sewer services to homes and businesses. Because access to property and services impart value to land, local governments typically require developers of land to build streets and cede them to the public.

The maintenance and operation of local streets is also supported with general funds of local governments using revenue from real estate taxes on residential, commercial, and industrial property. In recent years, many local

Table 4-1.   Ownership of American Roads, 2003

Units as indicated

Road category	Miles (thousands)	Percent of national total	Percent of category
Rural			
Counties	1,624	40.9	53.5
Towns, townships, municipalities	581	14.6	19.2
States	653	16.4	21.5
Federal	120	3.0	4.0
Other jurisdictions	56	1.4	1.8
Total rural	3,034	76.3	100.0
Urban[a]			
Counties	157	4.0	16.6
Towns, townships, municipalities	647	16.3	68.8
States	120	3.0	12.8
Federal	4	0.1	0.4
Other jurisdictions	13	0.3	1.4
Total urban	941	23.7	100.0
Grand total	3,975	100.0	. . .

Source: Federal Highway Administration, *Highway Statistics, 2003* (Department of Transportation, 2004), table HM-10.

a. "Urban" is used by the Department of Transportation to include a census-designated place with a population between 5,000 and 50,000, or a designated area with a population greater than 50,000.

Table 4-2.   Highway System Travel, 2003

Units as indicated

Road category	Miles traveled (billions)	Percent of national total	Percent of category
Rural			
Interstate	270	9.3	24.9
Other principal arterial	245	8.5	22.6
Minor arterial	171	5.9	15.8
Major collector	203	7.0	18.7
Minor collector	60	2.1	5.6
Local	135	4.7	12.4
Total rural	1,084	37.5	100.0
Urban			
Interstate	433	15.0	23.96
Other freeway and expressway	200	6.9	11.05
Other principal arterial	426	14.7	23.57
Minor arterial	349	12.1	19.32
Collector	154	5.3	8.52
Local	245	8.5	13.58
Total urban	1,807	62.5	100.0
Grand total	2,891	100.0	. . .

Source: FHWA, *Highway Statistics, 2003*, table VM-2.

governments have also used similar financial support to provide local public transit services, which can be viewed as a source of basic accessibility.

Although most transportation facilities are formally built, owned, and operated by local and state governments, the federal government's role in transportation grew significantly during the last century, and in many ways, actions undertaken by the states reflect national transportation and environmental policies. The federal government directly builds and owns few roads, most of which are on federal lands, but the Constitution enumerates a federal responsibility for "interstate commerce."

After World War II, the National System of Interstate and Defense Highways, consisting of more than 40,000 miles of high-quality highways, was made possible by a substantial increase in federal fuel taxes and excise taxes on vehicles and components, such as tires. Gradually, while the states were still ostensibly making the most important decisions, the federal government required them to fulfill certain requirements in order to receive coveted federal funds. States must now plan their highways and transit facilities in accordance with federal planning guidelines and must meet federal environmental protection requirements. Because the federal government oversees the health and well-being of its citizens, it also regulates the safety features, energy consumption, and pollution production of vehicles that are produced by private companies for private owners.

Under the Constitution, however, most government functions not specifically assigned to the federal government reside with the states. In the early part of the twentieth century, states' roles in transportation grew dramatically as automobile and truck travel expanded much faster than population and as the provision of intercity highway connections became necessary and expensive. Most heavily traveled, long-distance roads in the United States, and many transportation facilities serving other modes of travel, are owned and operated by state departments of transportation and overseen by commissions of citizens appointed by state governors or legislatures.

States differ greatly in their transportation practices. Nevertheless, many similarities run through their approaches. Fees for the use of the transportation system, in the form of transit fares, highway tolls, state fuel taxes, and vehicle registration fees, finance many transportation projects. Some states borrow money by issuing bonds to finance new transportation capacity. User fees are often used to repay this debt, but in some instances, bonds are backed by the general revenues of the states.

Metropolitan planning organizations (MPOs) and other regional players constitute another element of the system. Most Americans are far more aware of local, state, and federal governments than they are of regional agencies, yet these entities are gradually becoming major players in transportation decisionmaking. Metropolitan areas contain many government jurisdictions, and many trips commonly cross local boundaries—as do the troublesome environmental and social impacts of transportation. Although regional agencies rarely have the authority to levy taxes or raise their own funds, they have in some cases gained formal authority over state funds spent within their jurisdictions, and this gives them considerable financial power.[1]

For decades regional MPOs decided how federal transportation funds would be spent within fairly tight limits as determined by federal and state laws and narrowly specified funding categories. These agencies gained substantial new influence with passage of the Intermodal Surface Transportation Efficiency Act (ISTEA) of 1991.[2] This law reduced federal limitations and increased the flexibility with which regional agencies could allocate funds among types of projects.[3] States have also acted in recent years to increase the role of regional planning agencies. In California, for example, three-fourths of federal and state highway and transit funds are designated by state law to be spent in accordance with priorities set by the MPOs.

Challenges Facing Transportation Revenues

For eighty years federal and state motor fuel taxes have paid most of the costs of building and operating major roads in the United States. As public policy gradually came to favor a "balanced" transportation system, highway user fees also contributed increasingly to the construction and operation of public transit systems. But now there is a major change under way, and most citizens are not even aware that it is happening.

With federal and state fuel taxes rising much more slowly than travel volume and system costs, legislators are looking for new money to help build, operate, and maintain the transportation system. But instead of raising fuel taxes or introducing new forms of user fees to cover these needs, lawmakers are forcing local governments to raise nonuser funds locally and, in effect, are changing the basis of transportation finance to resemble more the situation that existed before the invention of user fees. Cities, counties, and transit districts are all increasingly turning to "local option transportation taxes" to fund new transportation investments. The most visible examples of these in recent years have been voter-approved sales taxes to fund particular roads and rail transit projects.[4]

Figure 4-1. Revenue Sources for Highways, 2002[a]

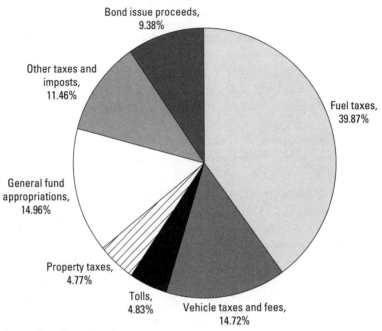

Source: See table 3-1, this volume.
a. Total = $135,916,333,000.

State legislators and federal lawmakers have recently responded to the real decline in user fee revenue in several ways. They have encouraged local transportation tax measures, increased borrowing to support transportation programs, and promoted more vigorous competition among states for available federal funds. They have avoided, however, the most promising direction for improving transportation finance: expanding implementation of user fees.

Figure 4-1 summarizes the diversity of revenue sources for highways. Although state user fees and the return to the states of federal user fees continue to provide a majority of revenues, this share has decreased over time, and other sources are becoming increasingly significant. Table 4-3, using data assembled by the Surface Transportation Policy Project, shows how dramatic the change has been in just five years. While revenue from user fees increased by 18 percent between 1995 and 1999 and remains the largest single source of revenue, local transportation taxes grew three times as fast during this period. In short, America's system of transportation finance is quietly but steadily being restructured.

Table 4-3. Changes in State and Local Transportation Revenue, 1995–99

Billions of dollars, except as indicated

Type of revenue	1995	1999	Change	Percent change
State borrowing	4.3	8.3	4.0	93.0
Other local taxes, including sales taxes	4.5	7.1	2.6	57.8
Other state taxes	6.6	8.6	2.0	30.3
Local general funds	12.3	15.9	3.5	28.5
Local property taxes	5.2	6.4	1.2	23.1
State user fees	36.2	42.7	6.5	18.0

Source: Surface Transportation Policy Project, *Measuring Up: The Trend toward Voter Approved Transportation Funding* (Washington, 2002).

Declining Reliance on the Gas Tax

The first major influence on the nation's changing transportation finance system is its declining reliance on the gas tax. Fuel taxes are usually levied as a charge per gallon of fuel sold. Generally, they do not increase automatically when the cost of living rises, as do sales and income taxes. Instead, they must be increased by legislative action. Although these taxes were in the past enormously popular—because many constituencies believed the benefits of transportation investments to be worth their costs—this is no longer true, and legislators appear to be willing to do almost anything but raise motor fuel taxes. Indeed, while twenty-eight states have raised their gas taxes since 1992, only Wyoming raised it enough to keep pace with inflation, and in real terms, the average gas tax rate declined by about 17.5 percent since then.[5]

California provides a vivid example of what is happening in most states. Between 1947 and 1963, the California fuel tax increased three times (as did the federal fuel tax); after that, however, neither was raised for more than twenty years. Since 1982 the California gas tax has been raised only once by the legislature and once again by vote of the people because the governor refused to endorse an increase without a referendum. In 1957 the California fuel tax stood at 6 cents per gallon. If it had risen at the same rate as inflation in the cost of all goods and services, the state fuel tax would today be 32.5 cents per gallon rather than its current 18 cents per gallon, which lags its 1957 buying power by 14.5 cents. California is not unique. On average, fuel taxes in the fifty states would have to rise about 11 cents per gallon just to recoup their 1957 buying power.[6]

Although these figures are stark, the financial situation is actually even worse. Overall, new vehicle fuel economy was about fourteen miles per gallon in 1974, and today it stands at about twenty-eight miles per gallon.[7] The result is that, as less tax revenue per gallon is generated, Americans drive about twice as many miles per gallon; therefore, fuel tax revenues have plummeted when measured per mile of driving. What is more, congestion is worsening throughout the nation as revenues from user fees level off in current dollars, decline in buying power, and decline even more per vehicle mile traveled.[8]

Another problem is that the cost of roads and other transportation facilities has risen dramatically even as the revenue to support them has declined. Building and maintaining roads and transit facilities require spending on land, labor, capital equipment, and materials, all of which cost more than in the past. The *Engineering News-Record* construction cost index, for example, tracks the average cost in twenty cities of a mix of major ingredients in the cost of transportation facilities: common labor, steel, lumber, and concrete. Between 1957 and the middle of 2004, the index increased nearly tenfold.[9] Although there was undoubtedly a gain in the productivity of construction expenditures during this time, it is nonetheless clear that revenues have declined dramatically in relation to costs.

Finally, according to the Federal Highway Administration (FHWA), the percent of travel occurring under congested conditions—defined as travel times moving at less than free-flow conditions—increased from 31.7 percent in 1997 to 33.1 percent in 2000.[10] Growing congestion not only slows traffic down, it also pollutes the air and consumes precious fuel.[11] The FHWA expects vehicle miles of travel to increase by another 42 percent between 2003 and 2020, with the growth rate for heavy trucks increasing faster than that for lighter vehicles.[12] Congestion will surely worsen at some locations, and funding is also needed to address safety needs and the deterioration of older pavements and bridges.[13] Faced with these escalating costs, the steady erosion of revenue from the motor fuel tax as a source of transportation finance is troubling.

Increased Reliance on Local Transportation Taxes

As gas tax yields sag, reliance on local transportation taxes surges. Numerous local government ballot measures have been taking up the slack left by the stagnation of fuel tax revenues at the state and federal levels. Before 1980 few states permitted or encouraged towns or counties to levy their own special-purpose transportation fees, except for the property taxes traditionally used for neighborhood streets and county roads. In the 1970s major metropolitan areas adopted permanent sales taxes to support new transit systems, and in the 1980s several states authorized local jurisdictions to hold elections to enact measures to raise revenues for transportation purposes. The pace accelerated during the 1990s, with twenty-one states either adopting new laws authorizing local-option transportation taxes or witnessing dramatic expansion in their use.[14]

During 2002 American voters considered forty-one separate ballot measures to raise money for transportation, of which only nine were statewide elections and only a handful involved user fees such as fuel taxes.[15] Some local governments have enacted vehicle registration fees (arguably a user fee but more accurately a form of property taxation), taxes on real estate sales, local income or payroll taxes earmarked for transportation, and taxes on new real estate developments.

Despite these variations, the most common approaches taken (used in about half of the measures) were local sales taxes.[16] Sales taxes have a broad base, and because they apply to the purchase of many goods, the rate of increase can be relatively low. This tends to make sales taxes more popular than increases in user fees, which are more concentrated because they fall on fewer people. One county in California, for example, estimated that a 1 percent countywide sales tax increase would produce as much added revenue for transportation as would a motor fuel tax increase of 16 cents per gallon.[17]

Local sales taxes weaken the role of the states and in several ways are less equitable and less efficient than user fees. User fees, after all, directly impose on travelers and system users the costs of building and maintaining the facilities from which they benefit and the indirect costs of resource depletion, air pollution, and other transportation "externalities." Moreover, user fees induce more efficient behavior, unlike sales and property taxes. If bridge tolls are increased, for example, some travelers decide to carpool or shift to public transit for the journey to work.[18]

Higher fuel taxes also encourage the purchase of more fuel-efficient vehicles. Sales and property taxes, on the other hand, do nothing to encourage more efficient or socially responsible use of the transportation system. Furthermore, our cities and towns need local sales and property taxes to provide essential services for which user charges are unavailable or undesirable, such as for schools and libraries. Revenues from sales taxes, in particular, also tend to drop dramatically in periods of recession, just when government needs increased revenues the most. So, although more local governments are turning to them, and reliance on them is increasing, local transportation sales taxes present a challenge for public policy.

An Explosion in Borrowing

Borrowing is also on the upswing. As table 4-3 indicates, state borrowing was the fastest growing source of revenue for transportation projects and programs in recent years. Proponents of various forms of borrowing prefer to call this approach "innovative financing," usually through loans or bonds.

A few states have created "infrastructure banks" that provide low-interest loans and other forms of credit enhancement for transportation projects.[19] Others have developed financial instruments that enable them to borrow against anticipated future federal appropriations and future revenues from a variety of taxes earmarked for transportation.[20] Borrowed money, however, is not really revenue at all since it must be repaid later using revenues from either taxes or user fees. And, of course, the state must also bear the cost of interest, which, if funds are held for twenty or thirty years, often exceeds the value of the principal.

Borrowing is often worthwhile, for example, when early construction of a project saves construction costs and when revenues later in the life of the project are likely to exceed the interest payments. It is appropriate to fund some capital projects with borrowed funds, and systematic analysis can show when the benefits of doing so exceed the costs. But borrowing is not always justified, and it is troubling that elected officials operating under term limits increasingly prefer borrowing simply because it defers the implied tax increases to a future date, presumably after they have left office.

The Politics of Spending Highway User Fees

Spending issues also enter into the finance picture. If funds collected from tolls and motor fuel taxes are actually "user fees," they are akin to a price charged in exchange for the benefits received from the roads. If this is so, complex philosophical and political questions arise about how the funds should appropriately be spent. Many believe that funds collected in these ways should be strictly reserved to pay costs associated with the construction, maintenance, and operation of highways. Employing such funds to cover state expenditures for health care or education would seem to many observers to be an inappropriate use of these revenues.[21] Others believe that public funds should be used for any public purpose deemed appropriate by elected officials. Some also argue that expenditures on transit and bicycle paths improve the overall efficiency of highways and should be permitted for highway user fees. Many environmentalists contend that highways impose "unpriced" externalities, such as air pollution on entire communities, and therefore the funds should be broadly available for any public purpose.[22]

Clearly, this debate varies from state to state. Some states have primarily urban populations, while others are largely rural. Levels of congestion differ greatly from place to place. Some states host a great deal more through traffic by nonresidents than others do. Some states experience mainly automobile travel while others see more goods movement. Some make extensive use of toll roads while others rely entirely on motor fuel taxes. Some states directly fund mass transportation systems and operations, while others finance mass transit entirely through local governments and special districts. It is not surprising, therefore, that states take different positions on the issue of eligible uses of fuel tax revenues. Thirty states restrict the use of motor fuel tax receipts to the planning, development, building, operation, maintenance, and administration of highways.[23]

Research is needed to clarify relationships between transportation patterns and conditions in states and their stance on how user fee revenue is spent. It is likely, however, that there are large differences of opinion within states, reflecting different philosophical positions and competing priorities of interest groups, even more than the uniqueness, history, and traditions of each state. Regardless of the current status of state spending policies, this question is certain to be central in policy debates on transportation finance in every state as well as at the national level.

Increasing Competition for Federal Funds

Finally, because it is becoming increasingly difficult for states to raise their motor fuel taxes, competition among the states for federal dollars is becoming ever more intense. The proceeds of the federal gas tax, presently set at 18.4 cents per gallon, are distributed to states based on "allocation formulas," which differ somewhat from one federal program to another.

For example, federal funds to maintain interstate highways are divided among the states based on a formula that equally weighs their miles of interstate highways, vehicle miles of travel on interstate highways, and annual contributions to the federal Highway Account attributable to commercial vehicles. Federal funds available for the Congestion Mitigation and Air Quality program are distributed to states based on the populations living where federal air quality standards have not been attained or in maintenance areas (locations that have only recently attained federal air quality standards).[24]

As shown in table 4-4, some states receive far more in federal highway funds than they contribute to the federal Highway Trust Fund (HTF), while

Table 4-4.   Highway Trust Fund Account Receipts and Apportionments, by State, 1998–2003[a]

In millions of dollars, except as indicated

State	Payments	Apportionments and allocations	Percent of apportionments to payments	Cumulated percent since July 1956
Alaska	364	2,330	640	668
District of Columbia	192	700	365	407
South Dakota	567	1,344	237	209
Rhode Island	461	1,069	232	224
Montana	778	1,797	231	236
North Dakota	551	1,255	228	206
Hawaii	425	958	225	337
Vermont	429	816	190	207
West Virginia	1,237	2,241	181	193
Delaware	463	776	168	155
Idaho	973	1,478	152	166
Wyoming	861	1,287	149	177
Connecticut	1,772	2,621	148	171
New York	6,977	9,056	130	124
Pennsylvania	6,927	8,532	123	117
New Mexico	1,495	1,770	118	130
Wisconsin	3,213	3,640	113	96
New Hampshire	797	902	113	132
Minnesota	2,356	2,664	113	124
Nevada	1,217	1,353	111	138
Kansas	1,847	2,014	109	109
Iowa	1,940	2,105	109	113
Utah	1,449	1,571	108	143
Arkansas	2,329	2,523	108	102
Alabama	3,474	3,745	108	110
Oregon	2,106	2,257	107	117
Washington	3,221	3,395	105	140
Maryland	3,037	3,174	105	132
Maine	899	938	104	112
Virginia	4,848	5,036	104	109
Nebraska	1,315	1,348	103	111
Mississippi	2,332	2,384	102	100
Illinois	5,766	5,808	101	108
Massachusetts	3,180	3,185	100	152
Kentucky	3,278	3,190	97	103
Missouri	4,331	4,199	97	95
Colorado	2,351	2,261	96	120
California	17,454	16,621	95	96
Louisiana	2,965	2,810	95	115
North Carolina	5,233	4,939	94	89
Tennessee	4,238	3,991	94	97
Michigan	5,912	5,506	93	91
Ohio	6,461	6,006	93	92
Indiana	4,419	4,102	93	89
South Carolina	3,119	2,892	93	90
Oklahoma	2,877	2,656	92	88

(*continued*)

Table 4-4. Highway Trust Fund Account Receipts and Apportionments, by State, 1998–2003[a] (*continued*)

In millions of dollars, except as indicated

State	Payments	Apportionments and allocations	Percent of apportionments to payments	Cumulated percent since July 1956
New Jersey	4,988	4,571	92	99
Arizona	3,267	2,975	91	109
Florida	9,008	8,117	90	90
Georgia	6,726	6,059	90	92
Texas	14,746	13,199	90	86
Total	171,171	180,166	. . .	. . .
	. . .	. . .	105	110

Source: Federal Highway Administration, *2002 Highway Statistics*, tables FE221 (2003) and FE221b (2004).

a. Payments into the fund include only the net highway user tax receipts and fines and penalties deposited in the Highway Account of the HTF. Payments into the HTF attributable to highway users in each state are estimated by the Federal Highway Administration.

others receive less than they have contributed. According to figures from the Department of Transportation, between 1956 and 2002, Alaska received more than 6.5 times the federal highway funds it contributed to the HTF in motor fuel and other user fees, while Texas received only 86 percent of the funds paid within its borders.

The political debates that shape new transportation legislation are often dominated by the efforts of "donor" states, such as New Jersey and Arizona, to revise allocation formulas to capture larger shares of their federal contributions, while recipient or "donee" states, such as Montana and Hawaii, argue that the most fair allocation formulas are those that maintain their large shares. Of course, a reasonable observer might expect some redistribution to be appropriate and might ask whether a federal transportation financing program that returns all money to the states in which it was collected is, in the end, likely to produce a result little different from fifty separate state funding programs.

Similarly, by capping spending, the federal government for some years allowed the balance in the federal Highway Account to grow by billions of dollars annually, claiming that by spending less on highways in a given year than it collected, it was contributing to deficit reduction. The states worked tirelessly to end this practice and succeeded in incorporating into TEA-21 the Revenue Aligned Budgetary Authority. RABA, as it is known, requires "spending down" the balance in the Highway Trust Fund by tying federal funding to the level of the HTF, thereby liberating more federal money for the states.

This tactic seems to have backfired to some extent, however. As the national recession proceeded, and gas tax revenues decreased, income to the HTF fell, creating a "negative RABA" effect—meaning that since spending must reflect income into the Highway Account, it now had to decrease rather than to increase. This threatens to further intensify competition among the states for larger slices of the federal pie during the current reauthorization debate.[25] Indeed, the federal reauthorization discussion has been dominated by members of several donor states seeking a 95 percent return of their Highway Account contributions.

Strategies for Renewing Transportation Revenues

Considering these issues, alternative strategies for supporting transportation revenues are garnering more and more attention. This section describes two such strategies.

Aligning Charges with Costs Imposed by Different Users

Transportation programs at the state and federal levels that rely to a considerable extent on user fees continue to face long-term, complex, and politically charged problems. User fees, including vehicle registration and license charges, fuel taxes, truck weight and distance charges, and tolls should, in principle, be structured such that the fees recovered from different classes of vehicles reflect the costs borne by governments to provide those vehicles with the opportunity to travel.

For example, heavy trucks impose costs on the highway system that significantly exceed those of light-duty vehicles, such as family automobiles. Heavy vehicles increase construction costs by requiring more gentle grades and curves and substantially thicker pavements than lighter vehicles.[26] Maintenance costs are also high on highway segments that carry large volumes of heavy vehicles. In recognition of these higher costs, states demand that heavy trucks pay higher vehicle registration fees and, where tolls exist, pay higher tolls. Most heavy trucks are powered by diesel engines, with fuel economy rates well below those of cars. Trucks thus pay taxes on diesel fuel that are higher per mile of driving than light vehicles.

Many studies demonstrate that the current system of user fees involves numerous cross-subsidies of some groups of vehicles by others.[27] Table 4-5 summarizes data recently published by the federal government resulting from its latest "Highway Cost Allocation Study." The table shows that when user

Table 4-5. Ratio of User Fee Payments to Allocated Costs for All Levels of Government

Vehicle class and registered weight	Federal	State	Federal and state	Local	All levels
Autos	0.9	1.0	1.0	0.1	0.7
Pickups and vans	1.2	1.2	1.2	0.1	0.9
Buses	0.1	0.8	0.5	0.0	0.4
All passenger vehicles	1.0	1.0	1.0	0.1	0.8
Single-unit trucks					
<25,000 pounds	1.4	2.2	1.9	0.1	1.5
25,001–50,000 pounds	0.6	1.0	0.8	0.0	0.6
>50,000 pounds	0.5	0.5	0.5	0.0	0.4
All single units	0.8	1.2	1.1	0.1	0.8
Combination trucks					
<50,000 pounds	1.4	1.7	1.6	0.1	1.3
50,001–70,000 pounds	1.0	1.3	1.1	0.1	0.9
70,001–75,000 pounds	0.9	1.1	1.0	0.1	0.8
75,001–80,000 pounds	0.9	0.9	0.9	0.1	0.8
>80,001	0.6	1.0	0.9	0.0	0.7
All combinations	0.9	1.0	0.9	0.1	0.8
All trucks	0.9	1.1	1.0	0.1	0.8
All vehicles	0.9	1.0	1.0	0.1	0.8

Source: Federal Highway Administration, *1997 Federal Highway Cost Allocation Study: Final Report* (Department of Transportation, 1997).

fees paid to all levels of government are estimated, different types of vehicles pay dramatically different proportions of the costs they impose on the highway system. In the aggregate, single-unit trucks weighing more than 50,000 pounds contribute in user fees only 40 percent of the estimated costs of their use. Autos contribute 70 percent of their costs; pickup trucks and vans, 90 percent; and single-unit trucks weighing less than 25,000 pounds contribute 150 percent of their costs through the taxes and fees that they pay.[28]

The mispricing of highway use is of enormous consequence. Small, Winston, and Evans have shown that an optimal system of road user charges, coupled with appropriate construction standards, could save money for everyone.[29] If charges were levied fairly in proportion to the costs imposed by vehicle type, and those charges vigorously enforced, and if roads were constructed to more demanding standards, savings in road maintenance and replacement costs over time would be great enough to permit lower user fees for all classes of vehicles. The transition period would span several decades, however, because it would take time to rebuild all the roads to the necessary standards.

Of course, this issue is politically explosive, and it is difficult to achieve even marginal changes in the direction of full cost recovery from user charges on each class of vehicle. The trucking industry is intensely competitive, and many trucking companies are small family businesses. Increases in charges for heavy trucks increase business risk, especially if charges are much higher in some states than in others. Although trucking interests point out that higher costs would necessarily be passed on to consumers of the goods that are moved by truck, others cite the efficiency, environmental, and congestion benefits of higher trucking costs. The latter would be an incentive to shift a larger share of long-distance freight movements to the rail system.

Of course, it remains difficult to convince any state to change its user fees to any significant extent. Because interstate truckers travel very long distances and their vehicles have large fuel tanks, if one state were to raise motor fuel taxes more than its neighbors, trucks would likely buy fuel in neighboring states. In the past, political compromises that involved higher user charges for trucks also resulted in approval for using even larger and heavier trucks, which, to a certain extent, lessened the effectiveness of the new policies.

Widespread Adoption of Electronic Toll Collection Systems

It seems safe to say, then, that the nation probably will be unable to rely on fuel taxes to finance roads or transit systems in the long term. The current development of hybrid engines that dramatically improve fuel economy is only a hint of changes likely to come. The world's supply of petroleum is finite, and we are already developing a variety of biofuels and other synthetic fuels. Fuel cells are also seen by many as a likely source of power for the future, and they may not, in the longer term, use petroleum-based fuels. At the very least, a changing and uncertain relationship between travel and the consumption of petroleum-based fuels lies ahead.

Of course, hydrogen or biofuels could be taxed just like gasoline, but doing so would likely conflict with other policy goals, such as reducing pollution and achieving energy independence. Undoubtedly, in the long term, charges will be based on road use rather than fuel use. However, every reasonable projection of technological change indicates that gasoline and diesel fuel will dominate the market for surface transportation fuel for at least two decades and probably three. Traffic will continue to grow and funds will be needed for transportation infrastructure construction, operation, and maintenance.

To meet those needs, many predict a greater role for tolls (which now make up about 4.8 percent of total revenue sources). Electronic toll collection (ETC) is expanding dramatically and is probably the way users of transportation facilities will be charged in the future. Travelers will eventually pay electronically for each use of the system, with charges reflecting the cost of using particular facilities at particular times of day by vehicles with particular characteristics. Almost 95 percent of all toll collection lanes in U.S. major metropolitan areas already have ETC capability, and the FHWA expects nearly total coverage by the end of this year.[30]

Economists have long argued that the only way to completely solve the congestion problem is through congestion-related pricing made possible by ETC systems. Economic theory says that the price of traveling should be higher at the places and during the times of day when demand for highways (and benefit from using them) is greatest. If a bridge toll, for example, cost three times more during periods of highest congestion than in the middle of the night, some travelers would surely be more likely to use public transit, form car pools, use less crowded alternate routes, or delay less essential trips to off-peak hours.[31] And in fact, several dozen travel corridors throughout the world currently use variable pricing for travel, including a small handful in the United States. Congestion pricing has been successfully used in Singapore for more than twenty-five years, and London implemented congestion pricing in 2003.[32]

Although transportation experts have discussed congestion pricing for decades, one of the major obstacles to its implementation has long been the technical difficulty of collecting tolls. Building toll plazas and varying the charges with time of day and class of vehicle are complex, expensive, and politically problematic. Recent advances in information technology, however, now make such pricing much more technically feasible. Small, inexpensive transponders enable each motorist to be charged a different fee to use each segment of road at a particular time of day. The charges can appear on monthly credit card bills.[33]

The technical capacity now exists to integrate into one system the mechanisms for financing our highway system and managing congestion. Charging more than we now do for the use of the busiest roads at the busiest times of day, and quite a bit less than we now do at other times and places, would be the fairest and most efficient way to raise the funds needed for operating and expanding the capacity of the transportation system. At the same time, the charges could be utilized to meter the use of the system to dramatically control congestion.

Some argue that the accounting system needed for congestion pricing will be an invasion of privacy, but it is possible to prevent this by using numbered accounts. Others argue that congestion pricing discriminates against the poor. Yet the current system of transportation finance is not at all neutral with respect to income, and a system of direct charges for actual benefits gained from using the system is inherently fairer than a complex system of cross-subsidies. For many trips, the proposed approach would lower trip costs compared with the current means of pricing travel. It would also surely be possible to offer discount rates to the poor.

Policy Recommendations

Choosing the best financing mechanisms for transportation is a difficult balancing act. Today, citizens demand not only that the finance system raise needed revenue but that it also include incentives to promote economic activity, provide improved access for people of all ages and income groups, and discourage environmental damage. It is essential that charges and fees for the use of transportation systems produce needed revenues, but it is also important that they incorporate incentives and price signals to attain other program and policy objectives, including efficiency and equity. In view of that, here are four recommendations for improving the equity and efficiency of our nation's system of surface transportation finance.

Increasing Transportation Revenues Should Be a State Rather than Local Responsibility

User fees continue to be among the most effective, efficient, and equitable approaches to transportation finance. In the short term, fuel taxes are the most readily available user fees, and states should raise fuel taxes to support transportation programs rather than to further devolve funding responsibility to local governments through local tax measures.

However, state legislators and members of Congress seem intent on avoiding any action that could be interpreted as a tax increase. They find it difficult to agree on an optimal allocation of user fees among classes of vehicles, and they find it painful to confront controversy over the allocation of highway user fees to public transit systems. All of this has increased lawmakers' reluctance to raise state and federal motor fuel taxes, despite the fact that these, for decades, were viewed not as taxes at all but as charges appropriately levied against those who benefit from the system and whose travel imposes costs on it. To a certain extent, this trend in the states is exacerbated by the influence of term limits. Legislators seem unwilling to raise motor fuel taxes because they know they will soon be out of office, and they do not wish to leave higher fuel taxes as their legacy.[34]

In short, transportation finance is increasingly dominated by a politics of expediency, as state legislators continue to shift burdens onto local-option transportation taxes and borrowing. More and more the choice between one type of revenue-raising mechanism and another is based entirely on revenue production and short-term acceptability to the voters. Overlooked as the responsibility for revenue production devolves back to local government is the fact that the revenue mechanisms are becoming simultaneously more inefficient and inequitable. States need to reassume responsibility for ensuring the adequacy and fairness of transportation funding.

States Should Explore and Plan for Use of Electronic Toll Collection Systems

Although motor fuel taxes have been the primary means of raising transportation revenues for more than eighty years and will remain viable for some time to come, their days may be numbered for practical reasons that reach beyond the political. Increasing concerns about global climate change and experimentation with alternative fuels suggest that over time we can expect dramatically improved vehicle energy efficiency. It is also increasingly likely that in the foreseeable future vehicles will be powered by a much wider variety of fuels. Although it cannot be said with certainty, many are betting that hydrogen will, before long, be the basis of automotive power.

In view of this, Congress and state legislatures should be urged to consider increases in fuel taxes during the reauthorization debate and in coming years, even though in all likelihood this type of user charge will gradually become obsolete. Legislators, in this respect, should keep one eye on the short term, during which fuel taxes should be given more attention than they have had lately, and focus the other eye on the longer term, when fuel taxes are likely to become far less useful.

Tolls were originally understood to be a direct and appropriate form of user charge, but they were expensive and annoying to collect.[35] Now we have finally perfected electronic toll collection, a technology that makes it feasible to collect tolls unobtrusively and inexpensively. Motorists by the millions are using "EZ Pass" on the East Coast, "Fastrak" on the West Coast, and a variety of electronic toll devices in between. The success of this approach is a clear glimpse of the future. In fact, a recent study concluded that electronic toll collection is feasible on a much larger scale than it has been thus far deployed. Its authors believe that issues that, at first glance, appear to present insurmountable political hurdles, such as personal privacy, can be overcome without undue difficulty.[36]

Eventually, electronic toll collection could possibly supplant fuel taxes as the principal means by which states finance the construction, maintenance, and operation of highways. As recognized in the 1920s, directly charging users at the time and place of use is the fairest and most efficient way of financing transportation systems. Electronic toll collection could also reduce the complexity of different charges for different classes of vehicles. Similarly, a change over time to electronic user fees could correct other inequities in the current system of user charges. For example, fuel taxes tend to overcharge urban travelers relative to rural drivers and those who travel off-peak relative to those who drive at rush hour.[37]

Pricing Strategies Should Promote More Efficient Use of the Transportation System

Financial strategies must always be considered in light of their potential to produce revenue, but consideration should also be given to the opportunity to use prices and charges to increase the efficient use of the existing transportation system. State and federal transportation funding programs can promote electronic toll collection as a means of increasing capacity by improving the efficiency with which the existing transportation system is used. Efficiency gains from toll collection come not just from the simple flat fees applied for the use of a facility. Rather, the real gains from greater reliance on tolling will flow from the opportunity to use price differentials to promote more efficient use of the system.

One example would be using higher tolls on existing toll bridges and highways at the most congested hours and lower tolls when demand for travel is lowest. Another example is "high-occupancy toll" lanes, a variety of high-occupancy vehicle lanes. Where the latter have unutilized capacity, they can be made available to single-occupant vehicles for a fee via electronic toll collection. This enhances state highway system revenue and reduces congestion on the parallel, mixed-flow lanes without requiring much construction. A similar application of tolling that has the potential to increase efficiency is that of allowing heavy trucks to pay fees for the privilege of bypassing ramp meters at freeway entrances.[38]

Pricing Strategies Should Reflect the Costs of Different Services

In keeping with the principle that pricing can be used to induce behavior that makes more efficient use of the transportation system, it follows that, in many instances, the most appropriate way of achieving this is to set charges that reflect the social marginal cost of the use of the facility. Heavy trucks should eventually be charged more to travel on a toll road than light-duty vehicles because they impose heavier costs on those facilities; peak-hour users of roadways should be charged more than off-peak users because they impose higher marginal costs on society by traveling at the most crowded hours. Off-peak travelers, on the other hand, should receive a price break because they impose lower costs on transportation facilities.

Conclusion

The transportation system is the ultimate public-private partnership. Cars and trucks are almost all privately owned, whereas the roadways are almost all public property. Americans fund highways and public transit systems through a complex partnership between many government bodies, continually influenced by numerous private, corporate, and civic interests. Governments at many levels interact with one another to build and manage the transportation system.

Given this complex arrangement, coupled with bureaucratic inertia, it will certainly be a challenge to fully achieve the ideals suggested here of a revenue system that also helps manage the transportation system. It is reasonable, however, to hold as an ideal the development of a system of user fees that produces adequate revenue to build and manage the transportation system while simultaneously promoting efficiency and equity. There will always be a need to balance these goals against the political process that, after all, epitomizes the art of the possible. On the other hand, the rapid development of technology to levy transportation charges means that the process of charging is no longer a barrier preventing progress toward this ideal. Building public understanding of the many possibilities for better service at lower cost through a system of transportation fees is the first step on what will undoubtedly be a long journey.

Notes

1. Martin Wachs and Jennifer Dill, "Regionalism in Transportation and Air Quality: History, Interpretation, and Insights for Regional Governance," in *Governance and Opportunity in Metropolitan America*, edited by Alan Altshuler and others (Washington: National Academy Press, 1999), pp. 253–80.

2. Reauthorized in 1998 as the Transportation Equity Act for the Twenty-First Century (TEA-21). TEA-21 allocated $217 billion in federal funding to transportation spending over six years.

3. For example, although federal funds previously came as either highway dollars or transit dollars that had to be spent on projects devoted exclusively to one mode or the other, the Surface Transportation program and Congestion Mitigation and Air Quality program allow regional agencies to determine their particular mix of expenditures among transit and highways.

4. Todd Goldman and Martin Wachs, "A Quiet Revolution in Transportation Finance," *Transportation Quarterly* 57, no. 1 (2003): 19–32.

5. See Puentes and Prince, chapter 3 in this volume.

6. Matthew Adams and others, "Financing Transportation in California: Strategies for Change." Report UCB-ITS-PWP-2000-6 (Berkeley: Institute of Transportation Studies, University of California, 2000).

7. Figures are for automobiles and do not include new pickup trucks, vans, or sport utility vehicles, which collectively average 20.5 miles per gallon. See Stacy Davis and Susan Diegel, *Transportation Energy Data Book,* 23d ed. (Oak Ridge, Tenn.: Center for Transportation Analysis, Oak Ridge National Laboratory, 2003).

8. Jeffrey Brown and others, *The Future of California Highway Finance* (San Francisco: California Policy Research Center, 1999).

9. McGraw Hill Construction, "Construction Cost Index History, 1908–2004," *Engineering News-Record* (http://enr.construction.com/features/coneco/subs/ constIndexHist.asp [2004]).

10. FHWA, *2002 Status of the Nation's Highways, Bridges and Transit: Conditions and Performance—Report to Congress* (Department of Transportation, 2002).

11. Martin Wachs, "Fighting Traffic Congestion with Information Technology," *Issues in Science and Technology* 19, no. 1 (2002): 43.

12. House Committee on Transportation and Infrastructure, "Statement of Mary Peters, Administrator, Federal Highway Administration," 107 Cong. 2 sess. (May 21, 2002).

13. Martin Wachs, "A Dozen Reasons for Raising Gasoline Taxes," *Public Works Management and Policy* 7, no. 4 (2003): 235–42.

14. Goldman and Wachs, "A Quiet Revolution."

15. Surface Transportation Policy Project, *Measuring Up: The Trend toward Voter Approved Transportation Funding* (Washington, 2002).

16. This is up from about one-third of all transportation measures before voters in November 2000. See Phyllis Myers and Robert Puentes, "Growth at the Ballot Box: Electing the Shape of Communities in November 2000," discussion paper prepared for the Center on Urban and Metropolitan Policy (Brookings, February 2001).

17. Amber Crabbe and others, "Local Transportation Sales Taxes: California's Experiment in Transportation Finance" (Berkeley: California Policy Research Center, 2002).

18. Ibid.

19. Infrastructure banks give states the capacity to increase the efficiency of their transportation investment and significantly leverage federal resources by attracting nonfederal public and private investment. See FHWA, "TEA-21—Transportation Equity Act for the 21st Century, Fact Sheet: State Infrastructure Bank Program" (www.fhwa.dot.gov/tea21/factsheets/sibs.htm [February 2005]).

20. Grant Anticipation Revenue Vehicle bonds enable states to pay debt service and other bond-related expenses with future federal-aid highway apportionments.

21. In Texas, for example, a portion of the motor fuel tax is allocated to the support of education. See chapter 3.

22. Ian W. H. Parry and Kenneth A. Small, "Does Britain or the United States Have the Right Gasoline Tax," Working Paper EPE-003 (Berkeley: University of California Energy Institute, November 2002).

23. See chapter 3.

24. Transportation Research Board, *The Congestion Mitigation and Air Quality Improvement Program: Assessing 10 Years of Experience*. Special Report 264 (Washington: National Academy Press, 2002).

25. Surface Transportation Policy Project, TEA-21 and RABA: *Why Is There Less Money?* (Washington, 2002).

26. According to data from the American Association of State Highway and Transportation Officials, an 80,000-pound, five-axle truck causes as much pavement damage, on average, as nearly 10,000 passenger cars. See Senate Committee on Environment and Public Works, "Statement of William D. Ankner, Ph.D., Director, Rhode Island Department of Transportation," 107 Cong. 2 sess. (September 30, 2002).

27. See, for example, James W. March, "Federal Highway Cost Allocation Study," *Public Roads* 61, no. 4 (1998) (www.tfhrc.gov/pubrds/janpr/cost.htm [February 2005]).

28. Although table 4-5 presents aggregate data for the nation, states differ considerably in how they levy charges for the use of their roads, especially on heavy-duty vehicles, and the extent of cross-subsidization in some states is much greater than in others.

29. Kenneth Small, Clifford Winston, and Carol A. Evans, *Road Work: A New Highway Pricing and Investment Policy* (Brookings, 1989).

30. FHWA, *Tracking the Deployment of the Integrated Metropolitan Intelligent Transportation Systems Infrastructure in the USA: Final 2002 Results* (Department of Transportation, 2004).

31. Mark Burris and Ashley Yelds, "Using ETC to Provide Variable Tolling: Some Real-World Results," paper presented at the Intelligent Transportation Society of America annual meeting, Washington, D.C., 2000.

32. During the first two weeks of London's congestion pricing program, which went into effect on February 17, 2003, bus ridership rose by 300,000 per day and average bus speeds rose 15.4 percent. Juliette Jowit, "Success of London Road Toll to Affect Bus Timetables," *Financial Times* (London), March 19, 2003, p. 10.

33. More than 10 million toll transponders have been issued to drivers in North America. Intelligent Transportation Society of America and Department of Transportation, *National Intelligent Transportation Systems Program Plan: A Ten-Year Vision* (2002).

34. Crabbe and others, "Local Transportation Sales Taxes."

35. Jeffrey Brown, "Reconsider the Gas Tax: Paying for What You Get," *Access* 19 (Fall 2001): 10–15.

36. David Forkenbrock and John Kuhl, *A New Approach to Assessing Road User Charges* (University of Iowa Public Policy Center, 2002).

37. Rural roads involve much greater surface area mileage and maintenance needs per capita or per mile of driving than urban roads (see tables 4-1 and 4-2). Urban roads

produce most of the traffic and, hence, most of the fuel tax revenues, while rural roads constitute most of the physical system. Per unit of highway, the subsidy flows from urban places to rural ones.

38. Satyanarayana Muthuswamy and David Levinson, "Buying into the Bypass: Allowing Trucks to Pay to Use the Ramp Meter Bypasses," *Transportation Quarterly* 57, no. 1 (2003): 81–92.

5

Slanted Pavement: How Ohio's Highway Spending Shortchanges Cities and Suburbs

Edward Hill, Billie Geyer, Robert Puentes, Kevin O'Brien, Claudette Robey, and John Brennan

Roads and highways are physical and fiscal realities, joining water-lines, sewers, and telecommunications infrastructure in shaping America's metropolitan areas. Roads form the backbone of the regional transportation system, flowing seamlessly across municipal boundaries. They enable local housing and labor markets to function while connecting locally made goods and services to broader markets. Granted, infrastructure does not create development. But it permits and channels demand for land and buildings along specific corridors.

Transportation infrastructure has clear regional economic and social benefits, but its finance structure remains a patchwork and creates huge financial liabilities for the unlucky unit of government that must foot the repair bills. How infrastructure construction and maintenance is financed affects the budgets of municipal, county, and state governments and represents large contingent liabilities, especially for municipal governments.

A grant from the Cleveland Foundation supported this research. The authors wish to thank the foundation and its staff for its support, as well as the Ohio Department of Transportation and Department of Taxation for access to data and other materials.

Do the rules governing who pays and how much make sense given today's metropolitan needs and realities? Municipal governments are generally required to pay for roads within their borders no matter where the traffic originates, no matter the role the road plays in the larger transportation system, no matter the fiscal condition and tax load borne by local taxpayers. They are required to pay no matter the bonding capacity of the jurisdiction and no matter who pays the fuel and use taxes that generate federal and state highway funds. Most state governments pay only for state and county routes under the pretext that traffic on all other roads is local and not part of the official state road and highway system. A few states maintain constitutional or statutory prohibitions on state funding of roads in large municipalities or on spending motor fuel taxes on any activity other than road and highway construction.[1] Such statutes reflect a bygone era when the cornstalk brigades ran state legislatures, and they persist in an era of suburban legislative dominance. Holes in roads are directly connected to holes in municipal purses.

Ohio typifies those parts of the nation that were industrialized before the mid-1960s and struggle with outmoded transportation finance structures. The state is highly urbanized, with a mix of central cities, inner-ring "first" suburbs, and rapidly growing suburban and exurban areas. The state also contains a slice of Appalachia and a significant number of rural agricultural counties. Ohio has a fully developed interstate highway system that is being expanded at its margins through lane additions, while demand for maintenance continues apace. Although Ohio ranks thirty-fifth among the states in geographic area, its highway system of federal and state-designated roads is the tenth largest in the country, with the second largest inventory of bridges. The state's interstate highway system is the fourth largest in the country and carries the fourth largest amount of truck freight in the country.[2] Demands to use highway funds to attract and retain employers complicate highway spending decisions, as do demands to redirect highway dollars toward alternative transportation uses, ranging from mass transit to recreational bikeways.

However, in Ohio, as in other states, an anti-urban bias distorts how transportation dollars are spent. Urban areas often act as "donors," contributing more transportation funds than they get in return. In this fashion, transportation funds continue to flow disproportionately to rural parts of the state, even though urban areas have the preponderance of people, vehicles, gas tax payments, and roadway expenses.

This chapter documents the long-standing fiscal mismatch between transportation revenues and responsibilities in Ohio by examining the geographic pattern of state transportation spending between 1980 and 1998. In particular, it examines the spatial patterns of state transportation finance and spending—including current highway contracts, gas tax collections, and vehicle registration tax revenues—and compares them to indicators of transportation demand and need.

In doing so, this chapter seeks to decipher one state's confusing system of highway finance to determine whether state transportation dollars are being spent in ways that meet the myriad challenges—aging infrastructure, traffic congestion, and decentralizing economic development—faced by metropolitan areas. The chapter also seeks—since Ohio's system of transportation finance resembles that of many states—to throw light on spending patterns within numerous states. In the end, we argue that Ohio must take steps to ameliorate the current mismatch between transportation funding and roadway responsibility.

Highway Funding in Ohio

In Ohio, as in a number of other states, the system of transportation finance is a historical relic that was put in place initially to build the highway system. In 1904 the Ohio General Assembly created the State Highway Department to study the physical makeup of highways and their repair.[3] At the time, the state government faced two critical transportation challenges: to tie together major economic and population centers with a system of highways, and to end rural isolation by tying rural Ohio to urban growth areas.

In the early twentieth century, municipalities were constructing citywide arterials, connecting them to a few suburban municipalities.[4] Municipalities and urban counties had the ability to finance their own needs because they were home to most of the state's industrial and property wealth. They used a combination of local property taxes and municipal bonds to pay for road construction before gasoline taxes became available.[5] In fact, early annexations by central cities were often motivated by the desire of then-rural residents to gain municipal services, especially roads, municipal water, and sanitation services. Building these services required access to either the purse of the central city or to its bond floats. Rural townships and unincorporated places, by contrast, lacked the tax base to pay for these improvements and, frequently, so did their counties. Consequently, the state agreed to pick up the cost of county and state roads to connect isolated villages to regional economies. To pay for these projects, states such as Ohio instituted a tax on gasoline.

Today, transportation funding in Ohio is financed primarily through a variety of state and federal sources. The Ohio Department of Transportation's (ODOT) total biennium budget for the 2004–05 state fiscal years is

Figure 5-1. Ohio Department of Transportation Funding Sources, State Fiscal Years 1999–2003

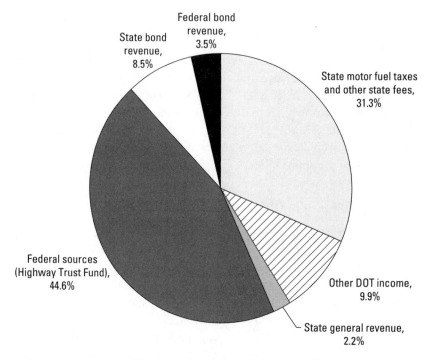

Source: Ohio Department of Transportation, *Financial and Statistical Report: Fiscal Year 2003* (Columbus, 2003).

$4.65 billion. Figure 5-1 summarizes the department's funding for fiscal years 1999 through 2003.

Gas Taxes

The federal revenues that flow to the state are derived from the federal gas tax, currently levied at 18.4 cents per gallon. These revenues flow directly into the Highway Trust Fund (HTF), which is administered by the Federal Highway Administration to support highway spending. HTF dollars are then redistributed to the states for transportation spending within the parameters, policies, and programs established at the federal level.[6] Other federal highway user taxes include taxes on diesel fuel, gasohol, special fuels, and various truck-related taxes, including the tire tax, truck and trailer sales tax, and heavy-vehicle use tax.[7]

Figure 5-2.   Ohio Motor Fuel Tax Rate, 1925–2004

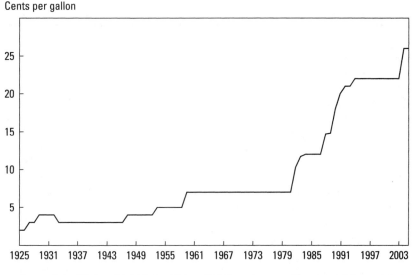

Cents per gallon

Source: Federal Highway Administration, *Highway Statistics,* various years (Department of Transportation).

Ohio's state gas tax (or motor fuel tax, which along with the federal gas tax is actually a motor fuel producers' or distributors' excise tax levied on dealers, wholesalers, and refiners) remained at 22 cents per gallon from 1993 to 2003, when it was increased to 26 cents (figure 5-2). The tax generates over $1.4 billion each year.[8] The motor fuel tax is also levied on diesel fuel and special fuels sold in Ohio. ODOT administers state highway programs in accordance with federal and state laws, policies, and procedures.[9]

In 2003 about 40 percent of the transportation revenues used by Ohio on its state-administered highways derived from state motor fuel taxes.[10] In fiscal year 2003, the state directly spent 70.7 percent of the $1.46 billion in revenues generated by the state gas tax, with 60.9 percent going into the state highway operating fund and 9.7 percent to the state highway bond retirement fund (table 5-1). The remaining funds were distributed to local governments based on the following statutory formulas:

—The county share ($127.7 million, or 8.8 percent of total state gas tax collections) was divided equally among all eighty-eight counties and was principally devoted to supporting county highway engineering staffs.

—The township share ($68.7 million, or 4.7 percent of collections) was divided equally among all state townships.

Table 5-1.   Ohio Gas Tax Distributions, Fiscal Year 2003

Units as indicated

Distributions	Millions of dollars	Percent of total
State		
Highway operating fund	887.1	60.9
Highway bond retirement	141.1	9.7
Total state	1,028.2	70.7
Local		
Municipalities	147.1	10.1
Counties	127.7	8.8
Townships	68.7	4.7
Total local	343.5	23.6
Local Transportation Improvement Program	65.8	4.5
Other[a]	18.5	1.3
Grand total	1,456.1	100.1[b]

Source: Ohio Department of Taxation, *2003 Annual Report* (tax.ohio.gov/divisions/communications/publications/annual_reports/publications_annual_report_2003.stm

a. Includes Grade Crossing Fund, Waterway Safety Fund, and distributions to the Ohio Turnpike Commission.

b. Value exceeding 100 is artifact due to rounding.

—The municipality share ($147.1 million, or 10.1 percent) was divided according to each municipality's share of statewide motor vehicle registrations.

It is important to note that in Ohio, as well as in twenty-nine other states, gas tax receipts are restricted to spending on the highway system only. In other words, the funds not only cannot be spent on nontransportation items such as debt reduction, but they cannot be spent to finance congestion and air quality projects, mass transit, or other options unrelated to highways.

One cent of the gas tax is dedicated to the Local Transportation Improvements Program, which was created by the legislature in 1989. These funds are available for local road, bridge, and culvert improvement projects and are administered in conjunction with the State Capital Improvement Program (SCIP). The SCIP (also known as the Issue 2 program) allows the state to use its general revenues to support and issue up to $120 million in infrastructure bonds each year. These bonds offer financial assistance (loans, grants, and credit enhancement) to local governments to improve their basic infrastructure, including roads, bridges, and culverts. Projects are selected for funding assistance on a regional basis by the integrating committees of the nineteen public works districts located throughout the state.

Motor Vehicle License Tax

The motor vehicle license tax (also known as vehicle registration fee) was first enacted in 1906 at $5 per vehicle. Subsequent changes instituted different fees for different types of vehicles and increased the rate.[11] In fiscal year 2003, vehicle license taxes generated $451.8 million.[12] All the money is earmarked for highway purposes. After bond retirement obligations and administrative expenses are met, license tax revenues are distributed as follows:

—34 percent to the municipal corporation or county of registration;

—47 percent to the county in which vehicle owner resides;

—9 percent to counties based on their relative share of county roads within the state;

—5 percent to townships based on the distribution formula discussed above; and

—5 percent equally among Ohio's counties.

Bonds and Other Revenue Sources

Ohio has used bond funds since 1954 to supplement the motor fuel tax, license fees, and other highway revenue sources. In November 1995 voters approved an amendment to increase the annual bond issuance limit to $220 million, with total outstanding debt limited to $1.2 billion. This increased bonding authority ended in 1997, and all related bonds will be retired by fiscal year 2005. ODOT's annual bond issuances were limited to $220 million from fiscal year 1996 through fiscal year 2000, after which annual bond sales cannot exceed $100 million per year.

ODOT also sponsors a variety of other programs that allow local governments to access federal funds. These programs include an urban paving initiative, an enhancements program, and county, city, and high-cost bridge programs. In fiscal year 2002, these programs totaled about $132 million, about one-tenth the amount generated from the state gas tax. Other local funding programs involve allocating federal funds to metropolitan planning organizations (MPOs) and to cities that are not large enough to have an MPO. These funds totaled $128.8 million in fiscal year 2002, down from $139 million in ODOT's 2001 capital program.[13] The MPO is composed of local elected officials, transportation system operators, and appropriate state officials. The sixteen MPOs in the state serve as regional forums for determining each region's transportation system needs, priorities, and financial resources. These planning processes are coordinated with the statewide planning process, the Transportation Plan and the Transportation Improvement Program. Local governments work with ODOT district offices as well as their MPOs to plan and coordinate road and bridge projects within their jurisdiction.

Purposes of the Finance System

There are three purposes for the current system of transportation finance in Ohio. The first is primarily economic: to facilitate trade and to connect places of work and residence. This argues for breaking away from county-based systems of highway decisionmaking (including engineering) to one that serves functional regional economies. The second is to provide funds to maintain the highway system that has been built over the past century. This argues for distributing funds based on traffic volume and for emphasizing the centrality of a roadway to a region's transportation system. The third purpose, in terms of the gas tax, is to internalize the cost imposed on society by the various users of the system. This includes the direct costs of wear and tear by different types of highway users, and it argues for including the external costs of impacts on air quality and other environmental resources that are generated by highway traffic. The remainder of this chapter assesses how Ohio's system of transportation finance fulfills these purposes.

Assigned Responsibilities for Ohio's Roads

Despite this array of funding sources, Ohio's roadway funding system creates a fundamental fiscal mismatch between jurisdictions with differing needs and responsibilities. In Ohio, local governments are generally responsible for maintaining, improving, and preserving the streets, highways, and bridges that are not the state's responsibility. The 2,345 local governments in Ohio are identified either as municipalities (there are 940 of these), townships (1,317), or counties (88). Municipalities are incorporated places with powers of local self-government, and municipalities with populations greater than 5,000 are considered cities. Townships are unincorporated areas of counties that provide a number of public services similar to municipalities. Some townships have larger populations than cities. Counties function as broad general-purpose governments in Ohio.[14]

Counties are responsible for county roads outside municipalities and for bridges on state and U.S. highways within municipalities that are over waterways. Incorporated municipalities or cities take care of roads in their jurisdictions (except the state roads and interstate highways). Townships are responsible for township roads; however, the major arterials within townships are frequently classified as county roads. Thus, unincorporated areas can rely on the county to provide services such as engineering, maintenance, and inspection of roads, which are financed by the county directly through taxes or indirectly by other revenues, such as grants.[15] By contrast, incorporated municipalities cannot rely on counties for such funding.

Counties are responsible for more than 58,000 lane miles of roadways and 27,000 bridges. Municipalities are responsible for 74,000 lane miles and 2,000 bridges. Townships oversee about 88,000 roadway miles but no bridges. A recent report from the Ohio Public Works Commission found that, together, these local governments need about $12 billion for their roads and bridges: municipalities need $8.2 billion, counties need $2.8 billion, and townships need $922 million.[16]

ODOT is responsible for coordinating the entire state highway system, including the interstate system, but it is only responsible for developing projects that are outside urban areas. Generally, this leaves municipalities with primary responsibility for all streets and highways except interstates, the counties with responsibility for county routes outside municipalities, and townships with responsibility for township roads.

State highways, as defined by section 4511.01 of the Ohio Revised Code, are "under the jurisdiction of the department of transportation, outside the limits of municipal corporations." The remaining streets and highways, including bridges, are the responsibility of the municipalities, counties, and townships. The state takes responsibility for state highways that run through municipalities as long as they "look" and function like interstate highways. That is, they must be limited-access roads with entrance and exit ramps and with no impeding intersections. In practice, ODOT has accepted a much broader scope of work by helping municipalities with major highway and bridge projects.

Many of the roads ineligible for state support lie within the jurisdiction of municipalities but are part of much bigger networks. However, as this chapter demonstrates, cities receive a disproportionately small share of this revenue base, forcing them to use municipal income, property taxes, and local vehicle license tax revenues to pay for their portion of the region's transportation system. In addition, some wealthier inner-ring suburbs dedicate all of their estate, or inheritance, tax receipts to these capital accounts.

ODOT has made funding fairer by implementing policies and programs to help local governments meet their maintenance responsibilities and has improved the way funding is distributed to its district offices. The Ohio General Assembly has also recognized this fiscal mismatch to some extent and, over the last twenty years, has initiated programs and revenue sources to assist municipalities with their responsibilities. The Ohio Public Works Program, the Local Transportation Improvement Program, and local vehicle license tax options all provide funding opportunities to local governments for road improvements. These funding sources, however, remain small and piecemeal compared with the funding sources that cities cannot directly access or that send millions of dollars disproportionately to rural areas on the suburban fringe.

The problems with this intergovernmental fiscal arrangement range from potential fiscal distress to distortions of development patterns. As existing roads age, they require not only periodic resurfacing but eventual comprehensive rebuilding. Therefore, older cities face a dilemma: do they undertake the repairs and rebuilding and endanger their budgets and bond ratings, or do they let the streets and roads deteriorate and endanger their economic and residential base? Another problem stems from the fact that the apportionments of gas tax revenues to local governments do not reflect the relative needs of different areas. For example, in Ohio the county portion of the distribution formula disburses funds equally to the state's eighty-eight counties without regard to population, vehicle registrations, traffic volumes, gas tax payments, or miles of roadway. This ensures that counties with modest needs garner the same funding as counties with vast needs.

Current state laws fail, moreover, to recognize the fiscal burden that municipalities face in maintaining older roadways. Nor do state laws recognize important management differences between urban and rural areas. For example, county highway departments receive funding from the state to support their engineering staffs, while municipalities receive no such funding. This puts central cities and inner-ring suburbs (especially low-income suburbs) at a severe disadvantage in creating roadway funding proposals and bid documents and in supervising construction projects.

Analysis of State Highway Spending

This section examines the distribution of highway spending within Ohio to determine whether current laws and allocations create an anti-urban bias. To determine how Ohio has been spending its highway dollars, we relied on several sources, outlined in the appendix. Primarily, we analyzed a database maintained by ODOT that identifies all highway contracts let by the state from 1980 to 1998. The database includes location, dollar amount, and type of activity. The activities are grouped into three categories: new construction, rehabilitation, and maintenance. (See appendix for descriptions.)

To assess the fit between need and spending in Ohio, the analysis considers highway spending per
—average daily vehicle miles traveled (VMT) on the entire road and highway system,
—estimated dollar volume of retail gasoline sales in each county,
—total vehicle registrations in each county, and
—total lane miles in each county.

These indicators not only approximate demand for highway investment funds but are themselves sources of significant portions of those funds. They are calculated for each county and then aggregated by county type: rural, urban, or suburban. The federal government also uses these indicators to allocate highway funds to the states.

Although it would seem that highway spending for expansion (new construction), maintenance, and rehabilitation would be higher in counties with greater roadway use, this is not the case. This analysis shows that Ohio's rural counties have fared significantly better than either urban or suburban counties on almost all the indicators of state spending. Road and highway spending in Ohio does not reflect the responsibilities that municipal governments have in maintaining and improving the roadway system.

The following is an examination of each of the indicators. The annual data are first graphed for each indicator during the nineteen-year period examined, and then they are aggregated and presented in a table of expenditures by the type of county.

Highway Spending Compared to Average Daily Vehicle Miles Traveled

With wear and tear on roads comes demand for highway maintenance and improvement dollars. This demand is best approximated by average daily VMT on the state highways and municipal roadways in a given year. If the system of highway expenditures is indeed efficient, then expenditures should closely parallel use. However, in Ohio it does not. In most years, rural counties spent more on state transportation relative to average daily VMT (combining travel on both the designated state system and municipal streets) than did suburban or urban counties. Rural counties received the highest relative amounts of state spending, based on average daily VMT, for all but four years from 1980 to 1998.

Figure 5-3 shows annual highway construction expenditures for each 1,000 daily highway miles driven over the entire roadway system by type of county in 1999 inflation-adjusted dollars.[17]

Figure 5-3. New Highway Construction and Major Preservation Spending per Thousand Daily VMT, by County Type, 1980–1998

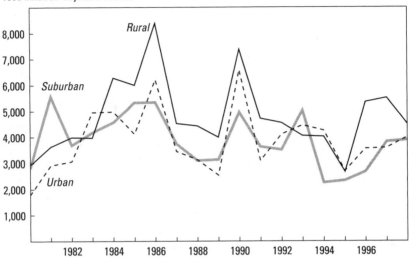

1999 inflation-adjusted dollars

Source: Authors' database constructed from agency records (see appendix).

Totaling highway contracts over the nineteen-year period reveals the clear rural bias in funding (table 5-2). Total highway spending is similar for suburban and urban counties, and both receive far less than rural counties— and even less than the state average. Table 5-2 shows that rural areas obtain more than urban and suburban counties in every category except new construction, for which the urban counties actually ranked highest.[18] Overall, highway spending between 1980 and 1998 in rural areas exceeded that in suburban counties by 25 percent and that in urban areas by 24 percent.

Table 5-2. Total State Spending per Thousand Daily VMT on the Total Roadway System, 1980–98

Constant 1999 dollars

County type	Maintenance	New construction	Rehabilitation	Total
Rural	13,481	11,591	66,305	91,377
Suburban	12,704	9,186	50,970	72,860
Urban	11,590	14,284	47,767	73,641
State average	12,366	12,076	52,944	77,386

Source: Authors' calculations based on data provided by the Ohio Department of Transportation.

Map 5-1.   Index of Capital Expenditures (1980-1998) per Average VMT, Ohio Counties (1982, 1987, 1992, 1997)[a]

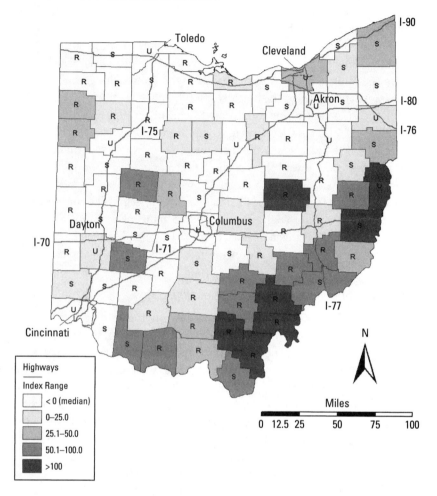

Source: Ohio Department of Transportation and Bureau of the Census. Prepared by Center for Public Management, Maxine Goodman Levin College of Urban Affairs, Cleveland State University.
a. R, rural; S, suburban; U, urban.

Map 5-1 depicts total highway spending from 1980 to 1998 per average VMT. These are the same data as displayed in figure 5-3 and table 5-2, but they were converted into an index to simplify interpretation. The index represents the balance between the demand for highway spending (road use) and the amount spent, as calculated from the percentage difference between each county and the median county in highway construction contracts let per average mile driven.[19] The median counties are Hancock and Muskingum. Light-colored areas in map 5-1 represent counties with index values below the median, and these areas grow darker as the index value increases.

The map shows that the Appalachian counties in the southeast corner of the state enjoyed the highest spending levels per vehicle mile traveled. The lowest relative spending is in the suburban and rural counties along Ohio's three major interstate highways: the north-south I-75 in the western portion of the state that carries traffic from southeast Michigan through Cincinnati (the "auto alley"); I-71 from Cleveland to Columbus to Cincinnati (the "three C" corridor); and the east-west Ohio Turnpike (I-80).[20] Ohio's urban counties were grouped in the lowest three spending categories. The counties housing Akron, Canton, Cincinnati, Columbus, Lima, Mansfield, and Toledo all fell below the median (shown in the lightest areas on the map). The counties that are home to Dayton and Youngstown fell between the median and 25 percent above the median. Cuyahoga County, home to Cleveland, is 42 percent above the median, and Steubenville's county is in the highest spending bracket.

Highway Spending Compared to Gasoline Sales

Transportation funds are generated mainly from the tax on gasoline sales. Gasoline sales by county, therefore, are a good indicator of the demand for vehicle use—and thus the demand on the roadway network—in a particular place. Unfortunately, we could not use data on actual gasoline tax collections because the Ohio Department of Taxation neither tabulates the data nor makes them available to the public.[21] Therefore, local contributions to gas taxes are approximated from total retail sales at gasoline stations by county, using data from the U.S. Economic Census.[22] To estimate sales values for the intercensus years, a moving average was calculated. The economic census provides data on total sales by retail gasoline stations but does not specify motor fuel sales; therefore, receipts from repairs and sales of groceries and sundries are also included in the data. Despite these problems, the census offers the best approximation of where motor fuel tax revenues are generated by county. Comparing these data to county data on highway contracts is an excellent, if admittedly rough, measure of spending equity.

Employing these measures, we find large discrepancies between types of counties where highway contracts are let and types of counties where retail gasoline sales take place. Figure 5-4 shows that rural counties again had the highest spending levels in all but two years between 1980 and 1998 relative to sales at gasoline stations.

Figure 5-4.   New Highway Construction and Major Preservation
Spending per Retail Sales at Gasoline Stations, 1980–98

1999 inflation-adjusted dollars

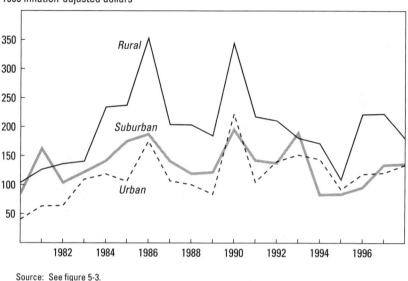

Source: See figure 5-3.

When these statistics are totaled for the nineteen-year period, highway
spending in rural counties exceeded that in suburban and urban areas by
46 percent and 62 percent, respectively. Rural investments in road maintenance, new construction, and rehabilitation exceeded those of all other types
of counties (table 5-3).

Map 5-2 reveals clear disparities between rural and urban-suburban
locales in highway contracts let per average dollar of retail gasoline sales.
Urban and suburban counties produce considerably more in retail gas sales
than they receive in ODOT contracts.[23]

Table 5-3.   Total Highway Spending per Retail Sales at Gasoline Stations,
1980–98

Constant 1999 dollars

County type	Maintenance	New construction	Rehabilitation	Total
Rural	551	474	2,712	3,738
Suburban	445	322	1,785	2,552
Urban	362	446	1,493	2,301
State average	423	413	1,812	2,649

Source: See table 5-2.

Map 5-2. Index of Total Spending by ODOT (1980–1998) per Average
Dollar of Gas Sales, Ohio Counties (1982, 1987, 1992, 1997)[a]

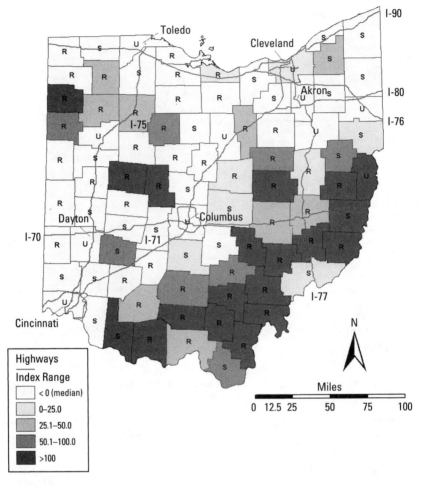

Source: See map 5-1.
a. R, rural; S, suburban; U, urban.

Highway Spending Compared to Registered Vehicles

Vehicle registrations by county also indicate demand on roads. The value
of highway contracts per registered vehicle was the highest in rural areas in
every year since 1983 but one. Spending in suburban areas exceeded those
in urban areas in twelve of the nineteen years analyzed (figure 5-5).

Figure 5-5.   New Highway Construction and Major Preservation
Spending per Registered Vehicle, by County Type, 1980–1998

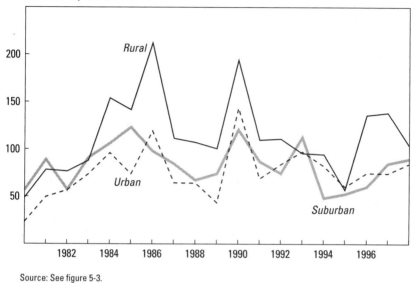

1999 inflation-adjusted dollars

Source: See figure 5-3.

Total highway spending in rural areas during the nineteen-year period
exceeded spending in suburban and urban areas by 34 and 48 percent, respectively. Only in new construction did urban counties outspend others (table 5-4).

Highway Spending Compared to Lane Miles of Roadway

Urban counties contain only 21 percent of the state's total roadway lane
miles (see appendix, table 5A-2). However, urban areas receive more highway investments per lane miles than suburban and rural areas (figure 5-6).

Table 5-4.   Total Highway Spending per Vehicle Registrations, 1980–98

Constant 1999 dollars

County type	Maintenance	New construction	Rehabilitation	Total
Rural	369	317	1,815	2,502
Suburban	326	236	1,309	1,871
Urban	267	329	1,100	1,695
State average	306	298	1,308	1,912

Source: See table 5-2.

Figure 5-6.   Highway Contracts per Lane Mile, by County Type, 1980–1998

1999 inflation-adjusted dollars

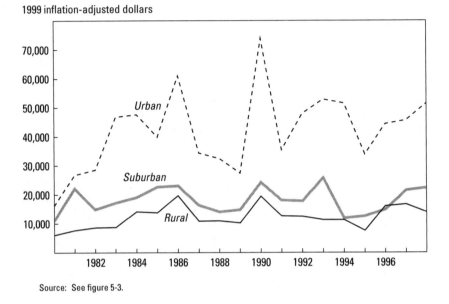

Source: See figure 5-3.

This is not because urban areas contend with the greatest need but because it is more expensive to build and rehabilitate highways in urban areas than in rural areas. In addition, two of Ohio's most populous counties, Cuyahoga and Hamilton, possess extensive bridge networks, which tend to be much more costly to rehabilitate than regular roadways.

During the nineteen-year period, total highway spending by lane mile was highest in urban counties, followed by suburban, and, finally, rural counties. These trends were consistent in all three spending categories (table 5-5).

Table 5-5.   Total Highway Spending Contracts per Lane Mile, 1980–98

Constant 1999 dollars

Category	Maintenance	New construction	Rehabilitation	Total
Rural	34,367	29,549	169,030	232,947
Suburban	60,171	43,510	241,411	345,092
Urban	125,732	154,957	518,195	798,884
State average	62,742	61,271	268,633	392,646

Source: See table 5-2.

To be sure, no one perfect piece of data measures the demand, or "need," for highway funds, the degree of redistribution by locale, or the impact of highway spending on the budgets of different levels of government. However, the indexes we have compiled demonstrate a consistent anti-urban bias in Ohio's highway programs. That urban areas receive more highway dollars per lane mile than other jurisdictions does not make highway financing equitable. It only verifies that urban roads are expensive to build and repair. The other three indicators are better measures of the amount of vehicle use on the roadway network. That urban areas consistently receive far fewer highway dollars than other areas for their vehicle miles traveled, number of registered vehicles, and demand for gasoline shows that urban areas are getting the short end of the financial stick relative to the wear and tear on their roads.

One cause for this bias is the disqualification of arterials within municipalities from receiving state and motor fuel tax funds. The array of special programs that have been instituted is insufficient to offset this fundamental bias and to overcome a historical legacy of inequity in highway building. A second source of bias lies within highway expenditures for maintenance. Given the first bias, this is no surprise: if there are incentives within funding programs to overbuild in rural counties, then requirements to maintain what was built will create a rural tilt in maintenance programs. This rural bias is further exacerbated by the distribution formulas for how the gas and registration taxes are allocated to local governments.

Behind the Spending Trends: Disparities in Distribution Formulas

Almost 60 percent of Ohio's highway funds come from the gasoline tax and vehicle registration. A significant portion of these revenues is distributed to local governments to build, improve, and maintain their roadways. The formulas used to distribute these revenues are also biased toward rural areas.[24]

In this section, we analyze funds distributed to local governments (counties, municipalities, and townships) from the gas and vehicle registration taxes. Funds were totaled by county; grouped as rural, suburban, or urban; and then compared to the three indicators of highway funding demand (vehicle miles traveled, retail sales at gas stations, and vehicle registrations) and to the number of lane miles of roadway. Once again, when revenue distributions from these taxes were compared with every indicator of demand, urban counties fared the worst and rural counties the best. These trends are reflected in tables 5-6 and 5-7.

Table 5-6.   Gas Tax Distributions by County Type, 1984–99[a]

Constant 1999 dollars

County type	By vehicle registrations	Per average daily VMT	By retail sales at gasoline stations
Rural	899	29,519	1,348
Suburban	466	16,744	636
Urban	325	12,259	441
State average	485	17,505	673

Sources: Authors' calculations based on data provided by the Ohio Bureau of Motor Vehicles, Ohio Department of Transportation, Census of Retail Trades, and Bureau of the Census.

a. Registered vehicles, vehicle miles traveled, and gas sales are averages over the 1984–99 period.

Table 5-7.   Vehicle Registration Tax Distributions by County Type, 1984–99[a]

Constant 1999 dollars

County type	By vehicle registrations	By average daily VMT	By retail sales at gas stations
Rural	40.09	1,507	60.22
Suburban	28.14	1,137	38.47
Urban	23.70	956	32.32
State average	28.62	1,137	39.84

Sources: See table 5-6.

a. Registered vehicles, vehicle miles traveled, and gas sales are averages over the 1984–99 period.

This discrepancy occurs because county and township distributions of the gas tax (as discussed earlier) are split evenly between jurisdictions. In other words, Cuyahoga County (1.4 million people) receives the same share of the gas tax collections as rural counties such as Harrison County (15,000 people). Only municipalities received funding based on an appropriate indicator—the municipality's share of statewide motor vehicle registrations.

The distribution formula for the motor vehicle registration tax also favors less-populated counties. Distributions from the registration tax are lowest in urban counties, higher in suburban counties, and highest in rural areas when compared with vehicle registrations, vehicle miles traveled, and retail sales at gasoline establishments.

Although 81 percent of the vehicle registration funds are distributed to the county in which a vehicle is registered, 19 percent are not. Furthermore, 14 percent of the total is allocated according to the relative proportion of county and township roads in the state. Such roads are not prevalent in urban counties owing to the fraction of land in urban counties that is incorporated. For example, Cuyahoga County has only 38 miles of county and township roads, while Guernsey County, a rural county in southeast Ohio, has 1,010.

Policy Recommendations

The analysis of transportation spending in Ohio reveals that rural counties receive more funds than urban and suburban counties, even though their highway needs and automobile use, as measured by vehicle miles traveled, retail sales at gasoline stations (a proxy for gasoline sales volumes), population, vehicle registrations, and lane miles, are less. Total contracting expenditures were highest in rural areas for all indicators except lane miles. These findings are important in policy debates of whether states receive their "fair share" of the federal gas tax.

When the highway system was being built, beginning in the 1950s through the mid-1990s, federal funding flowed disproportionately *to* rural states, states with rapidly growing populations, and states with undeveloped highway systems *from* more urbanized states and those with highway systems that were more advanced. This interstate redistribution of money allowed the national system of highways to be constructed. The traditional funding mechanism recognized that geographically large but less densely populated and poorer states had difficulty constructing and maintaining their portions of the interstate highway system and required federal gas tax funds in excess of what was paid in by local drivers.

As a result, many rural states with relatively low highway use received more federal gas tax revenues from the Highway Trust Fund than they contributed. (They were the "donee" states.) By contrast, many urban states, with greater highway use, contributed more than they received. (They were the "donor" states.) For example, in 1985 the average number of registered vehicles and VMT in the top ten donor states was roughly 6.7 million and 73 million, respectively, or nearly ten times the figures in the top ten donee states—727,018 and 7.5 million, respectively. Despite the disproportionate distribution, this formula was necessary to build and maintain political support for the interstate highway system program.[25] Once the interstate system was completed, the rationale for distributing money broke down, and the political compromise that built the system fell apart.

As a result, the Transportation Equity Act for the Twenty-First Century (TEA-21, passed in June 1998) guaranteed each state a return of at least

90.5 percent of its contributions to the Highway Account of the HTF. Proponents of this policy were, naturally, from those states that paid more money into the trust fund than they received under the old distributional rules. They argued that the new formula in TEA-21 would maintain the system in poorer and rural states while ensuring that the demands of the donor states were met. The pure politics that motivated the passage of the minimum guarantee funding rule is understandable. The rule acknowledges that the interstate system is largely complete and that it is time to change the way funds are distributed. In the debate around reauthorization of TEA-21, several states have pushed for a 95 percent return of their Highway Account contributions. The Senate incorporated this provision in its reauthorization bill.[26]

Despite the embrace of this funding issue at the federal level, similar rules generally do not exist at the state level. Our analysis shows that, in Ohio at least, urban counties are the donors of funds into state highway coffers, and rural areas are the donees. It is quite likely that the current system of highway taxes represents a fiscal drag on central cities and older suburbs because they have to maintain roads that are not part of the federal highway system and, in many cases, are not supported adequately by state funds. The rationale for the current system of highway finance may have made perfect sense when the highway system was constructed; however, it no longer makes sense as a way of maintaining that same system.

This unequal treatment is further exacerbated by biased formulas that disproportionately distribute the local government portion of the state gas tax and vehicle registration taxes to rural areas. These revenues overlap with the project database given that there is a local share within many of the projects that may contain gas tax or vehicle registration tax revenues. However, the negative impact on urban and suburban areas is compounded because federal and some state programs can only be accessed with an adequate local match.

Clearly, rural highways are necessary components of the statewide network.[27] Urban roads are no less important, however. Unfortunately, municipal governments have limited ability to raise revenues from the use of roadways within their borders. The primary sources of municipal funds are local income and property taxes, neither of which are related to traffic volumes or paid directly by those using the roadways.

It is incumbent on state government, then, to look comprehensively at how federal and state gas taxes—the primary sources of state and local highway revenues—are spent, allocated, and distributed. ODOT has made significant improvements during the last several years by changing the allocation formulas for districts, creating a more rational and less political process for programming "major new" projects, creating local funding programs, and providing assistance to local governments directly.[28] However, even with these amendments, equity remains elusive. The Mayors' Think Tank of Northeast Ohio finds that District 12, which includes Cuyahoga, Geauga, and Lake counties, is fourth largest in population but is next to last in money allocated.[29] There is only so much that can be done to overcome statutes written before the state and federal governments understood their role in the state and national highway systems.

The public policy challenge in the near future is to articulate an updated vision for funding highways and to establish goals and practices consistent with the economic and social realities of the early twenty-first century. Several policy responses would substantially ameliorate the current mismatch between funding and responsibilities.

Fix the Classification System

One approach would be to include major arterials in the state highway system, that is, the system ODOT maintains. These roads could be treated the same as interstate highways, which are part of the state highway system and are managed by ODOT. This would enable major municipal roads to immediately receive state funds. Alternatively, the state could model its funding programs on the federal program, which bases eligibility on a highway's functional classification rather than its location in an incorporated area. State and U.S. highways located within cities would generally be classified as principal or minor arterials or collectors, thereby putting them on equal footing with roadways of the same classification outside municipal boundaries.

Fix the Distribution Formulas

The methods for distributing the state gas tax to local governments must better match where travel occurs and where gasoline is purchased. It is essential to ensure that urban and metropolitan areas are not undermined by such formulas.

Continue Metropolitan Devolution

Another option would be to increase the programming and planning authority of the regional organizations, such as MPOs. Although these organizations have gained importance with each federal transportation authorization act, their programming authority remains incommensurate with their share of the population. ODOT's 2001 construction budget reflects MPO spending of $129 million, or 9 percent of the total. The population in counties encompassed by these MPOs totaled 7.9 million in 1998, or 71 percent of the state total. A more regional approach to planning and programming highway improvements could better match the regional nature of the networks as well as match revenues and responsibilities.

Free the Gas Tax for Balanced Spending

On a more basic level, Ohio should remove the restriction that tethers gas tax revenues exclusively to highway projects. The state should earmark a portion of these funds annually for transit and other projects for spending by local governments or MPOs.

Provide Better Data

Data should be released on where federal and state gas tax revenues are collected so that the public can better evaluate the spatial equity of highway spending.

Implications for Other State and Federal Leaders

Why should anyone except Ohioans care about the status of highway funding in Ohio? First, many, if not most, states have an anti-urban bias in highway distribution formulas. Ohio is an example, not an exception. In the congressional debate over the federal transportation law, members from donor states clamor to ensure that their state receives an equitable share of the gas tax dollars. These elected leaders should not lose sight of the donor-donee issue within their own states.

Second, federal transportation law should address the distribution formulas that omit major arterial city streets. This is a federal issue because Highway Trust Fund money supports this pattern of spending.

Third, highway spending formulas that favor new construction in rural areas contribute to the spread of low-density development through de facto development subsidies. Low-density development is not necessarily objectionable, and Ohio, with an economy that specializes in manufacturing and distribution, depends on truck transportation and a well-functioning interstate highway system. However, highways have distorted the pattern of property values within the state.

Fourth, gas tax funds may not be productive if they are restricted to state and interstate highways. Excluding major municipal roadways may compromise the overall system and possibly place the state at a disadvantage in attracting and retaining businesses.

Finally, as mentioned, Ohio, along with twenty-nine other states, forbids spending gas tax receipts to operate transit within the state. Such restrictions are overly burdensome to municipalities, which must seek other limited sources of transit funding to achieve a balanced transportation network.

Conclusion

Ongoing debates about federal transportation law present an opportunity to acknowledge that a historic event has taken place in American social and economic history: the interstate highway system has been completed. This landmark event demonstrates that a half century of dedicated, consistent capital investment can result in a stronger and wealthier nation. Now the time has come to declare victory and move on—on to a more stable system of infrastructure finance (not just highway finance) that maintains this precious gift of the World War II generation.

It is also time to recognize that it was the citizen-taxpayers of our older metropolitan areas who disproportionately paid for the construction of the highway system that made possible the economic miracle of the rural areas as well as the booming southern, western, and mountain states. Now is the time to level the playing field so that the donor metropolitan areas are not disconnected from the economy that they helped build.

Appendix 5A

Methodology

To conduct this study, we assembled a number of databases including, most importantly, ones tabulating all highway contracts let by the Ohio Department of Transportation (ODOT) from 1980 to 1998. The state's database was restructured while we were doing this research, and, therefore, highway contracts after 1998 are not yet available. The ODOT highway contract database contains county location, dollar amount, highway name, type of activity, year, and other descriptive information for each project contracted out during the period. We did not examine local spending (which is fed by vehicle registration fees) since the purpose of this research was to examine state funding priorities. Localities spend their transportation revenues largely within their jurisdiction.

The project activities were grouped into three categories: new construction, rehabilitation, and maintenance. New projects include those that expand capacity, such as the construction of new highways, lane additions, and new interchanges. Rehabilitation projects are major reconstructions and redevelopment projects, including bridge and culvert replacements and resurfacing projects. Maintenance projects include bridge repairs, lighting, fencing, pavement markings, signage, and bridge and guardrail painting projects; in other words, projects that do not expand capacity and are not major rehabilitations.

Other databases used are described below, with the source shown in parentheses:

—Vehicle miles traveled (ODOT): For the state system, data are broken down by county and by vehicle type, and cover interstates, U.S. routes, and state routes. Data used were for the years 1982, 1987, 1992, and 1998. For the total system, data are broken down by county and by federal highway classification. Data were used from the years 1990 through 1999.

—County population (Bureau of the Census): Data were used from every year from 1980 to 1999.[30]

—Vehicle registrations (Ohio Bureau of Motor Vehicles): The data used covered the total number by vehicle type from 1981 to 1999, and the total number by county for 1982, 1987, 1992, and 1998.

—Lane miles of roadway on the state highway system for 1998 (ODOT).

—Statewide motor vehicle fuel tax and fuel use tax information (Ohio Department of Taxation) from 1980 to 1998.[31]

State gas tax receipts or gas sales by county were not available through the Ohio Department of Taxation. Therefore, we used retail sales at gasoline service stations from the Census of Retail Trade as a proxy for where gasoline is purchased. The data were available by county for 1982, 1987, 1992, and 1997.[32] The major weakness of these data is that gasoline stations are defined as those that have more than half of their dollar sales in gasoline, which means that nearly half of their sales may be something other than gasoline. We assumed that the proportion of nongasoline sales is consistent across the state.

Counties are the unit of analysis because much of the data we use were only available at that level of government. We were particularly disappointed that information about the collection of gasoline taxes is not available for local governmental units (municipalities and townships). The state of Ohio collects motor fuel taxes from wholesalers, not retailers.

Each county was classified as rural, suburban, or urban based on its geography with regard to a metropolitan statistical area (MSA). Those outside an MSA were considered to be rural. The counties within MSAs were divided into two groups: the central county of the MSA was considered to be urban, and all other counties within the MSA were labeled as suburban. Table 5A-1 lists the individual counties and their rural, suburban, or urban classification. Table 5A-2 shows the lane mile calculation by county type.

Because counties in this chapter are classified as a whole and urban counties have urban and suburban components, our classification scheme biases the analysis to undercount funding flows to rural areas, suburbs, and townships, and overcount flows to cities. In other words, our findings of anti-urban bias are minimums.

Current Ohio Highway Spending Programs

ODOT is charged with maintaining a safe, effective, and accessible transportation system in Ohio, including highways, aviation, bicycles and pedestrians, transit, and rail transportation. For highway responsibilities, its first priority is to preserve and maintain the state highway system, and its second mission is to make investments in and improvements to the current system to ensure public safety and encourage economic development.[33]

ODOT's capital fund budget totaled $1.3 billion for highways in 2001. The investments are designated as system preservation, major new projects, local programs, and "other" (which includes other transportation modes and programs, such as Appalachian development and demonstration projects). Figure 5A-1 shows the percentage distribution of ODOT's 2001 capital budget, and projected budgets to 2005, among these capital project categories.

System preservation funding, which is the largest category, is divided between pavement projects, with $305 million in contracts during fiscal year 2001, and bridge projects ($186 million). These funds are allocated to the twelve ODOT districts based on formulas that consider pavement and bridge conditions, lane miles of roadway, square footage of bridge surfaces, traffic volumes, and percentage of cars and trucks. The district offices then determine how to best use those funds based on their knowledge of conditions, use, and role within the transportation network.

Major new projects consist of capacity projects at the state level, generally about $300 million a year. The Transportation Review Advisory Council (TRAC) decides which projects receive major new funding. The TRAC, which was created by the legislature in 1997 at the request of ODOT, is a per-

Table 5A-1.   Ohio Counties and Their Classification[a]

County	Type	County	Type
Adams	Rural	Licking	Suburban
Allen	Urban	Logan	Rural
Ashland	Rural	Lorain	Suburban
Ashtabula	Suburban	Lucas	Urban
Athens	Rural	Madison	Suburban
Auglaize	Suburban	Mahoning	Urban
Belmont	Suburban	Marion	Rural
Brown	Suburban	Medina	Suburban
Butler	Suburban	Meigs	Rural
Carroll	Suburban	Mercer	Rural
Champaign	Rural	Miami	Suburban
Clark	Suburban	Monroe	Rural
Clermont	Suburban	Montgomery	Urban
Clinton	Rural	Morgan	Rural
Columbiana	Suburban	Morrow	Rural
Coshocton	Rural	Muskingum	Rural
Crawford	Suburban	Noble	Rural
Cuyahoga	Urban	Ottawa	Rural
Darke	Rural	Paulding	Rural
Defiance	Rural	Perry	Rural
Delaware	Suburban	Pickaway	Suburban
Erie	Rural	Pike	Rural
Fairfield	Suburban	Portage	Suburban
Fayette	Rural	Preble	Rural
Franklin	Urban	Putnam	Rural
Fulton	Suburban	Richland	Urban
Gallia	Rural	Ross	Rural
Geauga	Suburban	Sandusky	Rural
Greene	Suburban	Scioto	Rural
Guernsey	Rural	Seneca	Rural
Hamilton	Urban	Shelby	Rural
Hancock	Rural	Stark	Urban
Hardin	Rural	Summit	Urban
Harrison	Rural	Trumbull	Suburban
Henry	Rural	Tuscarawas	Rural
Highland	Rural	Union	Rural
Hocking	Rural	Van Wert	Rural
Holmes	Rural	Vinton	Rural
Huron	Rural	Warren	Suburban
Jackson	Rural	Washington	Suburban
Jefferson	Urban	Wayne	Rural
Knox	Rural	Williams	Rural
Lake	Suburban	Wood	Suburban
Lawrence	Suburban	Wyandot	Rural

a. Metropolitan areas are based on the definitions as they existed in 2000 and consist of the Metropolitan Statistical Areas (MSA) and Primary Metropolitan Statistical Areas (PMSA) in the state of Ohio. Urban counties are those that contain the primary central city in an MSA or PMSA. Suburban counties are those counties in an MSA or PMSA that do not contain the primary central city. Rural counties are those counties that are outside of an MSA or PMSA. The assignment of counties to metropolitan areas under both the pre- and post-2000 definitional changes can be found at www.lmi.state.oh.us/maps/MapofMSAs2000.pdf (March 2005).

Table 5A-2. Lane Mile Calculations, by County Type

Units as indicated

County classification	Number of counties	Lane miles	Percent distribution
Urban	11	10,282	21.3
Suburban	28	16,068	33.3
Rural	49	21,851	45.3
Total	88	48,201	99.9[a]

Source: Ohio Department of Transportation; calculations by project team.
a. Value less than 100 is artifact due to rounding.

manent body of predominantly non-ODOT personnel whose responsibilities are to prioritize major new capacity projects, publish a selection process explaining how it prioritized the projects, and keep the major new capacity program in fiscal balance.

Figure 5A-1. Percentage Distribution of ODOT's Capital Funding Programs, 2001–05

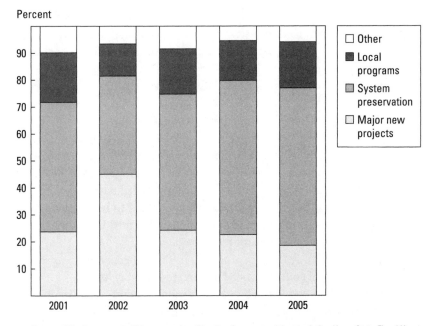

Source: Ohio Department of Transportation, "Funding Sources and Appropriation Uses, State Fiscal Years 2000 through 2004," *Financial and Statistical Report, Fiscal Year 2004* (www.dot.state.us/finanace/Annual/ Annual%20Statement%202004.pdf), and Ohio Department of Transportation, *2004–2005 Budget,* House Bill 87, final version (April 2003), p. 33.

The governor appoints six of the TRAC's nine members, the speaker of the Ohio House of Representatives appoints one, and the president of the Ohio Senate appoints one. ODOT's director serves as chairman. The TRAC's duties are limited to the project selection process for the major new projects program and are not related to the day-to-day operations of ODOT.

Current Federal Highway Programs

TEA-21 provided total authorizations of $217.8 billion for 1998 through 2003, the vast majority of which ($171 billion) went toward Title 1 federal-aid highway programs. Of that total, 92.7 percent, or $158.6 billion, was designated for the seven largest highway programs. These figures are summarized in table 5A-3.

These funds are apportioned to the states according to formulas that consider various combinations of lane miles, population, vehicle miles traveled, relative contributions to the Highway Trust Fund, and in the case of bridges, the relative share of total costs to repair or replace deficient highway bridges.

Federal aid eligibility is based on a highway's functional classification. The functional classification system is a means of classifying all roadways according to their role in the overall transportation network. Functional classification categories are

—rural: principal and minor arterials, major and minor collectors, and locals; and

—urban: principal and minor arterials, collectors, and locals.

Since the 1920s functional classifications have been used to assign facilities to a federal-aid highway system. Traditionally, a street, road, or highway was classified higher than a local in urban areas and higher than a local or minor collector in rural areas before qualifying for federal funds. TEA-21 changed this requirement slightly to allow federal aid to be spent on rural minor collectors—up to 15 percent of state rural funds. Urban and rural local access roads are ineligible for federal aid.

The primary highway funding programs in TEA-21 generally require a 20 percent state or local contribution. They are described below.

Interstate Maintenance. The 46,000-mile Dwight D. Eisenhower National System of Interstate and Defense Highways is a part of the National Highway System yet retains its separate identity. Because all remaining work to complete the interstate system has been fully funded by previous highway authorizations, this program ensures the continued maintenance and

Table 5A-3.   Summary of TEA-21 Funding Authorizations, 1998–2003

Units as indicated

Program	Dollars (billions)	Distribution (percent)
Title 1: Federal-Aid Highways		
Interstate Maintenance	23.8	. . .
National Highway System	28.6	. . .
Highway Bridge Replacement		
and Rehabilitation	20.4	. . .
Surface Transportation	33.3	. . .
Congestion Mitigation and Air Quality		
Improvement	8.1	. . .
Minimum Guarantee	35.0	. . .
High-priority projects	9.4	. . .
Other	12.4	. . .
Total Title 1	171.0	78.5
Title 2: Highway Safety	1.7	0.8
Title 3: Federal Transit Administration		
programs	41.0	18.8
Title 4: Motor Carrier Safety	0.6	0.3
Title 5: Transportation Research	2.9	1.3
Title 7: Miscellaneous	0.5	0.2
Total all programs	217.7	99.9[a]

Source: Department of Transportation, "TEA-21 Authorization Table Fact Sheet"
(www.fhwa.dot.gov/tea21/factsheets/factsht$.htm [February 2005]).

a. Value less than 100 is artifact due to rounding.

improvement of the system. States with no remaining interstate completion work may transfer surplus interstate construction funds to their National Highway System (NHS) fund account.

National Highway System. The NHS consists of 163,000 miles of rural and urban roads serving major population centers, international border crossings, intermodal transportation facilities, and major travel destinations. It includes the interstate system, other urban and rural principal arterials, and other strategic connectors.

Highway Bridge Replacement and Rehabilitation Program. This program provides assistance for eligible bridges located on any public road. Although a state may transfer up to 50 percent of its bridge funds to NHS or Surface Transportation Program (STP) apportionments, the amount transferred is deducted from national bridge needs for calculating apportionments in the following fiscal year.

Surface Transportation Program. The STP provides flexible funding that may be used by states and localities for projects on any federal-aid highway, including the NHS, bridge projects on any public roads, transit capital projects, and public bus terminals and facilities. A state may augment its STP funds by transferring from other programs. In addition, a portion of the Minimum Guarantee funds is administered as if it were STP funds. Once the funds are distributed to the states, 10 percent is set aside for safety construction activities, and another 10 percent is set aside for transportation enhancements.

Congestion Mitigation and Air Quality Improvement Program. This program provides a flexible funding source to state and local governments for transportation projects and programs to help meet the requirements of the Clean Air Act. Funding is available for areas that do not meet the National Ambient Air Quality Standards (nonattainment areas), as well as for former nonattainment areas that are now in compliance (maintenance areas). Funds are distributed to states based on county population and severity of air quality problems within the nonattainment or maintenance area.

High-Priority Projects Program. Specific projects (commonly known as demonstration projects) are eligible for funding under this program. These projects are those specifically identified by Congress and are included in the law itself. The funds do not expire and cannot be flexibly applied to other projects or programs.

Minimum Guarantee. The Minimum Guarantee program is designed specifically to ensure that states receive at least a 90.5 percent return on their contributions to the Highway Trust Fund. Most of these funds are administered as STP funds, with the remainder split by formula among the other major programs.

Notes

1. See Puentes and Prince, chapter 3 in this volume.

2. Ohio Department of Transportation, *Financial and Statistical Report: Fiscal Year 2002* (www.dot.state.oh.us/finance/Annual/Annual2002.pdf [February 2005]).

3. In 1882 the Ohio General Assembly created the Ohio Highway Commission to determine whether the state needed better roads. It concluded that public highways would be better left to local governments rather than to the state.

4. An arterial is generally a large road designed to handle a relatively large amount of traffic traveling at a relatively high speed.

5. Jeffrey Brown, "Reconsider the Gas Tax: Paying for What You Get," *Access* 19 (Fall 2001): 10–15.

6. The federal gas tax is divided as follows: approximately 15.44 cents accumulates in the Highway Account, with the remainder distributed to the Mass Transit Account (2.86 cents) and the Leaking Underground Storage Tank trust fund (0.10 cents).

7. Gasohol is a type of motor fuel that contains a mixture of gasoline and ethanol (about 10 percent alcohol) derived from cereal grains or grain by-products. Gasohol emissions contain less carbon monoxide than those from gasoline.

8. Before 1993 increases in the state gas tax were directly tied to inflationary pressures. However, use of this variable rate formula expired in the state fiscal year 1992–1993 budget bill.

9. In addition to the gas tax, two principal highway use taxes are charged to commercial vehicles operating within the state. The first is an annual license tax, based on the weight of the registered vehicle. The second is an additional 3 cents per gallon diesel surcharge. Commercial operators file a multistate tax return and pay the amount owed to each state based on fuel purchases and relative miles traveled in each state. The highway use taxes, which are dedicated to bond retirement, generate about $190 million per year.

10. Federal Highway Administration, *Highway Statistics 2003* (Department of Transportation, 2003), table SF-1.

11. Counties may levy a $15 per vehicle tax. Municipalities within counties that have levied the full $15 tax may levy an additional $5. Municipalities in counties that have not levied any permissive taxes may levy a $20 tax. Townships can levy a $5 tax regardless of the county's levy. Total local levies cannot exceed $20 per vehicle.

12. Ohio Bureau of Motor Vehicles, "2003 Tax Distribution Summary Statement of Motor Vehicle Registrations" (www.state.oh.us/odps/division/bmv/03-3taxdst.html [February 2005]).

13. Ohio Department of Transportation, "Central Ohio Transportation Workshop: Transportation Funding" (www.dot.state.oh.us/finance/budget/tranfunding.pdf [2002]).

14. Myron Orfield and Thomas Luce, *Cincinnati Metropatterns: A Regional Agenda for Community and Stability in the Cincinnati Region* (Minneapolis Metropolitan Area Research Corporation, 2001).

15. Hugh Hinton and Michael Beazley, *Analysis of the Fiscal Impact of Public Service Delivery Practices in Lucas County, Ohio* (University of Toledo Urban Affairs Center, 2002).

16. Motor Fuel Task Force, *Study of the Adequacy and Distribution of the Motor Fuel Tax: Final Report 2002* (www.ceao.org/Task%20Force%20Final%20Report%2012_11_02.pdf [February 2005]).

17. Vehicle miles traveled are average daily figures estimated by ODOT. These figures were unavailable for each year and therefore were estimated using the data available, as described in the methodology section of the appendix.

18. This is likely because rural and, to some extent, suburban highway construction costs far less than urban highways, mainly because of infrastructure displacement. Costs depend, generally, on degree of urbanization, terrain, and complexity. Typical urban highways cost up to five times as much as a typical rural highway, and in many instances are far greater. See John M. Cobin, "Market Provisions of Highways: Lessons from Costanera Norte" (www-pam.usc.edu/volume2/v2i1a3s1.html [1999]). The higher dollar amount of new construction in urban areas is almost entirely because of interstate highways, many of which contain many miles of bridges and overpasses.

19. The index was formed by subtracting the median value (by county) of total highway contracts let per average total miles driven from the value of total highway miles driven per average total miles in each county, then dividing that number by the median

and multiplying the total by 100. This allows the index to be interpreted as the percentage difference from the median amount. Spending data are the sum of spending over the entire time period, adjusted for inflation. Average daily vehicle miles traveled for each county is the average of use in 1982, 1987, 1992, and 1997.

20. "Auto alley" is so called because it links Detroit with auto plants and supply facilities in metropolitan Dayton and with the new concentration of plants in Kentucky and Tennessee.

21. Gasoline tank truck drivers record the data on fuel deliveries on their route sheets. The retailer pays the tax to wholesalers based on the volume of gasoline delivered, and the wholesaler then forwards this amount to the Department of Taxation. The department retains the route sheets but does not code the information or make it available to the public.

22. See www.census.gov/econ/census02.

23. Map 5-2 represents an index created by calculating the percentage difference in highway construction contracts let per average dollar volume of retail sales at gasoline stations (an approximation of the location of gasoline tax collections) between each county in Ohio and the median county.

24. This is true, with one caveat. There is some overlap between the state spending statistics and the distribution statistics that was impossible to sort out from the database. To the extent that local gas tax and state-collected registration tax distributions were used as a local match on a project that used state or federal funds, there will be some overlap between the two sets of analyses. On the other hand, the distribution formulas present a double disadvantage to municipalities because they then have less matching money for state and federal projects than the rural areas that receive greater amounts of these funds.

25. Ronald N. Johnson and Gary D. Libecap, "Political Processes and the Common Pool Problem: The Federal Highway Trust Fund," paper presented at the International Society for New Institutional Economics Annual Conference, September 22–24, 2000, Tübingen, Germany (www.isnie.org/ISNIE00/Papers/Johnson-Libecap.pdf [February 2005]).

26. *Safe, Accountable, Flexible, and Efficient Transportation Equity Act of 2004*, S. 1072, 108 Cong. 1 sess (May 15, 2003).

27. The extent to which their importance should skew the funding toward rural areas is unknown. The federal government's Appalachian Development Highway program has supported highway construction projects in the southeastern portion of the state as a means of promoting economic development and establishing a state-federal framework to meet the needs of the thirteen-state region. This program increases new construction dollars in an immediate sense and requires maintenance and rehabilitation spending thereafter. The program dollars are negligible, accounting for only 1.4 percent of ODOT's 2001 construction budget.

28. ODOT is made up of twelve regional districts.

29. Mayors' Think Tank of Northeast Ohio, "Policy Statement No. 5: Transportation Funding Issues" (http://dept.kent.edu/cpapp/mttpol5.htm [February 2005]).

30. Bureau of the Census, "Population Estimates" (www.census.gov/popest/counties/ [April 2005]).

31. Ohio Department of Taxation, "Tax Data Series: Motor Vehicle Fuel Tax" (tax.ohio.gov/divisions/tax_analysis/yax_dat_series/motor_fuel/publications_tds_motor. stm [April 2005]).

32. See data for indicated years at Bureau of the Census, " Economic Census, Census of Retail Trade" (www.census.gov/econ/census02 [April 2002]).

33. Ohio Department of Transportation, "Funding Sources and Appropriation Uses, State Fiscal Years 2000 through 2004," *Financial and Statistical Report, Fiscal Year 2004* (www.dot.state.oh.us/finance/Annual/Annual%20Statement%202004.pdf), and Ohio Department of Transportation, *2004–2005 Budget*, House Bill 87, Final Version (April 2003), p. 33.

PART THREE

Getting the Geography
of Transportation Right

6
Increasing Funding and Accountability for Metropolitan Transportation Decisions

Robert Puentes and Linda Bailey

Metropolitan areas matter. They are the engines of the new global economy. Supplier networks and customer relationships are regional rather than local in nature. Labor markets and commuting patterns cross jurisdictional and state lines. Firms make decisions on location and expansion based on regional advantages and amenities. Metropolitan areas are where most Americans live, work, and produce the majority of the nation's economic output. The services and revenues they generate drive state economies. When metropolitan America thrives, the nation thrives.

Threatening to undermine metropolitan areas' competitive edge in the global economy, however, is a daunting set of transportation challenges—crumbling infrastructure, deteriorating air quality, growing distances between jobs and workers, and increasing congestion and vehicle miles traveled. The lessons of the past decade show that existing transportation governance arrangements and structures are inadequate to meet the needs of metropolitan areas. If local and regional transportation challenges are to be effectively addressed, metropolitan areas need a greater say in the design and implementation of transportation policy.[1]

Fortunately, as Congress considers the future of federal transportation law, there is a burgeoning interest in increasing the decisionmaking ability of metropolitan areas. Organizations such as the American Association of State Highway and Transportation Officials have called for increasing certain funding for metropolitan areas, and political leaders such as King County (Washington) executive Ron Sims and Baltimore mayor Martin O'Malley have called for the creation of additional metropolitan-focused programs. In November 2003, Representative Eddie Bernice Johnson (Texas) introduced the Metropolitan Congestion Relief Act, which would address challenges in metropolitan areas.[2] As the debate around transportation continues, increased metropolitan decisionmaking and its benefits are indeed being advocated by many.

This chapter summarizes the extent of funding and program authority metropolitan areas are currently afforded. It does so by examining the evolution of metropolitan transportation decisionmaking and the role of metropolitan areas under current law. In the end, it argues that federal transportation law needs to expand existing funding sources and decisionmaking for metropolitan areas in order to fulfill the promises of previous reform efforts and to maintain a transportation system that works for twenty-first-century metropolitan America.

Background: Devolution and the End of the Interstate Highway Era

In a 1996 policy brief, Anthony Downs argued that federal efforts to devolve certain powers were going to the wrong levels; they were shifting to states and localities.[3] His argument was not that devolution itself was inappropriate but rather that many of the major problems in urban areas were regional in scope, and therefore they could not be solved by local jurisdictions acting independently.[4] He also maintained that states were too far from local communities to be effective in addressing such regional issues as housing, air quality, schools and education, and transportation. Devolution efforts need to focus on the metropolitan level.

By contrast, the nation's highway program has always been a "federal aid" program, with the federal government providing aid directly to states. At the outset of the program, and especially during the period after World War II, this arrangement clearly made sense. Based on his military experiences in this country and in Europe, President Dwight Eisenhower was profoundly interested in building and expanding the roadway network for the United States in order to "protect the vital interest of every citizen in a safe and adequate highway system."[5] Eisenhower's main concern in this regard was the completion of a 40,000-mile national system of defense highways connecting each state, to be built over a period of about thirteen years. The Federal-Aid Highway Act of 1956 articulated the federal responsibility in the program, declaring that the system was essential to the national interest.[6] The arrangement designated the federal government to pay 90 percent of the costs of the system.

In administering the program, the federal government would not separately own the highways but would coordinate planning and set standards in consultation with state officials. However, the vast majority of employees and contracts necessary to build and maintain the roads were to come from the state and local level. Over the years, this "intergovernmental transfer system" was one of the basic principles of the successful and steady promotion of highways.[7] This arrangement led successfully to the completion of the largest public works project in our nation's history.

As the highway system evolved and transportation planning became more sophisticated, Congress began encouraging regional collaboration. The Federal-Aid Highway Act of 1973 required states to dedicate a very small portion of the funds they received from the federal Highway Trust Fund for new regional entities in urbanized areas to carry out metropolitan planning activities.[8] The activities of these "metropolitan planning organizations" (MPOs) were still rather limited but nevertheless significant. Many saw the new MPOs as a means to counter, or at least put metropolitan areas on more equal footing with, the domineering influence of state transportation departments in pushing highway projects.[9]

By the 1980s federal interest in metropolitan planning and regional regulatory authority began to wane. During the Reagan administration, nearly every federal program designed to support regional planning was either sharply reduced or eliminated altogether. The share of federal operating funds for regional entities declined from 76 percent in 1978 to 45 percent in 1988.[10] MPOs were still charged by the Department of Transportation (DOT) with putting together a regional transportation improvement plan, but this activity generally consisted of nothing more than compiling projects developed and recommended by the state DOTs.[11]

Nevertheless, MPOs and other regional organizations remained in existence—but they had to become more entrepreneurial and focus on other activities. According to Myron Orfield, regional councils and MPOs began focusing on activities such as regional demographic data collection and technical assistance to local governments. As a result, when the federal funding dry spell of the 1980s came to a close, regional organizations had become very well attuned to the needs and priorities of their local jurisdictions.[12] This coincided with a new interest in metropolitan planning built primarily around environmental issues, as well as with increased pressures from suburban growth and development. In short, the stage was set for meaningful reform.

Federal Efforts to Support Metropolitan Transportation Decisionmaking

By the close of the century, as the interstate highway system neared completion, the federal government slowly refocused its highway program away from a pure interstate program to one that puts an emphasis on all modes—not just highways—and affords greater flexibility to states and localities as the primary determiners of how important investment decisions are made. These changes were emphasized in the first federal highway law of the 1990s: the Intermodal Surface transportation Efficiency Act (ISTEA).

ISTEA required that MPOs develop a twenty-year, long-range metropolitan transportation plan and a short-range transportation improvement plan (TIP). The purpose of developing these plans was primarily to aid in the selection of projects by requiring an inclusive and regionally representative process that gave adequate consideration to all modes. The TIPs from MPOs throughout each state are collected and, without modification, incorporated into the statewide transportation improvement plan. In both cases, to ensure the plans are fiscally realistic and do not revert to pre-ISTEA days when transportation plans were tantamount to "wish lists," projects in the plans include detailed discussions of how they will be funded. In addition, the long-range transportation plan and the TIP must both be developed through a process that emphasizes public participation and must conform to state air quality implementation plans.[13]

Aside from these changes in the metropolitan transportation planning process itself, ISTEA also recognized the wide diversity of metropolitan areas and the need to provide them with more control over transportation in their regions. ISTEA made two major changes in the way transportation decisions were made. One was the suballocation of state funds and decisionmaking to the local and metropolitan level. The other was the granting of flexibility in determining how transportation funds would be spent.

The rules requiring suballocation of funds were designed to put a small, but significant, amount of money directly in the hands of local officials for projects developed cooperatively through the metropolitan planning process, as well as increase funds for their day-to-day operations. As mentioned, when the federal highway program began, road funds were spent solely by state departments of transportation (DOTs), which received federal apportionments directly. Starting with ISTEA, however, metropolitan decisionmakers received direct authority over a portion of these funds.

The flexible funding provisions that permit highway funds to be spent on transit (and vice versa) were designed to allow spending based on locally defined goals and objectives rather than on rigid federal directives. This flexibility allowed states and MPOs to fund more integrated transportation systems, including transit options. These were profound changes in federal policy. With them came the recognition that the metropolitan transportation challenges of the twenty-first century are best addressed when investments are determined on the local or regional levels, in cooperation with the states.

Of course, neither the highway laws of the 1950s nor the reform efforts of the 1990s intended to remove or otherwise dilute the power of the states in favor of localities or metropolitan areas. Devolution and suballocation to metropolitan areas were meant to effect better decisionmaking by empowering metropolitan areas with increased funding and responsibility. States continue to wield dominant power and have the primary role in transportation programming and planning.[14]

To be sure, some states have always directed money for metropolitan spending. And, of course, all states spend considerable amounts in metropolitan areas, irrespective of how the funds are targeted or administered. But the importance of the metropolitan reforms under ISTEA underscores the point that the issue is not solely how much money is being spent in a particular place but, rather, how decisions controlling that spending are made. Clearly, many of the major battles between localities and states concern projects that communities actually oppose. So while state spending on metropolitan infrastructure is important, giving metropolitan areas the ability to conceive, design, and execute programs based on locally defined goals and objectives—as well as to decide which projects they did *not* want—is at the heart of the ISTEA reforms. There are four major programmatic elements of the federal surface transportation law that increased the ability of metropolitan areas to make transportation decisions.

Suballocated Surface Transportation Program

Of all the federal highway programs, the largest is the Surface Transportation Program (STP), which averaged about $5.6 billion annually through the first five years (1998–2002) of the Transportation Equity Act for the Twenty-First Century (TEA-21, enacted June 1998). The funds in the STP are also the most flexible of all the categorical programs on the federal ledger. This means that STP funds can be spent on a wide variety of transportation projects based on state, metropolitan, and local goals and objectives.[15] They can be used for building or improving highways and bridges, capital costs for transit projects, carpool projects, bicycle transportation and pedestrian walkways, safety improvements, traffic monitoring, planning, environmental protection, intelligent transportation systems, and research.[16]

Although STP funds are designed to be flexible and states are able to spend them on a wide variety of needs and objectives, only a portion of the funds are totally discretionary. The funds are programmed based on a complex formula that allocates 10 percent for safety-related programs and another 10 percent for transportation enhancement activities. Of the remaining 80 percent, 37.5 percent may be spent anywhere in the state, while 62.5 percent is split between small or nonurbanized parts of the state and urbanized areas with a population of over 200,000, in proportion to their relative share of the state's population.[17] The latter constitutes the metropolitan suballocated STP funds referred to in this chapter.[18]

Under the formula, TEA-21 funded $138.4 billion in road and bridge programs for fiscal years 1998 through 2002. Out of that amount, the STP program totaled $33.1 billion. STP suballocated to metropolitan areas was about $8.0 billion. In other words, during that time, current federal transportation law only ensured that 5.8 percent of all highway funds were under the direct decisionmaking control of metropolitan areas (figure 6-1).

This process of targeting funds specifically for urbanized, or metropolitan, areas is referred to as suballocation since the federal funds are allocated below the level of the state DOT—the traditional recipient for such funding. Since these funds are part of the STP, they are first apportioned to the states in accordance with a complicated formula based on the extent of the roadway system, amount of vehicle miles traveled, and estimated federal gas tax payments in each state. Metropolitan STP funds are then sent to the metropolitan planning organizations by the states. The state administers the funds for the other areas. Although the suballocated funds are directed to urbanized areas, the federal law directs local officials to work through MPOs in their administration.

Although devolving funds via STP suballocation gives MPOs and their regions more direct control of some money, interviews conducted with state and MPO officials in preparation of this brief showed that the spending of federal funds is still a negotiation between the MPO, which is responsible for the TIP, and the state DOTs, as arbiters over federal and state roadway funds. State DOTs have considerable influence over these plans, pushing some projects out twenty years while others are funded in the near term.

Figure 6-1.   TEA-21 Highway Program Apportionments, 1998–2002[a]

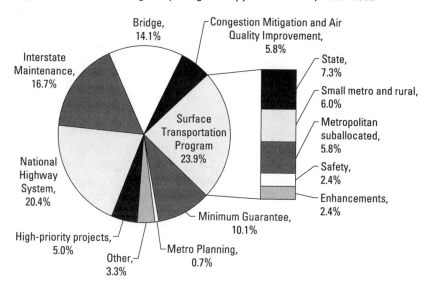

Source: Surface Transportation Policy Project analysis of Federal Highway Administration, *Notices,* N4510 series (www.fhwa.dot.gov/legsregs/directives/notices.htm [February 2005]).
a. Total = $138.4 billion.

The STP is also fed by the Minimum Guarantee program, which was designed specifically to ensure that states receive at least a 90.5 percent return on their contributions to the Highway Account of the federal Highway Trust Fund. Each state's share of the first $2.8 billion of Minimum Guarantee funds is administered as STP funds. Under TEA-21, however, neither the STP suballocation requirements nor the takedown for transportation enhancements and safety apply to this program.[19] This seems odd since the Minimum Guarantee program was intended to promote equity by ensuring states received their "fair share" of federal funds in proportion to receipts contributed in the form of gas taxes. Since in most states the vast majority of funds are generated in metropolitan areas, this omission ignores the spirit of the program.

Congestion Mitigation and Air Quality Improvement Program

Another federal program of paramount importance to metropolitan areas is the Congestion Mitigation and Air Quality (CMAQ) Improvement program. The primary purpose of the CMAQ program is to fund projects and programs in metropolitan areas that currently do not, or previously did not, meet federal air quality standards for ozone, carbon monoxide, and small particulate matter.[20] In 2001 those areas (referred to as nonattainment and maintenance areas, respectively) were home to more than 131 million Americans nationwide, almost half of the total U.S. population.[21] Under TEA-21, CMAQ allows states to disperse some $8.1 billion over the six-year life of the law (less than 6 percent of the total) to fund an array of activities.[22]

Funds from the CMAQ program can only be applied to projects that reduce vehicle emissions in metropolitan areas and cannot be used to fund road construction or widening projects (unless they have a carpool or high-occupancy-vehicle component). According to the DOT, the highest priority projects for CMAQ are transportation control measures that reduce the reliance on private vehicles for transportation needs.[23] These measures focus on alternative transportation, such as walking, biking, and public transportation, but CMAQ program funds are also spent on traffic flow improvements, such as signal timing or traffic monitoring.

A comprehensive assessment of the CMAQ program by the Transportation Research Board recently found that from a federal perspective, it is a highly decentralized program, where decisionmaking is devolved to the state and local level.[24] This is because, unlike other Federal Highway Administration funds, CMAQ money can only be spent in specific air quality nonattainment and maintenance areas. However, from a local perspective, although its funds are designed to be spent in metropolitan areas, CMAQ remains a state program, with the states playing the most important role.[25] The Transportation Research Board specifically cites the "significant state role" in some places as "a critical weakness of the CMAQ program."[26]

There is no guidance for how states should spend, or suballocate, CMAQ funds among their metropolitan areas. Interim regulations on CMAQ from the Federal Highway and Federal Transit administrations in 1998 specifically encourage states to suballocate CMAQ funds, but they do not provide any additional details except to explain that decisions over how to spend CMAQ funds should continue to be made through a cooperative process involving the state DOT, affected MPOs, local jurisdictions, and air quality agencies.[27] As a result, administration of CMAQ funds varies widely among the states.

Twenty-six states directly suballocate CMAQ funds to the metropolitan or local level. Several of these states, such as Texas and California, suballocate funds to nonattainment and maintenance areas using the same formula (based on population and severity of pollution) by which national-level CMAQ funds are allocated to the states. Generally, the funds are then discretionary for metropolitan areas to spend in any manner that results in congestion reduction or mitigation or air quality improvement. In fourteen states with CMAQ-eligible areas, the funds are retained by the state, and spending decisions are made by the state in consultation and cooperation with the metropolitan or local officials (table 6-1).[28]

Metropolitan Planning

In addition to the metropolitan focus in the Surface Transportation and CMAQ programs, federal transportation law also directly provides funds to MPOs to conduct various metropolitan planning activities. The Metropolitan Planning (PL) program provides funds for urbanized areas to carry out transportation plans and programs. Unlike the other metropolitan programs, which fund specific projects, PL funds enable MPOs to develop long- and short-range transportation plans, as well as special plans for managing metropolitan traffic. In other words, they are for MPOs to use in their day-to-day activities.

These activities represent the core of MPO duties. Indeed, in the law that lays out the purpose of the metropolitan planning component, the general requirements language is telling: "It is in the national interest to encourage and promote the safe and efficient management, operation, and development of surface transportation systems that will serve the mobility needs of people and freight and foster economic growth and development within and through urbanized areas, while minimizing transportation-related fuel consumption and air pollution."[29]

Despite the articulation of the federal role in these activities, overall funding is still relatively minute. Metropolitan planning funds are occasionally referred to as planning "takedown" funds since they derive from taking 1 percent off each state's core federal highway programs.[30] The federal transit program also contributes funds for metropolitan planning, but they come from annual appropriations rather than a takedown.[31] These two sources together constituted about $1.57 billion for metropolitan planning over the life of TEA-21, less than 1 percent of all the total funding.[32]

Transportation Enhancements

Another important program ushered in under ISTEA and continued in TEA-21 is the Transportation Enhancements (TE) program. As mentioned, the TE program is funded through a 10 percent set-aside from the STP, totaling about $3.3 billion (about 2.4 percent of the total) from 1998 through 2002.

Table 6-1. States' Suballocation of CMAQ Program and Transportation Enhancements (TE) Funds, 2003

States	CMAQ suballocation	TE suballocation
Alabama	Yes	No
Alaska	Yes	Yes
Arizona	Yes	No
Arkansas	No[a]	No
California	Yes	Yes
Colorado	Yes	Yes
Connecticut	No	No
Delaware	No	No
District of Columbia	No	. . .
Florida	Yes	Yes
Georgia	Yes	No
Hawaii	No[a]	No
Idaho	No[a]	No
Illinois	Yes	No
Indiana	Yes	No
Iowa	No[a]	Yes
Kansas	Yes	No
Kentucky	No	No
Louisiana	Yes	No
Maine	No	No
Maryland	No	No
Massachusetts	No	No
Michigan	Yes	No
Minnesota	Yes	Yes
Mississippi	No[a]	No
Missouri	Yes	No
Montana	Yes	Yes
Nebraska	No[a]	No
Nevada	Yes	No
New Hampshire	No	No
New Jersey	No	No
New Mexico	Yes	Yes
New York	Yes	No
North Carolina	No	No
North Dakota	No[a]	No
Ohio	Yes	Yes
Oklahoma	No[a]	No
Oregon	No	No[b]
Pennsylvania	Yes	Yes
Rhode Island	Yes	No
South Carolina	No	Yes
South Dakota	No[a]	No
Tennessee	Yes	No
Texas	Yes	No
Utah	Yes	No
Vermont	No[a]	No
Virginia	Yes	No
Washington	Yes	Yes
West Virginia	No	No

(continued)

Table 6-1. States' Suballocation of CMAQ Program and Transportation Enhancements (TE) Funds, 2003 (*continued*)

States	CMAQ suballocation	TE suballocation
Wisconsin	No	No
Wyoming	No[a]	No

Source: National Transportation Enhancements Clearinghouse, "Transportation Enhancements: Summary of Nationwide Spending and Policies as of FY 1999" (Washington, 2000), and updated via interviews in 2002 with state transportation department officials.

a. State has no nonattainment or maintenance areas.

b. Oregon merged its local and statewide TE programs into one statewide program in 2002 due to budget constraints.

Enhancement projects are broad-based, community-initiated projects that generally focus on mitigating the negative effects of the surface transportation system, such as the adverse impacts on pedestrians, scenic beauty, the environment, and historic structures. Projects eligible for funding include those that focus on walking and bicycling, historic preservation, scenic beautification, land acquisition, archeological research, and environmental mitigation projects. A recent report found that 55 percent of federal TE funds are spent on bicycle, pedestrian, and rails-to-trails projects; 24 percent on historic preservation and tourist centers; and 21 percent on landscaping, beautification, and environmental mitigation.[33] In short, the projects funded under the TE program are those not normally associated with the state DOT.[34]

Although, like the CMAQ program, there are no federal requirements in ISTEA or TEA-21 that direct states to suballocate TE funds, many states do suballocate or set aside TE funds to MPOs and localities. In fact, according to the National Transportation Enhancements Clearinghouse, twelve states sent all or a portion of their TE funds to substate jurisdictions.[35] Alaska, Colorado, Iowa, Ohio, Pennsylvania, South Carolina, and Washington suballocate all or a portion of TE funds to MPOs. California suballocates 75 percent to regional transportation planning agencies, and Minnesota suballocates to MPOs and area transportation partnerships. Montana suballocates to local governments. Florida and New Mexico suballocate TE to DOT districts, but as a report from the Rails-to-Trails Conservancy found, suballocating TE funds to DOT districts may actually have a negative effect on project selection, given these entities' historical focus on highway maintenance and construction and their difficulty in cultivating a meaningful level of citizen participation.[36]

These four programs have given MPOs and metropolitan leaders important abilities to plan and make decisions about transportation investments.

In the end, however, the degree of control they have acquired is relatively minor. Taken together, the four programs make up only 15.2 percent of the total road and bridge funding under TEA-21. Furthermore, metropolitan areas still do not have authority over all of these funds. The federal law only gives metropolitan areas direct control over metropolitan STP and PL funds—less than 7 percent of the total.[37] This represents a modest commitment to regions that collectively account for a substantial share of the nation's economic output and a large majority of all transit use, aviation passengers, and port tonnage, as well as being critical to the nation's freight rail and passenger rail capacities.[38] In light of this, the next section discusses some of the challenges facing metropolitan areas and outlines the case for greater enhancement of metropolitan decisionmaking in transportation.

The Case for Metropolitan Transportation Decisionmaking

According to the most recent census data, eight of every ten people in the United States live in the nearly 300 federally defined metropolitan areas.[39] Dominating this landscape are the largest areas—nearly six out of every ten Americans live in just the fifty largest. The top ten metropolitan areas—New York, Los Angeles, Chicago, Washington, San Francisco, Philadelphia, Boston, Detroit, Dallas, and Houston—house over 88.7 million people, or 31.5 percent of the total U.S. population. These metropolitan areas had an average population growth rate of 11 percent from 1990 to 2000.[40]

Not only are metropolitan areas where America lives, but they also drive the economy. Together, all metropolitan areas combined produce more than 85 percent of the nation's economic output; they also generate 84 percent of America's jobs.[41] In California, 97 percent of employment and output is generated within metropolitan areas.[42] More and more, metropolitan areas are where the business of American life is carried out. The transportation infrastructure is absolutely essential to literally keeping these metropolitan economies moving.

Metropolitan leaders from coast to coast are calling attention to a daunting set of transportation challenges that continue to be unmet. As mentioned earlier, these challenges threaten to undermine metropolitan regions' competitiveness. They are particularly important issues given the growing importance of metropolitan areas as competitive units of the world economy.[43] Goods and services are continuously moving at speeds and scales that heretofore were without precedence. Metropolitan areas are the hubs of our nation's network of production and consumption with multimodal and intermodal facilities that no longer adhere to the policy prescriptions of the interstate era.[44] Transportation planning and programming must reflect the new dominant model, while placing an even greater emphasis on meeting local challenges.

ISTEA and TEA-21 certainly made important strides to better align the geography of transportation decisionmaking with the geography of regional economies, commuting patterns, and social reality. To do that, the laws attempted to enlarge the responsibility of the regional MPOs in terms of transportation decisionmaking. However, as other chapters in this volume point out, that federal intent has largely been subverted.

Although ISTEA and TEA-21 were designed to move transportation decisionmaking out of the back rooms and boardrooms of the highway establishment, many state DOTs still wield considerable formal and informal power, retaining authority over substantial state transportation funds. The governors and some state DOTs still have veto authority over MPO-selected projects. Although large MPOs (in areas with populations over 200,000) also have authority to veto projects, the reality is that the state receives and manages all the federal transportation money, as well as large amounts of state transportation money, and the state's political leverage far exceeds that of the MPOs.[45] Furthermore, some states simply ignore local decisions and needs.[46] Such arrangements create an unfavorable climate for the flowering of federal policy reforms—and frequently cut against metropolitan interests.

There are several important reasons why some opposition to increased metropolitan decisionmaking remains. First, state governments and agencies are loath to relinquish control over any amount of funding or decisionmaking responsibility.[47] A General Accounting Office report found that this was a particular problem after ISTEA was passed.[48] Although state opposition to greater MPO authority is beginning to wane, several states continue to oppose greater roles and responsibilities for MPOs.[49] Second, unlike state DOTs, MPOs are not operational organizations. With few exceptions they are not equipped, nor do they intend, to make the jump from planning organization to operators of the system. Third, many MPOs are still struggling between parochial local interests and regional ones that are more "interlocal" in nature. Within many regions, local governments continue to compete with one another for their share of the metropolitan pie. In still other metropolitan areas, center cities, older suburbs, and minorities are underrepresented on MPO boards.[50] Finally, MPO as well as state capacity remains uneven. In a very real sense, the profession of transportation planning has failed to keep up with statutory and on-the-ground change in the 1990s.

Even in recent years, state transportation planning has largely remained the province of transportation professionals versed in engineering and concrete pouring rather than in urban planning, environmental management, or economic development—and that has hampered state and local implementation of the vision outlined in ISTEA and TEA-21.[51]

These concerns reflect the old approach to transportation planning and funding that ISTEA and TEA-21 attempted to reverse. There are at least five compelling reasons for making sure federal transportation law puts a greater emphasis on metropolitan areas.

First, *local governments within metropolitan areas own the vast majority of the transportation network.* In February 2003 a coalition of eleven national organizations, called Local Officials for Transportation, began pressing for a transportation agenda that, among other things, increases the role of local officials in transportation decisionmaking by suballocating greater resources to metropolitan areas.[52] Reflecting the principle of subsidiary, they contend that local officials are closer to the problems and challenges of metropolitan America and are therefore able to make better transportation decisions. However, according to the coalition, metropolitan areas make decisions on only about 10 cents of every dollar they generate.[53]

The coalition further contends that since local officials actually own and have direct responsibility over a large amount of the roadway miles, an argument can be made for a more proportional amount of funding.[54] Of course, owning the network does not necessarily translate into greater expenses. Costs depend, generally, on degree of urbanization, terrain, complexity, and classification. But typical urban roads cost up to five times as much as a typical rural road, and in many instances, the costs are far greater.[55] As Martin Wachs points out in chapter 4, an analysis of federal highway data shows that in 2002 local governments owned about 3 million of the 4 million miles of roads in the nation.[56] Local governments also own over half of all the nation's bridges and about 90 percent of the nation's transit systems.[57]

Second, *metropolitan transportation planning and programming is, by law, comprehensive and includes a wide range of stakeholders.* Local officials are the ones who ultimately make decisions on MPO plans and programs through a cooperative process that includes not just elected officials but a broad range of stakeholders. MPOs are required to involve local and regional transportation providers, transit agencies, freight shippers, airport authorities, maritime operations, Amtrak, port operators, and others within the metropolitan areas.[58] The inclusion of this diverse set of interests in metropolitan planning helps ensure that decisions on projects and spending are broadly reflective and not the sole dominion of the highway establishment.

To assess the quality of the metropolitan planning process, every three years the federal government is required to certify how well MPOs are meeting federal laws and regulations. In addition to the rules and regulations in ISTEA and TEA-21, the federal government must also evaluate how well MPOs are following clean air laws, the Civil Rights Act, the environmental justice executive order, and the Americans with Disabilities Act. Any MPO that is not certified can lose up to 20 percent of its federal funding.

State departments of transportation are not subject to certification by the federal government. TEA-21 does require that the statewide transportation improvement plan be reviewed every two years to ensure that it is developed in a manner consistent with the planning factors outlined in the law. However, there is no stated penalty for disapproval of the plan, nor is the failure to consider any factor reviewable in court.

A third reason to increase the decisionmaking authority and ability of MPOs is that *many states continue to penalize metropolitan areas in the distribution of transportation funds.* The current system of planning and programming, which is dominated by the states, has been criticized as undermining metropolitan areas. Federal funds are allocated in such a way that they favor rural areas over urban areas. In addition, state DOTs' traditional focus on highway maintenance and construction fosters metropolitan decentralization that negatively impacts cities and older suburbs.[59]

This penalty arises from several biases. The first bias follows from the fact that federal law allocates the vast majority of federal money directly to state DOTs. As mentioned, federal law directly suballocates less than 7 percent of program funds directly to MPOs and, even then, only to MPOs serving populations of over 200,000. In fact, while federal transportation spending increased from ISTEA to TEA-21, the share of funds suballocated to MPOs actually declined as a share of total highway spending.

A second bias follows from the way states distribute transportation revenues. Some states have developed distribution formulas based on transportation-related needs or on resident population, registered motor vehicles, and highway miles. However, others (such as Tennessee, Ohio, Arkansas, and Alabama) allocate a portion of funds evenly among their counties, regardless of their size, needs, and contribution to state funding pools.[60] This holdover from the states' past years of active rural highway construction ensures that built-out urban counties fail to receive a sensible share of funding.

Another bias owes to the simple fact that the states own a substantial portion of the roads in rural areas; by contrast, local governments generally own many of the roads and the transit systems located in metropolitan areas. This arrangement saddles local municipalities with sole responsibility for building and maintaining the roads in incorporated (more urban) places while states take care of roads in rural or otherwise unincorporated places on the suburban fringe.

Fourth, *states are not fulfilling the promises of federal law.* ISTEA and TEA-21 for the first time embedded in law the principle that America's metropolitan reality required an integrated, balanced, and regionally designed transportation system. As a framework the federal laws are sound. And yet, the laws themselves are only part of the picture. Unfortunately, implementation of the new federal statutes has been seriously flawed—and in basic ways unresponsive to metropolitan needs. Most notably, most states have failed to utilize the tools and discretion afforded them by ISTEA and TEA-21 to meaningfully address the worsening transportation problems present throughout their metropolitan regions.

One reason for this failure could be a lack of leadership and attention to these issues on the statewide level. As Anthony Downs mentioned in his seminal work *Stuck in Traffic,* "State agencies cannot act without regard for strong political forces. Even where a state agency provides a technically competent vehicle for achieving some policy, that policy will not be carried out unless significant and broad political support for it exists. Hence state agencies are poor vehicles for instituting new policies."[61]

In some states, the legislature determines many of the transportation priorities, similar to how Congress earmarks projects in legislation without regard for the metropolitan planning process.[62] This practice thwarts community involvement, raises the likelihood of unwanted projects, and may fail to meet the needs of disfavored districts.

Last, there is a *growing recognition that it takes more than transportation solutions to address transportation problems.* Whether or not we can build our way out of our transportation problems, it is becoming increasingly clear that solutions that depend solely on increasing or managing transportation capacity are not an adequate strategy. As renowned transportation expert Wilfred Owen observed back in 1956, the best way to address transportation problems must be through land use strategies that establish the growth and development patterns to which transportation issues are inexorably linked.[63] The recognition of this link is even stronger today. The DOT has stressed tighter coordination among land use, zoning, and housing authorities in order to address transportation challenges.[64]

Without such coordination, the DOT points out that transportation improvements "often lead to urban sprawl, which increases the amount of developed land and also the demand for transportation."[65] However, as a recent Transportation Research Board paper articulated, consideration of these effects on the statewide level has been "superficial at best."[66] The correct level for addressing these land use and transportation issues is at the metropolitan level, through the MPO structure. MPOs consist primarily of local elected officials that have direct control over local land use. Although MPOs themselves most often do not have authority over land use decisions, they are well situated to help review development applications, transportation elements of local comprehensive plans, and general land use issues in order to implement the best transportation strategies.

Of course, land use authority has long been, and is likely to remain, one of the most important and closely held powers afforded to local governments. However, at least twelve states have passed comprehensive growth management laws that delegate specific land use responsibilities to MPOs or regional entities, thus enabling the state to coordinate transportation planning at the metropolitan level. In addition, many MPOs also include state representatives and already work closely with local governments on issues such as housing, economic development, and social equity that have a profound impact on the transportation system.

Putting Devolution to the Test: State versus MPO Spending

Considering the diverse range of interests in each metropolitan area and the fundamental need for a multimodal and balanced transportation network, it is not possible to determine with any great level of empirical precision whether or not suballocated funds are better spent than those that are retained at the state level. Simply because a project is funded through suballocated STP funds or flexed from the CMAQ program does not make it a good project. Similarly, some standard highway projects clearly have metropolitan-wide benefits.

Given the discussion in the previous section, and considering that the initial intention of greater metropolitan decisionmaking was to ensure that projects more closely met locally defined goals and objectives, it is informative to examine differences in project selection with these funds. Although it is not easy to determine from a list of projects how well a transportation plan is meeting local needs, one fundamentally local transportation need is transit. The following analysis uses transit as a barometer of whether states or MPOs, given equally flexible funds, are more inclined to tend to local transit needs.[67]

The flexible funding provisions of ISTEA and TEA-21 refer to the programs identified in the legislation whose funds may be used for transit or highway projects. The significance of these provisions cannot be overstated. The bill drafters intended to give planners and decisionmakers at the state and local level the authority to transfer funds between highways and transit, with the direction of the transfers unspecified but to be determined by locally defined goals. Among other things, this freedom of financing greatly assists in the consideration of alternative solutions for achieving a more balanced transportation network.

To understand how states and MPOs differ in their project selection, we first examined the STP since it is a highly flexible program that is partially under the direct control of MPOs (in terms of the metropolitan suballocated portion discussed above). The data used for the analysis come from the Federal Highway Administration's Fiscal Management Information System (FMIS) and from the Federal Transit Administration. FMIS tracks all spending through the federal-aid highway program since its inception, by county, specifying fund source and type of work completed. The transit administration data are organized by urbanized area. To combine the two datasets, the FMIS data were summed at the metropolitan statistical area level, and the urbanized area data were assigned to a metropolitan statistical area.

The analysis reveals a number of interesting things about the spending patterns of MPOs and states. First, STP funds that MPOs controlled exclusively were much more likely to be applied to local transit needs than STP funds controlled by state DOTs. For fiscal years 1998 through 2002, MPOs spent 9.3 percent of all devolved STP funds on transit projects whereas only 2.5 percent of state-controlled STP funds were so allocated (table 6-2).[68] This figure represents only spending within metropolitan areas and excludes California, which suballocates three-quarters of its STP funds (see discussion below). If the states' rate of funding had matched that of the MPOs, transit agencies outside California would have seen an additional $1.2 billion over the past five years.

California is a special case. Starting in 1998, the state of California has suballocated all of its CMAQ funds as well as 75 percent of the remaining

Table 6-2. STP Funds Spent on Transit by Metropolitan versus State Decisionmakers, Metropolitan Statistical Areas, 1998–2002

Units as indicated

Decisionmaker	Transit obligations (dollars)	All STP-eligible obligations (dollars)	Percent of STP-eligible funds obligated to transit
Metropolitan (suballocated funds)	678,045,097	7,303,612,577	9.28
State (no suballocation)	441,553,790	17,972,860,003	2.46
California: state– metropolitan split (nonsuballocated STP funds)	578,060,302	2,765,162,662	20.91

Source: Original analysis using the Federal Highway Administration's Fiscal Management Information System (FMIS) and Federal Transit Administration data tables (2003).

program funds, including those from the STP. In California metropolitan areas, 21 percent of the STP funds were flexed to transit from 1998 to 2002.

Second, we identified which metropolitan areas spent large percentages of STP funds on transit. Table 6-3 lists the top twenty-five metropolitan areas that spent suballocated STP funds on transit. Although large, transit-oriented metropolitan areas such as Portland, San Francisco, and Boston are among the top twenty-five, the list also includes smaller areas such as Allentown, Fort Myers, and Des Moines.

It is important to distinguish between metropolitan areas that receive suballocated funds and those that do not. Recall that only metropolitan areas with populations over 200,000 directly receive STP suballocated funds. This accounts for 116 metropolitan areas. The other 161 metropolitan areas have to rely on distributions by their states. There may be more intangible benefits to MPOs that receive suballocated funds. Although all MPOs are theoretically included in project selection in their areas, even those using state funds, MPOs that receive suballocated funds may have more influence over nonsuballocated funds as well. In the 116 metropolitan areas receiving suballocated STP money, 6.7 percent of the *state's* STP funds went to transit; in the remaining 161 metropolitan statistical areas, just 1.3 percent of state-controlled STP money was flexed to transit.

Last, as discussed above, the CMAQ program was the primary source of funds flexed to transit under TEA-21, but the actual proportion was highly dependent on the decisionmaking structure surrounding the program in each

Table 6-3.   STP-Eligible Obligations Flexed to Transit, by Metropolitan Area, 1998–2002[a]

Units as indicated

Metropolitan area	Transit obligations from suballocated STP[b] (dollars)	All suballocated STP-eligible obligations (dollars)	Percent suballocated to transit
Portland-Salem, Ore.-Wash. CMSA	42,237,117	73,582,800	57.4
San Francisco-Oakland-San Jose, Calif. CMSA	108,819,161	231,459,285	47.0
Seattle-Tacoma-Bremerton, Wash. CMSA	46,036,550	115,574,486	39.8
Atlanta, Ga. MSA	72,808,800	182,875,369	39.8
Norfolk-Virginia Beach-Newport News, Va.-N.C. MSA	38,745,600	105,845,428	36.6
Los Angeles-Riverside-Orange County, Calif. CMSA	126,733,681	569,301,582	22.3
Boston-Worcester-Lawrence-Lowell-Brockton, Mass.-N.H. NECMA	32,762,314	162,635,569	20.1
Orlando, Fla. MSA	12,026,034	61,697,883	19.5
Birmingham, Ala. MSA	4,200,000	22,442,659	18.7
Denver-Boulder-Greeley, Colo. CMSA	9,000,000	54,276,381	16.6
Knoxville, Tenn. MSA	1,177,360	7,227,118	16.3
Fort Myers-Cape Coral, Fla. MSA	2,250,000	14,885,459	15.1
Chattanooga, Tenn.-Ga. MSA	3,393,741	24,611,758	13.8
Minneapolis-St. Paul, Minn.-Wisc. MSA	16,965,604	126,150,230	13.4
Raleigh-Durham-Chapel Hill, N.C. MSA	4,210,174	31,522,326	13.4
Richmond-Petersburg, Va. MSA	5,548,800	42,083,327	13.2
Daytona Beach, Fla. MSA	1,492,950	12,025,806	12.4
Sacramento-Yolo, Calif. CMSA	7,464,054	64,874,722	11.5
New York-Northern New Jersey-Long Island, N.Y.-N.J.-Conn.-Pa. CMSA	65,516,000	587,827,919	11.1
Lexington, Ky. MSA	1,216,000	12,456,916	9.8
Allentown-Bethlehem-Easton, Pa. MSA	1,442,140	15,759,465	9.2
Des Moines, Iowa MSA	1,850,687	20,386,881	9.1
Tampa-St. Petersburg-Clearwater, Fla. MSA	10,379,374	115,186,889	9.0
St. Louis, Mo.-Ill. MSA	12,264,041	136,414,159	9.0
Pittsburgh, Pa. MSA	3,562,000	57,759,695	6.2

Source: See table 6-2.

a. MSA, metropolitan statistical area; CMSA, consolidated metropolitan statistical area; NECMA, New England county metropolitan area.

b. Transit obligations include both funds flexed to the Federal Transit Administration and those spent directly on transit by the transportation agency.

Table 6-4. CMAQ Suballocation and Rates of Flexing to Transit, 1998–2002

Units as indicated

Decisionmaker	Transit obligations from CMAQ (dollars)	All CMAQ obligations (dollars)	Percent of CMAQ funds obligated to transit
Metropolitan (states with suballocated CMAQ)	2,723,757,954	5,109,756,292	53.3
State (no suballocation)	418,458,826	1,352,059,237	30.9
State received minimum allocation of CMAQ[a]	33,727,830	381,250,875	8.8

Source: See table 6-2.

a. Each state receives a minimum of 0.5 percent of the CMAQ program regardless of their air quality status.

state. Overall, almost half (46 percent) of CMAQ funds nationwide were obligated to transit from 1998 to 2002. Again, twenty-five states suballocate CMAQ funds to the metropolitan level. This, as well as eligibility and area limitations on CMAQ funds, has a strong influence on how the money is spent. Table 6-4 illustrates how CMAQ spending patterns differ between states with and without suballocation. (These figures represent all CMAQ spending throughout the state, unlike the analysis of STP spending presented earlier.)

This analysis of spending patterns under TEA-21 makes it clear that metropolitan areas are more likely to respond to local transit needs than are state departments of transportation. While transit is only one indicator of local transportation needs, it does point out that local officials appear to be better attuned to the value of a balanced, comprehensive, and multimodal transportation system.

Policy Recommendations

This chapter highlights the importance of metropolitan areas and the genuine need to ensure that they have the appropriate ability to make important decisions about transportation investments. As Congress reevaluates transportation reform, and as states attempt to grow their own economies in the current bleak fiscal environment, it is critical that there be greater focus on the transportation needs and challenges of our metropolitan areas.

If the federal government is serious about making transportation investment decisions that reflect local needs, there must be real money on the table. When the MPO has more discretionary funding for local projects, local officials are more likely to participate in the process. The availability of these funds not only provides financing for vital local projects but also encourages local officials to get involved in the transportation decision-making for their region.[69] To ensure metropolitan areas remain strong and economically viable, Congress should consider the following measures.

Increase the Amount of Money Directly Suballocated to the Metropolitan Level

An expansion of local control through suballocation, combined with funding flexibility, would enable MPOs to meet the challenges of intermodalism, environmental enhancement, and inclusive decisionmaking processes. This chapter examined just one quintessentially local need—public transit service—and found that MPOs are much more responsive to local needs than are states. Congress should give MPOs greater resources and flexibility to tailor transportation solutions to the distinctive realities of individual metropolitan areas. Congress should substantially increase the funding that is suballocated to MPOs, where the majority of the transportation challenges remain and where the majority of funds are generated. Specifically, the entire portion of STP funds available for distribution after the takedowns for enhancements and safety should be distributed throughout the state by the population formula. Congress should also ensure that the STP funds that are fed by the Minimum Guarantee program are subject to the metropolitan suballocation requirement, as they were during the life of ISTEA. These funds were $2.8 billion per year during TEA-21. This does not necessarily require an increase in overall funding but recommends a shift in decisionmaking authority over existing funds.

Require States to Suballocate All CMAQ Funds Directly to Metropolitan Areas

Suballocation of CMAQ funds to MPOs in air quality nonattainment and maintenance areas would make the program more responsive and reliable to local areas. Although some eastern states such as Maryland have shown a commitment to spending on air quality improvements, Congress directly holds MPOs responsible for developing transportation plans and programs to help their regions meet federal air quality standards. MPOs should be given direct access to these implementation funds. The MPO planning process offers untapped opportunities to identify environmental issues and account for them in the process of defining project alternatives. With the implementation of the Environmental Protection Agency's new eight-hour ozone standard, a growing number of counties in metropolitan areas will be defined as nonattainment areas. Effective application of CMAQ funds to local needs will be crucial to the national effort to improve air quality. States, for their part, should remove the restrictions on using gas tax revenues for transit in order to leverage federal funds from programs like CMAQ and take better advantage of federal-level reforms.

Increase Metropolitan Planning Takedown to 2 Percent

Although new responsibilities, such as management and operations, have been added to MPO requirements by TEA-21, the percentage of highway program funding allocated for metropolitan planning has remained at the 1 percent level set by ISTEA. In addition, the Census Bureau confirms that almost 50 new MPOs will be created as a result of the continued urbanization of America over the last decade, bringing the total number up to 385. As more MPOs come online and as existing MPOs continue to grow, the same percentage of funding is being spread out over a larger base. The existing TEA-21 set-aside for metropolitan transportation planning should be increased from 1 percent to 2 percent. This will help keep pace with the almost 20 percent increase in MPOs resulting from the 2000 census, the increasingly urbanized U.S. population coming under the jurisdiction of existing MPOs, and the increased MPO responsibilities created by enhanced planning provisions and requirements. The administration's surface transportation reauthorization proposal—the Safe, Accountable, Flexible, and Efficient Transportation Equity Act of 2003—supports a roughly 52 percent increase in the takedown by including Minimum Guarantee in the programs from which planning funds are derived. The American Association of State Highway Officials and the Association of Metropolitan Planning Organizations also support an increase in these funds.

Establish a New Federal Framework for Accountability and Performance

In exchange for greater funding, Congress should subject MPOs to enhanced accountability measures. State and metropolitan transportation agencies should be required to maintain information systems that annually measure progress on indicators of national significance. These indicators might include slowing the growth in daily vehicle miles traveled, improving public health, improving air quality, lowering transportation costs, and expanding transportation options for target groups (such as the elderly or low-income workers). The law should also require transportation agencies to set annual performance objectives in each of these critical areas. These performance objectives (and progress toward meeting them) should be shared with the general public in an accessible manner. In this regard, the new federal law should establish consequences for excellent and poor performance. Congress should allow the DOT to maintain a small incentive pool to reward states and metropolitan areas that consistently perform at an exceptional level. The department could also improve project delivery by giving high performers relief from regulatory and administrative requirements. By the same token, the federal DOT should consider possible intervention strategies for consistent low performers. (In designating high and low performers, DOT should take into account the difficult challenges facing state agencies and MPOs in large metropolitan areas).[70]

Ensure Information Transparency and Accessibility

Congress should require that all recipients of federal transportation funds disclose their program and spending policies and decisions in a transparent, accessible, frequent, and continuous manner. State and metropolitan entities should, at a minimum, disclose their spending patterns by political jurisdiction and origins of the revenue used. Congress should also fulfill one vision of ISTEA: that information be presented in a comprehensive and easy to understand format. DOT provides extremely limited access to data on expenditures of federal funds. Even though the Federal Highway Administration's Fiscal Management Information System has been in place since the early days of the interstate era, published information on spending by recipient and program is limited and often several years behind. The raw FMIS data used to produce much of the quantitative analysis in this report are difficult to work with and are not available on the World Wide Web.

Conclusion

Local and metropolitan leaders throughout the nation are demanding more decisionmaking authority and more direct control over federal dollars in order to address a wide range of transportation challenges. Although major federal reform efforts of the 1990s did take steps to strengthen local authority, there is much more to be done. In most states, MPOs are well positioned to fulfill the metropolitan role that is necessary in transportation governance and finance. Yet to do that, states must allow MPOs to complete the transition from advisory bodies to fully empowered, functioning authorities.

It has been said that America is neither an urban nor rural nation but rather a metropolitan nation, where the majority of the population lives and works in large metropolitan areas that include both historic central cities and dispersed suburban development. The debate around the transportation legislation must reflect this reality.

Notes

1. It is an axiom of this chapter that decisions should be made at the most appropriate level of government and as close to those who will be affected by those decisions as possible. This is generally referred to as the well-established principle of subsidiary.

2. H.R. 3611, 108 Cong. 2 sess. 2 (2003). The bill was cosponsored by Representatives Earl Blumenauer (Oregon) and Ellen Tauscher (California).

3. In the context of federal transportation reauthorization, "devolution" has come to mean different things. During the debate over reauthorization of the Intermodal Surface Transportation Efficiency Act, then representative John Kasich (R-Ohio) and former senator Connie Mack (R-Florida) championed a reauthorization proposal that would effectively remove the federal government from all transportation planning and programming activities. Kasich and Mack argued that since the interstates were complete, so was the federal role. They further argued that the federal government was an impediment to efficient transportation decisionmaking. In this context, devolution referred to the transfer of powers from the federal government to the states. For the purposes of this chapter, devolution refers to a more iterative process of shifting authorities from the state to the metropolitan and local levels and does not at all suggest a reduced federal role.

4. Anthony Downs, "The Devolution Revolution: Why Congress Is Shifting a Lot of Power to the Wrong Level," Policy Brief 3 (Brookings, 1996).

5. President, "State of the Union Address," January 7, 1954.

6. Federal Highway Administration, *Status of the Nation's Highways, Bridges, and Transit: 2002 Conditions and Performance Report* (Department of Transportation, 2003), p. 23–2.

7. James A. Dunn Jr., *Driving Forces: The Automobile, Its Enemies, and the Politics of Mobility* (Brookings, 1998).

8. The term "urbanized" is used here as defined by federal statutes. The Bureau of the Census designates densely settled areas containing 50,000 or more people as urbanized. For detailed information, see Bureau of the Census, "Census 2000 Urban and Rural Classification" (www.census.gov/geo/www/ua/ua_2k.html [February 2005]).

9. See Marlon Boarnet and Andrew Haughwout, "Do Highways Matter? Evidence and Policy Implications of Highways' Influence on Metropolitan Development," discussion paper prepared for the Center on Urban and Metropolitan Policy (Brookings, August 2000), and Mark Solof, "History of Metropolitan Planning Organizations, Part II," *NJTPA Quarterly* (December 1996).

10. Myron Orfield, *American Metropolitics: The New Suburban Reality* (Brookings, 2002).

11. Paul G. Lewis and Mary Sprague, *Federal Transportation Policy and the Role of Metropolitan Planning Organizations in California* (San Francisco: Public Policy Institute of California, 1997).

12. Orfield, *American Metropolitics.*

13. Department of Transportation, *A Guide to Metropolitan Transportation Planning Under ISTEA— How the Pieces Fit Together*, FHWA-P.D.-95-031 (1995).

14. Senate Committee on Environment and Public Works, "Statement of Cynthia Burbank, Program Manager, Planning and Environment Core Business Unit, Federal Highway Administration, Department of Transportation," 107 Cong. 2 sess. (May 15, 2002).

15. See Robert Puentes, "Flexible Funding for Transit: Who Uses It?" report prepared for the Center on Urban and Metropolitan Policy (Brookings, May 2000).

16. 23 U.S.C. 133(b).

17. The portion of the federal law that directs state DOTs to spend STP funds in smaller urbanized areas does not actually require that states devolve control of the funds to these areas.

18. 23 U.S.C. 133(d). Note: the suballocation requirement does not apply to Alaska, Hawaii, or Puerto Rico, which have legislative exemptions. Nor does it apply to states that do not have any urbanized areas with populations over 200,000: Idaho, Main, Montana, North Dakota, South Dakota, Vermont, West Virginia, and Wyoming.

19. Federal Highway Administration, "Minimum Guarantee Fact Sheet" (www.fhwa.dot.gov/tea21/factsheets/minguar.htm [September 1998]).

20. Federal Highway Administration, "Congestion Mitigation and Air Quality Improvement Program (CMAQ) Fact Sheet" (www.fhwa.dot.gov/tea21/factsheets/cmaq.htm [September 1998]).

21. Surface Transportation Policy Project, "The CMAQ Program: Funding Cleaner Air," Decoding Transportation Policy and Practice 7 (Washington, 2003).

22. The CMAQ program totals $9.6 billion, including distributions from Minimum Guarantee funds and Revenue Aligned Budget Authority funds.

23. *Federal Register* 63, no. 206 (October 26, 1998): 57154-8 (FHWA-98-4317).

24. Transportation Research Board, The *Congestion Mitigation and Air Quality Improvement Program: Assessing 10 Years of Experience*, Special Report 264 (Washington: National Academy Press, 2002), p. 111.

25. Ibid.

26. Ibid. p. 240.

27. Ibid.

28. It is admittedly difficult to classify states based on a simple "yes" or "no" in terms of whether or not they suballocate CMAQ funds. Some states, such as South Carolina and Montana, created unique funding allocation systems using CMAQ resources. Other states play a strong role administering CMAQ funds in some metropolitan areas but not in others—such as those where a strong MPO exists. Still other states, such as Alaska, Ohio, and Tennessee, retain a portion of their CMAQ funds and suballocate the remainder.

29. 23 U.S.C. 134(a)1.

30. The 1 percent is calculated from the authorizations remaining after the administrative deduction is made from the following programs: Interstate Maintenance, National Highway System, Surface Transportation, Congestion Mitigation and Air Quality, and Highway Bridge Replacement and Rehabilitation. See 23 U.S.C. 104(f)1.

31. 49 U.S.C. 5303.

32. The Federal Highway Administration's metropolitan transportation planning funding was $1.13 billion, and the Federal Transit Administration's funding was approximately $400 million. Federal Highway Administration, "Metropolitan Planning Fact Sheet" (www.fhwa.dot.gov/tea21/factsheets/metropln.htm [September 1998]).

33. John W. Fischer, "Highway and Transit Program Reauthorization," Report RL31665 (Congressional Research Service, Library of Congress, December 11, 2002).

34. According to the American Association of State Highway and Transportation Officials, the transportation sector is the largest financial contributor to historic preservation and archeological projects conducted in the United States. House Committee on Transportation and Infrastructure, Subcommittee on Highways and Transit, "Testimony of John C. Horsley, Executive Director of the American Association State Highway and Transportation Officials, Regarding Expediting Project Delivery to Improve Transportation and the Environment Act,"107 Cong. 2 sess. (October 8, 2002).

35. National Transportation Enhancements Clearinghouse, "Transportation Enhancements: Summary of Nationwide Spending and Policies as of FY 1999" (Washington, 2000). Information updated by the Brookings Institution, June 2003. Note that Georgia suballocates to congressional districts, but the state makes the ultimate funding decision.

36. Robert S. Patten, "Enhancing America's Communities—A Status Report on the Implementation of the Transportation Enhancements Provisions of ISTEA" (Washington: Rails-to-Trails Conservancy, 1994). See also ntl.bts.gov/DOCS/eac.html [February 2005].

37. All MPOs receive PL funds, but only those in urbanized areas with populations over 200,000 receive metropolitan suballocated funds.

38. Senate Environment and Public Works Committee, *Hearing on Transportation Planning and Smart Growth*, testimony of Judith Espinosa on behalf of the Surface Transportation Policy Project, 107 Cong. 2 sess. (May 15, 2002).

39. According to the Office of Management and Budget, a metropolitan area generally refers to a core area with a large population center and the surrounding jurisdictions that are somehow linked with the core area—referring essentially to economic and social integration.

40. Bureau of the Census, "Ranking Tables for Metropolitan Areas: Population in 2000 and Population Change from 1990 to 2000 (PHC-T-3)"(www.census.gov/population/www/cen2000/phc-t3.html [July 31, 2002]), table 1, "Metropolitan Areas and Their Geographic Components in Alphabetic Sort, 1990 and 2000 Population, and Numeric and Percent Change: 1990 to 2000."

41. The economic scope of metropolitan areas is also remarkable. The ten largest metropolitan areas in the United States have a greater combined gross product than the smallest thirty-one states combined. The Detroit metropolitan area alone has greater gross product than more than half of the states. And within each state, the importance of metropolitan areas is also apparent. In almost half the states, a single metropolitan area accounts for at least a quarter of the state's economy. For example, Phoenix and Chicago each make up about 70 percent of their states' economies and employ about 70 percent of the workforce. When all the metropolitan areas within a state are aggregated, they make up at least three-quarters of the economy in thirty of the fifty states. Metropolitan areas make up 100 percent of New Jersey's economy. See

United States Conference of Mayors, "The Role of Metro Areas in the U.S. Economy" (Washington, 2002).

42. Metropolitan Transportation Commission, *TEA-21 Reauthorization: Infrastructure for a Stronger America: 24th Annual Report to Congress* (Oakland, Calif., March 2003).

43. Bruce Schaller, "Building Effective Relationships between Central Cities and Regional, State and Federal Agencies," National Cooperative Highway Research Program Synthesis Report 297 (Washington: Transportation Research Board, 2001).

44. For a discussion about the metropolitan scale of the global economy, see Peter Calthorpe and William Fulton, *The Regional City* (Washington: Island Press, 2001)

45. Bruce McDowell, "Improving Regional Transportation Decisions: MPOs and Certification," discussion paper prepared for the Center on Urban and Metropolitan Policy (Brookings, September 1999).

46. House Transportation and Infrastructure Committee, *Hearing on Highways and Transit Needs: The State and Local Perspective*, testimony of Knoxville mayor Victor H. Ashe, 108 Cong. 1 sess. (May 7, 2003).

47. See Anthony Downs, *Stuck in Traffic: Coping with Peak Hour Traffic Congestion* (Brookings, 1992), p. 138.

48. General Accounting Office, *Urban Transportation: Metropolitan Planning Organizations' Efforts to Meet Federal Planning Requirements*, RCED-96-200 (1996).

49. Todd Goldman and Elizabeth Deakin, "Regionalism through Partnerships? Metropolitan Planning since ISTEA," *Berkeley Planning Journal* 14 (2000): 46–75.

50. Thomas Sanchez, "An Analysis of the Spatial Makeup of Metropolitan Decisionmakers" (Brookings, forthcoming).

51. For a discussion of how to enhance the education of transportation professionals, see Susan Handy and others, "The Education of Transportation Planning Professionals," Research Report SWUTC/02/167522 (Center for Transportation Research, University of Texas at Austin, 2002).

52. The Local Officials for Transportation coalition includes the American Public Works Association, Association of Metropolitan Planning Organizations, International City/County Management Association, National Association of City Transportation Officials, National Association of Counties, National Association of County Engineers, National Association of Development Organizations, National Association of Regional Councils, National League of Cities, Public Technology, Incorporated., and the U.S. Conference of Mayors.

53. Ron Thaniel, "Barr Leads Mayors' Call for Dealing with National Crisis in Metropolitan Congestion" (www.usmayors.org/USCM/us_mayor_newspaper/documents/12_09_02/barr_leads.asp[December 9, 2002]).

54. It is important to note that states continue to "own" freeways and other arterial highways where some of the heaviest traffic volumes take place.

55. See John M. Cobin, "Market Provisions of Highways: Lessons from Costanera Norte," *Planning and Markets* 2, no. 1 (1999).

56. See Wachs, chapter 4 in this volume.

57. Federal Highway Administration, *Status of the Nation's Highways*, chap. 2.

58. Federal Highway Administration and Federal Transit Administration, The *Metropolitan Transportation Planning Process: Key Issues* (Transportation Planning Capacity Building Program, Department of Transportation, 2001).

59. Gerald Frug, "Beyond Regional Government," *Harvard Law Review* 115, no. 7 (2002): 1763–1836.

60. See Hill and others, chapter 5 in this volume.

61. Downs, *Stuck in Traffic*, p. 131.

62. McDowell, "Improving Regional Transportation Decisions."

63. Wilfred Owen, *The Metropolitan Transportation Problem* (Brookings, 1956), p. 218.

64. Senate Committee on Environment and Public Works, "Statement of Cynthia Burbank."

65. Bureau of Transportation Statistics, *Transportation Statistics Annual Report 1996* (Department of Transportation, 1996).

66. Neil Pedersen, "Multimodal Transportation Planning at the State Level: State of the Practice and Future Issues" (Washington: Transportation Research Board, 1999).

67. A recent report found that the federal flexible funding provisions are a key element in helping local officials meet their transportation needs. See Robert G. Stanley, "Use of Flexible Funds for Transit under ISTEA and TEA-21," Transit Cooperative Research Program Synthesis 42 (Washington: Transportation Research Board, 2002).

68. Ten states' MPOs (Alaska, Hawaii, Idaho, Maine, Montana, North Dakota, South Dakota, Vermont, West Virginia, and Wyoming) received no STP-eligible funds—determined by a federal formula based on population characteristics. Only those states with MPOs receiving STP funds are included in the figures for MPOs.

69. Senate Committee on Environment and Public Works, "Testimony of Dr. Ronald Kirby, Director of Transportation Planning, National Capital Region Transportation Planning Board," 107 Cong. 2 sess. (May 15, 2002).

70. There is substantial federal precedent for such an accountability framework. Congress, for example, established a management assessment system for public housing agencies and created a performance measurement and reward system in the 1996 welfare reform law. The transportation system of governance and finance shares many similarities with these other areas of domestic policy—and should operate under similar accountability.

7

The Need for Regional Anticongestion Policies

Anthony Downs and Robert Puentes

Everyone hates traffic congestion. It wastes time and fuel and adds to air pollution. It also generates widespread frustration that even results in violence induced by "road rage." Congestion is especially aggravating because all attempted remedies seem to fail: traffic delays keep getting worse. This violates the axiom of American culture that all problems have solutions. "Why don't they do something about it" is an often heard outcry.

Why *don't* they solve this problem? Because rising traffic congestion is an inescapable condition in nearly all large and growing metropolitan areas throughout the world—from Los Angeles to Tokyo, from Washington to Paris, from Atlanta to São Paulo. Peak-hour traffic—that is, rush hour traffic congestion—is an inherent result of the way modern societies operate and the widespread desires of their residents to pursue certain goals that inevitably overload existing roads and transit systems every day.[1]

Nevertheless, there is enormous public pressure to do something about traffic. But traffic congestion is a condition embedded in the basic structure of American cultural values, governance institutions, economic organization, political beliefs, and lifestyle preferences. So "doing something about it" requires launching a multifaceted set of actions on many fronts simultaneously.

Even just trying to describe what kinds of actions might have some impacts is complicated.

To start, congestion can be tackled by either supply-side or demand-side tactics. Supply-side tactics include increasing road capacity and transit capacity and better managing incidents and accidents. In short, these tactics are designed to expand the means that travelers can use for commuting and other trips. They are implemented by public agencies such as state departments of transportation (DOTs).

Demand-side tactics are designed to reduce or manage the number of persons or vehicles traveling during peak periods, or change the mode or length of the trip. They include pricing and market-oriented strategies; land use policies such as concentrating jobs in clusters, increasing residential densities, and changing the jobs-to-housing balance; and local growth management policies. Local and state governments have the primary responsibility for these measures.

The problem with both of these groups of strategies is not in the tactics themselves but in the manner in which they are implemented. Traffic flows are regional in nature, not local or statewide. Only the coordination of transportation improvements with land use planning on the regional or metropolitan level could result in the most rational policies toward congestion. That is one of the reasons Congress established metropolitan planning organizations (MPOs) to oversee surface transportation planning in major metropolitan areas.

But effective anticongestion policies also involve many elements other than the planning and creation of new infrastructure elements. Examples are converting two-way streets into a system of one-way streets, coordinating traffic signals, using ramp metering to control vehicle flows onto expressways, adopting taxes or other regulations concerning parking during peak hours, changing residential density patterns in new-growth areas, adopting tax breaks that encourage high-density in-fill development or redevelopment of older neighborhoods, and managing a system of roving patrols on expressways that quickly remove accidents or stalled vehicles from traffic lanes. Other forms of regional organizations besides MPOs are necessary to establish and manage these and other similar tactics aimed at reducing traffic congestion across a region.

The increased focus on traffic and its impact on metropolitan America presents an excellent opportunity for Congress to respond to the growing demand for congestion relief. This chapter is intended to put some geographic context into the debate around traffic congestion by exploring institutional forms for carrying out congestion-relieving tactics. In the end, it recommends adopting truly regional policies dealing with key aspects of the many forces affecting traffic congestion.

Background: Capacity for Regionalism Today

Across America interest in possible regional remedies to various community problems has risen sharply in the past decade.[2] More and more citizens, government officials, and other observers are becoming convinced that the predominant governance system in American regions, which consists of many small, highly fragmented local governments, is not capable of dealing with a variety of problems effectively. These problems include air pollution, widespread shortage of affordable housing, lack of open space, rising infrastructure costs and higher taxes to pay them, inadequate public schools in many large cities, continuing isolation of the poorest households in deteriorating inner-city neighborhoods—and rush hour traffic congestion.

The problems themselves are spread too widely over each region as a whole and are interconnected across too many localities in each region to be effectively dealt with by individual governments acting separately. Since the dominant system is not working well, perhaps it is time to explore some other arrangement. The major alternative is some type of regionalism or metropolitanism.

Many tactics that would be effective in counteracting peak-hour traffic congestion similarly cannot be carried out by individual local or state governments. These tactics require regional design, implementation, or administration (where "regional" refers to an entire metropolitan area). In most U.S. metropolitan areas, however, no effective regional governmental agencies exist. Moreover, local governments frequently oppose the creation of such agencies.[3]

The current federal transportation law, the Transportation Equity Act for the Twenty-First Century, and its predecessor, the 1991 Intermodal Surface Transportation Efficiency Act, sought through devolution to better align the geography of transportation decisionmaking with the geography of regional economies, commuting patterns, and social reality. To do that, the laws undertook to enlarge the responsibility of the MPOs it had brought into being in 1962. Although these regional bodies were originally research organizations charged with advising state DOTs, Congress subsequently charged MPOs with developing coordinated plans for uses of federal and other ground transportation funds within each region and for overseeing what happened to those plans.[4]

This was surely an appropriate course of action. The need to coordinate the planning and construction of new ground transportation facilities at the regional level is blatantly obvious because so many personal and vehicle movements within each region cross jurisdictional boundaries. However, the powers to implement those plans were left in the hands of other agencies—particularly state DOTs.

In the past, state DOTs acted as the main regional coordinators in the absence of other formal integration mechanisms. But that approach suffered from serious drawbacks. It focused almost entirely upon roads, usually ignoring public transit, walking, and bicycles. It often failed to include any systematic way to receive or evaluate requests from individual localities for projects within their boundaries. It also frequently did not take into account the reactions of localities to proposed projects that would pass through their territories. It had no effective means of coordinating new transportation infrastructure with proposed new land use developments or future growth areas, or with local growth control or growth management policies. It often lacked formal mechanisms for soliciting and responding to citizen views about proposed projects. And it rarely had any formal mechanisms for coordinating the policies of highway departments in adjoining states when a region encompassed land within more than one state.

In recognition of these shortcomings, Congress expanded the role of previously created MPOs and charged them with creating regionally integrated plans for future ground transportation infrastructure projects. This goal seems clear, but achieving it effectively is extremely difficult. As urban economist George Sternlieb was fond of saying, "The words drip easily from the lip, but putting them into practice is something else." Regional intermodal planning of such a multifaceted activity as ground transportation is an extraordinarily complicated and difficult process, especially in a democracy that emphasizes citizen participation. Making that process work effectively will take many years of experience, flexible experimentation, and outstanding leadership—if it can be done even then.

Most large regions and many small ones have created MPOs. Each MPO has, in turn, launched a regionally coordinated ground transportation investment planning process. This process is designed to formulate, evaluate, develop consensus for, and adopt plans for constructing or modifying specific ground transportation projects throughout its region. Since many of those projects will have crucial impacts upon future levels of traffic congestion within the region, MPOs are a vital part of creating effective anticongestion policies at the regional level.

Anticongestion policies adopted by only one community are not likely to be very effective—even within its boundaries—unless they are closely coordinated with similar policies adopted in most other communities nearby.[5]

Regional implementation is particularly important for policies focusing on peak-hour road pricing. No local government could reduce congestion throughout a region by adopting peak-hour road pricing solely within its own boundaries. Regional implementation would also be vital in establishing a network of high-occupancy vehicle lanes, keeping average settlement densities in areas of new growth above some minimal level, building new roads or expanding existing ones, creating "cash out" programs concerning employers who provide free employee parking, and raising gasoline taxes.[6]

True, a few remedies could be effectively carried out by individual local governments acting alone. For example, a single local government with a large territory can coordinate traffic signals on its main streets, institute systems of one-way streets, pressure developers and employers in large job centers to establish traffic management associations, and create roving response teams to clear roadways quickly after traffic accidents. But all these tactics would also be much more effective if implemented consistently throughout a metropolitan area.

Furthermore, traffic congestion could best be attacked by using several complementary tactics simultaneously. For example, improved traffic signal coordination could be linked to rush hour road pricing so that traffic diverted from new toll roads would flow efficiently on nearby free-access roads.

Although it is quite clear that the present fragmented power arrangement is not working well, regional remedies are still rather limited. This is because certain aspects of such remedies rouse strong opposition to their enactment and have hindered their evolution. Therefore, few places have adopted them long enough to test whether they are in fact superior to fragmented governance.

Regional Efforts to Combat Congestion: Challenges and Opportunities

This section discusses some shortcomings and challenges accompanying efforts to address congestion on the regional level. The main issues concern the nature of regionalism and the function of MPOs.

Complexity and Equity

Tackling problems at the regional level in a democracy involves extremely complex and difficult activities—more difficult than those required to operate our present fragmented governance system. Many more divergent interests must be consulted and persuaded to cooperate than is the case with local governments acting separately. So the politics of achieving consensus on effective policies is much more complex and time consuming at the regional level. Coping with problems at the regional level also involves technically more complex policies than those confined to the local level. Hence the personal and leadership skills and technical abilities required to make regionalism work are hard to find.

Kathryn Foster summarizes what has been learned so far about the effectiveness of regional arrangements of all types: "Governance systems based on many local governments tend to promote participation and have lower service costs than do regionalized systems. Evidence remains inconclusive that regionalized governance systems are necessarily superior to localized ones in achieving equity or economic growth, although conventional wisdom and perception favor regional arrangements."[7]

Simply because a transportation plan is regionally developed by representatives from specific parts of each metropolitan area does not necessarily mean they will arrive at socially equitable distributions of the funds they are responsible for allocating. Just because a person living in one part of a region, and chosen to represent that part on a regional agency, is now serving on an agency with regionwide responsibilities is no guarantee that this person will actually adopt a truly regional perspective, rather than narrowly representing the parochial interests of his or her own district. For one thing, newly developing suburban areas often have transportation needs that differ radically from those of central cities. While some suburban areas clamor for increases in road and transit capacity, in central cities there is an often a dire need for maintenance and renewal of existing facilities.[8]

However, since suburban portions of most metropolitan areas have larger representation on regional bodies such as MPOs, they are able to craft regional transportation plans that focus on expanded and new transportation infrastructure rather than on rehabilitation or repairs. Indeed, a 1994 study found that nearly eight out of ten center cities were underrepresented on the boards of their local MPOs in terms of voting power. That is, the voting strength of the center city was lower than the city's percentage share of MPO area population.[9] Furthermore, very few MPOs grant any type of voting power to nongeographic entities such as transit agencies, port authorities, or environmental agencies.[10] As a result of these distortions, Martin Wachs and Jennifer Dill believe that "transportation funds have almost always been more available from both state and federal sources for capital investments—new roads and transit lines—than for maintenance, repair, or system operations. Thus, we believe that the transportation system has been 'overcapitalized.' More money has been spent on new facilities and equipment than would have been the case had monies been fungible between capital, operations, and maintenance applications."[11]

The main beneficiaries of new roads and transit lines have been suburbanites. They who have higher average incomes than city dwellers are the main users—and fare payers—on public transit systems. After examining the redistributive impacts of state gas tax funds used for transit operations in the San Francisco Bay area, Brian Taylor found that "the larger, inner-city transit operators in the Bay Area carried the overwhelmingly largest share of the passengers and received a dramatically smaller share of the program's resources. Conversely, smaller, more localized suburban transit operators received a far larger proportion of the subsidy dollars under this program than their regional share of transit ridership might suggest they ought to receive."[12]

Uncertain Effectiveness

The situation described above suggests that creating effective regional remedies for traffic congestion and other urban ills is still an emerging process. It is still not certain which remedies to which problems will prove definitely superior to the status quo under existing fragmented governance. Right now, the situation is analogous to the story of the singing contest in a mythical kingdom: The competition had been narrowed down to two final contestants, and the king was to make the final judgment about who would win. Immediately after hearing the first contestant sing, the king awarded the prize to the second contestant—without hearing the latter! Many citizens contemplating existing regional problems similarly conclude that present fragmented remedies are so bad that regional ones are bound to be better—without yet having tried the latter.

Therefore, although this chapter recommends trying many regional traffic-congestion remedies for the same reason, it is important to recognize the somewhat tentative and experimental nature of those recommendations. Regional remedies are worth trying, but there is as yet no guarantee how effectively they can be made to work.

Herculean Tasks for MPOs

The difficulty of this process is clear from the requirements Congress established for MPOs. Congress declared that each MPO must

—create a long-range, twenty-year strategic plan for regional transportation investment, taking into account all modes of ground movement—roads, transit, walking, and bicycles—and including both passenger and freight movements;

—create a short-range, current program of specific transportation improvement projects that have been evaluated as the best feasible alternatives and subjected to a process of citizen participation;

—establish widespread regional consensus among citizens, local governments and elected officials, and business and other private-sector leaders in support of both the long-range plan and the current program. This requires ongoing collaborative planning and close partnerships between the MPO and these other elements of society;

—coordinate the MPO's planning with that of all affected state and local government agencies, especially the state's department of transportation and environmental protection agency;

—build a sense of regionwide responsibility—a "regional ethos"— among MPO members, even though most of them are political representatives of specific local governments within the region;

—take full account of the likely effects of all planned projects upon air quality in accordance with the 1990 Clean Air Amendments Act;

—develop specific systems for managing congestion, intermodal relations, transit maintenance, safety, bridge maintenance, and pavement maintenance;

—use the latest techniques of analysis, evaluation, and behavioral modeling in carrying out all the other steps set forth above;

—follow all existing regulations for funding requests for both the Federal Highway Administration and the Federal Transit Administration, even though they are quite different; and

—do all this within limited budgets for both capital (paying for the infrastructure projects) and operations (hiring and running the necessary staff) and without any direct powers to implement the plans it creates, since implementation is left to other agencies.

Actually performing these tasks has proved a tremendous challenge to the officials running MPOs, as indicated by several evaluations of their activities conducted by outside observers.[13]

Strengthening MPOs

A major recommendation of several MPO evaluations was that the Department of Transportation (DOT) should establish, fund, and proactively promote a much more extensive program for expanding the technical and other capabilities of existing MPOs. This program should be aimed at both MPO staffs and other participants in the MPO planning process. Moreover, DOT needs to better integrate its own agencies' relationships with MPOs. At the time of these evaluations, the Federal Highway Administration, Federal Transit Administration, and Federal Aviation Administration—which have never fully coordinated their own overall approaches to individual metropolitan areas—had disparate, unnecessarily duplicative, and poorly coordinated procedures for interacting with and assisting MPOs.

In response to these recommendations, the DOT in November 2001 established a metropolitan capacity-building program. Its stated mission is "to help metropolitan area decisionmakers resolve the increasingly complex issues they face when addressing transportation needs in their communities. This comprehensive program for training, technical assistance, and support is targeted to state and local governments, transit operators, and community leaders."[14] This program is surely a step in the right direction, but how well it will work remains to be seen.

The above comments certainly do not mean that the MPO planning process should be abandoned. To the contrary, they indicate that achieving the multiple goals of that process is extremely difficult and will therefore entail a long period of experience and experimentation. In addition, Congress and the federal agencies concerned must be willing to adapt current regulations to the lessons that emerge from experience. Despite these difficulties, it is most likely that developing regional transportation planning will, in the long run, prove superior to continued fragmented planning among uncoordinated local governments.

Therefore, advocates of regional anticongestion strategies should seriously consider developing some type of regional transportation entity with responsibilities that surpass those currently afforded to MPOs. The agency's jurisdiction should ideally include the planning, construction, and operation of the metropolitan area's principal roads, bridges, tunnels, and mass transit systems. It would be able to review and coordinate local land use policies and set pricing schemes for parking and tolls. This could be a newly created regional authority or a fully evolved MPO. Establishing such a regional infrastructure agency would require action by the state or other governments concerned.

Clearly, this kind of an entity is easiest to create when the entire metropolitan area lies within one state. If regional public agencies with the genuine power to affect traffic congestion are ever to exist, this is probably the form most will take.

Other Possible Institutional Arrangements

MPOs deal mainly with building new transportation infrastructures; hence they are not the only organizations necessary to implement effective anticongestion policies at the regional level. Many such policies involve changing the behavior of existing governmental agencies, private bodies, or individual drivers. Examples include encouraging more ride sharing and transit ridership, adopting zoning laws that prevent very low density development in outlying areas, providing subsidies for high-density in-fill development, and creating high-density development zones around transit stops. These tactics would also be most effective if planned and managed at the regional level, but they are largely not within the purview of MPOs. So other institutional forms are needed to implement such tactics throughout an entire metropolitan area.

These regional anticongestion tactics are of two types: those concerned primarily with transportation itself (such as ramp metering or taxing parking facilities) and those concerned primarily with land use as it affects transportation (such as promoting high-density development around transit stops). Most Americans have quite different attitudes toward these two types of tactics. As Kathryn A. Foster in her excellent study explains, "Americans generally embrace regionalism when it promises material gains through improved service delivery or tax-reducing mergers but reject it when it redistributes resources, promotes racial and class mixing, or jeopardizes local land use prerogatives."[15]

To put it another way, Americans will accept relatively strong regional arrangements for primarily physical or economic activities much more readily than for social ones—including control over land use. Therefore, the type of regional arrangement most appropriate for any anticongestion tactic depends on whether that tactic is transportation oriented or land use oriented.

Foster divided all regional arrangements into two major categories: structural arrangements and nonstructural ones.[16] Table 7-1 shows those arrangements relevant to regional anticongestion policies. Each of these regional forms is discussed in greater detail below.

Structural Arrangements

Structural arrangements are those that involve some sort of formal governmental or legal entities with direct and specific decisionmaking authority. These arrangements entail primarily physical or economic activities.

Full Metropolitan Governments. These arrangements include city-county mergers and "pure" metropolitan governments. Their main advantage in

Table 7-1. Institutional Arrangements for Addressing Regional Traffic Congestion

Arrangements	Types	Examples
Structural	Full metropolitan governments	Jacksonville, Fla.; Indianapolis and Marion County, Ind.; Louisville–Jefferson Country Metro Government, Ky.
	Multipurpose regional entities	Portland Metro, Ore.; Twin Cities Metropolitan Council, Minn.
	Single-purpose regional entities	Port Authority of New York and New Jersey; various transit agencies
	State government agencies	Highway departments
	Federal or federally mandated agencies	MPOs; air quality management districts
Nonstructural	Voluntary cooperation among autonomous local governments	Councils of government
	Comprehensive plan preparation as part of a state-mandated planning process	Varies
	Joint public-private coordination, planning, and policy-promotion agencies	New York metro area Regional Planning Association, Chicago Metropolis 2020

Source: Based on Anthony Downs, *Stuck in Traffic* (Brookings and Lincoln Institute of Land Policy, 1992), chap. 10, and Kathryn A. Foster, "Regionalism on Purpose," Policy Focus Report (Cambridge, Mass.: Lincoln Institute of Land Policy, 2001), figure 9.

dealing with congestion is that they provide some broad, regional level control over all basic local governmental functions. However, this form has a fatal drawback: it has virtually no political support because it involves regional control over all land uses. Such control is often opposed by both suburban residents and by central-city elected officials. That leaves almost no one in favor of these arrangements. Hence no region has a pure metropolitan government, and only a handful have arrangements based on city-county mergers. It is important to note that even in places where large-scale consolidation has occurred, the newly formed government is still much smaller than the area served by the MPO. Jacksonville, Florida, for example, is the largest city in the contiguous United States since it merged with Duval County in 1968. The consolidated city-county is 757.7 square miles in land area; however, the MPO that serves Jacksonville—the First Coast Metropolitan Planning Organization—covers nearly 1,118 square miles.

Multipurpose Specialized Regional Entities. These arrangements typically combine regional control over major physical infrastructure—such as transportation and sewer and water systems—in one organization. Since these activities are closely interrelated functionally, managing them within a single organization makes sense. Moreover, these elements can strongly address congestion by affecting where new housing and other development will be created. Therefore, a single institution controlling these elements can significantly influence land use decisions relevant to transportation without removing formal control over these decisions from local governments. Thus such an institution is politically far less threatening to suburban communities than full metropolitan governance. One primary example is the Metropolitan Council, a regional planning agency that covers the seven main counties in metropolitan Minneapolis-St. Paul. The Met Council, as it is known, was first created over thirty years ago and oversees metropolitan systems for aviation, transportation, parks and recreation, and wastewater treatment.[17]

Single-Purpose Regional Entities. In some U.S. metropolitan areas, all public transit has been turned over to special regional agencies that run the bus lines, commuter rail lines, and fixed-rail mass transit systems. In other areas, regional agencies are responsible for key highway-oriented facilities, such as bridges and tunnels. In the New York City area, the regional port authority operates bridges, tunnels, bus terminals and bus lines, port facilities, and the main airports. Where such specialized regional agencies already exist, they can, under some circumstances, carry out regional anticongestion policies.

For example, regional transit agencies could improve the service and facilities of those systems to divert traffic from highways. Such agencies could also try to encourage high-density residential and commercial development in the vicinity of their major stations. These tactics are not in themselves likely to reduce congestion significantly, but they might be useful as parts of a larger and more comprehensive strategy. The Washington Metropolitan Area Transit Authority has an active program specifically to facilitate transit-oriented development near its rail stations and promote other smart-growth principles.

Where a regional transportation agency already exists, its scope for implementing congestion-reducing tactics is even greater. For example, in San Francisco the Metropolitan Transportation Commission is responsible for setting tolls for the state-owned bridges in the area.[18] Conceivably and with sufficient political courage, the commission could employ peak-hour tolls on these bridges to dissuade many auto commuters from using them. That proviso emphasizes again the importance of creating widespread public support for regional anticongestion policies among citizens and political leaders. It will not do any good to establish the institutional mechanisms to effect those policies unless such support has been generated in advance.

In a handful of regions, other institutional entities have been created that consist of partnerships among public agencies to deal with issues of traffic management, incident response, and traveler information.[19] These ad hoc organizations—generally referred to as regional operating organizations—are, as the name indicates, involved solely in the operations side of managing the regional transportation network and are generally not involved in planning.[20] So while they may be effective in dealing with day-to-day traffic issues, they are not likely to have any significant impact on long-term metropolitan congestion. However, given their potential for improved operations (as opposed to additional capital investment), regional operating organizations have a potentially important role in congestion mitigation strategies.

State Transportation or Highway Departments. State transportation or highway departments have long been responsible for much transportation facility planning, financing, construction, and operation throughout many metropolitan areas. They have three huge advantages in carrying out regional anticongestion policies: their jurisdictional territory encompasses the entire metropolitan area, unless it includes parts of more than one state; they already possess established capabilities and channels of finance, information, and political influence; and their agencies have access to large continuing flows of money to finance transportation activities and investments.

Therefore, such agencies could improve highway maintenance, build new roads or expand existing ones, add high-occupancy vehicle lanes to existing roads, coordinate traffic signals, and install ramp meters on expressways and arterials. Some state agencies could even install areawide peak-hour road pricing systems if the federal government removed current restrictions on charging peak-hour tolls on interstate highways.[21]

However, many of the above activities—such as building new roads—must now be coordinated with each region's MPO. In fact, according to the Transportation Equity Act for the Twenty-First Century, one of the key tasks for MPOs is to "promote efficient systems management and operation."[22] So the state government could no longer act alone regarding those activities. Moreover, state agencies are poor vehicles for instituting new policies that require citizens and officials to change their long-established behavior. Leadership in creating such change rarely comes from public officials in a democracy because they are essentially followers of existing public opinion. In fact, this characteristic is one of democracy's greatest strengths. However, this means that adopting new methods—especially controversial ones—requires intervention from some other agent of change.[23]

Federal or Federally Mandated Regional Agencies Other than MPOs.
The federal Clean Air Act is a potentially powerful regional force that might
affect traffic congestion. That law established air quality standards for all
U.S. metropolitan areas. The federal Environmental Protection Agency
requires state governments to create plans for cleaning up the air in "nonattainment areas" where air pollution exceeds acceptable levels. Nonattainment areas have boundaries that are generally similar to those of
metropolitan and consolidated metropolitan areas. Therefore, a state can set
up a regional organization to coordinate air quality improvement throughout an entire metropolitan area. Moreover, acting through such state-
created agencies, the federal government can override or preempt certain
local ordinances related to air quality. However, part of this function has
now been delegated to MPOs, which are charged with considering the possible air pollution impacts of any transportation facilities they propose and
conforming to the requirements of the Clean Air Amendments Act of 1990.

Vehicle emissions are a primary cause of air pollution. Long average commuting trips in general, and traffic congestion in particular, increase the
emissions discharged into the atmosphere. So air quality improvement
agencies have become concerned with traffic flows, especially in California.
Consequently, the California Air Resources Board has proposed regulations
that would require major changes in driving and commuting behavior over
large territories. For example, it has proposed that a significant fraction of
all vehicles be powered by fuels other than gasoline by the year 2010. Achieving that goal would require enormous changes both in the automobile and
petroleum industries and in household behavior. There are thirty-six air districts in California charged with enforcing these regulations in collaboration
with their local MPOs.

Such federally empowered agencies could (in theory) implement many
of the potentially most effective anticongestion tactics at regional levels. For
example, they could impose peak-hour road pricing and parking charges
throughout a metropolitan area. Thus federally rooted antipollution agencies are potentially one of the strongest instruments for carrying out regional
anticongestion tactics. In November 1998 the California Air Resources
Board amended existing low-emission vehicle regulations to extend passenger car emission standards to light trucks and sport utility vehicles, starting
in the year 2004.[24]

Such agencies could adopt and carry out regional anticongestion tactics
effectively only if two conditions prevail. First, each agency's leaders must be
convinced that specific regional anticongestion tactics are absolutely necessary

to reduce their air pollution to acceptable levels. This is not a forgone conclusion. There has been so little experience with regional application of these tactics that no one can be sure just how they would affect air quality. Moreover, there is always a lot of resistance to regional approaches, and so a strong case must be made that these tactics would greatly reduce air pollution before any regional air quality improvement agency will adopt them. Developing such a case is an important task for proponents of anticongestion tactics.

Second, most of the citizenry must voluntarily accept and follow these regulations. Past U.S. experience has repeatedly shown that strong and widespread citizen rejection of laws that require major behavioral changes may severely undermine their effectiveness. This can occur even if the agencies concerned have unchallenged legal authority to pass and enforce such laws. If many citizens ignore or flaunt such laws, it may be impossible for these agencies to enforce them. That happened in connection with the prohibition of alcoholic beverages during the 1920s and early 1930s. It is now happening concerning the importation and use of illegal drugs. Even massive, federally financed efforts to prevent illegal drug distribution and use have not come close to stopping either. A similar defiance of laws governing vehicle speed limits occurs throughout the nation every day.

Thus widespread citizen opposition to severe limitations on the design, purchase, and use of cars and trucks could very well undermine the effectiveness of federal efforts to impose those limitations. Such opposition would soon be communicated to elected officials, who could restrict the powers of air quality improvement agencies to pass and enforce those laws. However, it is too soon to predict that this will actually happen if a regional air quality improvement agency tries to implement unpopular anticongestion tactics. Despite possible citizen resistance, the already legally established powers of such agencies to act across an entire metropolitan area provide a potentially effective means of carrying out regional anticongestion tactics.

Nonstructural Arrangements

As opposed to the structural type, nonstructural arrangements are much weaker since they have less power to compel their participants to engage in a certain set of activities. Therefore, these forms are more likely to be acceptable for mainly land-use-oriented tactics.

Voluntary Cooperation among Autonomous Local Governments. This is the least satisfactory type of arrangement, with the fewest applications for fighting congestion, because it cannot compel local governments to coordinate their behavior closely or to monitor and adjust that behavior. Yet voluntary cooperation through arrangements such as councils of government could coordinate upgrading of local streets, timing of traffic signals, conversion of local streets to one-way flows, and incident management strategies, as well as possibly negotiating and coordinating consistent land uses. However, where anticongestion policies require controversial decisions—for example, benefits and costs often have to be allocated across many communities—this arrangement does not work well.

Comprehensive Plan Preparation as Part of a State-Mandated Planning Process. Several states require all their local governments to draw up comprehensive land use plans as part of a statewide planning system. These systems are designed to achieve state goals pertaining to the environment, transportation, open space, and housing. The state legislature first establishes broad goals and then directs all local, county, or regional governments to draw up comprehensive plans pursuing those goals within their own boundaries. This process is normally managed by a state-level agency. It has final coordination and approval power over the plans drawn up by lower-level bodies. By combining state-level goal setting and coordination with detailed local or regional level planning, this process uses the best traits of governmental bodies at each level. By late 2000 such processes had been adopted by Hawaii, Maine, Oregon, Florida, New Jersey, Maryland, Pennsylvania (at the county level), Rhode Island, Tennessee, and Washington.[25] It is separate from the MPO processes in these states but may be coordinated with the MPOs.

Such a comprehensive planning process could be used to carry out regional anticongestion policies under some circumstances. One such policy is confining all future urban development to average gross residential densities above some minimum level—say, 2,500 persons per square mile. This would shorten average commuting journeys compared with those in areas with much lower densities. A state could adopt such a minimum-density policy for all its metropolitan areas. Other anticongestion policies this process might entail are clustering high-density housing near rapid transit and commuter rail stations, stimulating formation of transportation management associations, encouraging more people to work at home, and instituting an areawide "cash-out" program related to free parking provided by employers.

Private Civic and Policy-Promotion Agencies. Americans have long been noted for forming associations to achieve joint purposes. As Alexis de Tocqueville pointed out, "In no country in the world has the principle of association been more successfully used or applied to a greater multitude of objects than in America."[26] One type especially important in changing public policy has been the regional civic organization that transcends individual community boundaries. An example is the United Way organizations that raise and distribute charitable contributions across the nation. In terms of organizations that work to address traffic congestion, examples include the San Francisco Bay Area Council, Chicago Metropolis 2020, and the greater New York Regional Planning Association.

This type of organization has three principal advantages in creating a regional basis for anticongestion policies. First, it can draw together members of both private and public organizations, including business firms, labor unions, nonprofit associations, universities, government agencies, and public legislatures and executives. That is to say, it can provide a forum in which members of these groups come together and discuss joint concerns outside their official organizations.

Second, it can establish any geographic jurisdiction its members desire, including entire metropolitan areas. This can be done by a mere declaration of purpose; it requires no official approval by anyone else.

Third, such an agency can take controversial stands without making its individual members commit themselves to those stands. Each member can claim that "the organization" did it or blame all the other members. This permits such an organization to take much more controversial collective positions on issues than many of its members would be willing to endorse individually in public. Hence this kind of entity is an ideal vehicle for changing public opinion to support some controversial new policy. It can espouse innovative positions ahead of existing public opinion, without exposing its individual members to accusations of ignoring that opinion. That is why so many regions have adopted this form for conducting "visioning" processes to formulate very long range plans for future growth and development.[27]

The two obvious disadvantages of such organizations are that they have little or no money and no governmental powers. Hence they have almost no ability to actually carry out whatever public policies they support, and their roles are confined to influencing public opinion and persuading those who do have money and power to adopt the policies they favor. They can therefore act as agents of change by convincing the public and its leaders that some problem is serious enough to demand concerted action; formulating, analyzing, and discussing possible remedies; and promoting those they believe would be most effective.

The three aforementioned functions are all vital to the acceptance of regional approaches to traffic congestion. It is crucial that some type of regional association outside of government strongly supports such strategies if they are to be adopted anywhere. If such a regionwide organization already exists to deal with other issues, perhaps it can expand its functions to cope with traffic congestion, too. Or else a new organization should be formed for this purpose. The membership should consist of top-level officials in large establishments and other citizens' groups in the metropolitan area, plus governmental leaders who can influence key transportation and land use policies.

Both private- and public-sector leaders should be involved from the start. Such an organization needs an initial convener to interview relevant stakeholders to determine who should be involved in its deliberations. After an "inner circle" of possible participants has been identified, there needs to be a preliminary written statement of the problems on which to focus and possible selection of a professional facilitator. If the consensus-building process is carried out skillfully within clearly defined written rules, the participants will become unified by sharing in the deliberative analysis of congestion problems, examination of possible solutions, and arrival at final recommendations. The whole process should be oriented toward creating a consensus across several issues and subissues (dealing with more than one increases opportunities for different participants to achieve positive gains from the joint result) in which all—or nearly all—participants regard themselves as better off than without any agreement. Their common experience in the process, plus the benefits they gain from the final agreement, will secure their emotional commitment to supporting their final recommendations in the face of the inevitable resistance. Then there should be one or more rounds of having the participants review the consensus with their separate organizations, and possibly modifying it to take account of suggested changes. Finally, the organization should launch a concerted campaign of information and political pressure urging adoption of the regional approaches it recommends.[28]

It is important to note that when such organizations are formed to consider a region's future, they typically define their subject matter beyond just traffic congestion, including land use and environmental issues as well. This shifts the focus of their deliberations away from traffic congestion to broader issues on which it is much more difficult to gain public support for regional policies than it would be concerning traffic congestion alone.

The above analysis of how to organize to promote regional anticongestion policies does not imply that congestion can best be attacked by creating a single regional agency as the czar over all anticongestion policies. Instead, it might be desirable to have different congestion-reducing policies run by different local and regional agencies that organized themselves in ways best suited to their individual tasks. But if several anticongestion agencies are created at the regional level, they should certainly be linked through both formal and informal relationships.

Prospects and Outlook for Regional Anticongestion Agencies

In almost every U.S. metropolitan area, attempts to implement effective regional anticongestion tactics will be met with resistance. Any organizations created for this purpose could work well only if they exercised authority and powers now divided among many local and state government agencies—and most agency officials are likely to strongly oppose any reduction in their present powers. Local governments are particularly loath to yield any control over their land uses to outsiders. Indeed, the main function of many U.S. local governments is to control land use patterns so as to benefit their existing homeowning residents by maintaining or increasing the market values of their property.[29] Yet many tactics for reducing peak-hour congestion would require shifting at least some local power over land use to a regional agency.

To a great extent, the MPO structure has accomplished this goal regarding the planning and construction of major infrastructure investments. But the authority of MPOs does not extend to operating those investments or controlling other types of anticongestion policies, as noted earlier. Hence additional regional efforts are necessary to make use of all potentially effective anticongestion tactics.

The most important actor in the potential development of effective regional agencies is the state. State governments encompass entire metropolitan areas or large parts thereof; hence they should not exhibit the same narrow parochialism as local governments. In most metropolitan areas, the territory of regional agencies would lie entirely within a single state.[30] And only state governments have the constitutional authority to create such regional agencies. Unfortunately, most state governments have been unwilling to do so to combat traffic congestion. In fact, most states have not embraced federal transportation efforts and devolved sufficient powers and responsibilities to metropolitan areas.[31]

One reason is that such an agency would have to be given powers that are now partly exercised by other state agencies—particularly state DOTs. Officials in those other agencies would be reluctant to give up any of their present authority. In addition, no state legislature is willing to incur the wrath of most local governments unless the legislators have strong incentives to do so. State legislators are themselves elected from local districts, and they are often linked personally and politically to existing local governments. Moreover, since state representatives are seldom elected from districts large enough to encompass an entire metropolitan area, their viewpoints are also quite parochial.

At the same time, certain gains might motivate state legislators to establish regional anticongestion agencies over the objections of local governments. The main gain would be reducing traffic congestion in the long run, but this positive outcome would be spread over residents and firms in all parts of the metropolitan area. For each beneficiary, it would be only a small part of the general benefits received from all state government actions. Hence few beneficiaries would decide how to vote for state legislative candidates on the basis of this issue alone.

In contrast, the potential loss of local sovereignty from the creation of such regional agencies would be seen by many local officials as a major threat to their welfare. So how each state legislator voted on this issue would heavily influence the amount of support he or she received from local officials at the next election. In the minds of most state legislators, the potential loss of support caused by their favoring creation of strong regional agencies would outweigh the gains from reducing traffic congestion.

This does not mean states will never create effective regional anticongestion agencies, simply that such actions will be rare. Even when they occur, some resistance will persist within both state and local governments. Underlying that resistance is the fundamental belief among many citizens that reducing traffic congestion is far less important than pursuing other social or personal goals. Therefore, if reducing congestion means they must change behavior they have cherished for other reasons, they may prefer to endure congestion—while, of course, still complaining loudly about it.

What would cause the relevant public officials to adopt regional tactics in spite of the above drawbacks? First, traffic congestion must become so widespread and so intolerable that a large fraction of the metropolitan area's citizenry regards it as a crisis. Second, key state and local officials—especially the governor—must believe that carrying out regional anticongestion tactics is essential to remedying this crisis. Third, there must be some credible institutional structure available through which to implement those regional tactics.

Need for a Crisis

In a few metropolitan areas, peak-hour congestion is so bad that reducing it is widely perceived as the central issue facing local governments. Hence the governor and state legislators are strongly motivated to appear to be doing something about this problem in order to be reelected.[32] Otherwise, they are unlikely to act effectively since the political leaders in a democracy fear asking the citizenry to make fundamental changes in established institutions or behavior. People can be induced to do so without enormous resistance only if they believe they must to alleviate a crisis that is either already present or imminent. Elected officials are, in turn, unwilling to ask the public to make basic changes unless they believe the public thinks itself threatened by such a crisis.

Most such crises involve some sudden disruption of normal life. They must pose serious, obvious, and immediate threats to the welfare of a large percentage of the population. But peak-hour traffic congestion does not change dramatically over night; rather, it gets a little worse each day. Since each commuter's route differs from those traveled by most others, people do not all encounter the same degree of congestion simultaneously. Thus there is no widespread common perception concerning just how bad traffic congestion has become as of any particular date.

In 1999 Georgia governor Roy Barnes was faced with such a crisis in the Atlanta metropolitan area. By the end of the 1990s, only Los Angeles and San Francisco metropolitan area drivers experienced more congestion each day than those in Atlanta.[33] Air pollution had become so severe that the region was faced with the loss of millions of dollars in federal transportation funds, as mandated by the federal Clean Air Act. As a result, the 1999 governor's race in Georgia was dominated by discussions of growth and transportation where Barnes made finding a metropolitan solution a cornerstone of his campaign.[34] After his election, he created the Georgia Regional Transportation Authority (GRTA) and gave it broad powers to improve air quality, curb sprawl, and address traffic congestion by, among other things, giving it the ability to veto state and local transportation plans.[35]

But generally, without any sudden crisis to galvanize public officials into action, they are reluctant to ask citizens to make the painful changes necessary to alleviate peak-hour congestion. True, after congestion has become bad enough long enough, more and more citizens and their political leaders may decide it has passed some invisible threshold of acceptability. If enough citizens reach this conclusion, some elected officials will propose the kinds of actions described in this chapter.

Need for Belief that Regional Remedies Are Essential

Even when congestion reaches crisis stage in metropolitan areas, key officials must be convinced that strong regional agencies are essential to addressing the problem. Otherwise they will prefer other approaches that do not require such drastic behavioral changes. The belief that regional remedies are essential is not widespread.[36]

A critical function of public-private anticongestion groups is to nurture and strengthen this belief in the minds of relevant public and private leaders. This is probably best accomplished by emphasizing the inadequacy of existing congestion-related policies formulated and carried out by highly fragmented local governments. Making this point will also require linking traffic congestion problems to the nature of land use and related decisions controlled by fragmented governments. The general public needs to become more aware of the fact that traffic congestion is closely tied to the prevalence of low-density settlement patterns encouraged by local government land use planning decisions—and by the public's own settlement preferences.

Need for Credible Regional Institutions

Even if the first two conditions exist, one or more credible institutional structures for implementing regional congestion remedies must also exist within the metropolitan area. The possible forms of such structures were discussed earlier. This condition implies that all key segments of the metropolitan area must lie within a single state because almost all regional bodies with effective action powers can only be created by state legislatures. If a metropolitan area is in two or more states, it will be extremely difficult to create any institutional structures able to implement anticongestion tactics throughout the region. Rivalries among political leaders and agencies in different states and the legal difficulties of creating interstate compacts will greatly complicate that task.

This condition also implies that both regional structures and the widespread belief that they are essential should be created before traffic congestion produces a crisis. Then when such a crisis appears, regional policy responses can be launched immediately. That will permit effective action to start before public concern with the crisis wanes. This is critical because the public's attention rarely remains focused on any one issue very long.[37] Therefore, persons promoting effective anticongestion tactics should start building a foundation for regional responses well before congestion reaches maximum intensity.

In the long run, severe peak-hour traffic congestion can only be effectively combated with the aid of at least some regional anticongestion tactics. But it is extremely difficult to create the political support and institutional structures necessary for such an approach. To do so, proponents will have to overcome massive resistance from local governments, existing state agencies, and a majority of citizens who do not want to stop commuting alone in their cars.

To accomplish this task, proponents will have to act in advance of any widely perceived congestion crises. Achieving success also demands persisting—perhaps for many years—in spite of continual failure. After all, not one of the more than 340 metropolitan areas in the United States has yet adopted a comprehensive, regionally based strategy for attacking traffic congestion, insofar as we know. This does not mean that all efforts to achieve a regional approach should be abandoned as hopeless. But it does mean that persons attempting such efforts must be prepared to endure failure for a long time. Their motto must be, "Never give up!"

Conclusion

Because traffic congestion is essentially a regional phenomenon, regional approaches are necessary to coping with it as effectively as possible. Up to now in the United States, the complexity of such approaches and their conflict with deeply embedded attitudes favoring fragmented local governance over land uses have both impeded effective anticongestion policies. The time has come not only to reexamine these obstacles to effective action but to overcome them by adopting truly regional policies dealing with key aspects of the many forces affecting traffic congestion.

Notes

1. For a comprehensive discussion of the causes of congestion, its dynamics, and its relative incidence in various parts of the country, see Anthony Downs, *Still Stuck in Traffic: Coping with Peak-Hour Traffic Congestion* (Brookings, 2004).

2. See Bruce Katz, ed., *Reflections on Regionalism* (Brookings, 2000).

3. Anthony Downs, "The Devolution Revolution: Why Congress is Shifting a Lot of Power to the Wrong Levels," Policy Brief 3 (Brookings, 1996).

4. For more discussion on federal efforts to support metropolitan transportation decisionmaking, see Puentes and Bailey, chapter 6 in this volume.

5. The main exception concerns some policies adopted by very large central cities.

6. Raising gasoline taxes would be most effective if done by the federal government, rather than by state governments, because many metropolitan areas contain parts of more than one state or are quite close to another state. If one state increased its gasoline tax to a level much higher than that in a nearby state, motorists would patronize service stations in the states with the lower prices. That would vitiate the impact of the tax increase and economically injure service stations in the state that raised taxes. Among the metropolitan areas or consolidated regions that cross state lines are New York City, Boston, Philadelphia, Chicago, Minneapolis-St. Paul, St. Louis, Kansas City, Cincinnati, Providence, Washington D.C., and Portland, Oregon. Only states in which major population centers are relatively distant from neighboring states could successfully avoid this problem. Probably the most important among such states are California, Florida, and Texas, in which a sizable fraction of U.S. population growth has occurred since 1970.

7. Kathryn A. Foster, "Regionalism on Purpose," Policy Focus Report (Cambridge, Mass.: Lincoln Institute of Land Policy, 2001), p. 18.

8. Martin Wachs and Jennifer Dill, "Regionalism in Transportation and Air Quality: History, Interpretation, and Insights for Regional Governance," in *Governance and Opportunity in Metropolitan America,* edited by Alan A. Altshuler and others (Washington: National Academy Press, 1999), pp. 253–80.

9. Seth Benjamin, John Kincaid, and Bruce McDowell, "MPOs and Weighted Voting," *Intergovernmental Perspective* 20, no. 2 (1994): 31–36.

10. Todd Goldman and Elizabeth Deakin, "Regionalism through Partnerships? Metropolitan Planning Since ISTEA," *Berkeley Planning Journal* 14 (2000): 46–75.

11. Wachs and Dill, "Regionalism in Transportation."

12. Brian D. Taylor, "Unjust Equity: An Examination of California's Transportation Development Act," *Transportation Research Record,* no. 1297 (1991): 85–92.

13. These evaluations include U.S. Advisory Commission on Intergovernmental Relations, *MPO Capacity: Improving the Capacity of Metropolitan Planning Organizations to Help Implement National Transportation Policies* (Washington, 1995), p. A-130; W. M. Lyons, "The FTA-FHWA MPO Reviews—Planning Practice under the ISTEA and the CAAA," Paper 94-0639 (Department of Transportation, 1994); and Paul S. Dempsey, Andrew Goetz, and Carl Larson, *Metropolitan Planning Organizations: An Assessment of the Transportation Planning Process. Report to Congress* (National Center for Intermodal Transportation, University of Denver and Mississippi State University, 2000).

14. Federal Highway Administration and Federal Transit Administration, "The Transportation Planning Capacity Building Program" (www.mcb.fhwa.dot.gov [February 2005]).

15. Foster, "Regionalism on Purpose," p. 1.

16. Ibid, p. 9.

17. Ted Mondale and William Fulton, "Managing Metropolitan Growth: Reflections on the Twin Cities Experience," case study prepared for the Center on Urban and Metropolitan Policy (Brookings, September 2003).

18. Operating through the Bay Area Toll Authority.

19. Valerie Briggs, "New Regional Organizations," *ITS Quarterly* 2, no. 3 (1999): 35–46.

20. Jonathan Gifford, "Introduction to Regional Operating Organizations," In *Organizing for Regional Transportation Operations Conference Proceedings* (McClean, Va.: Booz, Allen, Hamilton, January 27, 2003), p. 10.

21. Some parts of interstate highways do charge tolls, mainly portions incorporated into the system from preexisting toll roads. Examples are the Pennsylvania Toll Road, the Ohio Toll Road, the toll road system around Chicago, and the parts of Interstate 95 through Delaware. However, the federal government is now very reluctant to permit placing tolls on any additional parts of the interstate system.

22. Alex Taft, "The Metropolitan Planning Organization Role in Management and Operations," AMPO White Paper (Washington: Association of Metropolitan Planning Organizations, 2001). It is also important to note that all three reauthorization bills currently before Congress contain a variety of provisions for enhancing and facilitating systems management and operations activities.

23. For a study of bureaucratic resistance to change, see Anthony Downs, *Inside Bureaucracy* (Little, Brown, 1967).

24. California Air Resources Board, "LEV II—Amendments to California's Low-Emission Vehicle Regulations" (www.arb.ca.gov/msprog/levprog/levii/factsht.htm [November 23, 2004]).

25. This list is taken from page 17 of David R. Godschalk, "Smart Growth Efforts around the Nation," *Popular Government* 66, no. 1 (2000): 12–20. Godschalk included Georgia and Vermont in his list, but they have been omitted here because local government participation in their plans is voluntary.

26. Alexis de Toqueville, *Democracy in America*, vol. 1 (Knopf, 1972), p. 198. This tendency was more recently celebrated in Robert N. Bellah and others, *Habits of the Heart: Individualism and Commitment in American Life* (Harper and Row, 1985).

27. The processes most useful for creating and managing such organizations are comprehensively analyzed in Lawrence Susskind, Sarah McKearnan, and Jennifer Thomas-Larmer, *The Consensus Building Handbook: A Comprehensive Guide to Reaching Agreement* (Thousand Oaks, Ca.: Sage Publications, 1999).

28. This description of the consensus-building process was taken in part from Susskind, McKearnan, and Thomas-Larmer, *The Consensus Building Handbook*.

29. This point is best made in William Fischel, *The Home-Voter Hypothesis* (Harvard University Press, 2001).

30. However, those metropolitan areas that encompass parts of more than one state include some of the largest in the nation, such as New York, Chicago, Philadelphia, Boston, Washington, and Minneapolis-St. Paul.

31. See Katz, Puentes, and Bernstein, chapter 2 in this volume.

32. For a detailed analysis of how this arrangement works in a democracy, and why it is an advantage of democracy over other systems, see Anthony Downs, *An Economic Theory of Democracy* (Harper and Row, 1957).

33. David Schrank and Tim Lomax, *2003 Annual Urban Mobility Report* (College Station, Texas Transportation Institute, 2003), exhibit A-14.

34. Orlyn Lockard, "Solving the 'Tragedy': Transportation, Pollution and Regionalism in Atlanta," *Virginia Environmental Law Journal* 19, no. 1 (2000): 161–95.

35. Hank Dittmar, Barbara McCann, and Gloria Ohland, *Realizing GRTA's Potential: Lessons from Around the Country* (Washington: Surface Transportation Policy Project, 1999). The crisis in Atlanta was so bad that even the Georgia DOT and the Atlanta Regional Commission (the area's MPO) publicly supported GRTA.

36. However, it is important to note that a 2000 General Accounting Office survey of over 1,500 cities and counties found that more than eight out of ten respondents support federal incentives for communities to pursue regional solutions to manage growth. General Accounting Office, *Community Development: Local Growth Issues—Federal Opportunities and Challenges*, GAO/RCED-00-178 (2000).

37. See Anthony Downs, "Up and Down with Ecology: The Issue-Attention Cycle," in *Political Theory and Public Choice: The Selected Essays of Anthony Downs*, vol. 1 (Northampton, Mass.: Edward Elgar), pp. 100–12.

PART FOUR

Meeting Societal Needs in Transportation

8

The Long Journey to Work: A Federal Transportation Policy for Working Families

Evelyn Blumenberg and Margy Waller

Evidence from the 2000 census and other sources indicates that decentralization of economic and residential life remains the dominant growth pattern in the United States. Suburban areas continue to capture the lion's share of population and employment growth. America has rapidly become an "exit ramp" economy with office, retail, and commercial facilities increasingly located on the suburban fringe.[1] Consequently, travel is increasing from suburb to suburb—a far cry from the stereotype of suburbs as simply bedroom communities for workers commuting to traditional downtowns.

Across the 100 largest metropolitan areas, on average, about 22 percent of people work within three miles of the city center and more than 35 percent work more than ten miles from the center. In metropolitan areas such as Los Angeles, Detroit, Tampa, and Chicago, the latter category exceeds 60 percent.[2]

Low-income families have also dispersed, yet many remain concentrated in central-city neighborhoods. Families that live in dense urban neighborhoods can be within a short walk, drive, or bus ride to most destinations. However, for those who live in more isolated residential areas—whether in the central city, rural areas, or suburbs—jobs and services can be remote, particularly for families who do not have access to automobiles.

Years of disinvestment in the inner city, the lack of affordable housing, and residential segregation have contributed to the geographic isolation of the urban poor. While the number of people living in high-poverty neighborhoods declined by 2.4 million in the 1990s, this was primarily due to the strong economic conditions that persisted throughout the decade rather than to changes in transportation policy.[3] The concentration of poverty remains an important public policy concern, one exacerbated by the lack of viable transportation options to meet the changing structure of metropolitan areas. Meanwhile, suburban and rural employment is often many miles from dispersed suburban and rural populations. Thus the transportation challenges facing working families are numerous:

—decentralization of jobs and low-income families away from the central city to low-density suburban neighborhoods reduces the effectiveness of traditional, fixed-route public transportation;

—a high percentage of low-income families remains concentrated in central-city neighborhoods distant from suburban employment opportunities;

—low-income adults without access to automobiles often face lengthy travel times, even within the central city;

—for the suburban and rural poor, access to employment may be the most difficult, especially for those families without automobiles;

—while access to automobiles is very high, even among low-income households, some low-income families have low levels of auto access and remain transit dependent; and

—many low-income families own old and unreliable vehicles and therefore are saddled with the high costs of insurance, repair, maintenance, and other fees.

Numerous studies suggest that improved transportation services can enhance economic outcomes among the poor. However, there is no one-size-fits-all transportation policy for working families. Metropolitan areas are diverse. So too are low-income families, who live in a wide array of neighborhoods and have varied transportation resources. Not surprisingly, therefore, meeting the transportation needs of working families requires a mix of transportation solutions and the federal funding flexibility to creatively pursue varied national, regional, and local policy strategies.

In recent years new sources of federal funds have helped agencies initiate new transit services aimed at moving low-income adults into the labor market. These services need to be evaluated and, if effective, adopted more widely. In contrast, far less policy attention has been devoted to increasing automobile access among the poor. Given the strong connection between cars and employment outcomes, auto ownership programs may be one of the more promising options and worthy of expansion.

Transportation, therefore, links American families and their livelihoods, and, as such, sound transportation policy is also sound economic policy. Of course, transportation policies for working families must be developed in the context of broader efforts to help improve the mobility, economic vitality and environmental quality of twenty-first-century metropolitan America.[4] Federal transportation reform efforts have already ushered in a new era punctuated by innovative and integrated thinking about how transportation connects to other community priorities, such as housing, economic development, and air quality.

Congress has numerous opportunities to improve low-income transportation policy as part of several federal laws. Both the federal surface transportation law and the work-based welfare law have long since expired, although Congress has extended both many times to keep them in force. Also awaiting reauthorization are the Assets for Independence Act, the national demonstration of Individual Development Accounts, and the Workforce Investment Act.[5]

This chapter examines the transportation and job access challenges facing low-income workers and welfare recipients. It also offers specific policy responses to those challenges based on a menu of options, including fixed-route transit, paratransit and other door-to-door services, and automobile programs. Implicit in these recommendations is the assumption that these programs and services should be developed collaboratively, allowing regional and local stakeholders to collectively define and develop programs that are in the best interest of their communities.

Background: Work-Based Welfare Policy and the Transportation Needs of Working Families

The work-based welfare law passed by Congress and signed by former president Bill Clinton in 1996 created Temporary Assistance to Needy Families (TANF) block grants to states. States use the $16.5 billion per year in block grant funds to provide cash assistance, child care, training, and other welfare-to-work services to welfare recipients and low-income working families.[6] The 1996 law created work participation requirements for states and welfare recipients, as well as a time limit on receipt of federally funded assistance. These changes in welfare policy motivated policymakers and researchers to focus on the transportation barriers faced by welfare recipients and low-income workers.

After signing the historic welfare law in 1996, former president Clinton proposed several new transportation initiatives to assist low-income families in getting and keeping jobs. As part of the proposal for reauthorization of the federal surface transportation act (the Transportation Equity Act for the Twenty-First Century, or TEA-21), the Clinton administration recommended the creation of a new transportation program that would target additional funds to agencies providing transit services to welfare recipients and other low-income workers.

Elected officials of both parties, especially local leaders, advocated for the proposed new transportation funds because they were concerned that low-income residents would have difficulty finding work unless they had better access to suburban jobs. Pennsylvania senators Arlen Specter and Rick Santorum cosponsored an amendment to the transportation bill in 1998 to create what became known as the Job Access and Reverse Commute (JARC) program. At an event announcing the amendment, then mayor of Philadelphia Ed Rendell said, "The jobs that are available for which [welfare recipients] qualify are out in the suburbs. The people who need these jobs are located so far away and do not own automobiles. Our transportation system is inadequate to get them out to the suburbs."[7]

The JARC program authorizes up to $150 million annually for a national competition to support new or expanded transportation services that connect parents on welfare and other low-income workers to jobs and employment-related services. "JARC is intended to establish a coordinated regional approach to job access challenges."[8] According to the program design, the Department of Transportation (DOT) awards 60 percent of program funds to applicants from urbanized areas with populations of at least 200,000. The local metropolitan planning organization (MPO) must approve proposals submitted to the DOT. Another 20 percent is awarded to state-selected applicants from urbanized areas with populations below 200,000. The remaining 20 percent is awarded to state-selected applicants from rural areas. The federal statute requires a collaborative planning process among states, MPOs, transportation providers, county welfare and employment agencies, and other relevant stakeholders for funded projects.

Members of Congress added the JARC program to TEA-21 on the theory that inadequate transportation is a significant barrier to employment for the poor. They argued that improved public transit and paratransit (usually provided with vans) would increase the mobility of low-income adults and better enable them to find and retain employment. In the JARC statutory language, Congress acknowledged that public transit is not a practical or cost-effective solution for all low-income households.[9] Therefore, policymakers also adopted program changes to assist poor families with car ownership: for example, TANF block grant funds can now be used to purchase cars and auto insurance, a change that makes it possible for welfare recipients to own reliable cars and still be eligible for food, child care, and health coverage assistance.

Transportation: An Essential Link between Low-Income Workers and Jobs

Generally, three strategies can increase welfare recipients' geographic access to employment: urban reinvestment strategies designed to bring jobs closer to low-income communities; housing mobility strategies that move low-income residents closer to jobs; and transportation-based strategies intended to enhance mobility.[10] Although each strategy has different collateral benefits and costs, transportation policies, if properly targeted, can have a more immediate impact—which is important given the time limits on welfare receipt. Relocation—whether jobs or people—requires longer lead times. And although housing mobility has benefits unrelated to transportation, it can but does not necessarily reduce work commutes. The evidence suggests, therefore, that transportation solutions can provide an essential and, perhaps, more immediate link between low-income workers and employment.

Inadequate Transportation: A Major Barrier to Employment

Many low-income adults, welfare administrators, and employers identify transportation issues as significant barriers to employment. Low-income adults frequently mention the importance of transportation in their work lives. In a study conducted in Illinois, over 25 percent of former welfare recipients interviewed reported problems in getting or paying for transportation to work.[11] A similar study of welfare leavers in North Carolina found that 22 percent of unemployed respondents believed that transportation would be a problem if they were to find employment.[12] An overwhelming 61 percent of long-term welfare recipients in Iowa reported transportation barriers to work.[13]

Welfare administrators and employers also acknowledge the importance of transportation to the success of welfare-to-work programs. In Indiana and California, more than three-quarters of county welfare administrators surveyed reported that transportation is a significant barrier to the self-sufficiency of their clients.[14] In a Minnesota survey, 28 percent of employers identified transportation as the main barrier to hiring and retaining welfare recipients, with rural employers more likely than urban employers to identify transportation as a problem for their workforce.[15]

Finally, many employers report that their entry-level jobs are not accessible by public transit. In 1997 the Economic and Social Research Institute conducted a nationwide survey of employer attitudes toward entry-level workers.[16] The survey included 500 employers in industries that hired a greater than average number of entry-level workers, as well as two smaller samples of 100 each in Los Angeles and Milwaukee. Overall, 36 percent of employers reported entry-level jobs inaccessible by public transit. The subsamples, however, showed substantial variation across metropolitan areas. Only 13 percent of employers in Los Angeles were not accessible by public transit compared to 30 percent in Milwaukee.

Spatial Mismatch between Jobs and Low-Income Workers

The structure of metropolitan areas has gradually changed over time so that a majority of employment and residents are dispersed in suburban neighborhoods distant from the urban core. In 1910 the vast majority of metropolitan residents lived in the central city and only one quarter in the suburbs. Today, nearly two out of three metropolitan residents (62 percent) live in the suburbs.[17] Similarly, employment has also shifted outward toward suburban areas that, as of 1997, were home to 57 percent of metropolitan employment.[18] These trends are also reflected in metropolitan transportation patterns where, since the 1970s, the dominant commute flow has been from suburb to suburb. In 1960 travel within suburbs constituted only 10 percent of commutes.[19] This is far less than the 46-plus percent of all commutes that now begin and end in the suburbs.[20]

As economies and opportunity decentralize and the working poor remain disproportionately centralized, a "spatial mismatch" arises between jobs and people in metropolitan areas.[21] In suburbs entry-level jobs abound in manufacturing, wholesale trade, and retailing—and hold out opportunities for people with basic education and skills. However, the absence of viable transportation options—combined with persistent residential racial segregation and a lack of affordable suburban housing—effectively cuts off many inner-city workers from regional labor markets. Quite literally, low rates of car ownership and inadequate public transit keep job seekers in the urban core or central city from reaching many suburban jobs. Often, inner-city workers, hobbled by distance and poor information networks, are unaware of job openings outside of their neighborhoods.

The spatial mismatch is frequently cited as a primary explanation for the transportation barriers faced by poor families.[22] Many scholars, beginning with Kain in 1968, have provided compelling evidence that the spatial separation of housing and employment exacerbates the poverty of inner-city blacks.[23] Low-wage jobs are increasingly located further out in the urban periphery, and competition for the remaining central-city jobs can be fierce.[24]

Although the spatial mismatch hypothesis has been put to the test by a host of skeptical scholars, empirical support for the concept remains. For this reason, the spatial mismatch hypothesis has become the chief framework for understanding the transportation needs of all low-income, central-city residents, including welfare recipients. In fact, Congress cited the spatial mismatch hypothesis to justify funding of JARC, declaring that "Congress finds that . . . two-thirds of all new jobs are in the suburbs, whereas three quarters of welfare recipients live in rural areas or central cities."[25]

Work-based welfare policy has also prompted many scholars and transportation planners to examine the spatial location of welfare recipients and potential low-wage employment opportunities. These studies use maps to illustrate the high concentrations of welfare recipients residing in central cities, the growth in low-wage suburban employment, and, frequently, the weak public transit linkages between central cities and suburbs.[26] In other words, these studies, once again, underscore the relevance of the spatial mismatch hypothesis to low-income, central-city residents including, but not limited to, blacks.

Transportation Problems beyond Central-City Households

For transportation policy purposes, however, it is important to look beyond the spatial mismatch. While many low-income adults live far from employment opportunities, many others live closer to jobs yet still face transportation barriers. Again, 44 percent of the metropolitan poor live in the suburbs.[27] In addition, for low-income adults who remain in the inner city, there are still high concentrations of employment in some places.[28] Although some metropolitan areas—particularly in the Northeast and Midwest—have experienced a dramatic hollowing out of the urban core, this

Table 8-1. Access to Automobiles and Commute Mode, Metropolitan Areas, 2001

Percent

	Income status	
	Non–low income	Low income
Commute mode		
Personal vehicles	91	88
Transit	6	8
Walk	3	4
Other	1	1
Access to automobiles		
Households with vehicle	95	86

Source: Department of Transportation, *2001 National Household Travel Survey.* Households are considered low income if they have one to two persons and incomes under $10,000; three to four persons and incomes under $20,000; and five-plus persons and incomes under $25,000.

experience is far from universal. The decline in central-city Cleveland or St. Louis looks vastly different from that of Boston, San Francisco, New York, or Minneapolis.[29] Not surprisingly, studies find metropolitan variation in the extent and effects of the spatial mismatch.

However, living and working in the same part of the city, whether in the suburbs or the central city, does not necessarily reduce or eliminate transportation problems. Low-income workers tend to commute relatively short distances, far shorter, on average, than higher-income commuters.[30] Still, most low-income workers find employment outside of their immediate neighborhoods and require some form of reliable transportation by which to commute. Contrary to popular perception, most low-income adults commute by car (see table 8-1). Those workers fortunate to have access to automobiles can reach many employment opportunities within a reasonable commute time, regardless of where they live.

But not all low-wage workers have access to automobiles. Auto ownership rates vary substantially by income and race or ethnicity. Data from the 2000 census show that 10 percent of all households do not have vehicles, and those without vehicles are more likely to be in the lowest income brackets. Households with incomes below $25,000 make up 65 percent of households without vehicles.[31] In addition, blacks are overrepresented among zero-vehicle households: they constitute 12 percent of all households but 35 percent of households without cars.[32] Poor workers who are dependent on public transit—even when traveling within the central city—may live close to bus stops but often face lengthy commutes resulting from long waits at transit stops, cumbersome and time-consuming transfers, and infrequent service during off-peak hours.[33]

For the suburban and rural poor, access to employment may be most difficult, especially for those families without automobiles.[34] While most jobs are in the suburbs, they tend to be dispersed over large areas and can be inaccessible to low-income residential neighborhoods. Similarly, rural employment is often many miles from a dispersed rural population. Lower densities in these areas typically do not support the extensive transit networks found in many central cities, forcing most rural and suburban low-income commuters to rely on personal vehicles. Those without cars, however, can be the most isolated from employment.

Even for those low-income residents facing the central-city–suburb mismatch, policy solutions must consider the difficulty of traveling to distant, unfamiliar destinations. Long-distance travel on public transit is unlikely to be the best option for some low-income adults. Travel on transit from central cities to suburbs can be time-consuming, unreliable, and inconvenient. Single parents may have the most difficulty with these trips given that paid work is in addition to household responsibilities that they must manage without the help of a spouse. For example, a mother who takes two buses and more than an hour to get to a suburban job is in no position to depart quickly to pick up a sick child at school. Nor does transit easily accommodate the need to "trip chain," to make multiple stops at the child care center, the grocery store, and so forth.

Access to Reliable Transportation Improves Employment Outcomes

Numerous scholars find that reliable transportation leads to increased access to employment, higher earnings, and greater employment stability among the poor. The most compelling evidence centers on the positive relationship between access to automobiles and employment rates, hours worked, and mean monthly earnings.[35] Low-income households without cars are also more likely to experience unmet food and housing needs and have greater difficulty traveling for medical care.[36]

So far, most low-income car ownership programs are relatively new and small, and research evaluating their impact is limited.[37] However, surveys of workers who obtained cars from subsidized car ownership programs report higher wages and better jobs, improved quality of day care, more involvement with family and community, and more frequent participation in worship services.[38] In one study of a car ownership program in Vermont, researchers found that program participation significantly increased the probability of employment, as well as earned income.[39]

The evidence on the relationship between public transit and employment outcomes is more varied. Some studies show that access to public transit has a positive effect on overall employment rates and, more specifically, a moderate effect on transit use and employment rates among welfare recipients.[40] The evidence also suggests that black welfare recipients are much less likely than other recipients to be hired in jobs that are located distant from public transit stops, once again underscoring the negative effect of spatial isolation.[41]

In contrast, a recent study finds that access to fixed-route transit has no association with the employment outcomes of welfare recipients living in six metropolitan areas: Atlanta, Baltimore, Dallas, Denver, Milwaukee, and Portland, Oregon.[42] A study of Dade County, Florida, also shows that access to public transit has no effect on employment rates; however, it positively influences income, suggesting that better transit connections enabled residents to obtain higher-paid employment.[43] Although the magnitude of the effect of public transit on employment is still open for debate, many scholars acknowledge that car ownership is a much more powerful predictor of employment than availability of public transit.[44]

Transportation Services to Support Welfare and Employment Goals

One of the most commonly prescribed transportation remedies for the poor is programs to help facilitate reverse commuting—travel from central cities to the suburbs. In 2000, 9.8 percent of work trips went from the center city to the suburbs—the "reverse commute."[45] To facilitate travel from the urban core out to the suburbs, JARC has a special funding set-aside specifically for reverse commute programs, and many transit agencies are experimenting with a variety of these services.

However, improved reverse commute transit service will only address a small part of the transportation difficulties facing the poor. Currently, most reverse commutes—even among the poor—are made in private vehicles.[46] This is not surprising since fixed-route transit often has difficulty serving the reverse commute. Fixed-route transit works best in the inner city where there are dense clusters of jobs and residents. In the suburbs, employment is less often located adjacent to transit stops, and travel time from the central city is often lengthy.

The challenge for policymakers and planners extends beyond the reverse commute. It lies in targeting scarce funds to where they are most effective and avoiding costly projects that are unlikely to generate results. This challenge is complicated by the fact that there is no one-size-fits-all transportation solution. Improving the mobility of low-income adults requires a mix of transit and auto-related solutions.

Three strategies must be considered. First, enhance existing fixed-route public transit service in dense urban areas to improve mobility and access in neighborhoods where transit use is highest and residents are underserved. Second, provide demand-responsive service in areas where densities are too low to support fixed-route service but high enough to make this kind of service viable. Third, establish automobile ownership programs to assist low-wage workers whose travel needs cannot easily be accommodated by public transit. In fact, cars may be the most cost-effective transportation solution in areas where low residential and employment densities raise the costs of public transit—even demand-responsive service—beyond those of providing personal vehicles. Each approach has both strengths and weaknesses. To minimize the apparent weaknesses, policymakers must carefully craft these programs, drawing lessons from existing program evaluations.

Public Transit

Fixed-route public transit excels, and indeed has numerous advantages, in providing intraurban transportation. The urban core has high densities of jobs and residences and, within the central city, negative car-induced externalities (such as traffic congestion and inadequate parking), which detract from the advantages of private automobiles. In these central-city neighborhoods, low-income people tend to be underserved and could benefit greatly from improved intracity transit services.

In most cities, improvements mean increased investments in urban bus systems that carry the vast majority of low-income riders. A focus on inner-city buses, however, goes against the current mission of most mass transit agencies, where the emphasis is on luring choice suburban riders out of their automobiles and onto commuter rail systems.[47] Figure 8-1 illustrates that low-income transit users (households with incomes of less than $20,000) constitute nearly half of the bus and light-rail riders, while riders with very high household incomes (over $100,000) dominate the commuter rail category.[48]

Reverse commute solutions using fixed-route public transit have been widely attempted; however, these express bus routes can be quite costly for transit systems. The routes that tend to cover a larger share of their expenses

Figure 8-1. Income Distribution by Mode of Transit Users, 2001

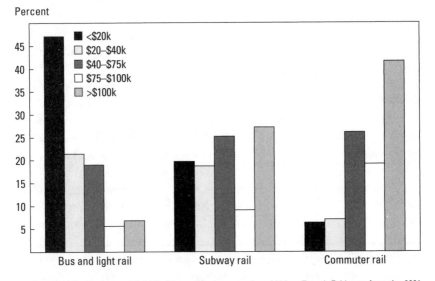

Percent

Source: John Pucher and John L. Renne, "Socioeconomics of Urban Travel: Evidence from the 2001 NHTS," *Transportation Quarterly* 57, no. 3 (2003), p. 63 (based on data from the *2001 National Household Travel Survey*).

from fares are those in which buses are crowded with passengers traveling short distances. Under these conditions, one seat will generate fares from a continuous stream of riders, thereby reducing the subsidy required to operate the service. Reverse commute service can be relatively inexpensive if it is provided as the "back haul" trip of cost-effective inbound service since buses typically must return to the beginning of a route. However, if reverse commute service is provided simply to transport inner-city residents to suburban locations, the costs of providing this express service will be very high. On these long runs, seats turn over less frequently and thus generate less income per mile traveled. Transit agencies may be forced to reduce services on better performing, intracity routes to cover the additional subsidies needed to provide suburban express service.[49]

Paratransit and Demand-Responsive Van Service

To sidestep some of the weaknesses of fixed-route transit, some transit agencies and welfare-to-work providers are implementing paratransit service—flexibly organized vanpools and shuttles that are provided on request. Most of these programs have yet to undergo extensive empirical evaluation. However, experience with paratransit service largely for the elderly and disabled shows that these types of demand-responsive programs can provide door-to-door service rivaling the convenience of the automobile, but at a very high cost. Data from the 2000 National Transit Database present the relative cost-effectiveness of public transit by mode. According to these data, the operating expense per unlinked passenger trip for demand-responsive service is $16.74, approximately eight times as high as that for bus ($2.19).[50] Even reverse commute bus service tends to be less expensive than demand-responsive transit service. In Los Angeles, for example, the cost per rider on even the most expensive reverse commute bus route is far below that of door-to-door van service.[51]

Some communities have successfully reduced the costs of paratransit services by using "mobility managers" who act as brokers for transportation services. In most communities, large public transit agencies are not the only providers of transportation services. Nontransit agencies and organizations, such as social service agencies, community-based organizations, churches and synagogues, and nonprofit organizations also provide transportation services to smaller, more specialized populations such as senior citizens, the disabled, veterans, welfare-to-work clients, and Medicaid recipients. Transportation brokers and mobility managers can provide a single point of contact for all users, rather than relying on case managers in each of the separate systems.

Furthermore, instead of maintaining separate systems for each target population, local governments that consolidate these multiple services can issue contracts by geographic area for greater efficiency. In a recent report, the General Accounting Office identified sixty-two federal programs that fund transportation services to transportation-disadvantaged populations.[52] Coordination across numerous programs is complicated by federal eligibility requirements and rules that vary with respect to eligibility, funding, reporting, safety, and programmatic goals.[53] However, consolidation, when it occurs, can allow transit providers to benefit from economies of scale and reduce costs per ride.[54]

But the problems associated with public transit often apply equally to paratransit solutions—even the best models. It is still difficult for parents to travel long distances to work—with limited means of quick return in an emergency—and to make stops for groceries or child care along the way. Other types of demand-responsive service such as taxis, for example, could help circumvent many of these problems and increase the mobility of the poor. Taxi service, often provided to low-income riders through user-side subsidies, can be cost effective since it relies on existing service.

Automobile Ownership

Increasingly, transportation solutions include improving access to private automobiles for working-poor families. Cars have many obvious benefits, which is why more than 86 percent of all trips—regardless of purpose—are made in automobiles.[55] Cars allow flexibility, accommodating schedules that may include complicated nonwork travel and unforeseen travel requirements. This is particularly important since only 15 percent of all person trips are work trips.[56] Cars also decrease travel time by avoiding long wait times at bus stops, multiple stops, and the circuitous routes of public transit. Cars also allow commuters to more easily travel during off-peak hours—such as nights and weekends—when transit service may be limited. Finally, cars provide door-to-door service, allowing women to avoid isolated bus stops and to travel in greater safety after dark.

Cars contribute to well-known social costs, including traffic congestion, air pollution, sprawl, and the anxiety that accompanies increasing dependence on foreign oil, making some policymakers hesitant to support policies and programs that their constituents might see as contributing to these externalities. Clearly, transportation and environmental policies should broadly address the negative effects of widespread auto use. However, the potential contribution of low-income drivers to congestion and other auto-related problems is minimal. Since land use patterns in the United States dictate that automobiles are necessary for employment success, it seems neither fair nor pragmatic to condemn policies intended to encourage auto ownership among the poor while at the same time expect low-income adults to work their way out of poverty.

Cars can make travel easier and thereby improve employment, health, and other outcomes. However, vehicle ownership is also associated with other thorny issues that specialized auto programs need to address. For example, cars in low-income households are nearly 40 percent older than the average car.[57] These older vehicles are often less than a year away from extensive repairs and can be unreliable. Moreover, with auto ownership comes added costs and responsibilities, such as fuel, maintenance and repairs, auto insurance, and monthly loan payments.

In fact, many low-income adults cannot afford to purchase automobiles and have difficulty either borrowing one or carpooling with others. Frequently, low-income workers do not qualify for traditional automobile loans at prime rates, pricing many low-income workers out of the auto market. Others are forced to pay a premium when purchasing cars from dealers who charge subprime rates.[58]

Despite efforts to eliminate public policies that create a disincentive to car ownership, some state and federal decisions continue to raise the cost of car ownership for the poor. Before implementation of the 1996 welfare law, states could not provide cash assistance or other benefits to families who owned vehicles worth more than $1,500; many states sought federal waivers to allow higher "vehicle asset limits." The 1996 statute gave states the flexibility to change or eliminate the asset limit. Since then federal regulations have clarified that states may abolish the "vehicle asset limit" altogether in some federally funded work support programs. Many policymakers support this strategy, asserting that poor families should not have to choose between car ownership that enables the work commute and the receipt of work support services intended to help parents get and keep jobs.[59]

Most states have responded to these options favorably. All states raised or eliminated the vehicle asset limit for cash assistance. In addition, some states have eliminated the vehicle asset limitation for at least one vehicle per household or worker for other work support services provided with TANF funds. States have also liberalized their asset rules, including car rules, in Medicaid; twenty-one states have no asset test in their Medicaid programs for parents, and forty-four states have no asset test in their programs for children.[60] However, several states still maintain vehicle asset limitations, some set at a level well below the purchase price of a reliable vehicle. For example, nine states have retained the federal policy for food stamps, leaving the vehicle asset limit in place by counting the value of cars that exceed $4,560. Seven other states have increased the asset limit for the first car to between $8,000 and $15,000. By contrast, the vehicle asset limit would have to be $12,200 in order to have the same purchasing power that it had when it was set at $4,500 in 1977.[61]

Despite the difficulties associated with auto ownership, policies to increase access to private vehicles among the poor are essential. In central cities the problems associated with not having personal vehicles are at best only partly addressed by effective public transit systems. And in rural or suburban areas, where public transit is less available and less viable, cars may be the only realistic option.

Transportation Agenda to Support Welfare Policy and Low-Income Working Families

TEA-21 and its predecessor, the Intermodal Surface Transportation Efficiency Act, marked a dramatic change in federal transportation policy. In metropolitan areas across the country, that change is apparent in many tangible ways. More funding has been allocated to transportation alternatives, more attention has been paid to repairing and maintaining existing transportation infrastructure, and more integrated thinking has been initiated about the connection between transportation and other community priorities such as air quality, housing, and economic development. Moreover, these changes reflect the shift in market and demographic realities of the country.

Nevertheless, federal transportation policy must go much further in developing and maintaining transportation services for the working poor and those making the move from welfare to work. The JARC program and innovative use of TANF funds for transportation have created many new, if small-scale, services designed to overcome transportation barriers. Still, lack of adequate and affordable transportation remains a primary barrier to work for many low-income people.

Additional funds are necessary to meet the transportation needs of the disadvantaged. But the funds will do little good unless they can be flexibly deployed to address the diverse transportation needs of working-poor families whose access to employment and services varies significantly by metropolitan area, neighborhood, and transportation resources. The most effective plans likely will evolve through regional and local planning and coordination followed by rigorous program evaluation.

In this context of overall flexibility, transportation investments should support a menu of options, including improved public transit where it is an efficient and cost-effective solution; reorganized and streamlined demand-responsive service (vans, shuttles, and taxi programs); and subsidized car ownership. Moreover, the time is right for action. There are a number of program areas that present federal policymakers with clear opportunities to address the transportation barriers faced by working-poor families.

Surface Transportation Law

Since enacted, the JARC program has provided funding for many new transportation initiatives; however, it is underfunded and should be strengthened. In addition, public transit policy can be improved to better serve low-income and transit-dependent workers and welfare recipients.

Increase Funding for the JARC Program. The appropriation from TEA-21 is inadequate to meet the need for transportation assistance to low-income workers, and unfortunately, the fiscal year 2003 budget cut discretionary funding in the program below the level of grants made in previous years.

This need is exacerbated by recent state decisions to reduce or eliminate TANF-funded transportation services. In 2002 states spent $584 million in TANF and state matching funds on transportation, but some, such as Arkansas, Arizona, Montana, and Tennessee, recently cut these funds as a result of state budget difficulties and caseload increases during the recession.[62] Furthermore, the president's JARC program budget request for 2005 does not adjust for inflation.

Retain Competitive Grant Process. In addition, President Bush's proposal to reauthorize TEA-21 devolves administration of the JARC program to states, eliminating the national competition for funds. Turning the program into a formula grant to states will not increase the number of people served. Unless Congress significantly increases the funding level and provides clarification that states must distribute the funds using a formula that considers local needs, state administration may not work. Furthermore, the president's proposal would also require state administration of transportation funds for disabled and elderly persons. This programmatic approach could lead to consolidated state block grants for transportation assistance, blending the funding for targeted needy populations. Since all of these underserved populations need more assistance to overcome transportation barriers, pitting them against one another in the state budget process may result in underfunding one group as a result of the political popularity, or lobbying strength, of another. Analysis of the federal block grants enacted in 1982 shows that states substituted other criteria for income eligibility, reallocated funds that had been targeted to urban areas, and reduced costs by eliminating service components and standards.[63]

Establish an Equitable JARC State-Local Match and Eliminate Earmarking. Congress should also reduce the local 50 percent funding match requirement to 20 percent, which is consistent with the match for most other federal transportation programs. Although it helps facilitate interagency collaboration, the 50 percent match creates difficulties for some agencies that, in an era of state and local budget deficits, have had difficulty finding local funding matches. Finally, Congress should discontinue the earmarking of funds since this practice undercuts requirements for local planning coordination.

Allow More Flexible Use of JARC Funds for On-Demand Services. Increased flexibility in the use of JARC funds could facilitate the consolidation of paratransit services and, therefore, the better utilization of existing vehicle capacity. For example, the JARC program could also allow funds to pay for mobility managers since JARC funds are generally not available for operating expenses.

Mobility managers are instrumental to creating a seamless paratransit system, having both the incentive and ability to connect riders to the appropriate transportation resources.

Permit Use of JARC for Low-Income Car Purchase Programs. JARC funds should be made more available to local planners for programs intended to help low-wage workers purchase automobiles. Although Federal Transit Administration (FTA) funds are generally not available for automobile purchase programs, the FTA recently clarified that car lease programs can use these funds under certain circumstances.[64] However, low-income car ownership programs subsidize car purchases in a variety of other ways. Federal policy should support these locally developed approaches, which include matched savings and limited subsidy programs. Excluding these options from funding unfairly places rural communities at a particular disadvantage, since fixed-route transit and demand-responsive van service approaches for such locations are less efficient and, therefore, less available than in more urbanized areas.

Require that Transportation Planners Consider the Spatial Access Needs of All Workers. Statewide and metropolitan transportation planning is conducted in a manner that does not explicitly consider the job access and spatial mismatch problems within metropolitan areas. Furthermore, the transportation systems that currently exist are not designed to alleviate this mismatch. As such, Congress should mandate, as a requirement to receive federal transportation funds, that metropolitan and statewide transportation plans include job access needs assessment and strategies in order to provide maximum regionwide accessibility for low-income workers.

Enforce Mandated Evaluation of JARC and Ensure FTA Systematically Collects Data on Grantee Performance. Although the JARC program has resulted in many new transportation programs, without evaluating these services, it is impossible to examine whether they both meet the transportation needs of the working poor and are cost effective. Through TEA-21, Congress required the DOT to evaluate the JARC program and submit its findings by June 2000. However, the department has not completed this evaluation nor has it announced a date for release.[65]

Refocus Funding to Better Serve Transit-Dependent Communities and Individuals. Previous federal transportation reform efforts underscored the importance of multimodal transportation networks in metropolitan areas. Despite earlier reforms, federal policy and programs continue to place transit projects at a disadvantage. This has profound implications for welfare recipients and low-income workers—particularly those who rely on buses for their mobility and job access needs. Congress should take steps to ensure that federally funded transit projects specifically and explicitly serve the objective of providing job access to low-income workers and welfare recipients.

Ensure that Transit-Oriented Development Meets the Needs of Low-Income Families. With the reauthorization of TEA-21, the federal government has a unique opportunity to leverage the billions of dollars already invested in light rail and other rail projects in a way that serves low-income workers. A key criterion for allocating transit funding should be the consistency of local land use plans and zoning codes with transit-supportive land uses and provisions for affordable housing.

Welfare Law

While the 1996 welfare reform legislation included new funding for child care, and most communities have an existing, if inadequate, system to provide child care services, there is no comparable funding mechanism or infrastructure to address transportation barriers for those moving from welfare to work. A few small and nearly cost-neutral changes to the welfare law would at least acknowledge the need to address transportation barriers faced by low-income workers seeking to work.

Add a New TANF Provision to Fund a Competitive Demonstration Car Purchase and Ownership Program. There are a growing number of low-income car ownership programs across the country, but most of these are small, with limited funding and capacity. Many program operators face funding cuts as a result of state budget deficits and other funder cutbacks.[66] To ensure that these promising programs continue to provide services and grow, and to encourage replication of successful programs, Congress should create a new funding stream targeted to providing assistance with car ownership for low-income working families. Funded programs should provide financial education services to assist car purchasers with budgeting for car ownership and other asset development. In both 2002 and 2004, the TANF reauthorization bills passed by the Senate Finance Committee included a new section allowing limited authorization for flexible funding to create a car ownership program. Congress should include a similar proposal with mandatory funding in the final TANF reauthorization bill.

Oppose Unnecessary Increases in TANF Work Rates that Reduce State Flexibility and Resources to Create Transportation Services. Some reauthorization proposals include increased work rates for states and individuals. The Congressional Budget Office estimates that the House-passed legislation could cost as much as $9 billion over five years to create and administer new work programs for a larger share of the caseload and provide the additional child care necessary for those parents to participate.[67] Yet none of the legislative proposals increase TANF block grants above the levels established in 1996. Static funding for a decade would force state policymakers to cut additional services since the cost of providing them increases even when funding levels do not. Furthermore, in 2002 states spent beyond the amount of their annual block grant for the second year in a row, using savings accumulated during the early years of implementation when the welfare rolls dropped significantly and unexpectedly, and administrators had the resources to restructure their welfare programs. Now, unspent funds have, for the most part, evaporated, and states face large overall budget deficits. In the face of these budget difficulties, many states have already cut work support services, including transportation programs. Mandating changes in work requirements will further reduce the resources available for transportation and other work support services. The proposed changes to work rates would be expensive to implement, are not supported by research evidence, and would significantly and unnecessarily reduce state flexibility to provide transportation assistance (and other services).[68]

Allow TANF Funds to Match Individual Development Accounts for Car Purchases without Jeopardizing Benefits. States and localities need the option to use TANF money to match Individual Development Accounts (IDAs) so that low-income workers can buy cars without jeopardizing their eligibility for other federally funded support services. IDAs are savings accounts for low-income workers that provide an incentive to save by matching deposits with public and private money. Public and private funding provides operating resources to organizations that support low-income individuals who participate in IDA programs. The nonprofits generally provide financial literacy training in addition to other management services. The current TANF statute effectively limits using IDA accounts matched with TANF funds to three qualified expenses: homeownership, postsecondary education, and starting a business. While the Department of Health and Human Services has clarified that states may use TANF funds to match IDAs for other purchases, such as cars, the IDA might be considered an asset when eligibility is determined for other federal benefits such as food stamps. A technical amendment to the statute would eliminate this barrier and allow for the more flexible use of state TANF funds. Other federal programs already give program operators this flexibility. For example, TANF federal funds administered as part of the department's Office of Refugee Resettlement are used to match IDA savings for a car purchase. Adding cars to the list of qualified expenditures simply creates another option for local operators and low-income working families—not a mandate. A number of states (Connecticut, Maine, Oklahoma, Pennsylvania, and Tennessee, for example) have created such programs, but their implementation is hampered due to the TANF statutory problem.

Require States to Address Transportation Gaps in Their TANF Plans. At the local level, the required collaborative process for application to the JARC competition has forged important new institutional relationships among transit, public and private human service, and workforce development agencies. Staff from these agencies frequently work together to plan, fund, or operate new transportation programs and services.

However, there is no mandate that state agencies consider the transportation needs of low-income families and welfare recipients as they make funding recommendations and decisions for use of the TANF block grant and matching state funds. Therefore, states need to encourage human service agencies to better understand, communicate, and address the role of transportation barriers in welfare-to-work outcomes. Requiring that states identify these barriers and make plans to address them as part of the state TANF plan, at a minimum, could lead to better understanding and cooperation at the state level.

Other Program Changes

There are several other federal policy amendments that would enhance transportation options for low-income workers and welfare recipients. The changes listed below would increase choice, remove barriers, and provide information for program design.

Allow AFIA and New CARE Act Program Funds to Match IDA Savings for Car Purchases. The federal Assets for Independence Act (AFIA) funds a demonstration of Individual Development Accounts in which eligible uses are a home, an education, and starting a microenterprise. President Clinton proposed amending the act in 2000 to add car purchase as an eligible use of the grants. While the administering agency and the lead national organization agreed to the amendment, Congress adjourned without implementing the change. The other federal funding stream for IDAs, in the Office of Refugee Resettlement, already permits car purchases with IDA savings. A recent survey of AFIA programs and others interested in AFIA reauthorization found that most observers recommend expanding the eligible purchases, including for a car.[69] AFIA is pending reauthorization, and Congress should add car purchase as an eligible use when the law is updated. Also, if Congress reconsiders a new IDA program, such as the one proposed in the Senate's Charity Aid Relief and Empowerment (CARE) Act of 2003, it should add cars to the list of eligible purchases for the IDA tax credit program included in the act.[70]

Eliminate the Vehicle Asset Test from All Federally Funded, Means-Tested Work Support Programs. Despite efforts to reduce the "vehicle asset limit" barrier to eligibility for work supports such as health insurance, food stamps, and TANF-funded services, workers that own reliable cars are still unable to receive certain benefits in some places. Policymakers should strengthen these work support programs by ensuring that every able worker in a household has access to a reliable car without being forced to forgo other services. In 2001 President Bush proposed this change as part of a package of changes in food stamp reauthorization. Although Congress did not adopt the change for reauthorization, it can amend this part of the law at any time.

Create a Demonstration Program for Low-Income Workers Who Need Loans to Purchase Cars. Federal policymakers made it possible for many low-income families to become homeowners by creating a subsidized and guaranteed loan program for veterans, reducing the risk for lenders with Federal Housing Administration guaranteed loans and funding for home purchase training programs, subsidizing purchase with the Section 8 program, and other policies. Similarly, an auto lending demonstration program could develop financing strategies that eventually lead to a more open market for automobile purchases. A grant program to reduce bank loan risk might encourage lenders to get involved. Nonprofits could allocate part of the grant to a collaborating lending institution and provide car purchase and financial literacy training for participants. Congress could couple this demonstration with a donation of vehicles from the retired federal fleet (rather than selling the cars for proceeds) to grantee low-income car ownership programs.

Require Workforce Boards to Assess Labor Market Transportation Needs. As part of the Workforce Investment Act Reauthorization, state and local workforce boards serving disadvantaged, displaced, and current workers should be required to consider the transportation barriers faced by clients, particularly in labor markets served by more than one board. These barriers must be addressed in the development of local plans to make the most effective use of state and federal resources intended to help workers get and keep a job, as well as move up the job ladder.

Fund More Research. Congress should direct the Department of Health and Human Services and the DOT, as well as other agencies, to allocate additional funds to research on the transportation issues facing low-income families. Although the growing body of research on transportation and the poor has provided numerous insights into how best to address transportation barriers to employment, there is still much that we do not know:

—Although understanding has grown regarding the travel patterns and transportation needs of welfare recipients and other public program partic-ipants, far less is known about these issues as they relate to the broader low-income population.

—Access to automobiles is strongly related to employment. However, relatively little is known about how to provide cars to low-income families, who often have difficulty affording the initial and ongoing costs of automo-bile ownership. Nor have alternative approaches to providing access to auto-mobiles, such as car sharing or taxi voucher programs, been effectively examined.

—Fixed-route public transit works best in dense urban areas. Although public transit service in these urban neighborhoods is typically extensive, we must identify neighborhoods that remain underserved because they are located distant from public transit stops, because levels of public transit ser-vice are inadequate, or because transit service hours have not accommo-dated changes in the work schedules of low-wage workers.

—In job-poor residential neighborhoods, long travel times can be prob-lematic. Typically, MPOs have addressed this issue by emphasizing big-ticket capital projects. However, we need to better understand how innovations in line-haul transit services, such as bus rapid transit, can be used to serve the longer distance travel needs of low-income commuters. Also, continued research is needed on the application of new "smart" tech-nologies in the deployment of paratransit. These technological enhance-ments can improve the cost-effectiveness and efficiency of this type of service.

—Much of the research on transportation and the poor has centered on the journey to work and employment rates. While this research is impor-tant, a better understanding is needed about the relationship between trans-portation and other necessary—and often work-supporting—activities of low-income households, including job search and nonwork travel, as well as the effect of transportation on earnings, job turnover, housing choice and residential location, and access to medical and child care.

Conclusion

The 1996 work-based welfare law did not create transportation barriers for low-income parents and others, but the new culture of work for welfare recipients has brought greater attention to this issue, spotlighting the myriad difficulties low-income adults have traveling to work. The media now regularly cover the issue, oftentimes by riding along with single mothers on their long bus rides from center-city homes to suburban entry-level jobs. The growing body of research reveals that access to reliable transportation can improve employment outcomes for low-income inner-city residents, as well as for the rural and suburban poor. When the media's featured low-income worker says (as she almost always does) that she cannot wait until she can afford to purchase a car, we now know that she says this with intuitive knowledge of what the research bears out: car ownership is a much more powerful predictor of employment than public transit. Nevertheless, flexibility in our policy response is essential. A menu of transportation solutions—transit, paratransit, and automobile access—must be developed, enhanced, and implemented according to the transportation needs of low-income communities living in diverse settings. Sound transportation policy is also an investment in our nation's economic success.

Despite compelling evidence of the importance of transportation to the employment outcomes of low-income adults, the federal government has been much slower to invest in transportation services for working-poor families than in other work supports, such as child care and the Earned Income Tax Credit. Congress and the administration have numerous opportunities to make at least incremental improvements in the system of services that reduce transportation barriers. Building on the still inadequate system of work- and family-strengthening supports by addressing transportation needs is an imperative that should not wait any longer.

Notes

1. Bruce Katz, "Smart Growth: The Future of the American Metropolis?" CASE Paper 58 (London School of Economics, 2002).

2. Edward Glaeser, Matthew Kahn, and Chenghuan Chu, "Job Sprawl: Employment Location in U.S. Metropolitan Areas," Center on Urban and Metropolitan Policy Survey Series (Brookings, July 2001).

3. See Paul A. Jargowsky, "Stunning Progress, Hidden Problems: The Dramatic Decline of Concentrated Poverty in the 1990s," report for the Center on Urban and Metropolitan Policy (Brookings, May 2003).

4. See Katz, Puentes, and Bernstein, chapter 2 of this volume.

5. Individual Development Accounts (IDAs) are special savings accounts for eligible low-income households. IDAs are similar to 401(k)s except that they match deposits instead of offering tax breaks as the incentive to save; and individuals saving in an IDA do so with the help of a nonprofit organization that provides economic literacy training and a variety of support services to help improve financial management skills.

6. Margy Waller and Alan Berube, "Timing Out: Long-term Welfare Caseloads in Large Cities and Counties," Center on Urban and Metropolitan Policy Survey Series (Brookings, September 2002).

7. Rick Sarlat, "Mayor Calls for Deep Measures to Assist Welfare Recipients," *Philadelphia Tribune*, January 2, 1998, p. 1-A.

8. Federal Transit Administration, "Job Access and Reverse Commute Grants: Fact Sheet" (www.fhwa.dot.gov/tea21/factsheets/jobaccs.htm [September 1998]).

9. 49 U.S.C. 3037(a)(2).

10. Mark Alan Hughes, "Moving Up and Moving Out: Confusing Ends and Means about Ghetto Dispersal," *Urban Studies* 24, no. 6 (1987): 503–17.

11. George Julnes and Anthony Halter, *Illinois Study of Former TANF Clients, Final Report* (Institute for Public Affairs, University of Illinois, 2000).

12. Phil Richardson and others, *Evaluation of the North Carolina Work First (TANF) Program: 18-Month Follow-up of Welfare Leavers in Selected Counties* (Reston, Va.: Maximus, Inc., 2001).

13. Iowa Department of Human Services, *Long-Term Welfare Recipients' Barriers to Employment: Summary* (2002).

14. David J. Fein and others, *The Indiana Welfare Reform Evaluation: Program Implementation and Economic Impacts after Two Years* (Washington: Abt Associates and the Urban Institute, 1998); Amy Cox, Nicole Humphrey, and Jacob Alex Klerman, *Welfare Reform in California: Results of the 1999 CalWORKs Program Staff Survey*, MR-1181.0-CDSS (Santa Monica, Calif.: RAND Corporation, 2000).

15. Greg Owen and others, "Whose Job Is It? Employers' Views on Welfare Reform." Working Paper 184 (Chicago: Joint Center for Poverty Research, 2000).

16. Marsha Regenstein, Jack A. Meyer, and Jennifer Dickemper Hicks, "Job Prospects for Welfare Recipients: Employers Speak Out" (Washington: Urban Institute, 1998).

17. Frank Hobbs and Nicole Stoops, *Demographic Trends in the 20th Century*, 2000 Special Reports, Series CENSR-4 (Bureau of the Census, 2000).

18. Department of Housing and Urban Development, *The State of the Cities: Megaforces Shaping the Future of the Nation's Cities* (2002).

19. Alan Pisarski, *Commuting in America II. The Second National Report on Commuting Patterns and Trends* (Lansdowne, Va.: Eno Transportation Foundation, 1996).

20. Calculations by the Brookings Institution Metropolitan Policy Program. Percentage based on U.S. census data for all metropolitan areas.

21. See, for example, Keith Ihlanfeldt and David Sjoquist, "The Spatial Mismatch Hypothesis: A Review of Recent Studies and Their Implications for Welfare Reform," *Housing Policy Debate* 9, no. 4 (1998): 849–92, and Valerie Preston and Sara McLafferty, "Spatial Mismatch Research in the 1990s: Progress and Potential," *Papers in Regional Science* 78, no.4 (1999): 387–402.

22. It is important to note that spatial mismatch is not just a "people to jobs" problem but also a "jobs to people" problem caused, in part, by massive metropolitan decentralization, as discussed earlier.

23. John F. Kain, "Housing Segregation, Negro Employment, and Metropolitan Decentralization," *Quarterly Journal of Economics* 82 (1968): 175-97.

24. Harry J. Holzer and Michael A. Stoll, "Meeting the Demand: Hiring Patterns of Welfare Recipients in Four Metropolitan Areas," Center on Urban and Metropolitan Policy Survey Series (Brookings, May 2001).

25. 49 U.S.C. 3037(a)(2) and 3037(a)(9).

26. See, for example, Evelyn Blumenberg and Paul Ong, "Cars, Buses, and Jobs: Welfare Recipients and Employment Access in Los Angeles," *Journal of the Transportation Research Board* 1756 (2001): 22–31; Citizens Planning and Housing Association, *Access to Jobs in the Baltimore Region* (1999); Annalynn Lacombe, *Welfare Reform and Access to Jobs in Boston*, BTS98-A-02, report prepared for the Bureau of Transportation Statistics (Department of Transportation, 1998); New York Metropolitan Transportation Council, *Access-to-Jobs* (1999); David Sawicki and Mitch Moody, "Developing Transportation Alternatives for Welfare Recipients Moving to Work," *Journal of the American Planning Association* 66, no. 3 (2000): 306–18; and Mark Alan Hughes, "Employment Decentralization and Accessibility: A Strategy for Stimulating Regional Mobility," *Journal of the American Planning Association* 57, no. 3 (1991): 288–99.

27. Calculations by the Brookings Institution Metropolitan Policy Program from U.S. census data, 2003.

28. Qing Shen, "A Spatial Analysis of Job Openings and Access in a U.S. Metropolitan area," *Journal of the American Planning Association* 67, no. 1 (2001): 53–68.

29. Glaeser and others, "Job Sprawl."

30. Households with incomes of less than $20,000 make an average of 3.2 trips per day and average 17.9 miles traveled per day—well below the national averages of 4.0 trips and 26.9 miles. See John Pucher and John L. Renne, "Socioeconomics of Urban Travel: Evidence from the 2001 NHTS," *Transportation Quarterly* 57, no. 3 (2003): 49–77.

31. Federal Highway Administration, *Our Nation's Travel: 1995 NPTS Early Results Report* (Department of Transportation, 1995).

32. Ibid.

33. Blumenberg and Ong, "Cars, Buses, and Jobs."

34. According to the Surface Transportation Policy Project, only 4.3 percent of the nation's 4 million miles of roads are served by transit. Surface Transportation Policy Project, "Transit Growing Faster than Driving: A Historic Shift in Travel Trends" (Washington, 2002). Furthermore, the Federal Transit Administration estimates that 40 percent of rural counties have no transit service. In many other rural areas, only limited service is provided. Yet rural residents do rely heavily on public transit when it is available. See House Transportation and Infrastructure Committee, Subcommittee on Highways, Transit, and Pipelines, "Statement of Jenna Dorn, Administrator, Federal Transit Administration," 108 Cong., 1 sess. (May 21, 2003).

35. See Evelyn Blumenberg, "On the Way to Work: Welfare Participants and Barriers to Employment," *Economic Development Quarterly* 16, no. 4 (2002): 314–25; Robert Cervero and others, "Transportation as a Stimulus to Welfare-to-Work: Private versus Public Mobility," *Journal of Planning Education and Research* 36, no. 3 (2002): 50–63;

THE LONG JOURNEY TO WORK **223**

Sandra Danziger and others, "Barriers to the Employment of Recipients," in *Prosperity for All? The Economic Boom and African Americans*, edited by Robert Cherry and William M. Rodgers III (New York: Russell Sage, 2000), pp. 245–78; Paul M. Ong, "Work and Car Ownership among Welfare Recipients," *Social Work Research* 20, no.4 (1996): 255–62; Paul M. Ong, "Car Ownership and Welfare-to-Work," *Journal of Policy Analysis and Management* 21, no. 2 (2002): 239–52; Steven Raphael and Lorien Rice, "Car Ownership, Employment, and Earnings," *Journal of Urban Economics* 52, no. 1 (2002): 109–30. Michael Stoll and Steven Raphael, "Racial Differences in Spatial Job Search Patterns: Exploring the Causes and Consequences," *Economic Geography* 76, no. 3 (2000): 201–23; Brian D. Taylor and Paul M. Ong, "Spatial Mismatch or Automobile Mismatch: An Examination of Race, Residence and Commuting in U.S. Metropolitan Areas," *Urban Studies* 32, no. 9 (1995): 1453–73; Margy Waller and Mark Alan Hughes, "Working Far from Home: Transportation and Welfare Reform in the Ten Big States," Policy Report (Washington: Progressive Policy Institute, July 1999).

36. Mary E. Corcoran, Colleen M. Heflin, and Kristine Siefert, "Food Insufficiency and Material Hardship in Post-TANF Welfare Families," *Ohio State Law Journal* 60, no. 4 (1999): 1395–1422; and J. Zogby and P. J. Malin, *Children's Health Care and Transportation Access* (New York: The Children's Health Fund, 2001).

37. Carolyn D. Hayden and Mauldin Bronwyn, *On the Road: Car Ownership as an Asset Building Strategy for Reducing Transportation Related Barriers to Work* (Oakland, Calif.: National Economic Development and Law Center, 2002); Susan Crane and Judith Olsen, "Working Wheels: A Seattle Success Story," *Community Investments Online*, April 2003 (frbsf.org/publications/community/investments/0303/working wheels.html [2003]).

38. Lisa M. Brabo and others, "Driving out of Poverty in Private Automobiles," in *Rediscovering the Other America: The Continuing Crisis of Poverty and Inequality in the United States*, edited by Keith M. Kilty and Elizabeth A. Segal (New York: Haworth Press, 2003), pp.183–96; Marilyn T. Lucas and Charles F. Nicholson, "Subsidized Vehicle Acquisition and Earned Income in the Transition from Welfare to Work." AEM Working Paper 2002-24 (Cornell University, Department of Applied Economics and Management, 2002); Marty Schwartz, "Changing Lives," unpublished report for Carroll County Department of Social Services and the Abell Foundation, Baltimore, Maryland, June 2002.

39. Lucas and Nicholson, "Subsidized Vehicle Acquisition."

40. Paul M. Ong and Doug Houston, "Transit, Employment and Women on Welfare," *Urban Geography* 23, no. 4 (2002): 344–64; Thomas W. Sanchez, "The Connection between Public Transit and Employment: The Cases of Portland and Atlanta," *Journal of the American Planning Association* 65, no. 3 (1999): 284–96.

41. Harry Holzer and Michael A. Stoll, "Employer Demand for Welfare Recipients by Race," *Journal of Labor Economics* 21, no. 1 (2003): 210–41.

42. Tom Sanchez, Qing Shen, and Zhong-Ren Peng, "Transit Mobility, Jobs Access and Low-Income Labour Participation in U.S. Metropolitan Areas," *Urban Studies* 41, no. 7 (2004): 1313–31.

43. Gregory L. Thompson, "New Insights into the Value of Transit: Modeling Inferences from Dade County," *Journal of the Transportation Research Board*, 1753 (2001): 52–58.

44. Robert Cervero and others, *Reverse Commuting and Job Access in California. Market, Needs and Policy Prospects* (Institute of Transportation Studies, University of California, Berkeley, 2002); Mizuki Kawabata, "Job Access and Employment among Low-Skilled Autoless Workers in U.S. Metropolitan Areas," *Environment and Planning A* 35, no. 9 (2003): 1651–68.

45. Calculations by the Brookings Institution Metropolitan Policy Program. Percentages are based on U.S. census data for all metropolitan areas.

46. Cervero and others, *Reverse Commuting*. On average, nineteen out of twenty reverse commutes are estimated to be by car. However, low-income reverse commuters are much more likely to rely on transit to make these trips. Transit use among low-income commuters was 7.8 percent in Los Angeles, 5.1 percent in the San Francisco Bay area, 10.5 percent in San Diego, and 12 percent in Sacramento.

47. Mark Garrett and Brian Taylor, "Reconsidering Social Equity in Public Transit," *Berkeley Planning Journal* 13 (1998): 6–27.

48. For a discussion about the rail and bus disparities, see Thomas W. Sanchez, Rich Stolz, and Jacinta S. Ma, *Moving to Equity: Addressing Inequitable Effects of Transportation Policies on Minorities* (Civil Rights Project at Harvard University and the Center for Community Change, 2003).

49. Waller and Hughes, "Working Far from Home."

50. Data from Federal Transit Administration, "2000 National Transit Database: National Transit Summaries and Trends" (www.ntdprogram.com/NTD/ntdhome.nsf/Docs/NTDPublications [February 2005]).

51. Cervero and others, *Reverse Commuting*.

52. General Accounting Office, *Transportation-Disadvantaged Populations: Some Coordination Efforts among Programs Providing Transportation Services, but Obstacles Persist*, GAO-03-697 (2003).

53. Ibid.

54. Ibid.

55. Pucher and Renne, "Socioeconomics of Urban Travel."

56. Federal Highway Administration, "Changes in the Purpose of Travel over Time: A Snapshot Analysis of the National Household Travel Survey 2001," *Highway Information Quarterly Newsletter* (www.fhwa.dot.gov/ohim/hiq/hiqjul03.htm [July 22, 2003]).

57. Elaine Murakami and Jennifer Young, "Daily Travel by Persons with Low Income," paper presented at the National Personal Transportation Survey symposium, Bethesda, Maryland, October 29-31, 1997 (npts.ornl.gov/npts/1995/Doc/LowInc.pdf [October 26, 1997]).

58. Crane and Olsen, "Working Wheels"; Anne Kim, "Taken for a Ride: Subprime Lenders, Automobility, and the Working Poor," Policy Report (Washington: Progressive Policy Institute, November 2002).

59. Clinton Foundation, "Remarks by the President on Transportation and Working Families, February 23, 2000" (www.clintonfoundation.org/legacy/022300-speech-by-president-at-food-stamp-and-transportation-event.htm [February 2005]).

60. Unpublished April 2003 survey of state Medicaid directors (Washington: Center on Budget and Policy Priorities, 2003).

61. Ray Horng and Stacy Dean, "States' Vehicle Asset Policies in the Food Stamp Program" (www.cbpp.org/7-30-01fa.htm [February 2005]).

62. Sharon Parrott and Nina Wu, "States Are Cutting TANF and Child Care Programs" (www.cbpp.org/6-3-03tanf.pdf [June 3, 2003]).

63. George E. Peterson and others, *The Reagan Block Grants: What Have We Learned?* (Washington: Urban Institute, 1986.)

64. "Job Access Reverse Commute Grants," *Federal Register* 67, no. 67 (April 8, 2002): 16790–99.

65. General Accounting Office, *Welfare Reform: Job Access Program Improves Local Service Coordination but Evaluation Should be Completed,* GAO-03-204 (2002).

66. Parrott and Wu, "States Are Cutting TANF."

67. Congressional Budget Office, "Memorandum," May 8, 2003.

68. Senate Finance Committee, *Hearing on Welfare Reform: Building on Success,* testimony of Margy Waller, Brookings Institution, 108 Cong., 1 sess. (March 12, 2003).

69. Corporation for Enterprise Development, "Assets for Independence Act Reauthorization Survey" (www.idanetwork.org/initiatives/AFIA_survey_summary.pdf [March 2003]).

70. The Corporation for Enterprise Development's IDA network website reports that the CARE Act proposal would provide up to $450 million "in IDA Tax Credits to match the savings of working families and would allow for up to 300,000 IDAs to be created. . . . The IDA Tax Credit would work by providing financial institutions with a dollar-for-dollar tax credit for every dollar they contribute as matching funds for IDAs, up to $500 per IDA per year." Corporation for Enterprise Development, "Savings for Working Families Act of 2003" (www.idanetwork.org/index.php?section=policy&page= legislative_proposals.html [March 2004]).

9 The Mobility Needs of Older Americans: Implications for Transportation Reauthorization

Sandra Rosenbloom

In 2000, 35 million Americans, or 12.4 percent of the total U.S. population, were over age sixty-five, and almost 4.5 million (or 1.6 percent of the total population) were over age eighty-five. By 2030 the number of older Americans will more than double.[1] Almost all of those seniors will have been licensed drivers for most of their lives, including many seniors too disabled to walk far or use conventional public transportation. As a result, seniors in the future will be even more dependent on the car than today's elderly.

These unprecedented demographic changes have rarely received the attention they deserve because there are so many myths about how most older Americans live. Public policy discussions assume that either elderly people need substantial government assistance and many publicly provided services or they have no unmet needs and require little governmental attention. In fact, most older Americans have complicated lives and rarely fall on either end of the spectrum. Many older people drive but still face mobility barriers, or they suffer from physical or medical problems but still seek an active community life. Equally important, the elderly are a significant and growing component of many of the transportation problems we face as a nation—from metropolitan decentralization to congestion to environmental pollution—even as they eventually suffer disproportionately from those very problems. To address both the mobility needs of the elderly and the important societal problems to which they contribute, we must refocus and redirect a wide range of public policies to respond to the complicated opportunities and constraints older people face today. This chapter challenges the easy assumptions that underlie most policy debates on transportation and the elderly, describing how an aging society adds to a range of transportation problems and discussing special approaches and solutions necessary to meet the mobility needs of over 70 million seniors in the coming decades.

Demographic Trends with Important Transportation Implications

Both the number of older people and their share of the population are growing rapidly. Across the spectrum, older Americans will both create and face daunting transportation challenges because the majority will live, increasingly alone, in suburban or rural communities that foster a deepening dependence on the private car to sustain their mobility.

Population Growth and Characteristics

The number of elderly is growing both absolutely and relatively, as shown by the differences between figures 9-1 and 9-2. By 2030 more than one in five Americans will be over age sixty-five, and one in eleven of those individuals will be over age eighty-five.[2] Compare this to 1970, when less than 1 percent of the population was over age eighty-five. At the same time, fewer younger people are available to pay or provide for the growing service needs of the expanding elderly population.

Older women will continue to substantially outnumber men. Older Americans will also become more diverse; people of color are one of the fastest growing groups among those over age sixty-five.[3] In 1994 roughly one in seven American seniors was from a racial or ethnic minority; this number will more than double in the next few decades.[4]

Most of the elderly will be in good health and not seriously disabled. In fact, disability rates have been declining for decades among all cohorts of the elderly, owing to a combination of good nutrition, improved health care, better education, and higher incomes. In 1996 almost three-quarters of older people reported that they were in good to excellent health, and only one quarter reported being unable to conduct one of nine major activities of daily living.[5] Although disability rates increase with age, two-thirds of

Figure 9-1.   Population Pyramid, 1970

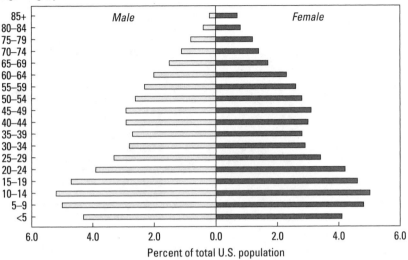

Source: Based on data from Bureau of the Census, "IDB Population Pyramids" (www.census.gov/ipc/www/idbpyr.html [September 30, 2004]).

those over age eighty-five reported being in good to excellent health. Overall, new generations of older Americans will be healthier for a greater percentage of their lives than those just a few decades ago.

However, a substantial portion of the elderly will eventually face increasing disabilities as they age. Almost 35 percent of those over age eighty in 1997 reported that their disabilities were severe enough to require assistance. Moreover, women and older people of color were significantly more likely to report serious health problems or disabilities. In 2000 over 40 percent of older blacks and more than 34 percent of older Hispanics rated their health as fair to poor (compared with 26 percent of white elders).[6]

As their degree of disability increases, those over eighty-five, and women in particular, will face several serious constraints with little family assistance. The majority of older women will live alone, some because they have never married, some because they have been widowed or divorced. In 1998 only 55 percent of women aged sixty-five to seventy-four were married; as a consequence, 41 percent of all older women were living alone compared with only 17 percent of comparable men. A 1995 study noted that "while most

Figure 9-2. Population Pyramid, 2030

Age range, years

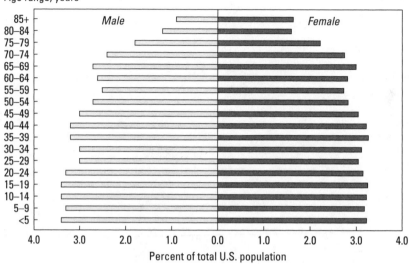

Source: See figure 9-1.

elderly men have a spouse for assistance, especially when health fails, most elderly women do not."[7] In fact, most older women will have no relatives or family members to provide support or assistance, given that the eighty-five-and-older cohorts in the upcoming two decades will have had fewer children than any previous cohort of the elderly.[8]

In addition, people of color, and particularly older women of color, are less likely to have the resources to buy assistance or the services and goods they need as they face mobility problems. In 1997 almost 14 percent of U.S. women but only 7 percent of men over age sixty-five lived below the poverty level.[9] Older women had a poverty rate almost 50 percent higher than older men, and those who lived alone had the highest poverty rate of all. In fact, over half of older Hispanic women who lived alone or with nonrelatives had incomes below the poverty line.[10] In 2000 almost 22 percent of older blacks and Hispanics were poor compared with fewer than 9 percent of elderly whites.

Residential Patterns

As figure 9-3 shows, almost three-quarters of the older population live within metropolitan areas, and over three-fourths of those live in the suburbs. This pattern has been intensifying for decades because of the aging-in-place

Figure 9-3.   Percent of U.S. Elderly by Residential Location, 2002

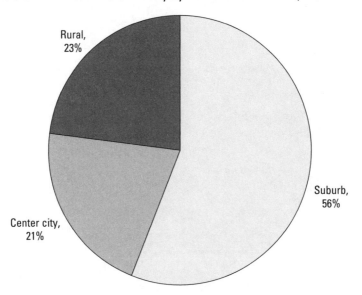

Rural,
23%

Suburb,
56%

Center city,
21%

Source: Senate Committee on Banking, Housing and Urban Affairs, *Hearing on TEA-21: A Lifeline for America's Citizens,* prepared statement of Lavada E. DeSalles, board member, AARP, 107 Cong. 2 sess. (July 17, 2002).

phenomenon: people remain in the homes in which they lived while rearing their children and holding jobs.

According to demographer William Frey, the suburbs aged more rapidly in the 1990s than the nation as a whole as a result of residential decisions made long ago.[11] Frey found that in 2000, those aged thirty-five to fifty-four accounted for 31 percent of the total suburban population, and most will likely remain in the suburbs as they grow older. Census data show that one- and five-year moving rates are lowest among those over age sixty-five and have been declining for years. Between 1990 and 1995, only 15.7 percent of those over age sixty-five moved, compared with almost 70 percent of those aged twenty to twenty-nine and 56 percent of those aged thirty to thirty-nine.[12] Moreover, Americans over age sixty-five today are only one-fourth as likely to move after they retire as were comparable elderly three decades ago.[13]

Transportation Patterns

Regardless of where they live, most older people are extremely dependent on the private car, either as a passenger or a driver, and increasingly the latter.

Figure 9-4.   Percentage of Trips by Mode of Transportation, Travelers Age 65 and Over, 2001[a]

Percent

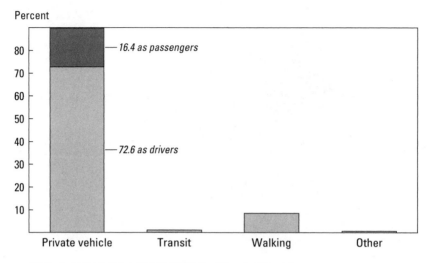

Source: Author's calculations from the 2001 National Household Travel Survey.

One indicator of the growing importance of the private car is the rate of licensing. In 1997 over 95 percent of all men and 80 percent of all women over age sixty-five were licensed drivers. By 2030 the gap between the sexes will have narrowed substantially given that 94 percent of women aged forty-five to forty-nine are currently licensed to drive.

As figure 9-4 shows, those over sixty-five make roughly 89 percent of their trips in a private vehicle, almost three-fourths of the time *driving* that vehicle. Even those over eighty-five make 87 percent of all trips in a private vehicle, driving themselves 60 percent of the time. In fact, data from the 2001 National Household Travel Survey show that older people make a greater percentage of their trips as drivers than do younger people.[14]

Conversely, use of alternative transportation modes has been dropping rapidly among the elderly for decades. In 1995 transit use among the elderly was, for the first time, less than that of younger people. In 1995 the elderly made only 2.2 percent of all trips by transit, but that figure fell by almost 50 percent between 1995 and 2001.

Although much policy debate about the elderly centers on their possible use of alternative public transit—such as special paratransit services or subsidized taxis—there is little indication that use of these options is large or growing among older people. In fact, taxi use (either private-pay or subsidized service) fell among the elderly from 1995 to 2001, while the use of other subsidized paratransit options was too small to break out in national data.[15] At the same time, there is substantial anecdotal information about the growing use of alternative private vehicle modes by the elderly, such as small electric vehicles, motorized scooters, and golf carts.[16]

Clearly linked to the growing dependence on the car is the growth in the number of trips and the mileage traveled, which have been increasing steadily among the elderly for more than three decades. Of course, whether more and longer trips are desirable is open to question. Most transportation planners and engineers define mobility in terms of the number of trips made, and an increase in trips is considered a positive social indicator.[17] However, others contrast mobility to access, or a measure of the ease with which people can reach needed goods and services.[18] Traveling more miles or making more trips by car may be an indicator not of improved mobility but of poorer access. At the same time, not all destinations are equal; people both young and old frequently bypass nearby stores, doctors, and religious institutions for preferred services often miles away. In reality, increased travel is probably a measure of both increased opportunities and decreased access for older people.

As much as they travel, older people make roughly 22 percent fewer trips than those under age sixty-five. A surprising amount of research refers to this difference, as well as to the drop in trips at retirement, as a reduction in mobility.[19] This again illustrates the problem of defining mobility as the number of trips made. In fact, the obvious difference between those younger and older than sixty-five is that the elderly rarely, if ever, make five roundtrips to work each week. The focus on the gap in trip making between the young and old obscures the fact that the elderly are very active until they reach age eighty or even older. In reality older people in many ways become more active than younger people when they retire. Older men take as many as 23 percent more nonwork trips and travel 6 percent more miles for nonwork purposes than men under age sixty-five.

Older women are also very active, but they take fewer nonwork trips than younger women. However, this pattern may change as more active cohorts of women age. Given increasing income, education, and job achievement among women over age forty today, it is likely that future cohorts of elderly women will more resemble men in their desire for an active postretirement lifestyle, in which travel plays an important role.

There are important variations by race and ethnicity in the travel patterns of otherwise comparable elders. Even when controlling for income and residential location, black, Asian, and Hispanic elders make fewer and shorter trips than white elderly and generally less often in a car. Moreover, there are greater travel differences between men and women within each of these ethnic and racial groups than there are between the groups or among whites. These patterns may be a complex combination of residential location, current or historical discrimination, and ethnic and cultural differences in attitudes and preferences. Certainly not all differences are problems that require remediation, but they do suggest a need to understand how older people from different backgrounds view travel and access, and the role family members are expected to and do play in the personal mobility of older family members.

Although most older people today drive to meet their needs, an important subset does not. Those living in the central city, older women (particularly over age seventy-five), the poor, those living alone, and ethnic and racial minorities are all less likely to be licensed to drive. Nevertheless, the car is a significant mode of transportation among those who do not drive. In 1995 the percentage of trips in cars (albeit fewer in number) made by those over age sixty-five without a license was almost as high as licensed drivers. Clearly, older people who do not drive depend heavily on others for rides and often on other older drivers.[20] Thus one older person losing a license (or ability to drive) may substantially reduce the mobility of several elderly individuals.[21]

Not having a license makes a substantial difference in the number and length of the trips older people make. For example, in 1995 licensed drivers aged sixty-five to sixty-nine made 87 percent more trips than comparable older people without a license. Even at age eighty-five, those with licenses make more than twice as many trips as those without a license. Of course, not all those differences represent transportation problems, given that trip making is an imperfect measure of mobility and most data conflate those who have never driven with those who gave up driving. Older people without licenses may have located in areas where they did not need to travel as often, they may live near family who bring them goods and services, or they may be too ill or otherwise disadvantaged to leave their homes. However, if increased trip making is ever viewed as an indicator of increased mobility, then a portion of the gap between licensed and unlicensed drives must signify immobility.

Challenges of an Aging Society

Most older people lead active lives dependent on the convenience and flexibility offered by the private car. Yet much policy debate seems to assume that older people contribute only marginally to the major transportation problems associated with increased reliance on the car. In fact, because of their lifestyles and growing reliance on the car, the elderly exacerbate several societal problems.

Environmental Pollution and Energy Consumption

The important role played by the private car in the lives of older people will have significant environmental implications. There is substantial evidence that traditional planning efforts underestimate the environmental impact of older drivers because those efforts assume that the relatively low licensing and travel rates seen among older people in the past will continue into the future.[22] Those rates, as suggested above, have been increasing substantially for decades. In 2030, if all older drivers only drove as much as did comparable individuals in 1995, the total number of vehicle miles among the elderly would more than double, simply because the population of older drivers would have increased substantially. If, however, as current trends suggest, older people increase the miles they drive to resemble the travel patterns of the cohort just ten years younger in 1995, the total number of miles driven annually would more than triple in the next three decades.

A large part of the increase in car travel will stem from the increasing number of women drivers. In 2010, if older women's trip rates equaled men's in 1995 and men's stayed constant (at the 1995 level), the elderly would make over 94 million trips per day. If, however, vehicle trip rates for older men and women were to continue to increase at the same annual rate as they did between 1983 and 1995, the number of daily trips would skyrocket to over 118 million in 2010 and 183 million in 2020 (or six times more than in 1995).[23]

In addition, the kind of trips older drivers make will exacerbate pollution problems. The shorter trips that the elderly typically make never allow their car engines to warm enough for pollution control devices to be effective, the so-called cold start problem. The catalytic converters on modern cars work best when both the catalyst and the engine exceed 600 degrees Fahrenheit; therefore, most emissions occur during the first 10 percent of a trip.[24] Even though the elderly make shorter trips, their auto emissions may be significant. Overall, data strongly suggest that older drivers will be

Table 9-1. Metropolitan Areas' Suburban Share of Elderly over Age
Sixty-five and Change in Population under Thirty-five, 1990–2000[a]

Percent, unless otherwise indicated

Rank in share of suburban population 65+	Metropolitan area	Suburban population 65+	Change in suburban population under 35
1	Sarasota, Fla.MSA	29.5	13.0
2	West Palm Beach, Fla. MSA	24.0	22.3
3	Tampa, Fla. MSA	20.5	11.9
4	Scranton, Pa. MSA	18.8	−11.0
5	Pittsburgh, Pa. MSA	17.9	−11.2
6	Tucson, Ariz. MSA	17.3	20.7
7	Monmouth, N.J. PMSA	16.9	3.4
8	Buffalo, N.Y. MSA	16.6	−9.6
9	Youngstown, Ohio MSA	16.3	−8.7
10	Fort Lauderdale, Fla.MSA	16.2	32.0
11	Allentown, Pa. MSA	16.0	−3.4
12	Providence, R.I.-Mass. NECMA	15.3	−6.3
13	Cleveland, Ohio MSA	15.0	−6.1
14	Phoenix, Ariz. MSA	14.9	47.5
15	Harrisburg, Pa. MSA	14.9	−2.8
16	Hartford, Conn. NECMA	14.5	−7.4
17	Springfield, Mass. NECMA	14.4	−9.0
18	Albany, N.Y. MSA	14.3	−8.3
19	Bergen, N.J. MSA	14.1	1.4
20	Bridgeport, Conn. NECMA	14.1	−3.5

Source: William H. Frey, "Boomers and Seniors in the Suburbs: Aging Patterns in Census 2000," Living Cities Census Series, Center on Urban and Metropolitan Policy (Brookings, January 2003).

a. MSA is metropolitan statistical area, PMSA is a primary metropolitan statistical area, and NECMA is New England county metropolitan area.

significant contributors to the damage done to the environment by the use of the private car.

Metropolitan Decentralization

Low-density development caused by metropolitan decentralization has long been recognized as a major and growing societal problem. What is often overlooked in these discussions is that the suburbanization of the elderly parallels the suburbanization of the U.S. population.

As table 9-1 shows, many metropolitan areas are experiencing rapid growth in the absolute *number* of suburban elderly, which often leads to a substantial growth in the *percentage* of the population over sixty-five. This has two causes. First, some areas, like Pittsburgh and Cleveland, have growing concentrations of older people in the suburbs because existing residents are aging in place while the percentage (and often the number) of younger

Table 9-2. Metropolitan Areas' Change in Suburban Population over Age Sixty-five and under Age Thirty-five, 1990–2000[a]

Percent, unless otherwise indicated

Rank in growth of percent of suburban population 65+	Metropolitan area	Change in suburban population 65+	Change in suburban population under 35
1	El Paso, Tex. MSA	83.1	39.5
2	Las Vegas, Nev.-Ariz. MSA	78.1	75.4
3	Colorado Springs, Colo. MSA	69.8	17.7
4	Honolulu, Hawaii MSA	53.4	−7.1
5	Tucson, Ariz. MSA	53.1	20.7
6	Phoenix-Mesa, Ariz. MSA	52.1	47.5
7	Austin, Tex. MSA	48.6	42.4
8	McAllen, Tex. MSA	47.3	50.7
9	Denver, Colo. PMSA	47.2	23.5
10	Jacksonville, Fla. MSA	46.6	16.2
11	Houston, Tex. PMSA	46.2	19.6
12	Albuquerque, N.Mex. MSA	43.0	12.1
13	Dallas, Tex. PMSA	41.5	28.2
14	Salt Lake City, Utah MSA	41.3	17.7
15	Baton Rouge, La. MSA	40.1	8.2
16	Atlanta, Ga. MSA	39.9	35.3
17	Memphis, Tenn.-Ark.-Miss. MSA	39.8	6.8
18	Sacramento, Calif. PMSA	39.6	13.5
19	Fort Worth, Tex. PMSA	39.2	14.1
20	Columbia, S.C. MSA	36.3	5.0

Source: See table 9-1.

a. MSA is metropolitan statistical area, PMSA is a primary metropolitan statistical area, and NECMA is New England county metropolitan area.

people is dropping. Second, some areas, like Houston and Tucson, have growing concentrations of older people both because existing residents are aging in place and because young retirees are migrating to the suburban (and even exurban) edges of their metropolitan areas.[25] Although most seniors do not move when they retire, the migration that does occur will reinforce suburbanization and sprawl in many rapidly growing states.

Although the metropolitan suburbs with the very largest share of older people are in Florida, the majority of suburbs with the highest share of seniors aged sixty-five and older are found in the Northeast, where the portion of the under-thirty-five population is declining most rapidly. By contrast, the "senior suburban growth centers" with the largest increases in elderly are all located in the Sunbelt, particularly in the Southwest, as table 9-2 makes clear. A 1996 national housing study by the American Association of Retired Persons found that, independent of where they actually lived, if they *had to move*, the majority of older respondents said they would move to low-density places. No more than

Map 9-1. Location of Metropolitan Tucson Retirement Communities

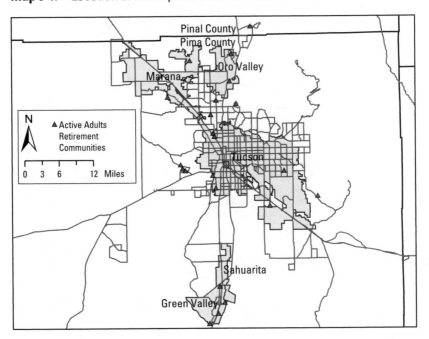

Source: Patricia Gober and Barbara Trapido-Lurie, Arizona State University.

one out of four respondents of any age wanted to live in what was defined as "the city." Only half of those currently living in denser central cities wanted to live in a comparable city environment if they had to move.[26]

Once in the Sunbelt, older people fuel suburban and even exurban sprawl. Most older people migrating to the Sunbelt choose fairly large homes in low-density areas, often in greenfield communities. Older buyers "want eight- to nine-foot ceilings, bigger garages, and a bathroom for each bedroom. Even people who don't cook want fancy kitchens."[27]

As a result of these trends, the elderly are becoming disproportionately represented on the suburban fringe. This is particularly true in fast-growing places such as metropolitan Phoenix and Tucson: in both metropolitan areas, the elderly represent almost one-third of new urban fringe residents. Maps 9-1 and 9-2 show the location of age-segregated communities in both areas; note that these communities where the elderly tend to congregate are located along the suburban fringes of the metropolitan area.

Map 9-2.   Location of Metropolitan Phoenix Retirement Communities

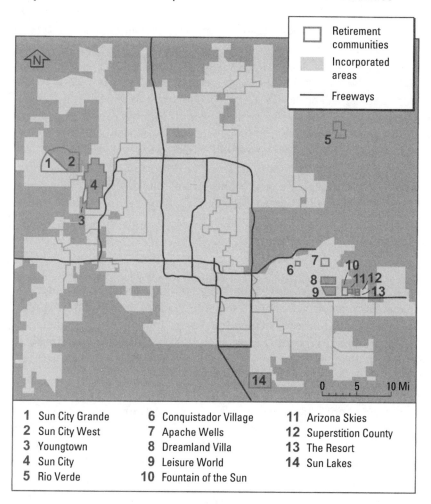

1 Sun City Grande	6 Conquistador Village
2 Sun City West	7 Apache Wells
3 Youngtown	8 Dreamland Villa
4 Sun City	9 Leisure World
5 Rio Verde	10 Fountain of the Sun

11 Arizona Skies
12 Superstition County
13 The Resort
14 Sun Lakes

Source: Morrison Institute, Arizona State University.

This phenomenon is not unique to Arizona. The Urban Land Institute found that the majority of so-called active adult retirement communities that attract after-retirement migrants are being built in the Sunbelt states and often on the suburban fringe, where land assemblage is easy and relatively less expensive. An average community of this type had just over 400 units, on 163 acres; the median size of the most popular detached home plan was 1,900 square feet.[28] And most of those choosing these homes are likely to arrive at the edge directly from outside the region.[29] According to the Milken Institute, it is the affluent "yuppie" elderly that will tend to locate on the metropolitan fringe, while less wealthy seniors likely will remain in their home cities and reside closer to the core.[30]

Over time metropolitan areas with large concentrations of older people aging in place will be faced with the need for an array of health and human services even as the percentage or number of working-age residents drops. William Frey suggests that these impacts will be felt most severely in the "snowbelt" communities that are continuing to lose their tax bases. However, many Sunbelt areas are attracting growth because, historically, they have low taxes and provide limited health and human services. Thus even if Sunbelt communities have stronger tax bases, they may not provide any better services for an aging population

Congestion

In the past two decades, traffic congestion has become a way of life in nearly every major metropolitan area. Metropolitan congestion is expected to increase as the number of vehicles, drivers, miles traveled, and intercity trucks grows and as regional economies continue to decentralize along low-density settlement patterns.[31] It is less recognized that older drivers are a growing component of many of these causes of congestion.

Of course, older drivers do not generally make work trips, and they tend to avoid both congested time periods and congested areas. Many cities, however, increasingly suffer traffic congestion for long periods of the day; the morning and evening peaks have lengthened substantially in the last three decades. Many cities also experience substantial midday peaks. In a report prepared for the Federal Highway Administration, the Texas Transportation Institute found that midday delays on the roadways are actually higher than the traditional rush hour periods in several metropolitan areas, including Los Angeles, Minneapolis, Phoenix, and Norfolk. In some cases, midday congestion is almost twice as bad as the morning peak period. The institute also found that cities that are congested during the peak hours also have a significant amount of midday delay.[32] As a result, older drivers can only avoid the worst of congestion; they do not generally travel in congestion-free periods.

In fact, older drivers make the bulk of their trips between 9 a.m. and 1 p.m., placing them on the road at the end of the morning peak and during the midday peak.[33] Moreover, although they tend to avoid freeways and thus contribute little to freeway congestion, older drivers may disproportionately affect arterial congestion (given that smaller streets have less capacity). Although far from the major cause of traffic congestion, older people do contribute to this societal problem because they make the majority of their trips during periods of moderate to heavy traffic.

Safety

An aging population both creates and faces safety problems with many modes of transportation.[34] Although the problems of the older driver are more frequently discussed, older pedestrians also face substantial dangers, which often makes it safer for them to be in a car than out on the street.

The safety consequences of an older driver population are a recognized problem. Older drivers are not only more likely to have crashes on an exposure basis (per trip or mile driven), they are also generally more likely to be at fault in a multicar crash and more likely to be killed or injured than are younger people in a crash of comparable magnitude.[35] At the same time, older drivers are less likely to be involved in crashes that kill someone else.[36] In addition, older drivers are substantially more law-abiding than younger drivers and far less willing to make risky maneuvers; they are also far less likely to drive under the influence of alcohol or illegal drugs. Experts have postulated that people today are better drivers and bring their safer habits with them into their retirement years. As a result, per capita crash rates have been declining among those over age sixty-five for decades.[37]

However, the large increase in the sheer number of older drivers, especially women, will cause an absolute increase in crash rates, even if per capita rates continue to drop. Moreover, a greater percentage of older drivers will be very old—over age eighty-five—and crash rates rise rapidly after that age. Because all older drivers appear to be increasing their trip making, their exposure will increase substantially, even if they are safer or more experienced than comparable drivers in the past.

Moreover, current per capita crash rates for older people are fairly low because older drivers self-regulate, that is, they change a number of things about their travel and driving behavior to accommodate loss of driving skills or problematic driving situations.[38] They often avoid congested areas, left turns, and peak-period travel or avoid driving at night or on unfamiliar roads or in bad weather. It is doubtful, however, that future generations of older drivers will self-regulate as much; accustomed as they are to the flexibility and convenience of the car, they simply may be unwilling to change their driving habits when doing so impedes their lifestyle.[39] If older drivers in the future fail to avoid problematic situations and perhaps engage in riskier behavior, per capita crash rates may well increase despite greater driving skills and experience.

In addition, older people are more susceptible to injury and death in the crashes that do occur.[40] Thus older people, who represent 13 percent of the U.S. population, constitute 18 percent of U.S. motor vehicle deaths. Moreover, people over age seventy-five have more motor vehicle deaths per 100,000 miles driven than any age cohort except those under twenty-five. The Insurance Institute for Highway Safety estimates that the doubling of the elderly population will mean that older people will be involved in 25 percent of all fatal car crashes within three decades.[41]

The aging of the population also brings several overlapping pedestrian safety problems. The most discussed are crashes between pedestrians and automobiles. However, improved data collection methods here and abroad suggest that both car-pedestrian crashes and falls are much higher than previously thought. Moreover, street falls may be the more significant of the two among the elderly.

In 2000 the pedestrian death rate for both men and women over age seventy was the highest of any age group. People aged sixty-five and over accounted for 22 percent of all pedestrian deaths and 32 percent of all nonfatal pedestrian injuries. People seventy and older, who constituted less than 10 percent of the population, accounted for 18 percent of pedestrian deaths. At the same time, pedestrian-car crash rates have been dropping substantially in the industrialized world over the last three decades. Most traffic safety researchers conclude that the decline is tied most closely to the fact that older people in developed countries are walking less and driving more.[42]

Debunking the Myths of Elderly Travel Needs

Transportation has been a recognized problem for the elderly for more than thirty years. In 1971 the first White House Conference on the Aging reported that transportation was one of the three greatest needs of older people.[43] Subsequent White House conferences have also ranked transportation problems as a major barrier. In 1988 the National Academy of Sciences convened a conference to undertake a "comprehensive study and investigation of problems which inhibit the safety and mobility of older people." They found that there were insufficient transportation resources for those unable or unwilling to drive.[44] In 1999 another national conference found that mobility gains among the elderly had been significant but only for those who could drive, and only for as long as they could do so.

Unfortunately, there are many misunderstandings about the mobility needs of older Americans. Most policy discussions tend to take an either-or stance: either they drive or they do not, either they are healthy and able-bodied or crippled and severely disabled, either they can use public transit or they cannot. Public policy has also tended to focus on only those with the most obvious and severe disadvantages. There are three important misconceptions about older people that must be overcome before appropriate policy and program strategies can be developed.

Myth One: As people age, they first lose the ability to drive; they then use public transit if it is available; when unable to use public transit they walk; and finally, unable to walk, they use special transit services.

Although widely believed, this "progression" is largely wrong. In fact, driving is often the easiest physical task for older people.[45] Long before they lose the ability to drive, older people may be unable to board or ride public transit or to walk to a bus stop or train station. Even though many may still be able to use special transit services, the overwhelming majority of older people, regardless of their stage of disability, are able to ride in a car and choose to do so first.

There is a dangerous corollary to the myth that the elderly opt for public transit or special transit services when they can no longer drive or use regular transit. In reality there are few special services available, whether provided by a transit operator or a social or human service agency.

First, special transit services are only available where there are regular transit services—which are almost nonexistent in rural areas and very limited in suburban areas, home to more than two-thirds of the elderly. Only 14 percent of the elderly who live in rural areas report having any kind of transit services within a half mile. As the Community Transit Association of America noted in one of their publications, "The past two decades have seen many forms of transportation virtually abandon rural areas. Small town residents often travel hundreds of miles just to access the nearest airport; intercity bus service is a shell of its former self; taxi service is scant and expensive; and passenger rail service often only streaks through the countryside in the middle of the night."[46] In a 1994 report prepared for the Rural Transit Assistance Program, the association found that two of five rural counties had no public transit, and another 25 percent had service equal only to one trip per month.[47]

Second, even in urban areas, many elderly people do not live close to existing bus lines and thus are ineligible by reason of geography for any special services that exist. In most communities, special transit services are only available within three-fourths of a mile of existing bus routes and only during regular bus route hours (as per the minimum requirements of the Americans with Disabilities Act [ADA]). Although most experts suggest that a quarter mile is a better measure of transit access for older people, in 1995 only 43 percent of the elderly in suburban areas reported living within a half mile of public transit.[48]

Third, most elderly people are ineligible for special transit services even if they live near existing bus routes. The complementary paratransit requirements of the ADA have put a tremendous burden on most urban paratransit systems; transit systems must provide a very high level of expensive service to those certified as ADA-eligible. In response, the overwhelming majority of metropolitan transit operators have severely restricted eligibility for those services. Many elderly do not qualify because their disability is not severe enough; being unable to drive or having minor handicaps rarely qualifies one for services.[49]

Most communities also host many small, special paratransit services provided by nongovernmental organizations, organizations supporting the aged, and public and private social services agencies. However, these providers generally transport only those involved in specific agency services and do not serve a large percentage of the elderly.[50] Overall, as currently financed and delivered, special paratransit services serve a very small proportion of a very large population and will serve an even smaller proportion of the growing elderly population in the future. They can and should constitute one part of a "family" of transportation services, but they are not the only or even a major strategy for meeting the mobility needs of older people.[51]

Myth Two: Older people who drive are mobile without assistance; those who cannot drive have substantial unmet needs.
Older people who drive still face mobility barriers. Long before they cease driving, people begin to adjust their travel patterns to address personal limitations by, for example, not driving at night or to congested areas. As suggested above, this self-regulation helps keep them safer.[52] However, most policy discussions fail to recognize how this behavior can negatively affect their lifestyle. We currently underestimate the impact of reduced driving and overestimate the impact of driving cessation because cessation is viewed as a single point in time after which mobility falls drastically. In fact, long before they give up driving, older people gradually lose mobility and independence as they gradually reduce their driving.

In a Tucson study that followed 1,300 older drivers for five years, those who ceased to drive one year after being interviewed made substantially fewer trips after cessation than they had in the previous year or than did those who continued to drive. The most striking fact, however, was that those who stopped driving were already making substantially fewer trips in the preceding year compared with those who continued to drive, even controlling for age, self-reported health status, and other variables.[53]

Myth Three: All loss of mobility skills is permanent; older people either have the skills needed to drive, use public transit, or walk—or they do not.

In reality, the mobility needs of the elderly are complicated. Public policy discussions in general often fail to recognize the varying abilities of older people. People may stop driving temporarily because of a heart attack or other serious illness but begin driving again as their health improves. Older people may need walkers and other mobility aids on some days but not on others. They may be able to travel by conventional public transit on a sunny day but need a ride on a rainy day. Thus they may require different options on different days or in different seasons of the year.

A corollary to this myth is that people who can drive will rarely use other modes no matter how those options are provided. This assumption reduces the incentive to focus attention on older drivers or older people who have mobility options. Indeed, most U.S. transit ridership among the elderly stems from those who do not drive. However, in Australia, Europe, and Canada, elderly car drivers make up a meaningful percentage of transit users.[54] When given a reasonable set of transportation options, older people in those countries appear to choose the best or most convenient mode for each trip.[55]

Thus it may be possible to structure public transit and other services to reduce car use among the elderly even if these options do not remove all need (or preference) for a car. The existence of such options before individuals cease to drive may make older people more willing and able to use other transport options when they do stop driving.

Legislative and Policy Solutions

As Congress and other policymakers at the state and metropolitan levels consider the reauthorization of the federal transportation law, they should both develop policies and programs that reduce the contribution older people make to important societal problems, such as congestion and metropolitan decentralization, and offer realistic mobility and access options. To do so, policymakers should recognize the different subsets of the elderly, including those who still drive, those who have given up driving, and those who never drove. Programs should consider where older people live and their ethnic, racial, and cultural backgrounds. To meet the mobility needs of the elderly, policymakers should consider the following actions.

Ensure that Metropolitan Planning Explicitly Addresses the Mobility Needs of the Elderly

There is a substantial and growing body of advocacy and planning research on the role of regional planning, community design, and metropolitan growth and development in ensuring people's mobility. However, little of that research focuses specifically on the elderly. Indeed, many advocates assume that anything that improves the design of neighborhoods overall will help the elderly. Unfortunately, these types of improvements may not help older people unless special attention is paid to their needs.[56]

Many efforts to integrate transportation and land use planning are designed to mix land uses, promote infill and central city redevelopment, and increase densities, all of which could increase the mobility and access of the elderly. Such development can locate a range of social and shopping opportunities nearer to home, reducing the elderly's need to travel far or by car. Multiuse developments that include housing might allow older people to conduct their daily activities largely within their own apartment building or complex. If such developments occur near their suburban homes, the elderly may be able to move from houses now too large into more appropriate apartments, remaining in their own neighborhood as they age.

However, such developments can also substantially change neighborhoods in ways that pose new or different problems for older people, such as increased noise and congestion, an influx of unfamiliar activities, and the potential for gentrification. Clearly, the impacts of these strategies are site specific and depend substantially on the attention paid to the housing and other details of relevance to the elderly. Planning for such development and redevelopment should ensure that older people, particularly those disadvantaged by extreme age, disability, or poverty, are not harmed by projects that are neither affordable nor accessible.

Walkable neighborhoods are also an essential element in several widely discussed public policies, from "smart growth" to community health. Neighborhoods designed and redesigned to make walking pleasant, safe, and secure might increase both the mobility and the health of older people.

There is considerable design and engineering research that shows communities how to improve pedestrian access by implementing pedestrian-friendly facilities and treatments, improving intersections, and adopting traffic-calming measures. These approaches, however, must be implemented with careful attention to the specific needs of older people.

The existing federal transportation law currently requires states to assess the pedestrian accessibility of their major road projects. It would be useful if this requirement were strengthened in the new legislation and if transit operators were charged with the same responsibilities for assessing the degree of pedestrian access to their services and facilities. Note that it has generally been held that the ADA only requires communities to provide accessible bus stops but not to ensure an accessible path to those stops. The Ninth Federal Circuit Court, however, recently found this to be an illogical interpretation of ADA mandates.[57] The decision may ultimately lead to the requirement that communities also provide accessible paths to transit stops, although local litigation will likely be necessary. It would be more effective to specifically mandate more comprehensive pedestrian accessibility in pending transportation legislation.

Ensure that Public Transit Services and Facilities Adequately Serve the Elderly

Over the last decade, older people have made substantially less use of public transit. However, research suggests that older people would make more use of transit if services were provided in ways that better met their needs. To do so, federal, state, and metropolitan policies and programs should encourage or require, as well as finance, four major categories of public transit development: improving conventional service, increasing safety and security in all parts of the system, enhancing communication and information, and providing additional services more carefully targeted to the elderly.

This would require additional funding. Unfortunately, the only element of the Transportation Equity Act for the Twenty-First Century explicitly designed for the elderly is the Section 5310 formula grants and loan for special needs of the elderly and persons with disabilities. Section 5310 provides transportation services in areas where transit service is unavailable, insufficient, or inappropriate.[58] The program provides benefits, although the amount is far too small ($456 million, about 1.1 percent of the total transit authorization) to be broadly effective.

Efforts to improve transit services for older people must focus not only on the more severely disadvantaged of the elderly (as Section 5310 does), but on the larger market of elderly travelers who can be convinced to use improved conventional services and new or different services that respond to their special needs. To improve conventional services, communities must first make transit safer and more secure for older people and provide better pretrip and en route information. They must also purchase more low-floor (accessible) buses; schedule more regular services, particularly in the off-peak hours; consider route restructuring to better serve the origins and destinations of older travelers; and even provide sporadic but scheduled services for shopping or other needs. These services should target neighborhoods with a growing elderly population as well as recreational vehicle and trailer parks.

Transit operators can also increase ridership among older people by changing the basic nature of the services offered. Some communities have been very successful with service routes and community buses—small, accessible, and scheduled buses in which the driver provides substantial assistance and all elderly travelers are guaranteed a seat. Community buses are also attractive because they are specifically routed to serve the origins and destinations of most interest to older people. Many systems have found that those who ride community buses are relatively healthy older people who are new to public transit or who used it only infrequently prior to the new services.[59]

Support Alternative Transport Options

There is a wealth of transportation resources and alternatives in many communities that are not well or fully used, many of which could become an important part of the transportation repertoire of the elderly if supported by state law and federal funds. First, supporting formal and informal volunteer networks and facilitating ride-sharing programs would increase transportation options for older people. Communities could help formal volunteer programs to overcome the liability and maintenance problems faced when they begin to carry any appreciable number of riders. Federal law could assist a public agency or the transit operator to develop group insurance coverage or to establish insurance pools. In addition, a transit operator or other public agency could develop ways for volunteers involved in formal systems to receive auto maintenance at reduced rates.

Community agencies or transit operators could encourage more informal volunteer service through voucher programs, as implemented in Mesa, Arizona, and Riverside, California. Currently, several federal transportation programs (Section 5311, Nonurbanized Area Formula Grant programs, and Section 5310, Elderly and Persons with Disabilities programs) can be used to pay for vouchers, although they rarely are. A 1999 study found that voucher programs were an effective way to use volunteers because they were less expensive than directly providing such services, and riders were usually offered longer service hours.[60]

In addition, communities could strengthen the role—and the safety, in some cases—of for-profit operators who provide mobility for older travelers by regularizing extralegal operations, expanding the role of the taxi, and cultivating additional entrepreneurs. Many neighborhoods and communities, particularly those of color, currently host a variety of jitney-type transportation providers, which may or may not be operating illegally. There is substantial anecdotal evidence that many riders of these informal services are older people.

To the extent possible, communities should standardize if not fully legalize such operations; if necessary, they can be prohibited from working outside the neighborhoods in which they have historically operated. Vehicle standards should be established and vehicles routinely inspected, and operators should be required to carry sufficient insurance. If they need assistance once their services are more formalized, communities can help lower insurance rates and maintenance costs. Moreover, communities should be encouraged to make better use of existing taxi operators, through user-side subsidies and contract programs. If lacking either taxis or informal providers, communities can help train and equip local entrepreneurs to provide needed services, particularly in specific neighborhoods.

Improve Highway and Street Infrastructure

The entire automobile-based infrastructure must be modified and enhanced so that older people can drive safely longer in ways that reduce or even eliminate the environmental and congestion-related features of their travel. Federal and state funds can be used to support programs and policies that make the road network safer, increase safe private vehicle use by qualified drivers, and help develop vehicles that are safer, cleaner, and easier to drive.

During the last decade, the Federal Highway Administration, in recognition of the aging of society and the problems that older drivers face, has prepared several handbooks and reference sources linking older road-user characteristics to highway design and operational and traffic engineering recommendations, suggesting specific roadway, signage, and traffic standards.[61] Federal funds should be used to encourage communities to update all aspects of the road system to conform to these important, but voluntary, older-driver design standards.

States should also be allowed to use their own and federal funds to assist safe, older drivers with financial difficulties to continue driving. A community can develop programs that provide assistance for a car's maintenance and fuel or even for its purchase. Given the car's contribution to a number of environmental problems, this may seem a quixotic approach, but it has been adopted in the United States as part of several welfare-to-work programs. Communities can also develop car-sharing programs for older people in independent living centers, trailer parks, or naturally occurring retirement neighborhoods. These communities can cooperatively buy and operate a small fleet of vehicles, allowing individual residents to reserve and drive them—and perhaps give up their own cars.

Finally, the federal government, in partnership with private industry, should take a more active role in developing cars that are safer, cleaner, and easier to drive. The vehicle emissions improvements that have been achieved by reducing car size or weight are particularly relevant for older drivers: smaller, lighter, or less protected vehicles may meet environmental mandates, but they also may increase the severity of the injuries incurred by older drivers in crashes.[62] In addition, because the U.S. government is one of the largest purchasers (directly or indirectly) of a range of mechanized disability aids, it should take an active role in evaluating the safety and other consequences of the growing reliance by older people on powered wheelchairs, golf carts, and electric scooters on roadways and pedestrian paths.

Conclusion

Older people are substantially more mobile today than ever before. Trip rates and distances have increased remarkably for all cohorts of the elderly. Whether cause or effect, these trends are directly related to metropolitan decentralization and the increasing dependency on the car. Although the mobility problems of older people who have never had a car or a license have consumed much of our attention, this group is a decreasing share of the total elderly population. The largest group of people facing substantial mobility losses in the future will be those who drove well into their senior years.

When older drivers lose the ability to drive or cannot easily secure rides from others, they will suffer substantial losses in mobility. If they have made perhaps irreversible housing and other decisions based on the mobility afforded by the car, they may suffer disproportionately more than those who never drove, given that the latter group may have made household decisions in ways that better support a car-free lifestyle.

Comprehensive and long-term solutions to the mobility needs of older people must take into account the great variability not only among people, but for the same person in different situations. Policies and programs must recognize the preference for a repertoire of travel options that give the elderly freedom and flexibility in the face of declining skills.

Policymakers must focus considerable attention and resources to meet the growing mobility needs of older travelers, and not simply as an equity or social issue. Solving the mobility needs of such a large and growing segment of the population is integral to answering several of the transportation challenges facing society. To do so, we must meet the varied needs of different subsets of the elderly, based on a realistic understanding of those needs, using cooperative strategies that forge partnerships between and among public- and private-sector agencies and actors.

Notes

1. Bureau of the Census, *Projections of the Population by Age, Sex, Race, and Hispanic Origin for the United States, 1999 to 2100, Middle Series* (Department of Commerce, 2002), table NP-D1-A.

2. Ibid.

3. Denise I. Smith, "The Elderly Population," in *1997 Population Profile of the United States.* Current Population Reports, Special Studies P23-194 (Bureau of the Census, 1998).

4. Bureau of the Census, "U.S. Population Estimates by Age, Sex, Race, and Hispanic Origin: 1990–93," Population Paper PPL-8 (Department of Commerce, 1994).

5. Activities of daily living include walking one-fourth mile, standing for up to two hours, sitting for up to two hours, climbing stairs, stooping or kneeling, reaching up, reaching out, grasping something, and carrying ten pounds. Federal Interagency Forum on Aging-Related Statistics, *Older Americans 2000: Key Indicators of Well-Being* (2000).

6. Department of Health and Human Services, *A Profile of Older Americans: 2002* (2002).

7. Bureau of the Census, "Sixty-Five Plus in the United States," Statistical Brief SB/95-8 (Department of Commerce, 1995).

8. Bureau of the Census, "Gender and Aging; Demographic Dimensions," International Brief IB/97-3 (Department of Commerce, 1997).

9. Department of Labor, Women's Bureau, *Facts on Working Women*, 98-2 (1998).

10. Department of Health and Human Services, *Older Americans.*

11. William H. Frey, "Boomers and Seniors in the Suburbs: Aging Patterns in Census 2000," Living Cities Census Series, Center on Urban and Metropolitan Policy (Brookings, January 2003).

12. Jason P. Schachter, *Geographical Mobility*, P23-200 (Bureau of the Census, Department of Commerce, 2000), tables 1 and 2.

13. Sandra Rosenbloom, "The Mobility of the Elderly: There's Good News and Bad News," in *Transportation in an Aging Society: Improving Mobility and Safety for Older Persons*, vol. 2, Technical Papers, TRB Conference Proceedings No. 27, 2004.

14. Ibid.

15. Ibid.

16. Jon E. Burkhardt and others, *Improving Public Transit Options for Older Persons*, vol. 2: *Full Report*. Transit Cooperative Research Program Report 82 (Washington: Transportation Research Board, 2002), p. 129.

17. John E. Eberhard, *National Perspectives on Transportation Options for an Aging Society* (National Highway Traffic Safety Administration, 2000).

18. Susan Handy and Kelly Clifton, "Evaluating Neighborhood Accessibility: Possibilities and Practicalities," *Journal of Transportation and Statistics* 4, no. 3 (2001): 67–78.

19. Federal Highway Administration, *Our Nation's Travel: 1995 NPTS Early Results Report* (Department of Transportation, 1997), p. 26.

20. Anita Stowell Ritter, Audrey Straight, and Ed Evans, *Understanding Senior Transportation: Report and Analysis of a Survey of Consumers 50+* (Washington: Public Policy Institute, American Association of Retired Persons, 2002).

21. Sandra Rosenbloom, "Women's Travel Patterns at Various Stages of Their Lives," in *Full Circle: Geographies of Women over the Life Course*, edited by Cindi Katz and Janice Monk (London: Routledge, 1993), pp. 208–42.

22. Sandra Rosenbloom, "Sustainability and the Aging of the Population: The Environmental Implications of the Automobility of Older People," *Transportation* 28 (2001): 375–408.

23. Ibid., and Sandra Rosenbloom and Agneta Ståhl, "Automobility among the Elderly: The Convergence of Environmental, Safety, Mobility, and Land Use Issues," *European Journal of Transport and Infrastructure Research* 2, no. 3-4 (2003): 197–214.

24. Environmental Protection Agency, *Federal Test Procedure Review Project*, Report 320-R-93-007 (1993).

25. William Frey, "Beyond Social Security: The Local Aspects of an Aging America," report prepared for the Center on Urban and Metropolitan Policy (Brookings, 1999).

26. American Association of Retired Persons, *Understanding Senior Housing into the Next Century* (Washington, 1996).

27. Susan Littwin, "Is America Meeting Our Needs?" *New Choices* 37, no. 6 (1999): 24.

28. Diane R. Suchman, *Developing Active Adult Retirement Communities* (Washington: Urban Land Institute, 2001).

29. Morrison Institute for Public Policy, *Hits and Misses: Fast Growth in Metropolitan Phoenix* (Arizona State University, 2000).

30. William H. Frey and Ross C. DeVol, "America's Demography in the New Century: Aging Baby Boomers and New Immigrants as Major Players," Policy Brief 9 (Santa Monica, Calif.: Milken Institute, 2002).

31. See Katz, Puentes, and Bernstein, chapter 2 in this volume.

32. Tim Lomax, Shawn Turner, and Richard Margiotta, *Monitoring Urban Roadways in 2000: Using Archived Operations Data for Reliability and Mobility Measurement*, FHWA-OP-02-029 (Department of Transportation, December 2001).

33. Nearly 90 percent of elderly drivers in Illinois said they frequently drove during off-peak hours (9 a.m. to 3 p.m.). Only about half also drove during the afternoon peak hours, and only one-quarter drove during the morning peak. See Rahim F. Benekohal and others, "Effects of Aging on Older Drivers' Travel Characteristics," *Transportation Research Record* 1438 (1997).

34. This paper uses the convention that safety refers to the risk of crashes and injuries from crashes; security refers to crime against people and the fear of being victimized.

35. A. M. Dellinger, J. A. Langlois, and G. Li, "Fatal Crashes among Older Drivers: Decomposition of Rates into Contributing Factors," *American Journal of Epidemiology* 155, no. 3 (2002): 234–41.

36. Insurance Institute for Highway Safety, "Older Drivers Up Close: They Aren't Dangerous Except Maybe to Themselves," *Status Report* 36, no.8 (2001); Patricia Hu, Jennifer Young, and An Lu, *Highway Crash Rates and Age-Related Driver Limitations: Literature Review and Evaluation of the Data Bases* (Oak Ridge, Tenn.: Center for Transportation Analysis, Oak Ridge National Laboratory, 1993); and Centers for Disease Control, *Older Adult Drivers* (Atlanta, 2003).

37. Leonard Evans, *Traffic Safety and the Driver* (New York: Van Nostrand Reinhold, 1991), pp. 19–43.

38. John W. Eberhard, "Safe Mobility for Senior Citizens," *IATSS Research* 20, no. 1 (1996): 29–37; Diana Persson, "The Elderly Driver: Deciding When to Stop," *Gerontologist* 33, no.1 (1993): 88–91; Darlene Yee, "A Survey of the Traffic Safety Needs of Drivers Aged 55 and Over," in *Needs and Problems of Older Drivers: Survey Results and Recommendations*, edited by James L. Malfetti (Falls Church, Va.: AAA Foundation for Traffic Safety, 1983), pp. 96–128.

39. Rosenbloom, "The Mobility of the Elderly."

40. Organisation for Economic Co-operation and Development, *Ageing and Transport: Mobility Needs and Safety Issues* (Paris, 2001), p. 39.

41. Insurance Institute for Highway Safety, "Older Drivers Up Close."

42. Organisation for Economic Co-operation and Development, *Maintaining Prosperity in an Aging Society* (Paris, 1998), and *Ageing and Transport.*

43. Department of Health, Education, and Welfare, Administration on Aging, *Transportation for the Elderly: The State of the Art*, Report HD-75-20081 (1975).

44. Sandra Rosenbloom, "The Mobility Needs of the Elderly," in *Transportation in an Aging Society: Improving Mobility and Safety for Older Persons*, Special Report 218, vol. 2 (Washington: Transportation Research Board, 1988), p. 10.

45. European Conference of Ministers of Transport, *Transport and Ageing of the Population*, Round Table 112 (Paris: Economic Research Centre, 1999).

46. Scott Bogren, "You Can Get There From Here," *Community Transportation* 16, no. 3 (1998): 10.

47. George Rucker, *Status Report on Public Transportation in Rural America, 1994*, FTA-IL-26-7001-95-01 (Federal Transit Administration, 1994).

48. Audrey Straight and Steven Gregory, *Transportation: The Older Person's Interest* (Washington: Public Policy Institute, American Association of Retired Persons, 2002).

49. National Council on Disability, "Negative Media Portrayals of the ADA," Policy Brief 5 (2003).

50. Rosenbloom, "The Mobility of the Elderly."

51. Ibid.

52. John W. Eberhard, "Safe Mobility for Senior Citizens," *IATSS Research* 20, no. 1 (1996): 29–37; Rahim F. Benekohal and others, *Highway Operations Problems of Elderly Drivers in Illinois*, FHWA-IL–023 (Springfield, Ill.: Illinois Department of Transportation, 1992); Persson, "The Elderly Driver"; and Yee, "Survey."

53. Sandra Rosenbloom, "Driving Cessation among the Elderly: When Does it Really Happen and What Impact Does it Have?" *Transportation Research Record* 1779 (2001): 93–99.

54. Sandra Rosenbloom and Jennifer Morris, "The Travel Patterns of Older Australians in an International Context: Policy Implications and Options," *Transportation Research Record* 1617 (1998): 189–93; European Conference of Ministers of Transport, *Transport and Ageing*.

55. It is important to note that the quality of transit service varies in different countries. The willingness to use transit depends a great deal on quality and availability of service.

56. Sandra Rosenbloom, *The Aging of Society and Smart Growth: The Hidden Links* (Drachman Institute, University of Arizona 2002).

57. See *Barden et al.* v. *City of Sacramento*, No. 01-15744 D.C., No. CV 99-0497 MLS Opinion, Appeal from the U.S. District Court for the Eastern District of California to the U.S. Court of Appeals for the Ninth Circuit, filed June 2, 2002, published 2004 (www.dralegal.org/cases/barden/usca-opinion.pdf).

58. 49 U.S.C. 5310.

59. Agneta Ståhl, "Providing Transportation for Elderly and Disabled in Sweden: Experience Gained and Future Trends," *Public Transport International* 40, no. 2 (1991): 180–201; Agneta Ståhl, "Mobility and Accessibility for Elderly and Disabled People in Sweden," *IATSS Research* 16, no. 2 (1992): 96–97; James J. McLary, Agneta Ståhl, and Steven Persich, "Implementation of Service Routes in the United States," *Transportation Research Record* 1378 (1993): 21-27; Sandra Rosenbloom, *Transit Markets of the Future: The Challenge of Change*, Transit Cooperative Research Program Report 28 (Washington: Transportation Research Board, 1998); John N. Balog, *Attracting Paratransit Patrons to Fixed-Route Services*, Transit Cooperative Research Program Report 24 (Washington: Transportation Research Board, 1997); and Lawrence J. Harman and Russell H. Thatcher, *Integrated Transit Service Design: An Overview: Broward County, Florida, Transit Options Project* (Washington: Project ACTION/NIAT, 1996).

60. Brad Bernier and Tom Seekins, "Rural Transportation Voucher Programs for People with Disabilities: Three Case Studies," *Journal of Transportation and Statistics* 2, no. 1 (1999): 61–70.

61. Federal Highway Administration, *Improvements in Symbol Sign Design to Aid Older Drivers*, FHWA-RD-95-129 (Department of Transportation, August 1995); *Traffic Operations for Older Drivers and Pedestrians*, FHWA-RD-95-169 (July 1996); *The Older Driver Highway Design Handbook*, FHWA-RD-97-135 (January 1998).

62. Evans, *Traffic Safety*.

PART FIVE

Other Important Metropolitan Transportation Issues

10

Highways and Transit: Leveling the Playing Field in Federal Transportation Policy

Edward Beimborn and Robert Puentes

Automobile trips dominate the way Americans travel. Conventional wisdom assumes that this is the result of a fair competition between all transportation modes operating under the same federal policies and rules.

However, the conventional wisdom is wrong. Federal policies that govern highway and transit projects are not the same. In fact, these two modes, which federal law specifically expects to work together in the development of a balanced multimodal system, are treated differently. This unlevel playing field has profound impacts on metropolitan America and on how cities, older suburbs, and newer suburbs grow and develop.

Imagine that the urban or metropolitan portion of the interstate highway system were built according to the same procedures as those used or proposed to build major transit systems. Under this scenario only 50 percent of the capital costs for major highways would be paid from federal sources rather than 80 or 90 percent. Cities would have to aggressively compete against one another for their highway funds based on the quality and justification of the proposed project. The rules for the competition would be subject to change without any input. Some states, cities, and metropolitan areas would never be able to build any highways, even if there was a pervasive desire by the public and the local officials to do so. Only a few highway segments could begin construction in any year.

If major highway projects were built under the same rules as transit, highways would need a congressional "sponsor" who would secure an earmark by competing with other members for scarce funds. Cities unable to get an earmark would have fewer freeways. Local governments would have to demonstrate that they have sufficient funds to pay for their share of the costs of building the highways. They would also have to demonstrate that they would be able to operate and maintain these highways, as well as their existing highways, into the future.

A substantial portion of highway funding would likely have to come from local property, sales, or income taxes. Often there would be limited state contribution to the costs. In many instances, public referenda would have to be conducted and be approved to get local authorization for project funding. Also, highway projects would have to compete with police, fire, education, and other programs for funding. In times of budget shortages, highways could be closed completely or eliminated.

The highway would need to be justified on an explicit measure of cost effectiveness. Agencies would have to specifically state how they would manage the land use impacts of their highways. Finally, intensive mandated study activities would have to precede the project and would be subject to an independent review by the federal government and an open comparison to other projects.

In short, if the rules that apply to new transit projects were applied to new highways, the latter would be very difficult to construct and subject to intense political scrutiny and debate. There would be fewer urban and suburban highways, and the shape of metropolitan areas in the United States would be radically different. Lifestyles of Americans, their mobility, and the health of the economy would be different from what they are now.

A common theme in transportation is that transportation decisions are best made by local elected officials at the metropolitan level. Decisions on the future form and nature of the transportation system are best made by those who are most affected and by those who have the best understanding of day-to-day transportation problems.[1]

Good local decisions require that various transportation options be compared equally and consistently on their merits. Local and metropolitan decisionmakers should then be able to choose the best set or combination of transportation strategies that meet local views, values, and directions. Thus local leaders should be able to pursue the best transportation alternatives for their communities, not the alternative that is simply the easiest to get funded or approved.

Unfortunately, this has not been the case with national transportation policy. Transit and highway systems are treated differently by federal policy, law, and regulations. Local governments are faced with major difficulties in obtaining funds for new transit systems, while at the same time highway funding can be obtained with relative ease. This unlevel playing field can distort decisions at the local level.

This chapter discusses the policy and regulatory barriers to considering and implementing new transit projects in comparison to the relative ease of highway development. In addition, it highlights the differences in the way new transit and highway programs are treated in federal legislation. Finally, it suggests reforms to level the playing field between highways and transit.

Background

The decades from the 1950s to the early 1990s were the halcyon years for highway planning and construction. During this time, through a massive expansion in federal highway assistance, the United States built a 46,000-mile National System of Interstate and Defense Highways—"the largest engineered structure in the world."[2] These highways literally changed the landscape of America.

The "interstate era," as it is commonly known, survived because of a broad consensus that was forged between transportation and political leaders, who were united in their belief that the highway system was essential and necessary to the health and security of the nation. However, according to a Federal Highway Administration publication, by the end of the 1980s that consensus had all but disappeared.[3]

At the same time that the interstate highway system was nearing completion, the nation's transit network had gone from a private industry that was publicly regulated to a public utility with its own demands for federal funding.[4] The federal transit program evolved from a relatively low bureaucratic level at the Department of Commerce to the Department of Housing and Urban Development (HUD) in 1964, to the Department of Transportation in 1968. There it became the Urban Mass Transportation Administration (later renamed the Federal Transit Administration, or FTA), an agency on bureaucratic par with the Federal Highway Administration, albeit considerably smaller and with much less funding.[5]

At the same time, the environmental movement began to directly challenge and question proponents of an expanded highway network. This movement, which was generally nonexistent in 1956 when the Interstate Highway Program began, advocated new national commitments that were often at odds with builders of the interstate system. Faced with considerable backlash over urban freeway expansion, city leaders also began to establish their own set of transportation goals and policy priorities.[6]

As a result, federal policy began to shift as well. One particular emphasis of federal transportation policy at this time was on promoting a level playing field for officials trying to wrestle with the challenge of creating a balanced, intermodal transportation network. A 1990 statement of national transportation policy specifically noted that subsidies, statutes, and regulations play an important part in distorting state and local transportation decisions.[7]

The congressional transportation reforms in the 1990s—the Intermodal Surface Transportation Efficiency Act (ISTEA) in 1991 and its offspring, the Transportation Equity Act for the Twenty-First Century (TEA-21) in 1998—sought to address these distortions. For example, when ISTEA was drafted and debated, the concept of equal matching funds for highways and transit was widely endorsed.[8] In the end, these laws gave states and metropolitan areas the certainty in funding and the flexibility in program design necessary to attempt a range of transportation solutions. Spurred on by these reforms, a small but significant number of states and metropolitan areas began experimenting with transportation policies that offered a more balanced mix between highway expansion and preservation, and between road building and transit expansion. Some of ISTEA's major reforms designed to bring more parity between highways and transit are described below.

More Equitable Matching Requirements

In the decades before ISTEA, a given amount of nonfederal money could leverage more federal highway dollars than it could transit dollars. The federal-aid urban system program was created in 1970 to address transportation problems in metropolitan areas by permitting the federal financing of urban highway and mass transit projects.[9] Transit projects that were financed with urban system highway funds generally received a 75 percent federal share of the urban systems funds. ISTEA's authors intended to remove this disparity of previous federal law by setting the federal-state match ratio for most highway and transit projects at 80 percent federal and 20 percent state and local. However, ISTEA retained the 90-to-10 federal-to-state matching ratio for interstate projects, and certain traffic and safety programs had a 100 percent federal share.

Funding Flexibility

The "flexible funding" provisions of ISTEA and TEA-21 refer to the programs identified in the legislation whose funds may be used for transit or highway projects. The significance of these provisions cannot be overstated. The bill drafters intended to give planners and decisionmakers at the state and local level the authority to transfer funds between highways and transit, with the direction of the transfers unspecified but determined by locally defined goals. Among other things, this freedom of financing has provided states and metropolitan planning organizations, as well as local political, corporate, civic, and constituency leaders, a greater opportunity to tailor transportation spending to regional needs and market realities.

To date, the experience with this flexibility has been limited. From 1992 to 1997, only four states (California, Massachusetts, New York, and Oregon) and the District of Columbia transferred more than one-third of available funds from highways to transit.[10] According to the FTA, in the ten years from 1992 to 2002, eight other states flexed no money to transit or a negligible amount.[11] While this program appeared to create opportunities for transit agencies and local areas to have more flexibility in how they spend their transportation dollars, the reality is that, except for a few notable exceptions, the process is hardly used by many states.

Major Investment Studies

ISTEA also sought to balance the process by which metropolitan areas considered major new transportation investments. Before ISTEA, states and metropolitan areas wishing to use federal funds to construct new large-scale transit systems were required to justify the project through a detailed analysis of alternatives and cost effectiveness, in addition to the environmental review required by the National Environmental Policy Act of 1969 (NEPA).[12] However, no such requirements were placed on new highway investments. Environmental impact studies for highways were often done after engineering started, and the analysis of cost effectiveness was not done at all.[13]

ISTEA specifically required the secretary of transportation to initiate a rulemaking proceeding to conform review requirements for transit projects to comparable requirements for highway projects. The resulting regulations required major investment studies (MIS) for any significant capital project that used federal funds. This generally included projects such as freeway or arterial widening or expansions of more than one mile in length,

Table 10-1. Comparison of Rules Governing Federal Transit and Highway Programs

Rules	Transit (New Starts)	Highway
Federal funding	Current federal law authorizes as much as an 80 percent federal share. FTA practice is to recommend only projects with a maximum 60 percent federal share, in accord with congressional appropriations committee direction. The Bush administration has proposed a 50 percent or less match in SAFETEA.[a]	Federal match is 80–90 percent depending on program.
	New Start money is highly competitive.	Program funds are allocated by formula.
	Nonfederal funds for transit are typically local, from varying sources; project funding must compete with other programs and may require referenda.	State funds are derived mainly from fuel and license fees. Normally a dedicated fund that cannot be used for nontransportation purposes.[b]
Project criteria and justification	Extensive list, including cost effectiveness, land use impacts, and financial plan.	Primarily environmental measures; no requirement for cost effectiveness or land use analysis.
Land use impacts	A key project selection criterion: "transit-supportive land use patterns."	Land use impacts of projects not considered.
Performance evaluation	Peer comparison is mandatory and reported to Congress.	Peer comparison is rare.
	A detailed process is used to compare alternative projects.	Alternative comparisons are optional at state level.
Information transparency and accessibility	Information and data are publicly accessible and transparent.	Information and data are difficult to access and unclear for the general public.

Source: Authors' analysis of federal transportation laws and reauthorization proposals.
a. Safe, Accountable, Flexible and Efficient Transportation Act of 2003.
b. Thirty states earmark gas tax revenues for highway or roadway projects only. The remaining states allocate a portion of revenues to other expenditures. See Puentes and Prince, chapter 3 in this volume.

or new rail transit lines or extensions of more than one mile in length. The MIS was intended, through alternatives analysis with extensive public input, to determine the best transportation strategy for a given corridor. However, as discussed below, TEA-21 eliminated the MIS as a planning requirement.[14]

Despite these advances initiated by ISTEA, federal rules remain stacked against transit (see table 10-1). The next section discusses the specific federal regulations that tilt the playing field and focuses on examples where rules and regulations exist, perhaps appropriately, for transit projects but not for highway projects.

Federal Policies that Create an Unlevel Playing Field

Consider a city or region that wants to upgrade its transportation system. A proper analysis of needs and opportunities would consider all reasonable options in a fair and balanced way. These would include both highway and transit options as well as policy changes. Costs of the alternatives should be thoroughly investigated as well as their impacts on the land use patterns of the region. Furthermore, the community should think about environmental impacts of the alternatives and how they affect the future economy of the area. The community should be able to decide what is best based on consistent policies and programs that do not tilt the decision one way or another.

Unfortunately, this is not the reality. There are major differences in how highway and transit projects are funded and administered. In fact, two separate systems govern these two transportation modes.

The FTA administers the New Starts program, the Department of Transportation's program for identifying and funding new fixed guideway transit projects (for example, rail, bus rapid transit, trolley, and ferry). Funds for this program are housed in the FTA's Capital Investments Grant and Loan program, which is also referred to as Section 5309 (of the U.S. Code). In addition to the New Starts program (which constitutes 40 percent of the capital program), Section 5309 also provides assistance for rail modernization (40 percent) and for bus and bus-related facilities (20 percent).[15]

Since the New Starts program is the way the federal government funds new transit projects, it is the primary transit program highlighted in this brief. The New Starts program provides discretionary financial assistance and has been used to expand or initiate hundreds of heavy-rail, light-rail, commuter-rail, and bus rapid transit systems that cannot be funded with formula, flexible, or local funds. It is intended to supplement the transit formula programs, which are not funded at a high enough level to allow metropolitan areas to pay for major fixed guideway investments. The term New Starts is a bit of a misnomer since it includes both expansions of existing systems as well the initiation of totally new transit technologies within metropolitan areas.

It is important to highlight this program to illustrate how unbalanced federal transportation policies can skew local, metropolitan, and state investment decisions. Every metropolitan area already has an important and extensive highway network. However, the process of building, widening, or extending this network differs fundamentally from doing the same to a transit system. For one thing, states do not seek permission to build highway projects. In fact, the U.S. code states specifically that the appropriation of highway funds "shall in no way infringe on the sovereign rights of the States to determine which projects shall be federally financed."[16] This is dramatically different from the situation that applies when areas want to construct new fixed guideway systems: they cannot spend federal funds on these projects unless they comply with rigorous federal requirements. The following section shows how highway and transit programs—especially New Starts— are treated differently by federal legislation and policy, and how those differences lead to an unlevel playing field and distort good local planning, management, and decisionmaking.

Federal Funding

In general, federal funding for highway projects is more secure and greater than that for transit projects, making the former easier to finance. As mentioned, the primary federal financial source for support of new transit systems is the New Starts program. TEA-21 authorized $8.2 billion in New Starts funding through fiscal year 2003, which is about 20 percent of the $41 billion for all FTA programs. It is important to note that only $6.1 billion was "guaranteed," and Congress has not provided any nonguaranteed funding for New Starts. Formula grants made up about half of all transit funding; they can be used for some capital investments (such as equipment and rolling stock, as well as planning, design, and evaluation work) but not solely for construction of major new systems or extensions.[17] (See table 10-2.)

The New Starts program is totally discretionary and highly regulated by the Department of Transportation. According to the General Accounting Office (GAO), New Starts funding is oversubscribed, and as a result, competition for these funds is intense.[18] Projects must progress through a regional review of alternatives, develop preliminary engineering plans, and meet FTA's approval for final design before final approval is given and the project is recommended for a multiyear full funding grant agreement.[19] It is not unusual for project funding applications to require many years to overcome each barrier and step. In TEA-21 Congress authorized nearly 200 separate transit projects, but very few of them will actually be built since the expenditure levels authorized were far less than required to fund them all.[20] It is important to note that the full funding grant agreement serves as a commitment of federal funds; however, each project's share of federal funds is subject to the annual congressional appropriations process.

Highway funds, conversely, are not competitive and do not require congressional earmarks. Receipts in the Highway Account of the federal

Table 10-2. Federal Transit and Highway Programs and Their Purpose, Federal Share, and Authorized Funding Levels[a]

Units as indicated

Appropriation or program	Program purpose or expenses	Federal share	TEA-21 funding	
			Millions of dollars	Percent of total
Federal transit programs				
Urbanized Area Formula grants (Section 5307)	Capital, planning, preventive maintenance, crime prevention and security, facilities and rolling stock, ADA paratransit, transit enhancements for urbanized areas	80; 90 for ADA or Clean Air Act purchases	18,033.8	44.0
New Starts discretionary grants (Section 5309)	Capital projects for new fixed guideway systems and extensions to existing systems, including property and right-of-way acquisition, initial acquisition of rolling stock, alternatives analysis	80 in federal law, 60 in congressional report language, 50 as proposed by Bush administration	8,182.4	20.0
Fixed guideway modernization discretionary funding (Section 5309)	Capital projects to modernize existing fixed guideway systems	80	6,592.4	16.1
Bus and bus-related discretionary grants (Section 5309)	Capital projects to replace, rehabilitate, and purchase buses and related equipment and to construct bus-related facilities	80	3,546.2	8.7
Other formula grants	Includes Alaska Railroad, elderly and persons with disabilities, and rural transit formulas	Generally 80–100; rural area operating expenses: 50	2,440.2	6.0
Transit planning and research	Metropolitan, state, and national planning and research; rural transit assistance; and cooperative research.	Generally 80–100	1,013.0	2.5
Job Access and Reverse Commute	Competitive grants to develop services to connect welfare recipients and low-income persons to employment and support services; eligible expenses include capital, operating, and maintenance	50	750.0	1.8
Administration		441.7		1.1
Total for transit		40,999.7		100

(continued)

Table 10-2. Federal Transit and Highway Programs and Their Purpose, Federal Share, and Authorized Funding Levels[a] (*continued*)

Units as indicated

Appropriation or program	Program purpose or expenses	Federal share	TEA-21 funding Millions of dollars	TEA-21 funding Percent of total
Federal highway programs				
Surface Transportation	Flexible funding that may be used by states and localities for projects on any federal-aid highway bridge projects on any public road, transit capital projects, and intracity and intercity bus terminals and facilities	80	33,332.7	19.5
National Highway System	Improvements to rural and urban roads that are part of the system, including the interstate system and designated connections to major intermodal terminals	80 (100 for Alaska and territorial highways)	28,571.1	16.7
Interstate Maintenance	Resurfacing, restoring, rehabilitating, and reconstructing most routes on the interstate system	90	23,809.6	13.9
Bridge	Replacing or rehabilitating deficient highway bridges; seismic retrofitting of bridges located on any public road	80	20,430.4	11.9
High-Priority Projects	Any project eligible for federal funds defined as demonstration projects in TEA-21	80	9,359.9	5.5
Congestion Mitigation and Air Quality	Funding projects and programs to reduce transportation-related emissions in air quality nonattainment and maintenance areas for ozone, carbon monoxide, and small particulate matter	80	8,122.6	4.7
Federal Lands Highway	Funding for coordinated program of public roads and transit facilities serving federal and Indian lands	100	4,066.0	2.4
Appalachian Development Highway System	Construction of the Appalachian corridor highways in thirteen states to promote economic development	80	2,250.0	1.3
Magnetic Levitation Transportation Technology Deployment	Construction of an operating transportation system employing magnetic levitation	66	1,010.0	0.6

(*continued*)

Table 10-2. Federal Transit and Highway Programs and Their Purpose, Federal Share, and Authorized Funding Levels[a] (*continued*)

Units as indicated

Appropriation or program	Program purpose or expenses	Federal share	TEA-21 funding Millions of dollars	Percent of total
Woodrow Wilson Bridge	Design and construction of a new bridge where Interstate 95 crosses the Potomac River	80–100	900.0	0.5
Corridor and border planning	Coordinated planning, design, and construction of corridors of national significance, to promote economic growth and international or interregional trade	80	700.0	0.4
Recreational trails	Development and maintenance of recreational trails for motorized and nonmotorized recreational trail users	80	270.0	0.2
Ferry boats and ferry facilities	Construction of ferry boats and ferry terminal facilities	80	220.0	0.1
National Scenic Byways	Supporting and providing discretionary grants for planning, designing, and developing scenic byway projects	80	148.0	0.1
Transportation System and Community Preservation	Funding for planning grants, implementation grants, and research to investigate and address relationships between transportation and community and system preservation	100	120.0	0.1
Value Pricing	Supporting the costs of implementing value pricing projects	80	51.0	<0.1
National Historic Covered Bridge Preservation	Rehabilitating, repairing, and preserving the nation's historic covered bridges	80	50.0	<0.1
Highway Use Tax Evasion	Support for state and federal efforts to enhance motor fuel tax enforcement	100	35.0	<0.1
Minimum Guarantee	Funding to states based on equity considerations; administered as STP funds	80	35,119.3	20.5
Other	Includes Puerto Rico highway program, railroad grade program, and safety programs		2,543.0	1.5
Total for highways			171,108.6	100.0

Source: Surface Transportation Policy Project, *TEA-21 User's Guide* (Washington, 1998); Federal Highway Administration, *Financing Federal-Aid Highways*, FHWA-PL-99-015 (Department of Transportation, 1999).
a. ADA, American with Disabilities Act; STP, Surface Transportation Program.

Highway Trust Fund are distributed to states based on "allocation formulas," which differ somewhat from one federal program to another. Once funds are allocated, the states can distribute them among projects as they see fit. Federal oversight is limited only to ensuring that they comply with federal guidelines and accepted design standards. This reduces the complexity and difficulty of the process of developing projects. With an assured source of funding, projects can be planned and implemented over time without concern for how they compare to projects in other states.

Another inequity exists in terms of the total percentage of costs the federal government is willing to contribute to highway and transit projects. As mentioned, ISTEA maintained an 80 percent funding ratio for formula and other discretionary programs but capped funding rates for transit New Starts at up to 80 percent of total project costs. In reality, actual funding rates are much lower. Congress recently directed the FTA not to approve New Starts projects with more than a 60 percent federal share.[21] In addition, the Bush administration's fiscal year 2004 budget reaffirms an earlier recommendation to reduce the federal match to 50 percent beginning in 2004.[22] In contrast, highway funding continues to enjoy a federal matching ratio of 90 percent for improvements and maintenance on the interstate highway system, and an 80 percent rate for most other projects. The Bush administration proposes that this ratio be at similar levels in the next reauthorization bill.[23]

Furthermore, the high federal match results in inefficient use of highway dollars. States often use state funds for their matching portion of highway projects, with little or no funding required from the local area.[24] Local officials sometimes view these projects as "free money" and eagerly seek to implement them. It is often tempting to load up the projects with costs and features that may not be needed but are easily accommodated when someone else is paying the cost. This can lead to inefficient use of federal resources and a failure to provide good stewardship for federal investments in highways.

In contrast, costs for most transit projects must be kept low since local sources of revenue must be identified, and commitments for operating costs and local shares of capital costs must be provided as a key project justification criterion. In the last year for which data is available, federal funds provided 47.2 percent of the capital funds used by transit agencies while state sources provided 10.7 percent and local sources provided 42.0 percent. It is important to note that at this time, the federal allowable share for all FTA capital projects was still at least 80 percent (see figure 10-1).

Figure 10-1. Funding Sources for Transit Capital Expenditures, 1990–2000

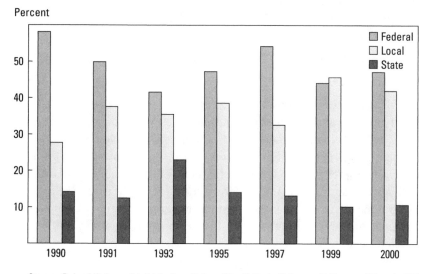

Percent

Source: Federal Highway Administration, *Status of the Nation's Highways, Bridges, and Transit: 2002 Conditions and Performance Report* (Department of Transportation, 2002), exhibit 6-27.

Local funds for transit services come from a variety of sources, depending on the community. Commonly used sources are sales taxes dedicated to transit, local income taxes, fuel taxes, or property taxes. In many cases the transit agency competes for these funds with other local needs such as education, health care, and police or fire protection. In places where the transit systems receive money from their state government, this can also come from a variety of sources: dedicated portions of a transportation fund or state general-purpose revenue sources such as income or sales taxes.[25] Here again, the transit agency has to compete with other state expenditure programs for funding.

When a city is contemplating a major new transit investment, it may need to put together a financial package that is subject to referendum for voter approval. Such packages may involve new sources of taxation such as a local sales, fuel, and income taxes or property tax assessments. These referenda can often be highly contentious, and there are many cases where communities have gone to the voters several times to gain approval.[26]

The end result of these funding inequities is that they sometimes lead to skewed investment decisions. A recent GAO report confirmed this when it found that the imbalance between the federal highway and transit match, in particular, could "bias the local decisionmaking process in favor of highway projects."[27] This conclusion was drawn from interviews the GAO conducted with project sponsors and those responsible for planning and programming transportation dollars.

Project Criteria and Justification

Unlike highway projects, new fixed guideway transit projects are subject to intense federal oversight and multiple project criteria and justifications. TEA-21 directs the FTA to evaluate and rate candidate New Starts projects as an input to federal funding decisions and at specific milestones throughout each project's planning and development. The FTA requires that a comprehensive planning and project development process be used to assist local decisionmakers in evaluating alternatives in specified corridors and to select the most appropriate improvement for the corridor. Planning and project development for New Starts projects is coordinated with metropolitan planning and NEPA review processes.

New Start proposals must undergo a comprehensive multiyear planning process subject to detailed regulations from the FTA. Aside from considering environmental impacts, New Starts projects must be reviewed for their impacts on employment, operating efficiency, cost effectiveness, land use policies, and level of local funding commitment.[28] For example, projects are judged on their ability to serve low-income households and generate employment near transit stations, as well as on how well the sponsoring agency has implemented polices to encourage transit-supportive development patterns. It is important to note that these criteria are broad and reach well beyond the transportation system itself. They do not subscribe to the belief that a transit project should be judged simply on its ability to reduce or solve a metropolitan area's congestion problems (see table 10-3)

The transportation subcommittee of the House Appropriations Committee, in its funding decision on the transportation appropriations bill for fiscal year 2005, has ignored this wisdom from the FTA and years of scholarly research. In going beyond the traditional role of the subcommittee, it admonished the FTA for not placing enough emphasis on congestion relief. Specifically, the report states that "reducing congestion on the roads must be one of the most critical elements for justification of building a new fixed guideway system or extending a current one."[29]

In addition, projects are subject to a rigorous cost-effectiveness process to evaluate the performance of the federal transit investment in terms of the

Table 10-3.   Federal Transit Administration Justification Criteria for a New Starts Project

Criteria	Measure(s)
Mobility improvements	Hours of transportation system user benefits
	Low-income households served
	Employment near stations
Environmental benefits	Change in regional pollutant emissions
	Change in regional energy consumption
	EPA air quality designation
Operating efficiencies	Operating cost per passenger mile
Cost effectiveness	Incremental cost per hour of transportation system user benefit
Transit-supportive land use and future patterns	Existing land use
	Transit-supportive plans and policies
	Performance and impacts of policies
	Other land use considerations
Other factors	Project benefits not reflected by other New Starts criteria

Source: Federal Transit Administration, "Planning, Development, and Funding for New Starts Projects" (www.fta.dot.gov/library/policy/ns/ns.htm [June 2005]).

incremental project cost divided by transportation system user benefits. User benefits consist of weighted travel time savings as determined by advanced travel forecasting models. FTA regulations are very extensive and provide very specific financial analysis techniques and assumptions; these allow a consistent comparison of projects at different locations.[30] Complying with these regulations can take several years of intense study, often costing millions of dollars.

The cost-effectiveness criteria are used to demonstrate that a project will attract new ridership and that those riders will benefit in terms of time, cost, and convenience. It allows the FTA to compare projects between communities and ensure that the projects chosen render the greatest return on federal investment. The House Appropriations Committee went further in its fiscal year 2004 transportation bill by saying specifically that the federal government should allocate transportation dollars in a manner that maximizes benefits relative to costs and that the FTA should "develop more stringent measures by which to rate New Starts projects."[31]

Without a doubt, these standards make for better transit projects. Agencies proposing projects are forced to think of how their projects will make better communities. The process of doing this is long and arduous. It requires an active planning process with participation of many groups and interests that have active political champions who often risk their careers on a project.

In sharp contrast, the level of analysis required for highway expansion or the construction of new facilities is less stringent. To comply with NEPA regulations, highway projects must evaluate environmental impacts if they could "significantly affect the environment."[32] In that case, an environmental impact statement or assessment is needed. The statements deal with issues such as noise and air quality effects and impacts on natural areas, such as wetlands, but the evaluation of the scope of the project and the criteria considered often stops there.[33] Seldom is there any attempt to deal with issues such as local employment impacts, services to low-income neighborhoods, or land use policy.

Cost-effectiveness analysis is used only to a limited extent and has been applied unevenly to highway programs. While some agencies attempt cost-benefit analyses for highway projects, others ignore this and propose and implement projects that have not had a cost-effectiveness test. Projects are chosen in a convoluted process that can be highly political and often inefficient. A recent GAO report points out that there are no federal requirements for using benefit-cost analysis for highway projects, nor does the Department of Transportation advocate any particular set of analytical tools. There are many reasons for this, including the challenges of quantifying some benefits and costs and the difficulties in building consensus for models, given the diversity of places and projects. The only area where such analysis is used is with the New Starts program.[34]

However, benefit-cost analysis has been advocated for highway projects for years. In 1977 the American Association of State Highway and Transportation Officials published a guide on conducting benefit-cost analyses for highway and other transportation projects.[35] Other textbooks, research reports, and publications discuss the importance of analyzing highway projects using benefit-cost techniques. Yet, as long as localities are able to purchase local benefits with state and federal funds, local governments have incentives to overstate highway project benefits and understate costs.

ISTEA established the major investment study process, which provides a sound basis for reaching major investment decisions in metropolitan areas by requiring a comprehensive analysis of all reasonable alternatives for addressing a transportation problem. ISTEA's metropolitan planning regulations required MIS analyses to evaluate the efficacy and cost-effectiveness of alternative investments or strategies in attaining local, state, and national goals and objectives. The MIS considered the benefits and costs of investments related to such factors as mobility improvements; social, economic, and environmental effects; safety; operating efficiencies; land use and economic development; financing; and energy consumption.[36] However, TEA-21 eliminated the MIS as a way to determine benefits and costs of major transportation investments. Yet major transit investments seeking New Starts funding are *still* required to go through FTA's requirements for an alternatives analysis, which are very similar to those of the MIS under ISTEA. Thus highway and transit project plans are not subject to the same degree of oversight.

Highways and transit projects are inherently different in what is perceived as benefits and costs, yet there is much that could be learned if highway projects were subject to similar criteria. Wise investment of highway funds should include a concern about what will be gained for the money expended. Hence decisionmakers and citizens would benefit from a transit-like review of highway projects.

Land Use Considerations

The relationship between land use and transportation is a fundamental concern in transportation policy. Everything that happens to land use has transportation implications, and every transportation action affects land use. Actions by transportation agencies shape land use by providing infrastructure to improve accessibility and mobility. This increases the utility of land and leads to more intensive land use. Land development generates travel, and travel generates the need for new facilities, which in turn increases accessibility and attracts further development. The question of whether transportation influences development or whether land use dictates transportation has been a matter of ongoing concern among transportation professionals since the beginning of transportation planning.[37]

Much has been written in recent years about urban sprawl, new urbanism, transit-oriented development, smart growth, and ways to effect a closer tie between land use and transportation. A comprehensive review of literature related to urban sprawl and its impacts concluded that there is general agreement that sprawl leads to more vehicle miles of travel, more automobile trips, and less cost-effective transit service.[38] There was also some agreement that sprawl engenders higher household costs for travel as well as greater social costs.

These principles have been well recognized by the FTA in its guidelines for New Starts and alternatives analysis. Local areas proposing major investments in transit are required to analyze land use impacts and to take proactive steps to ensure that transit investment is coordinated with land use. This is done to obtain a good return on federal investment by integrating transit service with economic development and residential activity.

Land use rightly is a local responsibility, and it is appropriate that federal and state agencies defer land use decisions to local governments. As mentioned, federal criteria require that transit projects be rated on whether they have transit-supportive land use plans and policies and on the impacts of these policies. These requirements can be challenging for a transit agency that must address land use considerations that are beyond its control. This is especially true with regard to commuter rail projects intended to operate in suburban communities that frequently put caps on residential or commercial densities. Nevertheless, the connection between land use and transportation is of paramount importance, and it is useful for a transit agency and local government to address these issues collaboratively.

No such land use provision exists for highway investments. Highways can have a profound impact on the pace and shape of metropolitan growth. Highway spending helps define the boundaries of metropolitan areas, determining where households and firms can locate their homes and facilities. In many metropolitan areas, transportation policies generally support the expansion of road capacity at the fringe of metropolitan areas and beyond, enabling people and businesses to live miles from urban centers but still benefit from metropolitan life. The spatial implications of these investments cannot be underestimated.

Highway projects often lead to development that generates additional traffic that negates the value and performance of highway improvements. Highways designed to move traffic efficiently become snarled with local vehicles needing to turn in and out of developments along the highway. If these developments are poorly planned, there are excessive vehicle conflicts, congestion, and safety hazards. The money spent for these projects is wasted as traffic builds up and creates a new set of problems that will require more expenditure of money. Furthermore, shifts in development from one part of a city to another can lead to wasted infrastructure and loss of jobs and economic activity elsewhere. Plans for highway projects need to consider how they will affect land use.

Local governments need to provide good stewardship of their transportation assets. Access management, interchange area planning, and better coordination between government units can make a difference in protecting highway investments. For example, access management provides a way to control the number and type of access points on major roads to help traffic flow better and more safely, but its use is scattered across the country, with no common federal policy or guidelines. There are no requirements that local governments consider land use effects for federal highway dollars, but it is an essential part of new transit investments. Highway programs could benefit substantially if local and state agencies were asked to show how their plans will protect the investment by better interfacing with land use.

Performance Evaluation

Furthermore, while transit agencies follow useful and important reporting and evaluation guidelines for their projects and systems, highway agencies have less effective procedures. Transit operators, regardless of whether or not they use New Starts funds, are required to submit annual reports of their performance, effectiveness, and cost-effectiveness to the FTA as part of the Uniform System of Accounts for use in the National Transit Database (NTD, formerly Section 15 data) requirements for continued federal funding. Transit agencies are very diverse, and to provide consistent data, all agencies must meet the same accounting and reporting requirements.[39] Each year, almost 600 transit operators report to the FTA on transit activities in more than 400 urbanized areas. Nationally, 85,000 transit vehicles, 7,000 miles of rail track, 2,000 rail stations, and 1,000 maintenance facilities are included in these reports. The NTD, as the repository for this information, serves as the primary tool to support transit operational and financial decisionmaking on a national level.

The NTD provides a comprehensive source of transit data and is used to support federal, state, and local public investment decisions. NTD data are used to apportion FTA funding among urbanized areas, according to legislatively mandated formulas. Furthermore, this information is used at various levels of government to guide policy development, assist in establishing national priorities, and shape public planning and strategic decisionmaking efforts. For example, the database has been recently changed to provide better reporting of safety and security information.[40]

This process allows transit agencies to use a consistent data set, compare their performance with peer agencies, and track trends over time. Agencies can quickly determine if their performance is improving or worsening and see how they are doing in comparison to similar agencies. This is an unquestionably useful procedure that leads to better management of transit systems.

Highway agencies have a different process. The Highway Performance Monitoring System (HPMS) provides data that reflect the extent, condition, performance, use, and operating characteristics of the nation's highways. Developed in 1978 as a national highway transportation system database, it includes limited data on all public roads, more detailed data for a sample of the arterial and collector functional systems, and certain statewide summary information. The HPMS includes a statistically drawn sample of over 100,000 highway sections containing information on current physical and operating characteristics as well as projections of future travel growth on a section-by-section basis.[41]

While the type of HPMS data is similar to that of the NTD, its use for evaluation of highway programs in relation to other peer agencies is only just beginning. Work has been done outside the Department of Transportation comparing states to each other and documenting trends over time.[42] This process is controversial, and some state and local agencies are reluctant to compare their performance to others. Consistency in collection methods and data varies among agencies, and many agencies feel that they are unique and cannot be compared to others.[43] Comparing highway agency performance is difficult and requires extensive effort to gather data from diverse sources. Transit agency peer comparisons are very easy, with consistent reports readily available on the Internet. Differences in the state of the art in collecting data and in attitudes toward use of this information lead to a different set of rules for transit versus highway systems. The transit evaluation processes are useful in general for transportation decisionmaking and should be applied equally to both modes.

Information Transparency and Accessibility

Finally, transit agencies must regularly disclose their spending and other data, or risk losing funding. Highway spending and other statistics, on the other hand, are more difficult to access and interpret.

Transit agency profiles are developed from the NTD, and they show transit system characteristics on a uniform basis as well as measures of performance and of effectiveness for services and costs.[44] These profiles are updated yearly for every transit agency in the nation and posted on the Internet in a clear format that is easy for the public to read and understand. The requirements for the NTD are codified in federal law, and receipt of certain transit funds is directly tied to compliance. Transit agencies risk the loss of Urbanized Area Formula program (Section 5307) funds if they do not comply with NTD reporting requirements.[45]

Conversely, extensive and detailed data collected by the Federal Highway Administration are not accessible by the general public over the Internet, nor are they presented in a format that the public can easily understand.

Indeed, the HPMS is a principal source of the data used by the FHWA to develop the annual *Highway Statistics* publication as well as the *Conditions and Performance Report* to Congress, both of which are available over the Internet. It is a stated objective of the HPMS that the database itself be "publicly accessible" and that the FHWA make it available over the Internet "in the short term"; however, this has yet to happen.[46]

The FHWA also maintains a Fiscal Management Information System (FMIS), which is a financial database of all highway projects that have been financed using federal funds. However, even though the FMIS has been in place since the early days of the interstate era, published information on spending by recipient and program is limited and often several years behind. The raw FMIS data used to produce much of the quantitative analysis in this report are difficult to work with and not available on the World Wide Web.

The end result is that it is very difficult to determine actual spending of federal transportation dollars for roadway projects. The federal government leaves it up to the states to build and maintain the nation's roadway network but does not require states to provide the public with detailed information about state investment decisions using those funds. It continues to be easier for the general public to determine where private institutions like banks and thrifts make investments (thanks to the federal Home Mortgage Disclosure Act) and to hold these institutions accountable than to know how transportation agencies spend their money.

Clearly, highways and transit are operating on an uneven playing field in terms of federal transportation policy. What is not as clear—though it seems intuitive—is whether these policies have resulted in any fewer transit projects than would have been built if policies were more balanced. This next section examines the recent situation in one metropolitan area—Milwaukee—to illustrate how federal policies can skew investment decisions on the state and local level.

Milwaukee Metropolitan Area Case Study

Milwaukee seemed like a logical choice for a new transit start. The city has areas of high density with mixed uses that were developed around a strong bus transit system and seemed like a natural for rail transit service. Jennifer Dorn, the FTA administrator, stated in a recent speech during a visit there that Milwaukee had sufficient population density to support rail transit.[47]

And unlike many other cities and metropolitan areas, Milwaukee remains fairly "centralized" in terms of metropolitan employment location.

Nearly two-thirds of the jobs are within ten miles of the central business district and over 20 percent are within three miles.[48] Overall, the city did lose residents during the 1990s, but the downtown area saw a slight increase in population as well as an increase in density.[49]

The metropolitan area also had a strong, visible champion of rail transit in Milwaukee mayor John Norquist. In the early 1990s, Mayor Norquist founded the Alliance for Future Transit in Milwaukee, a business organization designed to promote light-rail transit in the area. The transit agency in the area, Milwaukee County Transit System, was the twenty-fifth largest transit bus agency in the nation in 2001, with a good fare recovery rate: 34 percent of the agency's operating expenses came from passenger fares in 2001. It also had a solid management that was ready to run a system in coordination with good bus services to its community. The system received the Outstanding Achievement Award—the highest award a transit agency can receive—by the American Public Transit Association in both 1987 and in 1999.[50]

Furthermore, the area had an inside track to federal funding by the set-aside of nearly $300 million dollars of interstate cost estimate funds to be used for a new transit system for the area. This funding was explicitly set aside in the ISTEA legislation for transit purposes in the Milwaukee area.

The fixed guideway transit planning process in Milwaukee has a long and complex history. The metropolitan planning organization, the Southeastern Wisconsin Planning Commission, included major transit corridors as part of its long-range transportation plan for the region. The most significant effort in this regard was the Milwaukee East-West Corridor Study, conducted during the mid-1990s. The corridor included a regional medical center, two large universities, a major-league baseball stadium, Milwaukee's downtown and festival grounds, high-rise housing units, and neighborhood shopping centers. This corridor was earmarked in TEA-21 for one of 114 new rail projects to begin construction by 2003.

The study for this project cost millions of dollars, included hundreds of meetings, and involved over five years of effort. It followed FTA procedures and produced twenty-nine technical reports that fill up an entire bookshelf. All aspects of the alternatives were studied—impacts on air, noise, flooding, parks, wetlands, historic areas, properties, businesses, economic development, and natural areas, as well as costs, ridership potential, and policies to enhance land use around transit stops. In addition, extensive public meetings were held to define the project's scope and elicit reactions to the alternatives.

The study eventually resulted in a 430-page "working draft" of a major investment study–draft environmental impact study. This was issued for preliminary comments and reactions prior to an "official" draft environmental impact statement. This report described multiple alternatives of different light-rail or bus system alignments to be built in the area and included twenty-one letters from federal, state, and local agencies and the private sector regarding the project. Several of the most promising transit technologies were featured and were designed to address freeway capacity, serve low-income neighborhoods, and provide a focus for high-density urban development.[51]

However, the official draft environmental impact statement was never issued and was officially terminated by the FHWA in 2000.[52] These reports now gather dust as they sit on the shelves of the planners who worked on them. The project is all but dead in the water with just $91.5 million left of $289 million that was appropriated in 1991.

What happened? How could a process be so close to reaching a conclusion and then be cast aside? What value was there to spend so much time and money and effort by so many people to do all those complicated studies and then have it all come to naught? Opinions differ, but the process eventually fell apart on the issue of money and differences in federal funding policies for highways and transit. According to the FTA, the result was a lack of local consensus on funding options.[53]

A key issue was how to pay for the local share of the project. Transit in the Milwaukee area uses state transportation dollars and local funds for its nonfederal costs. Local funds come from the property tax and must compete with other government services for funds. Property taxes are high in Wisconsin, and local elected officials support increases at their political peril. In 1994 advisory referenda on the transit corridor project were voted down in five suburban communities. According to polls, most residents supported light rail and thought it would be reliable, provide environmental benefits, and help low-income people get to work. However, a majority also considered it to be too expensive.[54]

Wisconsin Department of Transportation officials said that there was no state money to be used for the nonfederal share of a light-rail transit project, but that state funds could be used for a highway project.[55] Money was available for highways but not for transit. Faced with no state funds, conflicts arose among central-city and suburban state legislators and local officials over who should pay the local share. Outlying suburban municipalities went on record opposing the project, despite reports that showed a light-rail system would not only contribute significantly to economic development in the city of Milwaukee but would also provide such benefits to the entire region.[56] No consensus or agreement could be reached. Eventually, state legislators prohibited any expenditure to even study the issue of light rail in the Milwaukee area, thus ending the process.[57]

Meanwhile, a highway study has been completed that recommends a $6.23 billion dollar expenditure to expand and reconstruct the regional freeway system—more than ten times the cost of the transit corridor project. Documents associated with the plan tout the fact that funding for the project will be the responsibility of the state (10–20 percent) and the federal government (80–90 percent) with no required funding from the localities.[58] This study has been adopted by the regional planning commission, endorsed by six of seven county boards (Milwaukee County being the exception), and written into state legislation.

Faced with a choice of no local costs for highways and substantial local costs for transit, the decision was easy, but it may not have been the best. No one knows what localities in the Milwaukee metropolitan area would have done if the rules governing new transit and highway projects were the same, leveling the playing field for both of them.

Recommendations

Congress should build upon the reforms solidified in ISTEA to level the playing field between highway and transit projects so that officials can make sound investment decisions based on metropolitan and local goals and objectives rather than skewed federal policies. In view of that, Congress should consider the following policy recommendations to ensure transportation investments meet the modern challenges facing metropolitan areas.

Establish Equivalent Standards for Both Transit and Highway Projects

Elements of the federal policies that govern transit investments can be used to benefit highway programs and help protect federal highway investments. In particular the following should be pursued.

Apply Land Use Requirements of FTA New Starts to Highway Projects Proposing Substantially Increased Capacity. Highways have a major impact on land use, and these effects should be considered, if for no other reason than to protect the value of federal investments from being undermined by poor land use programs and polices at the local level. The federal government only supports transit projects where local land use policies promote efficient development patterns. Decisionmakers should similarly consider whether highway projects generate or perpetuate past inefficient land use patterns. In any case, local and state governments should be explicitly required to deal with the land use impacts of both their transit *and* highway projects.

Improve Assessment of Highway Project Cost Effectiveness. Replacement and upgrading of existing highway infrastructure will require enormous sums of money, particularly in urban areas with aging freeway systems. This money should be spent efficiently and wisely. Therefore the process used to assess the cost-effectiveness of highway projects needs to be substantially improved. Federal funds for highways should be directed to projects where there is a clear demonstration that they will return value for money, the same as with transit projects.

Improve Data Systems. Improvements in data systems should be developed and implemented to permit better performance evaluation and peer comparisons for highway programs. This will allow highway agencies to better manage their systems and more quickly find best practices in other locations that can be used to increase their program's effectiveness.

Eliminate Impediments to Effective Transit Planning and Implementation

Federal transit policies should be modified to make planning and provision of transit service easier and more predictable for communities—and more competitive with existing policies for highways. The following recommendations would help achieve this goal.

Address Disparities in Federal Match Ratios. The disparity between the 50 percent federal match for transit and the 80 percent match for highways is far too dramatic to ensure proper local decisions. A community should not be faced with a choice between a transit project that requires new sources of local funds and a highway project where the balance of funds comes from state and not local sources. The 80 percent federal match for transit New Starts should be reestablished. Congress should also consider increasing the amount of funding in the New Starts program to respond to escalating demand.

Differentiate between New Starts and Extensions of Systems. The full New Start review process should be used only in places where a totally new system is being considered. Its use for extensions of existing systems is too cumbersome and could be simplified. Extensions should continue to be eligible for funding, but a more streamlined process should apply.

Amend Federal Law to Create a New Program for "Small Starts". Given the interest in many metropolitan areas in relatively low-cost transit projects, federal law should be amended to accommodate and expedite such small projects without the need for extensive and time-consuming analysis procedures. Current law exempts projects with less than $25 million in federal funds from some evaluation criteria. This should be expanded to projects seeking less than $100 million and include transit technologies such as bus rapid transit, streetcars, and commuter rail, as well as extensions to existing systems.

Conclusion

Highway projects and new transit projects are treated very differently in federal legislation and policy. This results in a double standard, with a relatively easy process for highway development and a difficult and complex process for transit.

When compared to highways, transit New Starts have a lower funding rate for capital projects, intense competition between areas for funding, no secure sources of nonfederal funding, and a complex and convoluted process for project approval. Furthermore, unlike highways projects, transit New Starts are required to demonstrate how they will be compatible with local land use, employment, and low-income community needs, and their sponsoring transit agencies are subject to accounting and financial reporting systems that enable peer comparisons with other agencies.

Congress and the administration must take the bias out of federal transportation policy so that decisionmaking on transportation alternatives can truly be local. The outcome of the transportation game should not be preordained by rules made in Washington. Instead, a level playing field between transit and highways, based on the best mix of both programs, can truly empower localities to do what is best for their metropolitan areas. At the same time, it would improve program accountability and funding efficiency in our nation's transportation program.

Notes

1. See Puentes and Bailey, chapter 6 in this volume.
2. Tom Lewis, *Divided Highways* (New York: Viking Press, 1997), p. 294.
3. Richard F. Weingroff, "Creating a Landmark: The Intermodal Surface Transportation Efficiency Act of 1991" (www.fhwa.dot.gov/infrastructure/rw01.htm [February 2005]).
4. Ibid.

5. James A. Dunn, *Driving Forces* (Brookings, 1998), p. 90; David Lewis and Fred Laurence Williams, *Policy and Planning as Public Choice* (Brookfield, Vt.: Ashgate Publishing, 1999), p. 46.

6. Alan Altshuler and David Luberoff, *Mega-Projects: The Changing Politics of Urban Public Investment* (Brookings, 2003), p. 18.

7. Department of Transportation, *Moving America: New Directions, New Opportunities: A Statement of National Transportation Policy* (1990), pp. 29 and 48.

8. Weingroff, "Creating a Landmark."

9. General Accounting Office, *Transportation Infrastructure: Better Tools Needed for Making Decisions on Using ISTEA Funds Flexibly,* GAO/WED-94-26 (1993).

10. Robert Puentes, "Flexible Funding for Transit: Who Uses It?" Trend Survey, Center on Urban and Metropolitan Policy (Brookings, 2000).

11. That is, less than $100,000 per year. Federal Transit Administration, "Trends in the Flexible Fund Program Annual Status Report FY 2002" (www.fta.dot.gov/grant_programs/specific_grant_programs/flexible_funds_highway_transit_flexible_funding/4329_9469_ENG_HTML.htm [February 2005]).

12. NEPA is a broad federal law that essentially sets the national environmental policy. It is directly relevant to transportation: for example, it requires examination and consideration of potential impacts on sensitive social and environmental resources as a condition for approval for a proposed transportation facility.

13. Surface Transportation Policy Project, *TEA-21 User's Guide* (Washington, 1998).

14. Section 1308 of TEA-21 eliminated the MIS as a separate requirement, instead directing that it be integrated into analyses required by NEPA.

15. See Federal Highway Administration, "Transit Capital Investment Grants and Loans Fact Sheet" (www.fhwa.dot.gov/tea21/factsheets/trcap.htm [September 1998]).

16. 23 U.S.C. 145(a)

17. For a more detailed discussion, see Transportation Research Board, "Financial Capital Investment: A Primer for the Transit Practitioner," Transit Cooperative Research Program Report 89 (Washington: National Academy of Sciences, 2003).

18. Eighty-five separate projects are competing for funds. General Accounting Office, *Bus Rapid Transit Offers Communities a Flexible Mass Transit Option,* GAO-03-729T (2003), p. 3.

19. General Accounting Office, *Transportation Programs: Opportunities for Oversight and Improved Use of Taxpayer Funds,* GAO-03-1040T (2003), p. 16.

20. TEA-21, P.L. 105-178, as amended by Title 9 of P.L. 105-206, chap. 3030. See also Altshuler and Luberoff, *Mega-Projects,* p. 216.

21. *Making Appropriations for the Department of Transportation and Related Agencies for the Fiscal Year Ending September 30, 2002, and for Other Purposes,* H. Rept. 107-308, 107 Cong., 1 sess. (Government Printing Office, 2001).

22. Office of Management and Budget, *Budget of the United States Government, Fiscal Year 2004—Appendix* (2003), Title 3—General Provisions, Sec. 321 (2003).

23. *SAFETEA, Safe, Accountable, Flexible and Efficient Transportation Act of 2003,* Administration Proposal (May 14, 2003), Title 2, Section 1301, p. 30, line 2, Federal Highway Administration.

24. However, it is worth noting that the burden of financing transportation programs is slowly shifting to local governments and voter-approved initiatives. For a detailed discussion, see Wachs, chapter 4 in this volume.

25. For a detailed discussion, see Transportation Research Board, "Characteristics of State Funding for Public Transportation-2002," Transit Cooperative Research Program Research Results Digest (Washington: National Academy of Sciences, 2003).

26. Richard Werbel and Peter J. Haas, "Voting Outcomes of Local Tax Ballot Measures with a Substantial Rail Transit Component," *Transportation Research Record,* no. 1799 (2002): 10–17.

27. General Accounting Office, *FTA Needs to Provide Clear Information and Additional Guidance on the New Starts Ratings Process,* GAO-03-701 (2003), p. 12.

28. Federal Transit Administration, "Planning, Development, and Funding for New Starts Projects" (www.fta.dot.gov/library/policy/ns/ns.htm [June 2005]).

29. House of Representatives, Committee on Appropriations, *Departments of Transportation and Treasury and Independent Agencies Appropriations Bill, 2005,* H. Rept.108-671, 108 Cong., 2 sess. (Government Printing Office, 2004).

30. Federal Transit Administration, "Reporting Instructions for Section 5309 New Starts Criteria, 3.4.1 Incremental Cost Divided by Transportation System User Benefits" (www.fta.dot.gov/library/policy/ns/2002/34.html [June 2005]).

31. House of Representatives, Committee on Appropriations, *Departments of Transportation and Treasury and Independent Agencies Appropriations Bill, 2004,* H. Rept.108-243, 108 Cong., 1 sess. (Government Printing Office, 2003).

32. *Code of Federal Regulations* 23, sec. 771.115.

33. Federal Highway Administration, "Guidance for Preparing and Processing Environmental and Section 4 (F) Documents," T 6640.8A, October 30, 1987 (environment.fhwa.dot.gov/projdev/impta6640.htm [February 2005]).

34. General Accounting Office, *Surface Transportation: Many Factors Affect Investment Decisions,* GAO-04-744 (2004).

35. American Association of State Highway and Transportation Officials, *A Manual on User Benefit-Cost Analysis of Highway and Bus-Transit Improvements* (Washington, 1977).

36. *Code of Federal Regulations* 23, sec. 450.318.

37. Center for Urban Transportation Studies, University of Wisconsin-Milwaukee, *An Overview: Land Use and Economic Development in Statewide Transportation Planning,* report prepared for the Federal Highway Administration (1999).

38. Robert Burchell and others, "The Cost of Sprawl Revisited," Transit Cooperative Research Program Report 39 (Washington: Transportation Research Board, 1998).

39. Volpe National Transportation Systems Center, "2002 Reporting Manual, Uniform System of Accounts" (www.ntdprogram.com/NTD/ReprtMan.nsf/Docs/USOA/$File/USOA.pdf [June 2005]).

40. Federal Transit Administration, *Report to Congress: Review of the National Transit Database* (Department of Transportation, May 31, 2000). See also www.fta.dot.gov/library/ntd/index.htm (February 2005).

41. Federal Highway Administration, "Overview of Highway Performance Monitoring System (HPMS) for FHWA Field Offices," Federal Highway Administration.

42. David T. Hartgen, *Ensuring Our Trust: Performance of State Highway Systems, 1984–2001*(University of North Carolina at Charlotte, 2003). See also John Locke Foundation, "The Looming Highway Condition Crisis: Performance of State Highway Sys-

tems, 1984–2002, 13th Annual Report" (www.johnlocke.org/policy_reports/2004020943.html [February 9, 2004]).

43. Eno Transportation Foundation, "Performance, A TQ Point-Counterpoint Exchange with David Hartgen and Lance Neumann," *Transportation Quarterly* 56, no. 1 (2002): 5–19.

44. See National Transit Database at www.ntdprogram.com/NTD/ntdhome. nsf/?Open (February 2005).

45. See *Code of Federal Regulations* 49, sec. 535 a(1).

46. Federal Highway Administration, *Highway Performance Monitoring System Reassessment*, FHWA-PL-99-001 (Department of Transportation, 1998).

47. Larry Sandler, "City Ripe for Better Transit," *Milwaukee Journal-Sentinel*, May 7, 2003, p. 9B.

48. Edward Glaeser, Matthew Kahn, and Chenghuan Chu, "Job Sprawl: Employment Location in U.S. Metropolitan Areas," Center on Urban and Metropolitan Policy Survey Series (Brookings, July 2001).

49. Rebecca R. Sohmer and Robert E. Lang, "Downtown Rebound," Census Note (Fannie Mae Foundation and Brookings, May 2001).

50. American Public Transportation Association, "APTA Award Winners 1983–2001" (Washington: undated) http://www.apta.com/services/awards/documents/awardshist. pdf.

51. James J. Casey, "The Politics of Congestion and Implementation: Milwaukee's Freeways and the Proposed Light Rail and Transit System," *Marquette Law Review* 78 (Spring 1995): 675–733.

52. "Termination of Draft Environmental Impact Statement; Milwaukee and Waukesha Counties, Wisconsin," *Federal Register* 65, no. 123 (June 26, 2000): 39464–65.

53. Federal Transit Administration, *Annual Report on New Starts: Proposed Allocations of Funds for Fiscal Year 2004* (Department of Transportation, 2003), appendix B.

54. Larry Sandler, "Light Rail, Heavy Debate," *Milwaukee Journal-Sentinel*, August 20, 1996, p.1.

55. Representative Thomas Petri, "Setting the Record Straight," June 12, 1998 (www.house.gov/ petri/weekly/jun12col.htm [June 2005]).

56. Marc V. Levine, *Light Rail in Milwaukee: An Analysis of the Potential Impact on Economic Development* (University of Wisconsin–Milwaukee, 1992).

57. Steven Walters and Larry Sandler, "Thompson Vows 255 Budget Vetoes: $43 Million to be Excised; Light Rail Funding Ban to Stay," *Milwaukee Journal-Sentinel*, October 27, 1999, p. 1.

58. Southeastern Wisconsin Regional Planning Commission, *A Regional Freeway System Reconstruction Plan for Southeastern Wisconsin* (Waukesha, Wisc.: 2003).

11

Protecting America's Highways and Transit Systems against Terrorism

Arnold Howitt and Jonathan Makler

In early April 2004, the Federal Bureau of Investigation and Department of Homeland Security issued a terse advisory, warning local officials of possible bombing attempts against buses or trains in American cities.[1] Since train bombings in Madrid in March had killed nearly 200 people and injured another 1,500, and a subway bombing in Moscow only one month earlier had killed at least 40 people, there had been widespread concern that the United States might be similarly vulnerable.

These were not new fears. Soon after the suicide jetliner attacks on the World Trade Center and the Pentagon on September 11, 2001, widely disseminated news photographs of armed National Guardsmen standing watch over the Golden Gate Bridge symbolized one focus of America's wariness— the vast surface transportation network that moves people and goods near and far throughout the United States.

Indeed, much vulnerability had been identified before September 11.[2] Transportation infrastructure, terminals, or vehicles can become terrorist targets, vehicles can be used as delivery mechanisms or weapons themselves, and the transportation system can provide mobility for terrorists or dangerous substances. Al Qaeda's terrorists used jetliners as weapons on September 11, and Timothy McVeigh used a rented truck loaded with fertilizer to blow up the Murrah Federal Building in Oklahoma City in 1995. Also in 1995, with only crude methods to disseminate the deadly chemical sarin, the Aum Shinrikyo cult killed twelve Tokyo subway passengers and employees (and injured or terrorized thousands more), and Palestinian terrorists have regularly blown up buses in Israel with horrifying results.[3] From 1991 to 2001, 42 percent of all terrorist attacks worldwide targeted rail systems or buses.[4]

Vulnerability, however, is not the only consideration. In thinking about ways of improving system safety, public policymakers and managers have to consider an important potential security-versus-service tradeoff. While the scale, accessibility, and networking of the surface transportation system create vulnerability, these attributes are essential to its mobility and economic functions.

The benefits of transportation in the United States stem from the ease with which travelers can move from home to work to shopping to social-cultural-recreational venues and also the ease with which goods and services can be delivered throughout the nation. Tightening security potentially threatens these benefits. Thus to the extent that steps to reduce vulnerability to terrorism compromise personal and economic mobility, the mere threat of terrorism imposes significant social and economic costs on the United States.[5] From a contrasting viewpoint, the surface transportation system can also play an important role in emergency response and recovery from a major terrorist attack.[6]

This chapter reviews measures both the federal government and states and localities have implemented since the September 11 attacks to enhance the security of highway and transit systems. Although a number of positive steps have been taken, we argue that protection of surface transportation has effectively been given secondary status. Policymakers and senior public managers see highway and transit systems as genuinely vulnerable to terrorist attack, but among the many potentially exposed elements of American society, these systems have not been given the highest priority for security funding or program development. Therefore, this chapter also explores a number of ways in which surface transportation security needs to be enhanced in the future.

In addition to the professional literature cited, this paper draws upon about four dozen personal interviews conducted by the authors with officials in several federal agencies (Federal Highway Administration, Federal Transit Administration, Transportation Security Administration), three state governments (California, Illinois, and Massachusetts), and three metropolitan areas (San Francisco, Chicago, and Boston). (See Appendix 11A for a complete list of participants.)

Surface Transportation Vulnerability and Preparedness Objectives

Surface transportation is significant as both a terrorist target and a critical element of the national emergency response system. The potential attraction for terrorists in attacking the surface transportation system is the opportunity to kill or injure large numbers of people, creating widespread fear and severely disrupting economic activity. Transportation facilities are ready targets for assaults with conventional or radiological explosives, chemical weapons, or infectious bioagents. Large numbers of vulnerable passengers congregate in terminals, travel in transit vehicles, and pass over and through infrastructure choke points such as bridges and tunnels. A large percentage of the nation's goods and services are delivered by truck and rail or stored in depots and warehouses served by the transportation system. [7] Beyond any immediate impacts on people or goods, moreover, a terrorist organization that targeted transportation facilities could achieve longer-term disruption by making passengers or shippers fearful or unable to use the system.

Surface transport vehicles could also be appropriated as terrorist weapons. Explosive-laden trucks, passenger buses, and even fixed-rail vehicles might be taken over, much as aircraft were on September 11. In addition, the transportation system is a potential vector of terrorist attack, carrying terrorists or dangerous chemicals or biological agents to the site of an attack on some other venue. [8]

Americans travel more than 2.8 trillion vehicle miles per year. They make about 9 billion transit trips per year, with the 30 largest bus or rail systems carrying more than 70 percent of the total. [9] Beyond its intensive use, though, surface transportation is extremely vulnerable because of the system's vast size, openness, and highly networked character. The United States has more than 160,000 miles of interstate and national highway system roadways, plus 3.8 million miles of other roads. [10] It has a total of 600,000 bridges and tunnels, of which 500 have been classified as critical facilities based on size, traffic volume, and strategic importance. [11]

Consequently, there are hundreds of sites in the United States where terrorist attacks on or by means of the surface transportation system could create hundreds or even thousands of casualties or severely disrupt economic activity. And there are many thousands of other locations where attacks could generate great fear and economic disruption, albeit with fewer potential casualties.

An alternative perspective is also worth noting. Aside from its attractiveness as a target, weapon, or vector of terrorist attack, surface transportation is also a crucial part of the emergency response system and an essential element in recovery from an act of terrorism. In the event of a serious attack on a particular locale, the surface transportation system would have to function well enough so that ambulances, fire equipment, law enforcement vehicles, and possibly construction equipment could rescue and move the injured to hospitals, quell fires, secure or demolish damaged structures, and maintain public order.

The system would also have to handle the potential evacuation—orderly or possibly panicked—of many people escaping real or perceived danger. Later, during the possibly extended process of economic and social recovery from a severe attack, it would be essential to restore the transportation system so that people and goods could again move freely.

This analysis suggests three preparedness objectives for the surface transportation system that are appropriate for terrorism as well as many natural and technological disasters:

—deterrence, prevention, and mitigation;

—emergency response and consequence management; and

—recovery.[12]

Deterrence, Prevention, and Mitigation

The first objective is to deter or prevent attacks from occurring or mitigate potential damage by anticipatory action. Measures to achieve this purpose include improved gathering, analysis, and dissemination of law enforcement and intelligence information about methods of possible terrorist attack or specific threats against particular places. They also include "target hardening" steps—for example, erecting physical barriers around vulnerable facilities, video surveillance, or preventive patrol by security guards. By making it more difficult to damage facilities or harm people, these steps reduce the likelihood that terrorists will choose to attack these targets and increase the probability that an intended attack will be thwarted or prove ineffective.

Emergency Response and Consequence Management

Another objective is institution of measures to prepare for effective emergency response to manage the consequences of an attack, should one occur.

These steps include planning for rescue, emergency transport, and medical care of the injured; evacuation and sheltering of people at risk; and fire suppression, containment of hazardous substances, or removal of blast debris, depending on the nature of the emergency.

Recovery

The third objective is recovery. An attack on transportation facilities would not only potentially harm many people but also disrupt the movement of people and goods within (and possibly between) centers of population and economic activity. This objective includes actions to restore public services and return physical structures, economic activities, and social life as closely as possible to preattack status.

Federal Action to Protect Surface Transportation

Galvanized by the attacks on the World Trade Center and the Pentagon and by the anthrax letters in the fall of 2001, the federal government has taken significant steps to bolster security and preparedness for terrorism, including enactment of major laws, creation of new institutions, reorganization of existing federal agencies, and large increases in federal funding. Overall, homeland security spending will have increased from $16.9 billion in fiscal year 2001 to $47.4 billion in fiscal year 2005. Nondefense homeland security spending will have increased from about $10 billion to $30 billion in that period.[13]

Transportation has been an extremely high federal priority, but given the circumstances, aviation, not surface transportation, has received the most intense attention from Congress, the White House, the Department of Transportation (DOT), and the newly created Transportation Security Administration (TSA), which was initially established in the DOT and subsequently incorporated into the Department of Homeland Security (DHS).[14] Although other components of the DOT, notably the Federal Highway Administration (FHWA) and Federal Transit Administration (FTA) (and other units of the DOT not discussed here), took steps to help state, regional, and local transportation agencies better protect their infrastructure and operations, they do not account for a large share of federal security spending—only $243 million in fiscal year 2005, which is an estimated 1.2% of projected *non*-DHS homeland security funding (see table 11-1).

Except for its aviation security responsibilities, the DOT was not in the first circle of federal agencies waging the war on terrorism. It was in a second circle that had to attend to acknowledged security vulnerabilities but

Table 11-1.   Federal Homeland Security Funding, by Agency, Fiscal Years 2003–05

Millions of dollars, unless otherwise indicated

Agency	2003, enacted	Percent of 2003 total[a]	2004, enacted	Percent of 2004 total[a]	2005, request	Percent of 2005 total[a]
Department of Homeland Security (DHS)	18,652.4	50.3	23,492.3	56.9	27,214.5	57.4
All other government agencies						
Department of Agriculture	299.9	1.6	326.6	1.8	651.1	3.2
Department of Commerce	111.6	0.6	131.2	0.7	150.1	0.7
Department of Defense	8,442.0	45.7	7,024.0	39.4	8,023.1	39.8
Department of Energy	1,246.9	6.8	1,362.5	7.6	1,496.9	7.4
Department of Health and Human Services	4,002.4	21.7	4,109.0	23.1	4,276.1	21.2
Department of the Interior	47.4	0.3	67.2	0.4	49.3	0.2
Department of Justice	1,892.5	10.2	2,165.8	12.2	2,581.1	12.8
Department of Labor	69.4	0.4	52.4	0.3	68.6	0.3
Department of State	632.7	3.4	701.3	3.9	954.8	4.7
Department of Transportation	382.8	2.1	283.5	1.6	242.6	1.2
Department of the Treasury	80.0	0.4	90.4	0.5	87.1	0.4
Department of Veterans Affairs	154.3	0.8	271.3	1.5	297.0	1.5
Corps of Engineers	36.0	0.2	103.4	0.6	84.0	0.4
Environmental Protection Agency	132.9	0.7	123.3	0.7	97.4	0.5
Executive Office of the President	41.0	0.2	35.0	0.2	35.0	0.2
General Services Administration	67.1	0.4	78.9	0.4	79.5	0.4
National Aeronautics and Space Administration	205.0	1.1	191.0	1.1	207.0	1.0
National Science Foundation	284.6	1.5	327.9	1.8	343.6	1.7
Social Security Administration	132.0	0.7	143.4	0.8	155.0	0.8
District of Columbia	25.0	0.1	19.0	0.1	15.0	0.1
Nuclear Regulatory Commission	47.0	0.3	66.8	0.4	57.0	0.3
Smithsonian Institution	82.8	0.4	78.3	0.4	76.0	0.4
Other agencies	50.7	0.3	62.6	0.4	144.1	0.7
Total funding excluding that for DHS	18,466.0		17,814.8		20,171.4	
Total funding	37,118.4		41,307.1		47,385.9	

Source: Executive Office of the President, *Budget of the United States Government, Fiscal Year 2005, Analytical Perspectives* (Government Printing Office, 2004), table 3-1.

a. Excluding DHS.

with less White House and congressional support and attention. Neither the Bush administration nor Congress, moreover, has made surface transportation a high priority in providing homeland security funds to state and local governments so that these jurisdictions could pay for protective enhancements to surface transportation security. For fiscal years 2001 to 2005, federal homeland security appropriations for state and local governments doubled from $2.7 billion to $5.5 billion. Much of this increase was for "first responder" programs (from $616 million in fiscal year 2001 to $3.6 billion in fiscal year 2005).[15]

In terms of transit security, the House and Senate each passed their own version of the Public Transportation Terrorism Prevention Act in late 2004. The bills would authorize $3.5 billion over three years in grants to transit agencies for detection equipment and other terrorism prevention measures.[16] Funds for the Senate version were to come from the DHS while the House version tapped the DOT. Neither was signed into law. The Senate also passed the Rail Security Act in 2004, which was to provide $1 billion in grants to state and local governments, rail authorities, and Amtrak.[17]

According to a House committee report, in fiscal years 2002 and 2003, the nation's aviation system and its 1.8 million daily passengers received $11 billion from the federal government for security. By contrast, in 2003 and 2004, public transit's 14 million daily riders received only $115 million specifically allocated for transit security grants (as part of an overall $1.4 billion from the Urban Area Security Initiative). In fiscal year 2005, another $150 million was added (from $1.2 billion more total funding). Intercity bus security was allocated an additional $40 million in total for fiscal years 2002 through 2005. Trucking security was given $5 million in fiscal year 2005.[18]

Another House report pointed out that the federal government has invested $9.16 per passenger for aviation security but less than one penny for each transit rider.[19] Some have noted that other expenditures, such as those for Amtrak rail improvements, should be factored in. Nevertheless, the disparities are stark. As Representative Tom Petri, chair of the House Subcommittee on Highways, Transit, and Pipelines bluntly put it, "Not enough is being invested in improving transit security."[20]

What accounts for this? Domestically, the congressional and executive branch agendas for preparedness have most prominently featured issues related to the tragedies of fall 2001. In addition to airline security, these issues include enhancing intelligence and law enforcement capabilities to thwart and apprehend potential terrorists; improving public health and emergency medical infrastructure to prevent, detect, or respond to bioterrorism and other forms of attack; and training and equipping state and local emergency response personnel.

Department of Homeland Security

In transportation security, by far the most important post–September 11 initiative was congressional passage of the Aviation and Transportation

Security Act of 2001, which established the TSA as a new unit in the Department of Transportation.[21] With the passage of the Homeland Security Act of 2002, the TSA was subsequently transferred to the new Department of Homeland Security, effective March 1, 2003.[22]

In addition to giving the TSA sweeping new authority over aviation, the Transportation Security Act declared that the new DOT undersecretary "shall be responsible for security in all modes of transportation" in the DOT and, under conditions of national emergency, shall coordinate all transportation functions. The undersecretary's general transportation security functions were potentially quite broad, including maintaining liaison with intelligence and law enforcement agencies, receiving and disseminating intelligence, assessing the nature and level of threat to transportation, developing security policies and plans, managing research and development programs, and inspecting security facilities and systems.

Despite these general grants of responsibility for transportation modes other than aviation, including highways and transit, the overwhelming thrust of 2001's Transportation Security Act—and hence the immediate concern of the TSA undersecretary—was the airline industry. Nearly the entire act consisted of a detailed set of responsibilities to be carried out to protect commercial aviation from future hijackings and other potential threats. The act, moreover, gave the TSA an aggressive schedule of specific tasks and deadlines for enhancing aviation security systems, directly hiring airport security personnel as federal employees, and managing the transfer of security responsibilities from the private firms that had previously contracted these functions. Fulfilling these aviation requirements within the time constraints set by Congress dominated the attention of the TSA in its first years. Funding commitments to aviation security remain the agency's principal responsibility, accounting for more than 95 percent of its budget request for fiscal year 2005.[23]

Primarily on account of the possibility of terrorists smuggling dangerous materials in international cargo or striking at the vessels themselves, Congress has also mandated that maritime security issues get more attention. In late November 2002, Congress enacted the Maritime Transportation Security Act, which required, among other provisions, maritime personnel-identification and vessel-tracking systems, vulnerability assessments, incident response plans for vessels and facilities, and a risk assessment of foreign ports.[24] The U.S. Coast Guard has assumed many of the responsibilities established under this act.[25] The act also included a grant program that supplemented and was integrated into an existing program administered by the TSA.

Outside of the aviation and maritime areas, the security administration has taken a systems rather than modal approach to transportation security, trying to identify and deal with elements of the overall transport system that seem most vulnerable and have the greatest potential for loss of life, property damage, and disruption of economic activity. Among other initiatives, it is developing two assessment tools to help the federal government and subnational jurisdictions assess threats, criticality, and vulnerability. It has also worked on a national transportation workers identification card program.[26]

To deal with surface transportation issues, as well as port security, the TSA in 2002 established an Office of Maritime and Land Security (OMLS). Overall, the development of the OMLS has lagged behind that of the aviation elements of the TSA and remains a small component of the agency; most of its development has come since late 2002. Out of the total TSA workforce of approximately 35,000 in 2004, the OMLS had fewer than 200 people to deal with both its port and land transportation focal areas.

One major OMLS project has been development of regulations, issued in May 2003, on tighter registration and credentialing of hazardous materials truck drivers.[27] The OMLS has also worked to prepare standards or guidelines for physical infrastructure protection and establish relationships with transportation stakeholders in state and local governments and the private sector. After the Madrid railroad bombing in March 2004, the TSA issued a rail-transit security directive to local agencies that required immediate implementation of fifteen specific security measures.[28]

These efforts are significant but do not compare to the initiatives taken in aviation. By sharp contrast, the agency's purview of surface transportation has only a general mandate from Congress and few personnel. It has had little grant money to help state and local governments defray the costs of new highway and transit security measures and, through matching, motivate them to commit their own funds. Moreover, as a consequence of having only a small surface transportation staff, the TSA has developed only nascent relationships with the thousands of public agencies and private business stakeholders—and the national associations—that play a role in surface transportation as either service providers or major system users.[29]

Department of Transportation

Much of the federal government's capacity for addressing transit and highway security issues resides in components of the DOT. Soon after September 11, a department-wide security working group formed that included representatives of all its modal administrations (as well as the TSA during the period when it was part of the department). It worked on cross-cutting issues such as providing more timely and extensive intelligence and security information from federal sources to transportation officials at the state and local levels. But the Federal Transit Administration and the Federal Highway Administration have taken the lead in their areas of responsibility.

Federal Transit Administration. Before September 11, the FTA, through its Office of Safety and Security, had provided a number of regional and local transit agencies with technical assistance in conducting security audits to identify weaknesses in infrastructure protection and security plans. The transit administration expanded its efforts after September 11, concentrating on those facilities thought to be most at risk of attack: about thirty of the largest transit properties, plus Utah where the Winter Olympics were held in early 2002.

Since the FTA is not primarily a regulatory agency, most of its efforts have involved technical assistance voluntarily accepted by interested transit agencies. It has now extended security assistance to about sixty transit agencies, with an emphasis on training needs and a set of twenty relatively low-cost action items that do not require expensive modifications to infrastructure.[30] These measures emphasize actions to improve management and accountability; identify security problems; screen employees in operational and maintenance positions; improve training and exercises; control access to sensitive documents, materials, and venues; and develop protocols for responding to different DHS threat advisory levels.

During 2002 and 2003, the FTA sponsored a series of seventeen two-day regional forums, seeking to draw transit agency staff and senior first responders from police, fire, and emergency medical service agencies. The forums focused on the role that transit could play as a component of an overall emergency response capability in the region; they were explicitly designed to integrate transit personnel into regional networks of emergency responders. The transit administration has subsidized and worked with major state and regional transit agencies in developing large-scale emergency response drills based on terrorism scenarios, so that collaborative relationships could be exercised and weakness diagnosed.

Through an extensive publications program, the FTA has sought to publicize and disseminate information about best practices adopted by individual local or regional transit agencies. It has also provided financing so that the American Public Transit Association, the principal professional organization of the transit industry, could establish a Surface Transportation Infrastructure and Analysis Center.[31] This facility, which became operational in early 2003, coordinates and shares information among transit systems and national intelligence agencies about possible terrorism directed against transit.

Federal Highway Administration. The FHWA, working closely with a special task force from the American Association of State Highway and Transportation Officials, has undertaken a number of security and emergency response projects, in many respects paralleling the activity of the FTA.[32] It also sponsored ten two-day regional forums to help highway officials establish closer relationships with first responders and focus the latter on response and recovery in highway emergencies. Three major exercises were conducted in border state regions. Various guidebooks and publications have been developed to provide transportation professionals nationwide with information on topics such as updating emergency plans and assessing the vulnerability of highway infrastructure. The FHWA has provided technical assistance to a number of areas judged by the DHS to have high-risk transportation infrastructure.[33]

As discussed earlier, both the transit and highway administrations have conducted security activities with only limited new appropriations and personnel. Most resources for new federal government transportation security functions have gone into building the TSA, which, as noted, has had a limited focus on surface transportation. Nor, except for providing money for major transit agencies to conduct emergency drills, have the FTA and FHWA had significant funds to provide grants directly to state or local transportation agencies to improve security.

The General Accounting Office has argued that with the transfer of the TSA to the Department of Homeland Security, its responsibilities, on one side, and those of the FTA and FHWA, on the other, have not been defined clearly enough by Congress or administrative agreements and that only loose operational coordination has been achieved.[34] While this state of affairs is not surprising, given the newness of this agency and the major reorganization that shifted it from the DOT to the DHS, it is imperative that the relatively few federal personnel and resources available for surface transportation be used as effectively and as compatibly as possible.

Intergovernmental Funding. One side of the intergovernmental financing picture has been the possible use of dedicated homeland security funds for transportation security purposes. Congress has authorized general-purpose grants to states and localities for homeland security functions as described above, but only a relatively small share has been dedicated to surface transportation.[35] State and local decisionmakers have been given broad discretion about how to utilize federal money to meet current security costs and bolster their protective capabilities, but with the exception of the dedicated funding noted above, they have generally not been required to devote funds to surface transportation.

The other side of the intergovernmental financing picture has been the possible use of general transportation funds for homeland security purposes. With the Transportation Equity Act for the Twenty-First Century (TEA-21) originally due to expire in 2003, the Bush administration developed draft replacement legislation for congressional consideration: the Safe, Accountable, Flexible and Efficient Transportation Equity Act of 2003 (SAFETEA).[36] This bill, which authorizes federal funding for highway and transit grants to the states, provides both general-purpose funds for transportation capital plans developed by state and regional transportation agencies, as well as some restricted-use funds for specific purposes—for example, congestion reduction and air quality improvement projects.

Although consideration was given to proposing set-aside funding for surface transportation security purposes, which could have been thematically highlighted in SAFETEA, the administration decided not to establish a dedicated security fund. The DOT reportedly was reluctant to see states required to use federal allotments for security, particularly once the TSA was transferred to the Department of Homeland Security. Instead, it drafted legislative language for the transit title of the bill that treated many transportation security expenditures as capital projects, allowing grantees to use SAFETEA funds even for some operational purposes; but use for security was not mandated. Under the highway title of the bill, SAFETEA does propose that security expenditures may be 100 percent federally funded rather than requiring a nonfederal match as other uses do.

Overall, therefore, the federal government has responded to the terrorist attacks in the fall of 2001 with many initiatives to strengthen its own agencies and to encourage and support improved capabilities at the state and local level. Surface transportation, however, has been a secondary concern, with aviation security, improvements in the public health and emergency medical systems, and more general issues of law enforcement and emergency response in the forefront of attention.

In support of the state and regional agencies that own and operate the nation's highways and transit systems, federal agencies have provided technical assistance and training and sought to enhance networks of relationships between state and local transportation officials and first response agencies. They have not been able to provide much targeted financial support, however, to defray costs incurred in response to the September 11 terrorist attacks and the subsequent heightened security alerts—let alone to provide dedicated subsidies for the capital costs of improving highway and transit system security.

Thus, in terms of the three transportation security objectives identified above, federal funding and technical assistance has helped states and localities primarily in regard to *emergency response* and *recovery* by providing some training to local responders, seeking to connect transportation agencies more effectively to traditional emergency response agencies, and stimulating more detailed planning. The *deterrence-prevention-mitigation* objective has been served mainly by provision of technical assistance in analyzing potential vulnerabilities and in somewhat improved methods of sharing intelligence and law enforcement information with transportation agencies, but it has not been served by significant amounts of dedicated capital funding.

State and Local Perspectives on Transportation Security

The September 11 jetliner attacks and the anthrax letters made senior state and local government leaders take stock of their security preparations and ponder the risks of being targeted by terrorists. State and local officials vary much more widely than federal officials in their overall security concerns, given perceived differential risks of attack among jurisdictions. Their capacity to act, moreover, varies widely as well, given great differences in personnel and fiscal resources.

The sense of urgency at the national level was extremely intense. Compared to elected leaders or executive officials of a state or city, federal government officials have a unique perspective on potential terrorist attacks. The president, Congress, and major federal agencies deal with terrorism in the context of their core defense, national security, foreign affairs, and justice functions. They are responsible and ultimately accountable for what they do to prevent or respond to a terrorist attack anywhere in United States territory—whether originating internally or from across its borders—or against American interests abroad.

By contrast, state or local officials are directly responsible for attacks only against their own jurisdiction. No doubt they are genuinely concerned about other locales, but they are not responsible in the same way that federal leaders or officials are. By definition, no state or local official faces a probability of attack as great as that faced by federal officials responsible for the entire nation. Nor does the international terrorism that threatens the United States arise in the context of basic state and local government responsibilities. No state or locality can afford to ignore the threat entirely, but officials in each jurisdiction are likely to make quite different assessments of the odds of attack, depending on their sense of risk. The governments of New York City, Washington, D.C., and a few other key locales regard their jurisdictions as highly at risk, but many others judge the odds of an attack against their own jurisdictions as much lower.

Because they own much of the national stock of transit and highway infrastructure, transportation agencies in most states undertook various short-term actions to tighten security, reassure the public, revise emergency response plans, and consider longer-term protective requirements. Nonetheless, like their federal counterparts, state and local officials identified mass transit and highways as possible targets but not one of their highest priorities among the many security issues that demanded attention. They had to rely primarily on their own financial resources, and budget constraints limited the scope and scale of their response.

In most states, the agencies taking the initiative on transportation security were state departments of transportation (SDOTs), with responsibility for the physical infrastructure of major roadways and related facilities, and the state police, typically with responsibility for highway safety and law enforcement—plus the special districts or authorities that owned or operated turnpikes or bridges independent of SDOT authority.[37] SDOTs often led systematic infrastructure vulnerability assessments, seeking to identify critical facilities, analyze how vulnerable they were to terrorist attack, project the consequences for people and the economy of their being destroyed or damaged, and thereby set priorities for protection. State police departments sought to develop more extensive crisis management capabilities through planning, training, and exercising. They also built enhanced information links between transportation agencies and law enforcement.

However, transportation security activities at the state level, mainly concerning state-owned and -operated surface transportation assets, and activities at the big city and metropolitan levels were only loosely coordinated with each other. Major cities and transit agencies frequently did parallel vulnerability assessment and emergency planning activities, particularly if they viewed themselves as prime terrorist targets.[38]

A number of states organized transportation security task forces—often subcommittees of multipurpose, umbrella state committees—to bring together major stakeholders concerned with surface transportation security issues. However, transportation was often a late or secondary priority of these statewide task forces.

In Illinois, a state terrorism task force was organized in 1999, primarily motivated by the Oklahoma City bombing. A transportation subcommittee, which eventually had a number of working groups, was not formed until 2002. In this state and others, even when consensus could be reached on a prioritized list of critical and vulnerable transportation facilities, action was limited because protective measures frequently required capital investments or major new operating costs that were perceived as fiscally infeasible in the absence of substantial federal financial assistance.

In California, each of the eight divisions of the California Highway Patrol was assigned to conduct a vulnerability assessment and develop protective plans for its area of operation. In the Bay Area, this effort led to a stakeholder task force that assessed the security needs of the Golden Gate Bridge and assigned responsibilities to each stakeholder—for example, which agency would respond to emergencies on which parts of the bridge and how the transportation of people and goods would be handled under different scenarios of damage and recovery.

Although state-level transportation security task forces or informal SDOT consultation usually included major regional and big city transportation stakeholders, the focus of the state-level efforts was primarily on prevention and emergency response for state-owned infrastructure, not on the overall metropolitan transportation system. With some exceptions such as California, coordination across jurisdictions and across levels of government tended to remain secondary.

In terms of emergency response capabilities, most states and cities had significant capacity in place before September 11. The overall emergency management system in the United States is a bottom-up system: local governments have initial responsibility for planning and response, with state resources—and ultimately federal assets—called into play only if local resources cannot cope with the demands of a particular emergency. Most jurisdictions had emergency plans designed for natural or manmade disasters that might require the transportation system to facilitate emergency medical response or evacuation of at-risk populations. They also had incident management systems, increasingly supported by intelligent transportation systems, for handling disruptions of normal operations; and they had plans and procedures for handling hazardous materials spills, developed through local emergency planning committees organized under Environmental Protection Agency regulations. After September 11, these plans and procedures were revisited and improved, and training on terrorism response was made available to transportation staff.

On the transit side, regional public transportation agencies were the key players. A survey of transit agencies by the American Public Transit Association in 2004 found that transit security-related investment needs approached $6 billion.[39] Because they saw significant risk of being targeted for terrorist attack, regional transit agencies were highly motivated to protect their passengers, employees, and vehicles, as well as their infrastructure.

Like their state transportation counterparts, transit agencies had some advantages in addressing security issues. In general, they already had written emergency response plans, regularly did emergency drills and disaster exercises, and therefore had at least basic working relationships with emergency response agencies and medical facilities. In many areas, under the federal Metropolitan Medical Response System program (which began before September 11 but expanded in its aftermath), transit agencies became better integrated into enhanced emergency medical plans for various types of terrorist attack.

In Boston, for example, the Massachusetts Bay Transportation Authority—an independent state agency that operates the regional subway and bus systems and contracts for commuter rail service—had good working relationships with the city's emergency response agencies and with state emergency management officials. Together they had regular safety drills and exercises and closely collaborated in planning major public events, such as the annual "First Night" New Year's Eve celebration and the massive annual Fourth of July concert along the Charles River. Both the city and the transportation authority improved their emergency operations centers to be ready for a major incident.

However, there were distinct limits to what transit agencies could do in terms of increased security actions. Post–September 11, they experienced fiscally painful spikes in operating costs as they intensively used personnel for extra protective duty, both for routine operations and special events, and made investments in modest physical security upgrades.

One key element of the deterrence-prevention-mitigation objective involves the development of law enforcement intelligence in useable form so that transit or other transportation agencies can be aware of potential and actual threats and better target their security resources in response. The much-criticized system of color-coded alert levels managed by the White House Office of Homeland Security and then by the DHS aimed at conveying such information. From the perspective of transportation agencies, the core problem in terms of law enforcement information was being included as a full participant in information exchange and receiving this information in timely fashion.

Most transit agencies around the country were either dependent on city police forces or had only small transit police staffs, and they lacked expertise on terrorism issues. Even such a relatively large transit system as San Francisco's Bay Area Rapid Transit District had only a small, dedicated police force of about 150 officers. This agency's relationships with city and state law enforcement agencies were a valuable asset, and contacts grew more extensive, frequent, and intense in the aftermath of September 11, although governmental coordination is still an issue.[40] Nonetheless, transportation and transit agencies generally remained peripheral to the information sharing process.

Like the federal government, state and local transportation agencies mainly focused on planning and relationship development for the emergency response and recovery objectives. Other than information analysis and vulnerability assessments and some tightening of access to facilities, transportation agencies were limited in their deterrence-prevention-mitigation activities.

Funding Constraints

However, for state and local agencies even the response-oriented activities had distinct limits. Surface transportation agencies perceived increased operating costs as unwelcome necessities in the extraordinary climate of fiscal stress that affected most states and localities in 2002 and 2003, which was characterized by large deficits and a general need for spending cutbacks. Most states and localities found it difficult to consider major new expenditures for transportation security, particularly capital investments, out of own-source revenues. Federal funds dedicated to homeland security were also quite limited, as discussed earlier.

It should be clearly noted, however, that transportation agencies potentially could have tapped funding available in TEA-21 for capital spending on security needs. The political dynamics of transportation fund allocation worked against this, however. Because TEA-21 funds could be used for a wide range of transportation purposes, security purposes had to compete with traditional transportation projects. Moreover, there was considerable reluctance to use general-purpose transportation funds for security purposes, even where the need was perceived as high, since many believed that the federal government would (or should) eventually provide dedicated homeland security subsidies.

On the other hand, when federal general-purpose homeland security funds were provided to state or local governments, there were numerous nontransportation claimants (for example, first responders or health agencies) lobbying for allocations of money to their own projects—often with well-established expectations about securing these funds. Thus, in many instances, transportation stakeholders did not want to use the general-purpose TEA-21 funds for security because they were seeking dedicated homeland security funds for this objective, but they also were typically unable to make strong enough claims on homeland security funds—relative to police, fire, and public health agencies—to capture much of a share. The result was limited federal fund allocation to transportation security.

Like their federal counterparts, state and local agencies have emphasized the diagnostic and vulnerability assessment dimensions of the deterrence-prevention-mitigation objective, without being able to implement the more expensive steps of making capital investments or increasing manpower allocated to this purpose. They have done far more in terms of the emergency response–consequence management and recovery objectives.

Overall, then, states have been modestly proactive on transportation security issues. They have been quite concerned about major facilities, such as the Golden Gate Bridge, that have high public visibility and are perceived to face substantial risk. They are concerned, too, about potential attacks on vehicles or people using their facilities, but they have found it hard to devise new protective measures. Given the scale of their systems in terms of miles of roadway and track and numbers of bridges and tunnels, providing guards or installing surveillance systems is likely to be ineffective and prohibitively expensive. And so they have concentrated to a great degree on their role as emergency responders, enhancing capacity that to some degree was already in place.

Policy Recommendations

Since September 11 most states, large cities, and transportation agencies have addressed terrorism in their overall emergency management plans and made those plans more thorough. They have assessed facility vulnerabilities, tightened procedures, and improved protection of buildings, terminals, and key infrastructure. Progress is not equal everywhere, nor are preparations as extensive as would be ideal; but real change has occurred, particularly in those locales that perceive a high risk of attack. Notwithstanding this improvement, much remains to be done.

The next tasks in enhancing surface transportation security are more difficult and must proceed in a less favorable political and organizational climate than the initial steps. This section suggests some surface transportation security policy issues that need attention in coming years.

Rethinking Federal Funding for Surface Transportation Security

The financing system for surface transportation security must be carefully assessed for whether its structure results in underinvestment in security. As discussed, transportation agency resource constraints are shaping policy decisions. Whatever form they take, prevention and protection measures are likely to require significant capital investments, particularly for infrastructure improvements, such as physical barriers or electronic surveillance equipment. Some protective measures may also require significant ongoing operating expenses, such as for security personnel to monitor video surveillance equipment.

In the stringent fiscal climate that the majority of states and localities face today, it is likely that the federal government will need to rationalize and enhance its role in providing funds so that states and localities will have support and fiscal incentives to take action. Federal funds can leverage commitments of state and local own-source revenues. As has been happening to a greater degree recently, the federal government and the states should make sure, moreover, that their limited fiscal resources are directed to areas of likely threat, reducing the tendency for geographically unrestricted funds to be very widely distributed, irrespective of degree of need.

Given a likely shortage of funds for improvements in transportation security, transit and highway officials must carefully prioritize desirable protective measures so that they can target the most pressing needs. Moreover, in planning activities at the state or city level, as at the federal level, transportation agencies are often regarded as secondary players compared to emergency managers, public safety, and law enforcement agencies. Transportation officials have a role in the discussions, but often at the periphery. Transportation agencies must develop stronger and more effective voices in state decisionmaking and resource allocation.

Confronting the Accessibility-Security Tradeoff

Our transit and highway systems are open. It is not practical to check every passenger and vehicle no matter how many monitoring devices or personnel are deployed.[41] However, the degree to which openness and accessibility of transportation can and should be subject to security trade-offs has by no means been settled. A future terrorist attack on a transportation venue might well result in legislation mandating sweeping changes in transportation access. Are access restrictions similar to those imposed on the air transport system feasible and effective for public transit or freight shipments? What consequences would they likely entail, both in economic and social terms? Are they acceptable given the current degree of threat and the impact on the essential functions performed by the vast transportation system? Such questions should be addressed and analyses undertaken so that policy is not made in a vacuum as a result of crisis.

Preventing Terrorism

Deterrence-prevention-mitigation measures for transportation facilities have not evolved as far as emergency response capabilities. On the state and local government side, there is a tremendous desire for timely, credible, and specific threat information—through the national threat alert system or directly communicated from law enforcement—so that protective measures can be deployed at time of need without wasting resources on needless equipment or operating expenses at other times. Although improvements can clearly be made, there is a real question as to whether such information will ever be available from federal law enforcement sources, given the significant obstacles to getting before-the-fact information about potential terrorist attacks.

Also important but far less developed are methods to ensure that local law enforcement personnel—who are in aggregate far more numerous than their federal counterparts—contribute effectively to surveillance and investigation of possible terrorist threats. Information developed by local law enforcement could well prove critical in stopping a future attack. Transit and highway security operations might well add important data, so they must be carefully integrated with other police operations. To achieve the necessary upward flow of law enforcement intelligence requires at least as much cooperation among levels of government as communicating threats that have been uncovered by federal agencies. Increased federal efforts are needed to help these agencies understand what kinds of information should be collected and what data are significant. That may require a further expansion of the number of transportation officials cleared to receive secret law enforcement information and classified intelligence data.

Federal Assistance for Technology Assessment

The feasibility and effectiveness of improvements in physical infrastructure are being debated. New technologies are being developed, tested, and refined.[42] These research and technology findings are frequently difficult for short-staffed state and local transportation agencies to monitor and review. It would be wasteful, moreover, for each state to perform this function on its own. Thus a strong federal role in identifying and testing innovative technology and providing technical assistance to states and localities is highly desirable. The federal government has a key role to play, too, in setting standards for technology and security practices, so that investments are not delayed by state and local uncertainty about what will later be required.

Emergency Preparedness

Because prevention may not be successful, emergency response–consequence management and recovery capabilities also need further enhancement—in the transportation context and others. These preparedness tasks include building deeper capacity. Training must go beyond awareness instruction to include more specialized skill development. Jurisdictions need the services of more than a single individual with these skills, moreover. As the anthrax letter attacks of 2001 showed, emergencies that extend over wider geographic areas or longer time periods can severely tax not only the overall pools of emergency responders but quite acutely the handful of substantive specialists equipped with expertise for a particular type of situation. Transportation agencies, moreover, need better capabilities for communicating with the public during such emergencies.

More integrated capacity is also needed for the future. The range of transportation agencies and operators in a large metropolitan area or state is significant, creating a major coordination problem within the transportation community itself. Yet there are many security concerns that would benefit from collective scrutiny, information exchange, and perhaps joint action. Metropolitan planning organizations (MPOs) could play a far larger role in this regard than they have to date—and also could be an important element in setting transportation security budget priorities. However, in the three areas we looked at intensively—Boston, Chicago, and the San Francisco Bay area—MPOs were not prominently involved in security activities, although the Metropolitan Transportation Commission in San Francisco has played a limited convening and coordination role. MPOs vary enormously in their structure and capabilities, but in many areas they might develop a stronger role in pulling together diverse agencies, stimulating discussion, articulating common concerns, and providing help in planning.[43]

Beyond the transportation arena itself, transportation agencies need to be better linked to other agencies that would respond to a terrorist attack. Crises have to be managed effectively across emergency response agencies—police, fire service, and emergency medical services—and include close links with the health care system, which itself does not have sufficient levels of coordination. For example, hospital emergency room staffs and public health infectious disease specialists may have to work together successfully in a bioterror attack. Improved integration should go beyond the public sector to include major private corporations or nonprofit organizations (universities, health care centers) whose personnel or facilities may be attacked or whose assets (trained personnel, facilities, and transportation capabilities) would be useful in a crisis. Integration of capacity must also span jurisdictional boundaries—effectively connecting big cities with smaller communities in the metropolitan area or state emergency response with more isolated communities. More comprehensive forms of mutual aid need to be developed to avoid either prohibitively expensive duplication of equipment or training by every municipality or substantial areas that lack important dimensions of protection.

Integration should include interoperability as well as relationship building and sharing of assets. Emergency radio systems, as has been frequently noted, do not typically allow firefighters from one jurisdiction to communicate with those from another, or even with police or paramedics from their own community. But interoperability implies more than the compatibility of equipment. It means the ability to work together effectively in emergencies, even when the units needing to mesh have not previously trained or exercised together. This requires work practices coordinated through common protocols such as the National Incident Management System, the adoption of which has been mandated by the Homeland Security Act as the template for emergency response by federal agencies and nationally.[44]

Building deeper, more integrated, interoperable emergency response capabilities is a far more difficult undertaking than improvements made to date. These future steps affect basic organizational operations by rank-and-file personnel, not merely planning or policymaking activities by senior officials. They require not only changes in single agencies but also coordination of networks of organizations that may not be hierarchically linked and managed. Effecting these changes is thus likely to be time intensive and costly in organizational as well as dollar terms. It will require significant commitments of line and management personnel at the expense of other activities and engagement of many agencies in negotiating new forms of collaboration.

Conclusion

As the United States looks to the future, the stakes of deciding how to improve transportation security are high. We do not know whether the nation will face repeated, horrific terrorist attacks—large or "small"—on U.S. territory. If the nation faces a continued severe threat, surface transportation systems may well become targets, perhaps regular targets. People's lives and welfare may depend on the steps taken to date and in the near future.

The novelty of the terrorist threat to American territory means that the nation has only begun to develop firm ideas about how greater protection might be secured in the surface transportation system and how these enhancements will be financed. This chapter has reviewed how transport agencies at different levels have responded since September 11 rather than focusing on the substance of the policy choices about enhancing security. Much more policy analysis must go on in that realm.

As we develop transportation security strategy, both proactively and in direct response to future events, we must also deal more clearly with the potential tradeoff between security and service accessibility. The many economic and social benefits of our surface transportation network depend, in important respects, on the openness of the system. As in other areas of homeland security policy, we must be cognizant of the costs as well as the benefits of enhancing security.

Appendix 11A

The following is a list of interviewees and their institutional affiliations at the time they were interviewed.

Boston-Massachusetts Region

Robert Calobrisi, Boston Emergency Management Agency, Boston Fire Department

Paul Christian, Boston Fire Department

Peter Cusalito, Weapons of Mass Destruction Civil Support Team, Massachusetts National Guard

Paul Evans, Boston Police Department

William Fleming, Police Department, Massachusetts Bay Transportation Authority

Michael Galvin, Boston Basic City Services

Brian Greeley, State Office of Commonwealth Security

Eric Hahn, Boston Police Department

John Hasson, Boston Emergency Management Agency, Boston Fire Department

Jerry Leone, U.S. Attorney's Office and Anti-Terrorism Task Force

Michael Leone, Massachusetts Port Authority

Stephen McGrail, Massachusetts Emergency Management Agency

Stephen Morash, Boston Emergency Management Agency, Boston Fire Department

Elaine Sudanowicz, Boston Transportation Department and Boston Emergency Management Agency

Richard Swensen, State Office of Commonwealth Security

Chicago-Illinois Region

Sara Alexander, Chicago Office of Emergency Management and Communications

Mike Chamness, Illinois Emergency Management Agency

Joe Gaspirich, Illinois Emergency Management Agency

James Getz, Illinois Department of Natural Resources, Conservation Police

Rick Guzman, Illinois Office of Homeland Security

Harmon Herbert, U.S. Coast Guard

James Kehoe, Chicago Fire Department

Tom Korty, Illinois Department of Transportation

Ed LeFevour, Chicago Department of Aviation
Fred Leonard, Metra Police, Northeast Illinois Regional Commuter Railroad Corporation
David Lozeau, Chicago Transit Authority
Bernero Martinez, Chicago Police Department
Rob Newbold, Illinois Department of Transportation
Kevin Phillips, Cook County Emergency Management Agency
Michael Snyders, Illinois State Police
Leslee Stein Spencer, Illinois Department of Public Health
Earl Zuelke, Chicago Police Department, Maritime Unit

San Francisco-California Region

Kathleen Bailey, California Office of Emergency Services, Coastal Region
Lucien Canton, San Francisco Office of Emergency Services
Phyllis Cauley, California Office of Emergency Services, Coastal Region
Richard Desmond, Jr., California Highway Patrol
Jeff Georgevich, Metropolitan Transportation Commission
Michael Griffin, California Office of Emergency Services, Coastal Region
Michael Guerin, California Office of Emergency Services, Law Enforcement Branch
Len Hardy, Bay Area Rapid Transit
Robert Hertan, San Francisco Municipal Railway (Muni)
Rick Linson, California Highway Patrol
Lisa Mancini, San Francisco Muni
Nancy Okasaki, Metropolitan Transportation Commission

Federal and Other

Bob Adduci, U.S. Department of Transportation, Volpe Center
Frank Buckley, Transportation Security Administration, Office of Maritime and Land Security
Theo Gamelas, Transportation Security Administration, Office of Maritime and Land Security
John Gerner, Federal Highway Administration, Office of Transportation Security
Rob Healy, American Public Transportation Association
Greg Hull, American Public Transportation Association
Tony Kane, American Association of State Highway and Transportation Officials

Susan Knisely, Federal Transit Administration, Office of Safety and Security

Charles Morton, Transportation Security Administration, Office of Maritime and Land Security

Brian O'Malley, Transportation Security Administration, Office of Maritime and Land Security

David Price, Federal Highway Administration, Office of Transportation Security

Harry Saporta, Federal Transit Administration, Office of Safety and Security

Steve Sprague, Transportation Security Administration, Office of Maritime and Land Security

Notes

1. Eric Lichtblau, "Warning of Possible Attacks on Big-City Buses and Trains," *New York Times*, April 3, 2004, p. A10.

2. National Research Council, *Improving Surface Transportation Security: A Research and Development Strategy* (Washington: National Academy Press, 1999); and Peter Guerrero, *Mass Transit: Challenges in Security Transit Systems*, GAO-02-1075T (General Accounting Office, 2002).

3. Steve Dunham, "Mass Transit Defends Itself against Terrorism," March 2002 (www.homelandsecurity.org/journal/articles/displayArticle.asp?article=47 [June 2005]); and Kelley Coyner, "Sustainable Transportation Security," paper prepared for the Executive Session on Domestic Preparedness, John F. Kennedy School of Government (Harvard University, 2004).

4. House Committee on Transportation and Infrastructure, Subcommittee on Highways, Transit and Pipelines, *Hearing on Public Transportation Security*, 108 Cong., 2 sess. (June 22, 2004).

5. Coyner, "Sustainable Transportation Security," and Transportation Research Board, "Deterrence, Protection and Preparation: The New Transportation Security Imperative," Special Report 270 (Washington: National Academy of Sciences, 2002).

6. Laura Higgins and others, "The Role of Public Transportation Operations in Emergency Management: Research Report," Research Report 1834-2 (Texas Transportation Institute, Texas A&M University, 1999).

7. Truck and rail modes together move over 80 percent of the nation's freight. Air moves about 3 percent of freight in value and less than 0.1 percent in terms of overall weight. Bureau of Transportation Statistics, *Commodity Flow Survey 2002* (Department of Transportation, 2004).

8. Coyner, "Sustainable Transportation Security."

9. General Accounting Office, *Mass Transit: Federal Action Could Help Transit Agencies Address Security Challenges*, GAO-03-263 (2002).

10. See Wachs, chapter 4 in this volume.

11. Douglas B. Ham and Stephen Lockwood, "National Needs Assessment for Ensuring Transportation Infrastructure Security," National Cooperative Highway Research Program Project 20-59 (Washington: Transportation Research Board, 2002); and Blue Ribbon Panel on Bridge and Tunnel Security, *Recommendations for Bridge and Tunnel Security* (Washington: American Association of State Highway and Transportation Officials, 2003).

12. Transportation Research Board, "Deterrence, Protection and Preparation."

13. Veronique de Rugy, "What Does Homeland Security Spending Buy?" Working Paper 107 (Washington: American Enterprise Institute, 2004).

14. General Accounting Office, *Transportation Security: Federal Action Needed to Help Address Security Challenges*, GAO-03-843 (2003).

15. De Rugy, "Homeland Security Spending."

16. *Public Transportation Terrorism Prevention and Response Act of 2004*, H.R. 5082, 108 Cong., 2 sess. (Government Printing Office [GPO], 2004); and *Public Transportation Terrorism Prevention Act of 2004*, S. 2884, 108 Cong., 2 sess., (GPO, 2004).

17. *Rail Security Act of 2004*, S. 2273, 108 Cong., 2 sess., (GPO, 2004).

18. House, *Public Transportation Security;* and California Institute for Federal Policy Research, *Special Report: Homeland Security Appropriations for Fiscal Year 2005 (Conferenced) and California Implications—October 2004* (Washington, 2004).

19. H.R. 5082.

20. Representative Thomas Petri, "Public Transportation Terrorism Prevention Bill Introduced in U.S. House" (www.house.gov/petri/press/terror_bill.htm [September 15, 2004]).

21. P.L. 107-71, 115 Stat. 597 (2001).

22. P.L. 296, 116 Stat. 2135 (2002).

23. De Rugy, "Homeland Security Spending."

24. P.L. 107-295, 116 Stat. 2064 (2002).

25. The Coast Guard was transferred from the DOT to the DHS along with the TSA under the Homeland Security Act.

26. General Accounting Office, *Transportation Security.*

27. *Code of Federal Regulations* 49, sec. 1572 (2003).

28. H.R. 5082.

29. The number of stakeholders includes state transportation departments in every state and territory, hundreds of separate transit agencies (including 30 major ones), about 50 commercial rail carriers, and 6,000 over-the-road trucking firms. See Coyner, "Sustainable Transportation Security"; and Bureau of Transportation Statistics, *Transportation Statistics Annual Report* (Department of Transportation, 2004).

30. General Accounting Office, *Transportation Security.*

31. Greg Hull, *Public Transportation Security Initiatives and Requirements* (Washington: American Public Transportation Association, 2003).

32. See the Special Committee on Transportation Security website (security.transportation.org [March 2005]).

33. General Accounting Office, *Transportation Security.*

34. Ibid.

35. See *Uniting and Strengthening America by Providing Appropriate Tools Required to Intercept and Obstruct Terrorism (USA PATRIOT ACT) Act of 2001*, P.L. 107-56, 115 Stat. 252 (2001); and *Homeland Security Act of 2002*, P.L. 107-296.

36. Proposed by the Bush administration, May 14, 2003.

37. Such agencies include the Port Authority of New York and New Jersey and the Golden Gate Bridge, Highway, and Transportation District. Some SDOTs also have primary transit responsibilities within their states.

38. General Accounting Office, *Transportation Security.*

39. American Public Transportation Association, *Survey of United States Transit System Security Needs and Funding Priorities* (Washington, 2004).

40. Brian M. Jenkins and Larry N. Gersten, "Protecting Public Surface Transportation Against Terrorism and Serious Crime: Continuing Research on Best Security Practices," MTI Report 01-07 (Mineta Transportation Institute, San Jose State University, 2001).

41. James Broder and Eva Lerner-Lam, presentation made at the teleconference on Exploring the Use of Roving Security Inspections to Increase Post 9/11 Rail and Bus Transit Security in the U.S. (Reston, Va.: Transportation and Development Institute, American Society of Civil Engineers, March 25, 2004).

42. Transportation Research Board, "Deterrence, Protection and Preparation."

43. Michael D. Meyer, *The Role of the Metropolitan Planning Organization (MPO) in Preparing for Security Incidents and Transportation Response,* report prepared for the Federal Highway Administration (Department of Transportation, 2002).

44. Annabelle Boyd and John P. Sullivan, *Emergency Preparedness for Transit Terrorism* (Washington: Transportation Research Board, 2000); Hank Christen and others, "An Overview of Incident Management Systems," *Perspectives on Preparedness,* no. 4 (2001): 1–10; and Arnold M. Howitt and Herman B. "Dutch" Leonard, "A Command System for All Seasons?" *Crisis/Response Journal* 1, no. 2 (2005):40–42.

CONTRIBUTORS

Linda Bailey
ICF Consulting

Scott Bernstein
*Center for Neighborhood
Technology*

Edward Beimborn
University of Wisconsin

Evelyn Blumenberg
*School of Public Policy and Social
Research, University of
California–Los Angeles*

John Brennan
Cleveland State University

Anthony Downs
*Brookings Institution Metropolitan
Policy Program*

Billie Geyer
Cleveland State University

Edward Hill
Cleveland State University

Arnold Howitt
Harvard University

Bruce Katz
*Brookings Institution Metropolitan
Policy Program*

Jonathan Makler
IBI Group

Kevin O'Brien
Cleveland State University

Ryan Prince
Louis Berger Group

Robert Puentes
*Brookings Institution Metropolitan
Policy Program*

Claudette Robey
Cleveland State University

Sandra Rosenbloom
*Drachman Institute, University
of Arizona*

Martin Wachs,
*Institute of Transportation Studies,
University of California–Berkeley*

Margy Waller
Brookings Institution

Federal Housing Administration
(FHA), 218
Federal Transit Administration (FTA):
analysis of regulations, 271; CMAQ
and, 146; emphasis on congestion,
270; federal allowable shares, 268;
history of, 259; low-income car pur-
chase and lease programs, 214;
MPOs and, 177; New Starts projects,
263, 264, 268, 270, 273; NTD and,
275; terrorism and security and, 291,
296–97; transit funds, 23
FHA. *See* Federal Housing
Administration
FHWA. *See* Federal Highway Adminis-
tration
First Coast Metropolitan Planning
Organization (Fla.), 179
First responder programs, 293, 296, 297
Fiscal Management Information System
(FMIS), 16, 277
Florida, 149, 184, 237
FMIS. *See* Fiscal Management Informa-
tion System
Fort Myers (Fla.), 157
Foster, Kathryn A., 174, 178
Frey, William, 231, 240
FTA. *See* Federal Transit Administration
Fuels. *See* Automobiles and trucks;
Gasoline; Taxes—fuel

GAO. *See* General Accounting Office
Gasoline: constituent parts of, 46–47;
consumption of, 54–55, 68, 84; retail
price of, 46–47, 74n3. *See also* Automobiles and trucks; Taxes—fuel
General Accounting Office (GAO):
FHWA, FTA, and TSA responsibilities, 297; New Starts funding, 264;
studies of highways and transit,
269–70, 272; study of MPOs, 21,
151; study of state gas taxes, 65–66;
study of transportation services, 209
Georgia, 58, 59
Georgia Regional Transportation
Authority (GRTA), 189

Golden Gate Bridge (San Francisco),
287, 301, 304
Government Accountability Office. *See*
General Accounting Office
Governmental Accounting Standards
Board (GASB), 28, 42n51
Government, federal: administration of
the Interstate Highway System, 141,
142; budget deficit of, 74n6; current
highway programs, 130–32; gas
taxes and, 7, 48, 51–56, 57, 74n6, 83,
87, 104, 121, 132n6; metropolitan
transportation decisionmaking and,
142–50; MPOs and, 153; regional
agencies, 182–83; research needs,
219; spending on transportation and
transit, 20, 21–22, 87–90, 263; terrorism and security and, 291–99,
304, 305; transit development and,
35, 263; transportation and, 3, 4, 5,
10, 78, 80, 159, 259–60; urban and
metropolitan policies of, 4, 141; user
fees and tolls, 50. *See also* Congress;
Transportation, Department of;
*individual governmental administra-
tions, departments, and agencies*
Government Performance Results Act
(*1993*), 25
Governments, local: accounting and
bookkeeping by, 28; gas taxes and, 7,
48, 66; highway funding and, 268;
land use issues, 155, 184, 187,
274–75, 281; MPOs and, 151,
152–53; number of transit passenger
trips, 20; road ownership and maintenance and, 22, 78, 80; sales taxes
and, 85; terrorism and security and,
292–93, 299–304, 305, 306; traffic
congestion and, 173, 183–84,
188–89; user fees and tolls, 50, 77
Governments, local—transportation:
federal programs and, 7, 13, 16, 261;
finance, 8, 29, 77, 81, 82–83, 84–85,
94–95, 102; networks and services,
10, 22, 209; policies, 6, 9–10, 20, 78,
152, 159, 258–60, 261, 269–70, 274;
reforms, 3–4, 16–17